Foreign
Policy
in
Transition

Contemporary Issues Series

Foreign Policy in Transition

A Critical Analysis of the Foreign Policy of the United States

Steven B. Hunt

NATIONAL TEXTBOOK COMPANY • *Skokie, IL 60077 U.S.A.*

Contents

Introduction

U.S. foreign policy is complicated. The U.S. deals with more than 150 sovereign nations and dozens of international organizations. Our own nation is constantly changing, and those 150 plus other nations and dozens of organizations are changing, which results in our foreign policies constantly shifting to adjust to a perpetually new international environment. When our policy shifts, it impacts in many ways because policies as well as nations are "interdependent" in today's world. Nothing is really simple about international relations.

The student of foreign trade and foreign aid will have the lesson of complexity driven home time and again this forthcoming year. *Foreign Policy in Transition* attempts to cover some of the key issues of policy change. Part I of this book looks at the critical issues of foreign trade from a U.S. perspective. The U.S. has, since the 1930s, generally promoted the idea of free international trade. Recent trade deficits, OPEC, various other commodity cartels, sensitive technology, and other problems, however, are making many re-examine the free trade philosophy. Part II of *Foreign Policy in Transition* looks at a particular aspect of trade and aid: arms. U.S. arms sales and arms aid have expanded more than 1500% in ten years. The essential question here is, should it have? Part III focuses on U.S. aid to totalitarian or repressive regimes. President Carter stresses a moralistic foreign policy which promotes human rights, but the U.S. supports a large number of governments which are markedly undemocratic. Do we really mean it when we proclaim human rights throughout the world or do our acts deny our rhetoric? Part IV offers a compilation of select bibliographic material related to all the issues related to U.S. aid and trade, many of which could not be examined in detail in earlier sections of the book.

I. U.S. FOREIGN TRADE: IS FREE TRADE FAILING?

U.S. foreign trade policy has been based on 1930's precedents supporting a free trade philosophy. We have retained some import quotas and tariffs and there are other barriers to trade, but as a member of GATT, the U.S. has espoused an open world market. The OPEC cartel and various world commodity arrangements, the EEC and Japanese trade barriers, and sensitivity of East-West trade, technological exports, and nuclear power, however, have all called into question the free trade philosophy. As our balance of trade and balance of payments fall into deficit and as U.S. workers lose jobs, more and more people are calling for an end to a world free market. Amazingly, both the rich nations and the poor nations, industrial exporters and raw materials suppliers, creditors and debtors, all want trade changes but in many different directions.

Part I opens with an examination of U.S. trade performance since 1970. Lawrence Fox, Vice-President for International Economic Affairs, notes that the U.S. market share of world trade has declined markedly since 1970. Particularly shaky, during this period of time, was the U.S. position vis a vis West Germany and Japan as concerns industrial goods and with OPEC as concerns oil. Fox has no immediate worries, but the 1970-77 period, particularly 1975-1977, was not a good one for the U.S.

In the second article, Robert Brusca reports a major resurgence of U.S. exports in 1978. Brusca argues that price competitiveness has been restored by the exchange rate changes of the past two years. He expects even more improvement in 1979. However, he admits such improvement is dependent on continued price competitiveness which, in turn, is dependent on Export Import Bank loan authorizations and improved R&D and investment in the U.S.

Geoff Wood and Doug Mudd, in "The Recent U.S. Trade Deficit— No Cause for Panic" continue the series of arguments sponsored by Federal Reserve Banks. They argue that temporary deficits in trade aren't necessarily historically all that bad. What would be bad, according to Wood and Mudd, would be a U.S. panic reaction, especially a reaction which included economically propping up particular sagging industries. They argue that such propping would be an ineffective waste of resources. In short, they support traditional free trade philosophy and hope that the 1975-77 trade debacle was a historical and temporary aberration.

Clifton Luttrell's "Imports and Jobs" would tend to support Brusca and Wood and Mudd. Luttrell contends that job losses in the trade field are obvious while job gains are relatively unobservable. Really, Luttrell thinks, the losses and the gains tend to balance out in the long run. Also, the quality of life in the U.S. is measurably improved by the addition of foreign goods.

The fifth article shifts emphasis from discussion of the U.S. trade record and its meaning to recent changes in the law and recognized trade problems. Kazimierz Grzybowski and his colleagues discuss the passage of the 1974 Trade Act. They state that the trade act extends the viability of GATT and, hence, of free trade. They recognize the 1974 Trade Act as a political compromise but see it returning free trade to the world or at least to the Tokyo trade negotiations.

Irene Elliott's "U.S. Role in East-West Trade: An Appraisal" continues the discussion of current problems and prospects for U.S. trade. Trade with communist countries has always been a serious and sensitive issue with political variables weighing as heavily as economic factors. Financial arrangements in East-West trade require incredible negotiations, and technological transfers to Eastern Europe are security worries. Despite the hazards, however, East-West trade has proliferated in the last ten years, and solutions are being found between profoundly differing economic systems.

Still, as Jack Baranson says, "Technology Exports Can Hurt Us." Past technology transfers have hurt the U.S. international competitive position and endangered national security. Baranson argues that we should restrict technology transfers much more closely and require sectoral review before allowing a particular type of technology to go abroad.

Stanley Metzger examines yet another problem in U.S. trade, the problem of cartels, combines, and commodity agreements. OPEC is the best known trading cartel, but there are hundreds. OECD, an organization representing a number of developed nations, and UNCTAD, an organization representing underdeveloped raw material exporters, alike have commodity agreements which infringe on free trade. International law supposedly has the power to resolve commodity conflicts, but, as usual in these matters, national interest supercedes the law. Metzger has little hope for a short term solution and expects the problem of cartels, combines, and commodity agreements to be with us for some time.

David Helscher reports on yet another problem area in U.S. trade; agriculture. Agriculture has been seen by some as the savior of U.S. trade. By charging more for our grain, it is argued, we can balance our oil and manufacturing debits. However, American agricultural trade policy has been fundamentally set for 25 years by the Agricultural Trade Development and Assistance Act, more commonly known as PL 480. PL 480 allows for food assistance on a cash or credit basis to "friendly" nations in need. Helscher points out that such friendly nations have even included Russia in the past and that profit motives and humanitarian motives concerning food aid are often in conflict. Helscher sees a complex future for American agriculture and PL 480, but he retains hope that the U.S. can feed many millions without making them dependent and simultaneously profit from it.

Mike Bauser comments on the last U.S. trade problem to be discussed in Part I when he writes about "U.S. Nuclear Export Policy." The U.S. has promoted for many years the idea of the peaceful use of the atom for energy. Simultaneously, however, the U.S. has been extremely security conscious concerning the dangers of the nonpeaceful uses of nuclear power. U.S. export policy has stuck on the safety side at the expense of more nuclear energy and a larger U.S. share in the nuclear energy market. Bauser argues our policy must balance out safety needs with power needs and economic market needs.

The last article in Part I returns to a government source, in this case a portion of a report on "U.S. Export Policy" published by the Subcommittee on International Finance of the Committee on Banking, Housing, and Urban Affairs of the U.S. Senate. In response to a series of problems discussed earlier in the report, the subcommittee suggests that the U.S. organize both industry and agriculture for exporting, that incentives be given to R&D and export investment, that the U.S. negotiate the reduction of trade barriers to U.S. goods, and that the U.S. government arrange for favorable financial conditions for exporters.

II. U.S. ARMS POLICIES: IS THE U.S. a MERCHANT OF DEATH?

The trade labyrinth will involve most students in the 1979-80 school year. However, the trade topic doesn't specify which trade policies are to be changed, for what reasons, or in what directions. Some students will necessarily get specific, and many may turn to a particularly thorny trade problem as the focus of their research, the arms trade conundrum.

The U.S. is the largest arms supplier in the world. We give away arms in the form of military aid, and we sell arms in trade. It used to be that this involved only a few millions of dollars worth of outdated surplus weapons in a given year. Today, however, the arms business is a multi-billion dollar international operation which includes sales of the very latest in weapons technology. In 1976 the Congress attempted to put some controls on the system with passage of the Arms Export Control Act; but the arms business is bigger than ever, and tens of thousands of people the world over, including many in the U.S., are asking if the U.S. is a merchant of death.

Part II opens with Lucy Wilson Benson, Under Secretary for Security Assistance, Science, and Technology, U.S. Department of State, attempting to explain how arms transfers fit as an instrument of U.S. foreign policy. Mrs. Benson argues that arms transfers perform many useful functions in U.S. foreign policy. They strengthen U.S. allies, maintain regional balances, gain the U.S. needed concessions, help our balance of payments, and offset Soviet influences. Mrs. Benson admits that the sales can be dangerous and that difficult cost benefit analyses in arms transfers are necessary, but says that the Carter administration will maintain arms transfers as a foreign policy tool.

In the second article, Archibald Alexander asks the critical question, "Arms Transfers by the U.S.: Merchant of Death or Arsenal of Democracy?" Alexander finds both pros and cons to arms transfers after reviewing the Arms Export Control Act of 1976. All in all, however, Alexander is opposed to the massiveness of U.S. arms shipments. He suggests energy conservation to reduce the need for financial remuneration via arms and international agreements curtailing arms transfers to reduce the need to match other arms suppliers.

Henry Billingsley discusses the particular instance of the F-16 sale to Iran. Supposedly, this sale should have been controlled by the Arms Export Control Act of 1976. Political and economic expedience, however, allowed for the sales despite Congressional disquietude. The recent power shifts in Iran make this sale in retrospect even more questionable. Uncomfortable thoughts assail one thinking of the American arms now being used by Vietnam in S.E. Asia, and one wonders what will happen to the billions of dollars of U.S. weapons in Iran.

The last article, "The Transfer of Arms to Third World Countries and Their Internal Uses" by Asbjørn Eide, pulls few punches. Eide sees arms transfers to Third World countries destroying social development and creating artificial economic dependencies. Eide is appalled and calls for Third World nations to take the lead in preventing the armaments habit and getting the U.N. to stop the U.S. and Soviet Union, the two nations he sees as the chief culprits in arms supply.

III. U.S. AID AND HUMAN RIGHTS: DO WE REALLY MEAN IT?

Many have noticed that U.S. rhetoric concerning foreign policy and U.S. action in foreign policy are not always congruent. Specifically, the U.S. has put forth the clarion call for human rights; yet we support South Korea, the Philippines, South Africa, Peru, et al., whose regimes are notoriously suppressive. Does the U.S. have a double standard? Can our "friends" suppress human rights without our notice while our enemies' least peccadillo is exposed? These questions are examined in the last section of *Foreign Policy in Transition.*

In the first article, Vita Bite analyzes human rights and U.S. foreign policy. She gives background on U.S. policy for 1973 – 76 and then explains the Carter human rights initiatives. She also comments upon recent legislation and its connection to foreign policy and human rights stands.

In the last excerpt of this year's analysis, Secretary Vance reports on the efforts of the administration in the human rights area and its effects on bilateral aid, security assistance, and international financial loans. His report is an annual one mandated by PL 92-105 and follows upon each year's hearings into foreign assistance legislation.

Steve Hunt
Lewis & Clark College
Portland, Oregon

I
U.S. Foreign Trade:
Is Free Trade Failing?

U.S. Trade Performance Since 1970

With Special Reference to Manufactured Goods

Lawrence A. Fox

PREFACE

Changes in the U.S. trade picture are important for the U.S. economy. Currently, U.S. exports and imports together equal about 14 percent of our GNP. In recent years, manufactured goods, supplies and equipment have constituted two-thirds of U.S. exports, and over half of U.S. imports. In the past two years, the traditional U.S. trade surplus in manufactured goods has been declining and the first quarter of 1978 shows a deficit of $3 billion.

Recent changes in the U.S. trade account have been difficult to evaluate in view of alteration in our traditional pattern of energy imports, currency changes, and other economic factors. Business cycle developments at home and abroad, inflation, high rates of unemployment and growing intervention by governments to affect trade flows make it necessary to achieve maximum benefits for the U.S. economy from trade.

President Carter has urged that U.S. industry and agriculture expand exports and has directed that a national export expansion program be undertaken. NAM, representing roughly 75 percent of the manufacturing output of the U.S., supports programs to increase exports and will be addressing through its International Economic Affairs Committee various policy aspects of this problem.

This report on U.S. trade has been prepared with particular emphasis on manufactured goods. The purpose of the report is to focus attention

From National Export Program Hearing before the Committee on Commerce, Science, and Transportation United States Senate, September 28, 1978, Serial No. 95-113, U.S. Government Printing Office, 1978.

on the facts and thereby to facilitate informed discussion of policy alternatives to improve U.S. trade performance.

LAWRENCE A. FOX
Vice President
International Economic Affairs

Highlights

The U.S. recorded its largest trade deficit in history in 1977—almost $27 billion in contrast with a trade deficit of $6 billion in 1976.

Manufactured goods export growth has been virtually flat for the past 2 years while manufactured goods imports have risen sharply. The first quarter of 1978 showed a deficit in the manufactured goods trade balance, in contrast with a surplus of $21 billion in 1975.

Manufactured goods exports of the Common Market, Germany and Japan to the world (excluding the U.S.) have grown more rapidly than U.S. manufactured goods exports since 1975.

The increase in the oil deficit was about $9 billion, less than half the total increase in the trade deficit from 1967 to 1977.

Agricultural exports totaled $19.6 billion in 1977, but agricultural export growth has been stagnant since 1975.

The U.S. trade balance declined in 1977 with all major areas of the world.

The trade deficit with Japan was $8.1 billion in 1977, in contrast to $5.4 billion in 1976.

The 1977 trade surplus with the Common Market declined by more than $3 billion from the 1976 level.

The U.S. trade balance with Canada—our largest trading partner—declined in 1977 by $1.6 billion.

Executive Summary

U.S. trade performance in the past 2 years contrasts with 1975, a year of vigorous export growth and net decline in U.S. imports, with the resulting trade surplus of $11 billion, the largest in U.S. history. Just as the 1975 figures reflect world business cycle developments, the declining U.S. trade performance is similarly influenced by the business cycle, but nevertheless it is evident that the U.S. trade balance has been undergoing a secular decline since the mid-1960s. The downturn since 1975 seems to be reestablishing an earlier trend that existed prior to devaluation, floating, and the worldwide economic disturbances of 1973-74. Oil, of course, is a major cause of the growing U.S. deficit, but not the only cause. Most notably, the U.S. trade surplus in manufactured goods declined from a peak of $21 billion. Agricultural exports have been stagnant. Imports have risen across the board.

General Trade Developments, 1976-77

The U.S. trade deficit in 1977 was $26.7 billion, four and one-half times the 1976 level. Exports were sluggish, totaling $120.1 billion, or 4.6 percent above 1976. Imports totaled $146.8 billion, or 21.6 percent above 1976. The annualized first quarter deficit for 1978 was $38.6 billion.

The increase in the oil deficit amounted to slightly less than half of the increase in the total trade deficit from 1976 to 1977. Major elements in the growing deficit other than oil were non-oil industrial supplies and materials, which went from a $2 billion surplus in 1976 to a $2 billion deficit in 1977 consumer goods, whose deficit grew from $11 billion to $14 billion; and capital goods, whose surplus shrank by $2 billion. Petroleum and petroleum products went from a 1976 deficit of $31 billion to a 1977 deficit of $40 billion.

Trade Trends by Commodity, 1970-77

The period since 1970 is sufficiently long to reflect the impact of the devaluation of the dollar, the consequences of floating exchange rates, and the worldwide economic disturbances of 1973-74. By 1975 the United States had largely absorbed the influence of dollar devaluation, but it had scarcely begun to adapt to the great changes wrought since 1973 by the increase in oil prices and the stagflation present throughout most of the world economy.

Imports

The largest non-oil import category is industrial supplies, which constituted one-third of total U.S. imports in 1977. This category grew at an average annual rate of 16 percent from 1970 to 1977. The last 2 years have seen higher-than-average growth rates, with a rate of 17.5 percent for 1977.

The second ranking non-oil import category is consumer goods, accounting for 21 percent of total non-oil imports in 1977. The average annual rate of growth for consumer goods imports from 1970 to 1977 was 17 percent. The U.S. economic recovery since 1975 has produced especially strong import growth, amounting to 34 percent in 1976 and 22 percent in 1977.

Capital goods constituted 13 percent of U.S. non-oil imports in 1977. Capital goods import growth averaged 20 percent per year from 1970 to 1977. Import growth picked up somewhat in 1977 after weak expansion in 1976.

Exports

The rapid deterioration in the non-oil trade account reflects the stagnation in major commercial export sectors combined with buoyant import growth. Taking inflation into account, the two top export categories—capital goods and industrial supplies and materials—which supply almost two-thirds of U.S. sales abroad, experienced negative real growth for 1976-77.

The downturn in the largest export category, capital goods, has received little attention, but if it persists it will entail major structural difficulties for the external account. Capital goods supplied one-third of all U.S. sales in 1977. The average growth rate from 1970 to 1977 was 16 percent per year. Since 1975 growth has come to a virtual standstill, falling to 2 percent in 1977. The second major export group is industrial supplies and materials, accounting for 28 percent of total exports in 1977. The growth rate for this group also declined since 1975, falling to 1.0 percent in 1977.

Trade Trends by Area, 1970-77

U.S. trade balances with all major areas except the EC and Communist countries have deteriorated since 1970. In 1977 the U.S. trade surplus with the EC amounted to $4.4 billion and with Communist areas to $1.6 billion. The greatest deficit was with Japan, amounting to $8.1 billion in 1977.

The largest supplier of the U.S. in 1977 was Canada, with $29 billion of merchandise sales, followed by the EC, with $22 billion of sales. The largest U.S. market in 1977 was the EC, absorbing $26 billion of U.S. goods, followed closely by Canada.

The most rapidly growing market area in recent years has been the Middle East. While the U.S. share of the Middle East market has been growing, it has not grown as rapidly as that of Germany or Japan in the period 1970-76.

Developing countries have become major suppliers of manufacturers to the U.S., providing one-quarter of total manufactured goods imported in 1977. Six rapidly industrialized countries* supplied two-thirds of all LDC manufacture exports to the U.S. in 1977. The share of developed countries in the U.S. market has fallen correspondingly, with Western Europe the largest current supplier.

Developing countries now buy 43 percent of U.S. manufactured exports. Developed countries purchase slightly more than half of U.S. exports, with Canada the largest single market. Communist countries remain comparatively unimportant as trade partners in manufactures, accounting for about one percent.

Comparisons in Trade Performance with Major Trading Countries

The United States remains the world's largest exporter and importer. However, in manufactured exports, the United States was overtaken by West Germany in 1970. Germany had 19.1 percent of world manufactured exports in 1976, compared with the U.S. share of 18.3 percent ($79 billion for the United States and $91 billion for Germany). Since 1970 Japan's market share for manufactures has risen rapidly, reaching 14.8 percent in 1976.

U.S.-Japanese trade in manufactures shows the greatest asymmetry of any major area, and the asymmetry has grown since 1970. In 1970, Japan accounted for 21.6 percent of U.S. manufactured imports and 6.6 percent of U.S. manufactured exports. In 1977, the comparable figure had risen to 23.5 percent on the U.S. import side and on the U.S. export side had fallen to 4.6 percent.

Lagging U.S. manufactured goods export performance is in part due to the slow economic growth rates abroad. But this explanation is incomplete. Export growth rates for the Common Market, Germany and Japan to the world excluding the U.S. have exceeded U.S. export rates since 1975. The conjunctural business cycle explanation thus must be supplemented by other analytical approaches.

U.S. Trade Performance Since 1970 With Special Reference to Manufacturers

This examination of the U.S. trade account addresses three major aspects of U.S. trade performance in the 1970s:

I. What has been the overall development of the U.S. trade account? Have there been significant changes in the commodity composition of imports and exports? In import sources and export markets?

II. What is the role of oil in the deterioration of the trade balance?

III. What has been the overall record of U.S. trade performance in manufactured goods? Where have the most important changes in U.S. imports and exports of manufactured goods occurred, both in terms of areas and commodities breakdown?

I. General Development of the Trade Account

U.S. trade performance in the past 2 years contrasts with 1975, a year of vigorous export growth and net decline in U.S. imports. Recent comparisons are bound to show declining performance when measured against a year such as 1975; but, with a longer perspective, it seems clear that the U.S. trade balance has been undergoing a secular decline since the mid-1960s (Graph 1, Table 1). The downturn since 1975 seems to be reestablishing an earlier trend that existed prior to dollar devaluation, floating, and the worldwide economic disturbances in 1973-74.

Graph 1
U.S. Total Trade Balance and
Trade Balance in Manufactured Goods, 1965-1977

(5 billion; exports f.a.s., imports transaction value f.a.s.)

Source: Commerce Department, International Economic Indicators.

Table 1.—U.S. Trade, 1970-77
(In billions of dollars)

	Imports	Exports	Balance
Year:			
1970	40.0	42.7	2.7
1971	45.6	43.5	−2.0
1972	55.6	49.2	−6.4
1973	69.5	70.8	1.3
1974	100.3	97.9	−2.3
1975	96.1	107.1	11.0
1976	120.7	114.8	−5.9
1977	146.8	120.1	−26.7
1978[1]	162.1	123.4	−38.7
1977:[1]			
I	141.6	117.9	−23.7
II	148.6	121.9	−26.7
III	149.4	122.5	−26.8
IV	146.9	118.1	−28.8
1978:[1] I	162.1	123.4	−38.7

[1]Annual rate; 1978 based on 1st quarter seasonally adjusted figures from FT-990 series.

Note: Beginning 1974, imports are based on F.A.S. transaction values; for 1970-73 imports are based on customs values. Imports are also available since 1974 on a C.I.F. basis, although not shown in this table. Exports are valued F.A.S. for all years shown.

Source: Commerce Department "International Economic Indicators" and FT-990.

The U.S. trade account when broken down by end-use category has deteriorated in every sector since 1976 except for "special category" military goods (Table 2). In addition to petroleum, relatively sharp deterioration has occurred in the trade balances for industrial supplies other than petroleum, automotive vehicles, and consumer goods. The capital goods category experienced a smaller decrease in its positive balance, from $27.4 billion in 1976 to $25.6 billion in 1977.

Table 2.—U.S. Trade, by "End-Use" Categories, 1970, 1976, and 1977
(In billions of dollars)

	Imports	Exports	Balance
Foods, feeds, and beverages:			
1970	6.2	5.8	- 0.4
1976	11.5	19.7	8.2
1977	13.9	19.6	5.7
Industrial supplies and materials:			
1970	15.1	13.8	- 1.3
1976	60.9	32.0	- 28.9
1977	75.6	33.5	- 42.1
Petroleum and petroleum products, excluding gas:			
1970	'2.8	.5	- 1.3
1976	'31.8	1.0	- 30.8
1977	'41.4	1.3	- 40.1
Other industrial supplies and materials:			
1970	12.3	13.3	1.0
1976	29.1	31.0	1.9
1977	34.2	32.2	- 2.0
Capital goods, excluding automotive:			
1970	3.8	14.4	10.6
1976	10.9	38.3	27.4
1977	13.4	39.0	25.6
Automotive vehicles, parts, and engines:			
1970	6.0	3.7	- 2.3
1976	16.2	11.2	- 5.0
1977	18.7	12.1	- 6.6
Consumer goods (nonfood), excluding automotive:			
1970	7.6	2.7	- 4.9
1976	18.4	7.9	- 10.5
1977	22.4	8.8	- 13.6

'Does not include crude petroleum imports into the Virgin Islands, which totaled $2,600,000,000 in 1977.

Note: 19707 Customs value; 1976 and 1977: FAS.

Source: Commerce Department, FT-990, table E-9, I-5.

The relative contribution of the end-use categories to export performance has not changed much from 1970 to 1977 (Table 3). The greatest decrease occurred in industrial supplies, which accounted for only 27.9 percent of 1977 exports compared to 31.9 percent of 1970 exports. Capital goods barely changed in its relative contribution, supplying 32.4 percent of 1977, an increase of 0.5 percent over 1970. Imports increased across the board in absolute terms. The relative contribution of end-use categories to imports altered significantly from 1970 to 1977 (Table 3). The greatest relative decline in import share was in foods, feeds, and beverages, from 15.5 percent of total imports in 1970 to 9.5 percent last year. The greatest increase occurred in industrial supplies, which accounted for slightly more than half of all imports in 1977, compared to 37.8 percent in 1970. This is caused, of course, by the increase in volume and value of oil imports. As a percentage of non-oil imports, the industrial supplies category remained stable from 1976 to 1977. Capital goods, on the other hand, increased from 10.2 percent of all U.S. imports in 1970 to 12.7 percent in 1977 (from $3.8 billion in 1970 to $13.4 billion in 1977).

The overall U.S. trade balance experienced a downturn with all major areas except the European Community and the Communist countries since 1970 (Table 4). In 1977, the EC still provided the U.S. with a trade surplus of $4.4 billion.* The only other major trade surplus in 1977 was with Communist countries in Europe and Asia, although this surplus declined to $1.6 billion from the 1976 peak of $2.5 billion. Trade with Japan and South and East Asia underwent serious deteriorating deficits since 1975, with these areas accounting for a combined U.S. trade deficit of $15.2 billion in 1977.

Table 3.—Changes in Composition of U.S. Imports and Exports 1970 and 1977

	Percent of total imports	Percent of total imports, excluding petroleum plus petroleum products excluding gas	Percent of total exports
Foods, feeds and beverages:			
1970.	15.5	16.6	13.4
1977.	9.5	13.2	16.3
Industrial supplies and materials:			
1970.	37.8	¹33.2	31.9
1977.	51.5	¹32.5	27.9
Capital goods, excluding automotive:			
1970.	9.5	10.2	31.9
1977.	9.1	12.7	32.4
Automotive vehicles, parts and engines:			
1970.	15.0	16.0	8.6
1977.	12.7	17.7	10.1
Consumer goods (nonfood), excluding automotive:			
1970.	19.0	20.3	6.3
1977.	15.3	21.3	7.3

¹Industrial supplies and materials, excluding petroleum and petroleum products, excluding gas.

Source: Commerce Department, FT-990.

Table 4.—U.S. Imports From and Exports To Selected Areas, 1974-77
(In millions of dollars)

	Imports	Exports	Balance
European Community:			
1974..	19.0	22.1	3.1
1975..	16.6	22.9	6.3
1976..	17.8	25.4	7.6
1977..	22.1	26.5	4.4
Japan:			
1974..	12.3	10.7	− 1.6
1975..	11.3	9.6	− 1.7
1976..	15.5	10.1	− 5.4
1977..	18.6	10.5	− 8.1
Near East:			
1974..	4.7	5.6	.9
1975..	5.4	8.9	3.5
1976..	9.1	10.0	.9
1977..	13.0	11.0	− 2.0
Western Hemisphere, excluding Canada:			
1974..	18.4	15.8	-2.6
1975..	16.0	17.1	1.1
1976..	17.1	17.0	-.1
1977..	20.9	17.9	-3.0
Canada:			
1974..	21.9	19.9	− 2.0
1975..	21.7	21.7	0
1976..	26.2	24.1	− 2.1
1977..	29.4	25.7	− 3.7
Communist countries, Europe and Asia:			
1974..	1.0	2.2	1.2
1975..	.9	3.1	2.2
1976..	1.1	3.6	2.5
1977..	1.1	2.7	1.6
East and South Asia, excluding Japan and Communist countries:			
1974..	10.2	9.2	− 1.0
1975..	10.2	10.1	− .1
1976..	14.6	10.2	− 4.4
1977..	17.8	10.7	− 7.1

Source: Commerce Department, "Trends in U.S. Foreign Trade," 1975 and 1977.

II. The Role of Oil in the Trade Deficit

Since 1970, the U.S. imports of crude petroleum have quintupled in quantity and have risen 26 times in value (from 500 million barrels in 1970 to 2.5 billion barrels in 1977; from $1.3 billion to $33.6 billion). Purchases of petroleum and petroleum products totalled $41.5 billion in 1977, compared to $2.8 billion in 1970.* The impact of dramatically increasing oil imports on the balance of trade has been the subject of abundant commentary. It is important to note, however, that while oil is one major problem in the trade balance, it is by no means the only one.

Simply subtracting oil from the trade flow does not permit an accurate assessment of the non-oil trade balance. Oil-exporting countries would not have greatly increased their purchases from the U.S. in recent years had they not benefitted from rising oil revenues. By subtracting total OPEC trade, a more realistic assessment of the evolving U.S. trade position is possible (Table 5). A Commerce Department staff report concludes that this alternate measure indicates that even though it is merely an approximation the trade balance "is not in a sharp surplus position as supposedly indicated by the 'non-oil' balance."** It is also significant that the "non-OPEC" trade balance also fell from a peak surplus in 1975 to a deficit in 1977.

Table 5.—U.S. Trade Balances, 1965-77
(In billions of dollars)

	Overall trade balance	Non-oil trade balance	Non-OPEC trade balance
Year:			
1965.	6.1	7.8	6.4
1966.	4.8	6.5	5.0
1967.	4.7	6.3	4.8
1968.	1.4	3.3	1.2
1969.	2.0	4.1	1.6
1970.	3.3	5.5	2.9
1971.	− 1.4	1.4	− 1.7
1972.	− 5.8	− 2.0	− 5.9
1973.	1.9	9.0	2.8
1974.	− 1.7	21.7	7.2
1975.	11.5	35.4	17.8
1976.	− 5.7	25.1	6.8
1977[1].	− 25.1	16.4	− 4.5

[1] 6 mo. seasonally adjusted, annual rate.

Note: See page 13 for definition of various balances.

Source: Commerce Department, Bureau of International Economic Policy and Research, Staff Economic Report, "The U.S. Trade Balance Less Oil: Is It Meaningful?" August 1977, p.6.

In addition, the U.S. trade account has not yet adjusted adequately to a world trading environment characterized by permanently higher oil prices. Other major exporting countries such as Japan and West Germany, already almost entirely dependent on imported oil, had "merely" to absorb the price increases and have done so in a remarkably short time. The United States, in addition, has had to factor into its trade increased oil and gas imports to make up for absolute declines in domestic oil production. The present U.S. system of differential pricing of foreign and domestic oil obviously is transitional and will evolve toward a system of world prices—but with results for the trade account that cannot be fully foreseen.

III. Trade in Manufactures

U.S. trade in manufactures in 1977 was generally unsatisfactory (Table 6). The trade balance for all manufactures (SITC 5 through 8) experienced a surplus of $4.8 billion, down from the surplus of $13.8 billion in 1976, and $21 billion in 1975. The first quarter of 1978 showed a deficit of $3.1 billion. Although it is unwise to use first quarter figures to project annual levels (the annualized deficit would be $12.6 billion), it is noteworthy that the first quarter of 1978 was the sixth quarter in a row which showed generally declining rates for the manufactures balance.

Table 6.—U.S. Imports and Exports of Manufactured Goods and Capital Goods
1970, 1976, 1977
(In billions of dollars)

	Imports	Exports	Balance
Manufactures (SITC 5, 6, 7, 8):[1]			
1970	25.9	29.7	3.8
1976	64.8	78.5	13.8
1977	77.2	82.0	4.8
1978 (1)	94.8	82.2	− 12.6
Chemicals (5):			
1970	1.5	3.8	2.4
1976	4.8	10.0	5.2
1977	5.4	10.8	5.4
1978 (1)	6.0	11.0	5.0
Manufactured goods by material (6):			
1970	8.4	5.1	− 3.4
1976	17.6	11.2	− 6.4
1977	21.4	11.3	− 10.1
1978 (1)	27.2	11.0	− 16.2
Machinery and transport equipment (7):			
1970	11.2	17.9	6.7
1976	29.8	49.5	19.7
1977	35.5	51.0	15.5
1978 (1)	44.4	51.2	6.9
Miscellaneous manufactured articles (8):			
1970	4.8	2.6	− 2.3
1976	12.6	6.6	− 6.0
1977	14.9	7.3	− 7.5
1978 (1)	17.3	9.0	− 8.4
Capital goods, excluding automotive:			
1970	3.8	14.4	10.6
1976	10.9	38.3	27.4
1977	13.4	39.0	25.7
1978 (1)	16.9	39.6	22.7

[1]Manufactures total includes reexports.

Note: F.A.S. except for 1970 where customs values are shown.

Source: Commerce Department, FT-990, and "International Economic Indicators."

A Trade in Selected Categories of Manufactures

Capital goods had a $25.7 billion surplus in 1977, down from the previous surplus of $27.4 billion. Further breakdown of the manufactures category shows that in 1977 chemicals (SITC 5),* manufactured goods by material such as steel and paper (SITC 6), and miscellaneous manufactured articles (SITC 8) encountered further deterioration of the 1976 deficits, with the greatest deficit increase occurring for manufactured goods by material, which fell from a $6.1 billion deficit in 1976 to $10.0 billion deficit last year. Machinery and transport equipment (SITC 7) posted a surplus of only $15.5 billion, down $4.2 billion from 1976.

Further examination of the groups losing ground in 1977 shows considerable weakness in two areas. Within the category of machinery and transport equipment, the transport equipment group had a 1977 surplus of only $0.7 billion, down $3.1 billion from 1976. The deficit in new automobiles grew by $1.3 billion, producing a deficit of $7.2 billion in 1977; but trucks and other vehicles also contributed to this decline. Within the category of manufactured goods by material, the balances for iron and steel and for paper worsened (from a deficit of $0.5 billion to $0.9 billion for paper; from a deficit of $2.4 billion to $4.1 billion for iron and steel). Within the category of miscellaneous manufactured articles, several subgroups accounted for the deterioration, including clothing, musical instruments and phonographs, and toys and sporting goods.

Table 7.—Relative Importance of Major Areas for U.S. Manufactures Trade, 1970 and 1977
(In percent)

	1970	1977
A. Source of U.S. imports of manufactures:		
Developed countries[1]	84.4	74.8
Canada	28.1	23.5
Western Europe[2]	34.7	27.8
Japan	21.6	23.5
Communist areas in Europe and Asia	.5	.8
Developing Countries[3]	15.1	24.4
Brazil, Hong Kong, Mexico, South Korea, Singapore, and Taiwan	8.6	16.2
B. Markets for U.S. exports of manufactures:		
Developed countries[1]	62.8	55.6
Canada	24.3	26.0
Western Europe[2]	31.9	25.0
Japan	6.6	4.6
Communist areas in Europe and Asia	.5	1.1
Developing countries[3]	36.7	43.3
Brazil, Hong Kong, Mexico, South Korea, Singapore, and Taiwan	9.5	11.2

[1]OECD countries.
[2]OECD in Europe.
[3]All countries excluding OECD countries and Communist countries.
Source: Commerce Department, FT 155, FT 455.

B. U.S. Trade Partners in Manufactures

The origin of U.S. imports of manufactures has changed significantly since 1970 (Table 7). Developing countries boosted their share of U.S. imports from 15.1 percent in 1970 to 24.4 percent in 1977, and within this group, six rapidly industrializing countries (Brazil, Hong Kong, Mexico, Singapore, South Korea, Taiwan) doubled their share of U.S. manufactured imports in that period (Table 8). Furthermore, these six countries have greatly strengthened their relative position among developing country exporters of manufactures: while these six countries accounted for one-half of all LDC Manufactured goods imported by the U.S. in 1970, they accounted for two-thirds in 1977. Taiwan was the

Table 8.—Relative Importance of Selected Developing Countries in U.S. Trade, 1970 and 1977

	1970	1977
A. Brazil, Hong Kong, Mexico, Singapore, South Korea, and Taiwan. Share (percent) of U.S. imports of:		
All goods.	9.6	11.8
Manufactured goods (SITC 5-8)	8.6	16.2
Chemicals (SITC 5).	2.8	3.7
Manufactured goods by material (SITC 6).	5.1	10.3
Machinery and transportation (SITC 7).	4.8	10.9
Miscellaneous manufactured articles (SITC 8).	25.6	41.8
B. Brazil, Hong Kong, Mexico, Singapore, South Korea, and Taiwan. Share (percent) of U.S. exports of:		
All goods.	10.1	11.4
Manufactured goods (SITC 5-8)	9.5	11.2
Chemicals (SITC 5).	11.4	16.4
Manufactured goods by material (SITC 6).	8.6	9.5
Machinery and transportation (SITC 7).	9.5	10.7
Miscellaneous manufactured articles (SITC 8).	9.8	9.5

Source: Commerce Department, FT 155, FT 455.

leader, with manufactured goods exports to the U.S. valued at $3.5 billion in 1977. Manufactured goods imports from developing countries totaled $12.5 billion in 1977 (Table 7).

Developed countries in general remain the major source of foreign manufactures for the United States, although their share decreased from four-fifths of U.S. imports in 1970 to three-fourths in 1977. Within the advanced countries, Western Europe remains the dominant supplier, followed by Canada and Japan. Only Japan increased its share of the U.S. market during this eight-year period, from 21.6 percent in 1970 to 23.5 percent in 1977.

Communist countries continue to provide a relatively negligible portion of U.S. imports of manufacturers, although their share increased from 0.5 percent to 0.8 percent.

The country distribution of U.S. exports of manufactures has followed the general pattern of changes shown by the sources of U.S. manufactured imports: Developing countries are becoming more important for the U.S. (although the increase in LDC shares for U.S. exports is smaller than for U.S. imports). LDC buyers purchased two-fifths of U.S. manufactured exports in 1977. Within the group of LDCs, the oil-exporting countries have more than doubled their relative shares for U.S. manufactured exports, from 5.9 percent in 1972 to 13.1 percent in 1976.*Developed country markets declined somewhat in relative importance, from 62.8 percent in 1970 to 59.6 percent in 1977. Within this group, Canada replaced Western Europe as the most important market in 1977, purchasing almost one-third of U.S. manufactured exports. Western Europe's share dropped from 31.9 percent to 25.0 percent.

Communist countries continued to purchase a relatively small amount of U.S. manufactured exports: 1.1 percent in 1977, an increase of 0.6 percent over the 1970 level.

The most striking aspect of the developed country statistics is the low level or share of U.S. manufactured exports to Japan. Japan accounted for only 6.6 percent of U.S. export sales in 1970, and this share fell by almost one-third to 4.6 percent in 1977. In comparing the origins of U.S. manufactured exports, one major asymmetry becomes apparent: In 1977 Japan supplied 25.0 percent of U.S. manufactured imports but purchased only 4.6 percent of U.S. manufactured exports. No other area shows such great imbalance between sales to and purchases from the United States.

U.S. trade balances in capital goods worsened in 1977 for every major area with the exception of the European Community (Table 9). Most severe was the deterioration in the deficit with Japan, where the balance dropped further into deficit by 200 percent. The surplus with Communist countries decreased by 38 percent, and with East and South Asia by 8 percent.

Table 9.—U.S. Trade in Capital Goods with Selected Areas, 1970, 1976-77
(In billions of dollars)

	U.S. imports from—	U.S. exports to—	Balance[1]
European Community (9):			
1970[2]	1.6	4.1	2.5
1976	3.8	8.4	4.5
1977	4.5	9.1	4.6
Japan:			
1970	.6	1.2	.6
1976	2.2	1.7	- .4
1977	3.0	1.7	-1.2
Near East:			
1970	0	.4	.4
1976	.1	4.4	4.4
1977	.1	4.2	4.2
Western Hemisphere, excluding Canada:			
1970	.1	2.4	2.2
1976	.9	6.6	5.7
1977	1.0	6.6	5.6
Canada:			
1970	.8	2.6	1.7
1976	1.7	6.1	4.4
1977	2.0	6.3	4.4
Communist countries, Europe, and Asia:			
1970	0	.1	.1
1976	.1	.8	.8
1977	.1	.6	.5
East and South Asia, excluding Japan and Communist countries:			
1970	.2	1.1	.9
1976	1.4	4.0	2.5
1977	1.8	4.2	2.3

[1]Discrepancies in balances due to rounding.

[2]Excludes Denmark and Ireland, for which data are unavailable; includes United Kingdom.

Source: Commerce Department, FT-990.

Table 10.—Trade in Manufactures: United States, Federal Republic of Germany, Japan, 1970, 1975-77

(In billions of dollars)

	United States			Federal Republic of Germany			Japan		
	Imports	Exports	Balance	Imports (CIF)	Exports (FOB)	Balance	Imports (CIF)	Exports (FOB)	Balance
1970..............	25.9	29.7	3.8	17.4	30.7	13.3	5.6	18.1	12.5
1975..............	51.1	72.1	21.0	50.0	79.6	29.6	11.5	53.2	41.7
1976..............	64.8	78.5	13.8	48.6	90.7	42.1	13.4	64.6	51.2
1977..............	77.2	82.0	4.8	¹56.3	¹99.5	¹43.2	¹14.4	¹79.5	¹65.1
1977:²									
I	69.8	80.3	10.6	55.0	98.9	43.9	13.8	68.5	54.7
II	78.4	85.5	7.1	55.6	101.5	45.9	15.2	75.9	60.7
III..............	79.0	79.3	.3	56.3	99.5	43.2	14.4	79.5	65.1
IV..............	81.7	82.8	1.1	³	³	³	³	³	³
1978:²									
I	94.8	82.2	-12.6	....					

¹1977, III at annual rates.

²At annual rates.

³Not available.

Note: F.A.S. except where noted.

Source: Commerce Department, "International Economic Indicators."

C. Trade Performance of U.S. and Selected Countries

The U.S. trade performance in manufactures was feeble compared to that of West Germany and Japan (Table 10). The U.S. surplus in manufactures has continued to decline sharply from its 1975 peak of $21.0 billion, and in the last quarter of 1977 the annual rate based on the fourth quarter alone was only $1.1 billion. In the first quarter of 1978, the annual rate sank to a deficit of $12.6 billion. In comparison, the manufactures trade balances of West Germany and Japan have continued to improve, with the projected 1977 surplus of Germany growing to $43.2 billion and that of Japan growing to $65.1 billion, based on the third quarter of 1977. When trade in manufactures for the United States, West Germany, and Japan is related to domestic production of manufactured goods, the export orientation of these major U.S. competitors becomes apparent (Table 11). Germany's imports, as a share of domestic production of manufactured goods, increased by 6.5 percent from 1970 to 1976, while the figure for German exports increased by 14.4 percent. For Japan, the comparable import statistic actually declined 0.4 percent, while the export figure increased dramatically by 15.5 percent. For the U.S., manufactured goods imports and exports as a percentage of domestic manufactured goods production increased 6.3 percent and 7.5 percent, respectively.

Table 11.—Relative Importance of Manufactured Goods Production, United States,
Federal Republic of Germany, and Japan, 1970 and 1976

	United States		Federal Republic of Germany		Japan	
	Imports	Exports	Imports	Exports	Imports	Exports
A. Manufactures trade as a percentage of domestic production of manufactured goods:						
1970...............................	11.2	12.8	22.6	39.9	11.6	37.6
1976...............................	17.5	21.2	29.1	54.3	11.2	53.1
B. Manufactures trade as a percentage of GNP:						
1970...............................	2.6	3.0	9.4	16.5	2.9	9.2
1976...............................	3.8	4.6	10.5	19.5	2.4	11.8

Sources: Department of Commerce, "International Economic Indicators; International Economic Report of the President, 1977," table 2: "Monthly Report of the Deutsche Bundesbank, December 1977, table 111-1: Bank of Japan, "Economic Statistics Monthly," December 1977, table 121-2(8): "IMF International Financial Statistics."

Table 12.—Comparison of Export Performance of U.S. and Selected Countries, 1975-77
(In billions of dollars)

	West Germany		European Community		Japan	
	Value	Percent change from previous year	Value	Percent change from previous year	Value	Percent change from previous year
A. Exports of manufacturers by West Germany, European Community, and Japan, 1975-77:						
To world:						
1957..............................	79.6	...	233.3	...	53.2	...
1976..............................	90.7	13.9	257.7	10.5	64.6	21.4
1977..............................	99.5	9.7	302.7	17.5	79.5	23.1
To world, excluding United States:						
1975..............................	74.6	...	219.3	...	42.2	...
1976..............................	85.5	14.6	242.9	10.8	49.6	17.0
1977..............................	92.8	8.5	284.6	17.2	61.4	23.8
B. U.S. exports of manufacturers, 1975-77:						
1975..............................	72.1	...	...	...	...	...
1976..............................	78.5	8.9	...	...	...	...
1977..............................	82.0	6.2	...	...	...	...

Note: 1975: FOB; 1976-77: F.A.S.
Source: Commerce Department, International Economic indicators; GATT, International Trade 1976-77, appendix table A plus D; European Community, Monthly Trade Bulletin; 1977 European Community figures projected from January-September 1977, with EUA 1 equals $1.124.

Table 13.—Deviations from Constant Share Norms for Manufacturing Exports,
by Trading Partners: 1970-73, 1973-76, and 1970-76
(In millions of dollars)

Partner and period	United States	Germany	Japan	United Kingdom	France	Italy	Belgium-Luxem-bourg	Nether-lands	Canada
United States:									
1970-73................	...	475	-7	296	132	-209	168	84	-1,325
1973-76................	...	-2,356	2,945	-614	177	320	-555	-163	928
1970-76................	...	1,663	2,996	-219	364	-385	-323	-24	-1,003

Table 13.—Deviations from Constant Share Norms for Manufacturing Exports,
by Trading Partners: 1970-73, 1973-76, and 1970-76
(In millions of dollars)

Partner and period	United States	Germany	Japan	United Kingdom	France	Italy	Belgium-Luxem-bourg	Nether-lands	Canada
Canada:									
1970-73	46	29	11	-149	37	1	23	-26	...
1973-76	583	-103	55	-387	-42	11	-34	-37	...
1970-76	649	-59	74	-609	14	12	0	76	...
Japan:									
1970-73	-157	121	...	-31	89	51	32	4	-76
1973-76	88	-152	...	-66	-32	1	-65	-18	-11
1970-76	-97	-19	...	-105	68	59	-32	-15	-91
Australia, New Zealand, South Africa:									
1970-73	-36	237	560	-361	-20	15	47	-4	-152
1973-76	340	-333	311	-720	106	-91	-21	-60	50
1970-76	261	41	1,189	-1,293	70	-69	46	-68	-175
EEC-9:									
1970-73	-3,902	1,943	1,006	-670	1,180	-612	549	850	-941
1973-76	-108	-1,733	732	1,050	-835	988	-541	-940	-305
1970-76	-6,025	1,141	2,224	53	948	37	338	375	-1,676
Other developed Europe:									
1970-73	-550	304	204	-192	181	-71	16	198	-34
1973-76	188	-399	330	-302	-143	167	41	-177	-13
1970-76	-635	61	635	-635	133	60	72	118	-62
Developing Europe:									
1970-73	-462	129	-9	-293	209	40	35	78	-39
1973-76	169	24	333	-125	-122	80	-68	-128	-13
1970-76	-498	212	318	-547	179	140	-16	-13	-71
Eastern Europe:									
1970-73	36	1,154	-40	-386	-55	-480	114	62	-12
1973-76	310	-1,236	1,202	-411	111	-389	-152	-132	-1
1970-76	379	846	1,144	-1,102	5	-1,244	51	-23	-24
Africa:									
1970-73	-237	122	428	-422	5	-68	-55	27	6
1973-76	171	-41	-176	230	407	14	-26	79	43
1970-76	-268	183	636	-555	403	-114	-130	125	53
Caribbean:									
1970-73	-43	76	450	-173	-109	-123	5	-26	-68
1973-76	19	-260	229	-108	23	-45	-28	-72	22
1970-76	-65	-127	1,055	-416	-182	-263	-26	-123	-94
South America:									
1970-73	-559	126	479	-119	139	-37	-47	57	-191
1973-76	704	-496	18	-113	-137	51	-112	-193	222
1970-76	-129	-274	796	-317	120	-7	-35	-98	-96
Middle East:									
1970-73	-117	92	391	-249	-392	125	51	37	35
1973-76	1,058	255	1,977	-1,319	-1,468	-244	-570	-167	59
1970-76	677	587	3,267	-2,171	117	117	-464	-65	185
Central Asia and Far East:									
1970-73	-287	54	931	-298	70	-128	-19	12	-94
1973-76	164	-203	-10	-649	439	-93	118	-108	-27
1970-76	-238	-142	-1,418	-1,122	548	-299	90	-94	-177

Note: The table compares the hypothetical export level—that which would be needed to maintain the market share—with the actual export level. A positive deviation indicates an increasing market share. A negative deviation indicates a decreasing market share. The size of the deviation indicates the amount of exports needed to regain the initial market share (in the case of a negative deviation) or the amount by which exports exceeded the level necessary to maintain the initial market share (in the case of a positive deviation).

Source: C. Michael Aho and Richard D. Carney, "United States Export Performance in the Post-Devaluation Period: Continuation of a Secular Decline?" Statement submitted to the Senate Committee on Banking, Housing, and Urban Affairs, Subcommittee on International Finance, Feb. 23, 1978, p.14A.

The argument is frequently made that the poor U.S. export performance in manufactures since 1975 is the result of slow economic growth abroad. The data in Table 12 indicates that at best this view is incomplete. The West German and EC manufactures export growth rates for 1975-76 are higher for the world excluding the United States than they are for the entire world; furthermore, these rates (plus the Japanese rates) are higher than the U.S. rate for 1976. In 1977, the EC rate is slightly lower (by 0.3 percent) for the non-U.S. world, and the Japanese rate is slightly higher (0.7 percent). Again, rates for all three exporting areas to the world excluding the United States are higher than the U.S. export growth rate. If the growth rate (conjunctural business cycle) argument were fully valid, one would have expected to see much more pronounced differences in the export records of these areas betwen the world and the non-U.S. world markets. Stated otherwise, Japanese, German and EC export growth rates to third countries would have been expected to be less buoyant than their exports to the United States. The United States, with faster economic growth, should have pulled in imports more rapidly than third countries.

The U.S. market share performance in manufactures in major areas of the world has been weak compared to other important exporting nations (Table 13). From 1970 to 1976, the U.S. share declined in every major area except Canada and the Middle East. Japan, on the other hand, advanced in every area. West Germany lost shares in several areas including the U.S. itself, Canada, South America, and the Far East. In the important Middle East market, Japan had the greatest share expansion compared with other developed nations, followed by the United States and Germany.

Growth Rates of U.S. Manufactured Imports and Exports
(Percentage change from previous year)

	Imports	Exports
1966	28.6	10.3
1967	9.7	9.9
1968	30.4	14.2
1969	11.7	12.5
1970	12.6	9.6
1971	17.4	3.7
1972	24.3	11.4
1973	19.0	32.7
1974	22.7	41.7
1975	− 7.4	11.6
1976	26.8	8.9
1977	19.1	4.5

Source: Commerce Department, "International Economic Indicators."

Since 1960 major changes have occurred in world market shares of manufactured goods exports (Table 14). In the decade of the 1960s, the

United States lost much of its market share, from one-fourth of world manufactured goods exports in 1960 to one-fifth in 1970. West Germany surpassed the United States in the early 1970s as the chief world exporter of manufactures. U.S. export growth of manufactured goods improved dramatically in 1973 and 1974, reflecting dollar devaluation and strong economic growth abroad (Graph 2). Afterward, export growth slackened, approaching the sluggish pre-devaluation growth rates, as other developed countries entered periods of low economic activity and the developing countries exhausted their import financing resources. U.S. sales of manufactured goods abroad reflected the downturn in foreign markets. Therefore, the major improvement in the U.S. trade balance in 1973-75, which many attributed almost entirely to dollar devaluation, was due to a great extent to traditional business cycle developments at home and abroad.

Table 14.—Shares of World Exports of Manufactures

	United States		Federal Republic of Germany	France	Japan	United Kingdom
	Excluding exports	Other				
1960.	25.3	22.8	18.2	9.1	6.5	15.3
1969.	22.5	19.3	18.7	7.8	10.7	10.7
1970.	21.3	18.4	19.0	8.3	11.2	10.1
1971.	20.1	17.2	19.3	8.3	12.7	10.6
1972.	19.1	16.3	19.3	8.7	13.5	9.7
1973.	19.5	16.7	20.3	8.7	13.3	9.0
1974.	20.2	17.7	20.2	8.2	14.8	8.2
1975.	21.2	18.9	18.6	9.0	14.2	9.0
1976.	20.5	18.3	19.1	8.9	14.8	8.4
1977:						
I'	19.9	18.1	19.3	9.2	14.5	8.7
II'	20.0	18.6	18.5	9.0	15.0	9.5

'Annual rates.

Source: Commerce Department, "International Economic Indicators," March 1978.

U.S. imports of manufactures, on the other hand, actually fell in 1974, as the United States entered its economic slump earlier than other major countries. By 1976, however, imports resumed their brisk pace, reflecting the U.S. recovery, while manufactured exports maintained their low growth rates. Thus, both U.S. exports and imports saw their growth rates interrupted in the early 1970s. A poor export trend in the present decade has been interrupted by two good years. It seems that since 1976 the unfavorable trends in U.S. manufactured goods trade are reestablishing themselves as weak export growth accompanies strong import growth. By 1976, the U.S. market share of world manufactured exports began to decline from the 1975 peak.

Other countries experienced great changes in their export position. The United Kingdom, for example, has lost one-third of its share of world

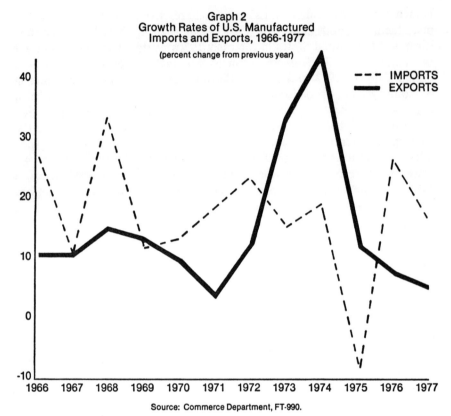

Graph 2
Growth Rates of U.S. Manufactured
Imports and Exports, 1966-1977

(percent change from previous year)

Source: Commerce Department, FT-990.

exports of manufactures since 1960. Japan has greatly increased its share, from 6.5 percent in 1960 to 14.8 percent in 1976. France has regained its 1960 market share after some weakness in its export performance in the early 1970s.

From 1970 to 1976, the U.S. has lost market shares in all four groups of manufactures (Table 15). The severest drop was in machinery and transport, followed by chemicals manufactures by material, and miscellaneous manufactures. Only foods and materials (except fuels) show an expanding market share. It is illuminating to note that, when this period is subdivided into 1970-73 and 1973-76, manufactures consistently lose shares in the earlier period and rebound in the latter one—but not sufficiently to regain their initial market share.

Note: The table compares the hypothetical export level—that which would be needed to maintain the market share—with the actual export level. A positive deviation indicates an increasing market share. A negative deviation indicates a decreasing market share. The size of the deviation indicates the amount of exports needed to regain the initial market share (in the case of a negative deviation) or the amount by which exports exceeded the level necessary to maintain the initial market share (in the case of a positive deviation).

Source: C. Michael Aho and Richard D. Carney, "United States Export Performance in the Post-Devaluation Period: Continuation of a Secular Decline?" Statement submitted to the Senate Committee on Banking, Housing, and Urban Affairs, Subcommittee on International Finance, Feb. 23, 1978, p.13A.

Table 15.—Deviations from Constant Share Norms at the 1-Digit SITC Level,
1965-70, 1970-73, 1973-76, and 1970-76
(In millions of dollars)

1-Digit SITC categories and period	United States	Germany	Japan	United Kingdom	France	Italy	Belgium-Luxembourg	Netherlands	Canada
Food (0):									
1965-70	− 1,690	396	129	− 57	239	− 232	288	− 346	− 562
1970-73	3,301	561	− 433	70	832	− 446	179	− 209	− 312
1973-76	− 2,258	− 27	− 411	− 8	− 920	89	− 83	430	− 264
1970-76	2,617	801	− 1,050	96	307	− 571	181	122	− 724
Beverages and tobacco (1):									
1965-70	− 93	11	− 1	20	47	44	− 8	20	19
1970-73	− 222	66	− 9	− 224	421	120	42	56	− 129
1973-76	164	104	45	− 21	− 356	19	14	34	− 72
1970-76	− 132	192	33	− 320	207	180	70	108	− 244
Materials (except fuels) (2):									
1965-70	− 53	− 23	− 37	− 27	− 208	− 95	− 151	− 31	44
1970-73	1,078	311	159	18	338	− 1	27	209	− 3
1973-76	− 1,418	− 100	− 119	− 175	− 290	− 39	− 184	− 135	− 541
1970-76	155	354	114	− 149	204	− 40	− 144	170	− 546
Fuels (3):									
1965-70	− 106	− 297	− 6	− 185	− 209	− 35	− 61	255	260
1970-73	− 1,232	− 123	5	4	72	44	71	818	642
1973-76	404	− 976	− 93	186	− 116	− 806	125	− 589	− 298
1970-76	− 2,395	− 1,255	− 80	194	48	− 706	287	1,270	1,159
Fats and oils (4):									
1965-70	− 179	25	− 15	− 5	16	9	14	45	3
1970-73	− 151	101	− 7	4	50	11	18	31	− 12
1973-76	6	42	− 1	− 3	7	4	26	0	12
1970-76	− 205	184	− 11	8	77	20	51	43	− 5
Chemicals (5):									
1965-70	− 613	254	223	− 386	− 103	− 211	257	310	29
1970-73	− 1,165	546	− 92	− 290	323	13	533	670	− 270
1973-76	158	− 1,088	− 4	108	− 514	20	91	195	170
1970-76	− 1,803	− 169	− 158	− 380	29	43	989	1,324	− 285
Materials manufactured (6):									
1965-70	− 514	657	616	− 1,029	− 390	− 219	6	− 38	− 88
1970-73	− 1,431	2,048	− 366	− 111	302	421	461	553	− 1,746
1973-76	440	− 1,390	2,687	− 1,582	239	822	− 2,489	− 142	− 313
1970-76	− 1,682	1,646	2,144	− 1,747	208	1,447	− 1,805	678	− 2,901
Machinery and transport (7):									
1965-70	− 2,257	− 729	2,519	− 3,257	552	489	− 117	− 413	2,988
1970-73	− 4,193	3,020	4,074	− 2,497	918	− 1,013	359	313	− 1,739
1973-76	1,019	− 4,791	5,179	− 1,790	1,372	− 383	43	− 55	− 1,171
1970-76	− 5,979	250	11,977	− 5,957	2,903	− 2,073	642	468	− 4,072
Miscellaneous manufactured articles (8):									
1965-70	− 586	77	268	− 218	− 174	401	− 11	78	91
1970-73	− 650	442	− 703	− 294	614	− 388	216	213	− 41
1973-76	491	− 360	90	− 42	− 537	708	− 327	− 43	− 16
1970-76	− 494	310	− 975	− 488	394	120	− 1	280	− 78
Not classified (9):									
1965-70	− 6	131	79	− 124	− 36	− 102	24	− 18	37
1970-73	− 246	62	169	25	− 49	2	80	− 20	− 64
1973-76	490	177	6	− 338	− 25	84	361	− 19	30
1970-76	− 914	283	299	− 295	− 110	88	499	− 54	− 81
Total exports:									
1965-70	− 7,123	1,246	3,757	− 5,091	− 772	− 25	− 1,412	− 5	1,734
1970-73	− 4,933	7,087	2,673	− 3,461	4,066	− 1,056	1,780	3,075	− 4,045
1973-76	− 1,723	− 6,997	7,280	− 3,499	− 2,379	− 1,056	− 3,006	874	− 1,933
1970-76	− 9,601	4,319	11,526	− 9,025	4,113	− 878	− 164	5,785	− 8,392

Table 16.—Changes in U.S. Exports by End-Use Category, 1970, 1975-77

Category	1977 value (billions)	1970-77 average annual rate	1975-76	1976-77
Grand total...	$120.16	15.7	6.9	4.5
Foods, feeds and beverages	19.59	18.9	3.3	− .5
Industrial supplies and materials	33.53	13.5	6.0	4.8
Capital goods, excluding automotive............................	39.05	15.3	8.1	1.9
Elec. mach., ex. consumer type	7.38	19.8	24.0	10.6
Generators, transf., and access. (switchgear, etc.)...............	1.64	25.2	30.8	9.4
Broadcasting and commun. eq. ex. telephonic and related elec. and electron. compon...	3.34	19.7	30.5	8.1
Telephonic eq. plus elec. apparatus n.e.c., incl. elec. furnaces, motors, cable, batt, X-ray, etc...............................	2.41	17.3	11.7	15.1
Non-elec. mach., ex. consmr.-type............................	25.46	15.1	5.3	3.1
Constr. and contracting mach. plus nonfarm factors, pts. and attach., n.e.c..	5.38	15.5	.4	− 9.5
Drilling plus oilfield eq.	1.34	23.4	4.3	− 17.2
Excavating plus paving mach................................	2.44	15.5	1.4	− 5.8
Nonfarm factors, pts. and attach............................	1.22	11.2	− 5.6	− 7.5
Non-elec. ind. mach., n.e.c.; pts. and attach., n.e.c..............	12.27	14.3	4.3	2.6
Power-gen. mach. ex. eng. for aircr. plus autos................	1.64	15.2	− 1.2	− 3.0
Mach. tools plus metalwkg. mach., n.e.c. plus pts..............	.89	7.7	.3	− 9.0
Spec. indl. mach., n.e.c., plus pts.	1.74	14.1	2.0	8.4
Measuring, testing, and control instruments plus pts.	1.92	14.4	8.9	16.1
Indl. mach., compon., plus pts., n.e.c., incl. pumps, compressors, valves, bearings, furnaces, etc...................	3.82	15.8	8.7	4.6
Ag. scien. plus bsns. mach., eq., plus fixtures; pts. and attach.......	7.81	16.4	12.1	15.0
Tractors, farm and garden, and pts. and attach.	.87	25.3	23.4	− 6.5
Ag. mach. plus pts., ex. tractors plus pts.	.71	21.7	1.7	2.9
Bsns. mach., ind. off., comput., copying, etc.	4.08	13.4	10.8	23.7
Scien., prof., med., plus hosp. instrum. plus eq................	1.06	21.0	18.3	16.4
Eq., tools, plus fixtures for photo and other service ind.	1.10	17.8	9.3	13.0
Civilian aircraft—complete, all types..........................	2.75	8.7	1.3	-14.3
Automotive vehicle, points plus engine	12.13	18.7	11.6	7.9
Consumer goods (nonfood, excluding automobile)	8.80	18.1	22.3	11.3
Consumer durables—manufactured (excluding automotive)	4.05	22.0	25.8	5.3
Consumer nondurables—manufactured.........................	4.74	16.7	19.0	17.0
Special category, domestic (military type) ....':...........	3.21	12.9	-13.1	23.4

Source: FT-990, table E-9. (1970 and 1975: Customs value; 1976 and 1977: F.A.A.)

D. U.S. Trade in Capital Goods

Within the capital goods category, the strongest export performer was electric machinery, which accounted for one-fifth of all capital goods exports in 1977 (Table 16). For the 1970-77 period, its average annual growth rate was 4.3 percent higher than the general capital goods rate. Electric machinery showed a vigorous export expansion in 1975-76 (10.6 percent). This is in marked contrast to the general decline in capital goods export sluggishness. The most vigorous electric machinery subgroup was generators, transformers and accessories (including switchgear), with a 1970-77 expansion record of 25.2 percent per year, on the average.

Non-electric machinery, supplying four-fifths of 1977 capital goods exports, grew at an average rate of 15.1 percent per year from 1970-77.

Strong performers within this group for the entire period include drilling and oil-field equipment and tractors and agricultural machinery, and scientific instruments. A pronounced drop in growth rates has been apparent since 1975 for drilling and oil-field equipment and tractors and agricultural machinery as large oil projects have been completed and LDC farm programs have encountered financing difficulties. An upturn is evident since 1975 for business equipment including computers and copiers, contrasting with a 1970-77 average-growth performance which ranked lower than the overall capital goods record. The absolute value of business machinery exports represents a major segment of capital goods sales, amounting to $4.08 billion in 1977.

Exports of civilian aircraft have traditionally made an important contribution to U.S. exports. In 1977 civilian aircraft sales amounted to $2.75 billion. However, the general growth of civilian aircraft exports from 1970 to 1977 was considerably lower than the general capital goods rate, averaging only 9.0 percent per year. Aircraft sales grew only 1.3 percent in 1975-76, and fell by 14.3 percent in 1975-77. Developments in 1978, however, indicate that this sector may have an expanding market in coming years.

U.S. sales of consumer goods and automotive vehicles out-performed capital goods sales, and export growth rates since 1975 have been much higher than capital goods rates. These two categories supplied $21 billion in export sales in 1977.

Capital goods sales are "lumpy," often related to large projects with long lead times. The downturn in U.S. capital goods exports since 1975 should not—taken in isolation—be given an undue importance. What does warrant careful consideration is the relatively moderate growth of capital goods exports throughout the 1970s and the rate of import growth. The capital goods export growth rate was below the expansion rate for total U.S. exports in this period, and also below the rate for foods, automotive vehicles, and consumer goods. On the import side, capital goods purchases grew at an average rate of 19.7 percent per year from 1970 to 1977, a growth rate which is one-third higher than the average rate of capital export expansion during this period.

Unfortunately, the end-use classification system which provides a capital goods breakdown is not used by other nations, so direct comparison of United States and foreign country performance in this sector is not possible. It has already been pointed out, however, that the United States has lost market shares for manufactured exports from 1970 to 1976, and examination of high-technology R + D-intensive manufactured exports by Aho and Carney indicates loss by market shares by the United States. Examining the two-digit breakdowns of the four SITC categories of manufactures for market share changes from 1970 to 1976, Aho and Carney found that only 9 out of the 30 subgroups showed gains. None of these 9 subgroups could be considered R + D intensive.[1] All of the traditionally R + D intensive subgroups lost market shares, and some of the greatest losses occurred in the most technically advanced categories such as chemical elements, plastics, electrical and nonelectrical machinery, transport equipment, and scientific instruments. Aho and Carney conclude:

"Since all of the deviations [indicating changes in market share] for the technically sophisticated products were negative between 1970 and 1976, this implies that those sectors did not reverse any losses caused by the excess demand inflation of the 1960s. In fact, in several of the categories the losses were accentuated even though the dollar was devalued."[2]

Thus, even allowing for the unsteady nature of capital goods sales, the development of U.S. capital goods exports over the past several years indicates that basic changes are occurring in the U.S. competitive position.

Capital goods imports from a relatively small but rapidly growing part of total U.S. imports. Such imports accounted for 9.1 percent of total imports in 1977, but the 1970-77 average annual rate of growth of capital goods exceeded that of any other end-use import category, excluding oil (Table 17). Furthermore, the U.S. has been importing capital goods at a considerably higher rate (19.7 percent per year) than it has been exporting capital goods (15.3 percent per year) for the 1970-77 period. The 1975-76 import growth rate dropped to 13.9 percent, but this climbed to 21.9 percent in 1976-77, higher than that of any other non-petroleum category except civilian aircraft.

The increasing expansion of U.S. purchases of capital goods from abroad, together with sluggish U.S. exports of such goods, has occurred throughout the 1970s and further underlines the need for analysis regarding competitive developments in this critical part of the manufactured goods sector.

Conclusion: Looking ahead

World trade slowed down more markedly in 1977 than in 1976, and most developed countries experienced minimal economic growth. The United States, with a relatively high domestic growth rate for 1977, enjoyed no real export expansion in the key manufacturing sector. Other major exporting countries, however, not only expanded their exports to the U.S. market, but to an even greater extent in markets outside the United States. On the other hand, U.S. imports grew 12 percent in volume compared to 5 percent for Germany and 2.5 percent in Japan. The United States increased its imports of capital goods in 1977 more rapidly than consumer goods.

Table 17.—Changes in U.S. Imports by End-Use Category, 1970, 1975-77

Category	1977 value (billions)	Percent change 1970-77 average annual rate	1975-76	1976-77
Grand total	$146.82	20.0	25.7	21.7
Foods, feeds and beverages	8.49	4.7	19.9	14.6
Industrial supplies and materials	75.62	25.0	25.0	24.1
Petroleum plus petroleum products, ex. gas	41.38	47.2	28.2	30.2
All other industrial supplies plus mat.	34.24	15.7	21.7	17.5
Capital goods, ex. automotive	13.35	19.7	13.9	22.0
Elec. mach., ex. consmr., plus pts............................	4.56	24.0	30.6	21.0
Non-elec. mach., ex. consmr.; transp. equip. excl. auto plus aircraft; pts. plus attach., n.e.s.	8.20	18.0	9.6	21.1
Mach. tools plus met. wkg. plus pts...........................	.54	16.1	– 0.2	22.2
Constr., text, plus other spec. indl. mach., plus pts.	1.53	16.0	8.7	30.7
Indl. nonelec. mach., eng., plus pts., n.e.s., incl. pumps, compressors, bearings, material handling eq., nonmtl. wkg. mach tools, etc.	2.51	19.1	8.3	21.4
Tractors (nonfarm), pts. plus attach.	.07	12.9	– 33.0	– 31.9
Tractors (farm plus garden), pts. plus attach...................	.66	20.0	7.1	20.6
Ag. mach. plus pts., ex. tractors plus pts......................	.52	16.4	4.4	2.1
Bsns. mach., incl. office, computing, copying, etc..............	1.51	18.1	26.1	17.5
Scientific, prof., plus service-industry eq. plus pts.; misc. transp. eq., n.e.s.	.88	20.0	12.7	32.9
Civilian aircraft, engines and parts............................	.59	17.6	– 25.8	45.2
Automotive veh, pts., plus engines	18.67	17.7	38.4	15.6
Consumer goods (nonfood), ex. auto	22.42	16.8	34.4	21.8
Consumer nondurables—mfd...............................	8.38	16.0	36.8	12.0
Consumer durables, ex. auto—mfd...........................	12.29	17.1	32.3	27.3

Note: 1970 and 1975: Customs value; 1976 and 1977: FAS.

Source: Commerce Department, FT-990, table 1-10 (1970), table 1-5 (1976-77).

It thus appears that basic difficulties may be surfacing in the industrial sector. Are rising capital goods imports and stagnant capital goods exports, for example, different aspects of a more fundamental underlying problem—low rates of capital investment in the United States? How important are foreign government export promotion programs, i.e., export-led growth policies to pay for oil imports and overcome unemployment? What of the role of interventionist government industrial policies designed to create high technology industries? Or state-trading or public sector projects in which governments intervene to determine trade flows and select buyers and sellers?

Until now, insufficient analysis has been devoted to the changing roles and composition of the manufactured goods sector in the U.S. trade deficit. Export expansion programs, import policies, conceptual approaches to economic adjustment and strategies of economic development in the United States—each of these policy areas may benefit from in-depth examination of current changes in trade in the manufacturing sector.

A more definitive understanding of the current trade deficit—not to mention policy recommendations designed to alleviate it—must include an evaluation of the relatively new development which this report has highlighted—the manufacturing sector's loss of market shares abroad, and at home as well.

Statistical Appendix

Trade balance figures and market share data are extensively used in this report, rather than absolute figures for exports and imports in order to overcome to the extent practicable the "money illusion." Inflation, of course, simply exaggerates the size of imports and exports.

Two classification systems are used in this report. The Standard International Trade Classification (SITC) was developed by the United Nations and is used by most trading nations of the world. It includes the following categories:

0 Food and Live Animals.
1 Beverages and Tobacco.
2 Crude Materials, except Fuels—Inedible.
3 Mineral Fuels, Lubricants, and Related Materials.
4 Oils and Fats—Animal and Vegetables.
5 Chemicals.
6 Manufactured Goods Classified Chiefly by Material (including paper, textiles except fibers and apparel, iron and steel).
7 Machinery and Transport.
8 Miscellaneous Manufactured Articles (including clothing, footwear, scientific instruments, clocks and musical instruments).
9 Commodities and Transactions not classified according to Kind (U.S. goods returned and shipments under $251).

The second system used in this report is the "end-use" classification, a U.S. government system based on combinations of two or more numbers of the Tariff Schedules of the United States Annotated. End-use categories are not used by other nations. However, they have the advantage of distinguishing between capital goods and consumer goods, and they are therefore useful in this type of study. End-use categories include:

Foods, Feeds and Beverages.
Industrial Supplies and Materials (including fuels, paper, textile supplies, iron ore and steel scrap, and iron and steel manufactures).
Capital Goods, except Automotive.
Automotive Vehicles, Parts, and Engines.
Consumer Goods (Nonfood), except Automotive.
Imports, Not Elsewhere Stated (including military aircraft and U.S. goods returned).

Geographical breakdowns follow the terminology established by the Department of Commerce, "Guide to Foreign Trade Statistics 1975," page 201.

*Brazil, Hong Kong, Mexico, Singapore, South Korea, and Taiwan.

*The U.S. balance to manufactured goods with the EC showed a surplus of $2.05 billion in 1977; the U.S. had a surplus in foods, feeds and beverages of $4.04 billion and a surplus in capital goods of $4.00 billion.

*Figures do not include gas. The Census Bureau statistics used here do not include oil imported in the Virgin Islands for U.S. consumption, which amounted to $2.6 billion in 1977.

**Commerce Department, Bureau of International Economic Policy and Research, Staff Economic Report, "The U.S. trade Balance Less Oil: Is It Meaningful?" August 1977, p.3.

*See statistical appendix for definition of SITC classification system and end-use categories.

*General Agreement on Tariffs and Trade. *International Trade 1976/1977* (GATT Geneva 1977), Appendix, Table A.

[1]The 9 subgroups were: fertilizers, explosives, leather manufactures, wood and cork, paper manufactures, textiles, furniture, handbags and luggage, and footwear.

[2]Aho and Carney, p.24.

United States Export Performance

Robert Brusca

Following a prolonged period of stagnation, the volume of United States exports registered one of its sharpest surges ever between January and November 1978. Export volume increased at nearly a 25 percent annual rate. That compares with an average increase of less than 1 percent per annum over the preceding three years.

The marked reversal in export performance requires explanation. Why did United States exports remain so weak up through early 1978? And why has the subsequent turnaround in exports been so pronounced?

Providing thoroughly convincing answers to these questions may be impossible. Over recent years this country's exporters—and potential exporters—have been faced with significant changes in dollar exchange rates, with sharply differing economic growth rates here and abroad, and with diverse trends in national inflation rates. In those circumstances, the profit incentives to export have undergone considerable change from one year to the next. And, in an atmosphere of continuing uncertainty, the varied responses of exporters to those changes in incentives have been unusually hard to foresee on the basis of simple statistical relationships drawn from the past.

Nevertheless, based on the initial results of empirical research in progress at the Federal Reserve Bank of New York, a number of conclusions can be made:

- Much of the weakness of United States export volume after the 1974-75 recession stems from the coincidence of slow growth of import demand in our major markets abroad, especially Japan and Canada, and relatively rapid economic growth in this country.

From *Quarterly Review,* Federal Reserve Bank of New York, Winter 1978-79, pages 49-56. Reprinted by permission of Federal Reserve Bank of New York.

- The United States' share of world markets deteriorated substantially in 1978 and 1977, largely because of a major erosion of the price competitiveness of our exports that occurred during the recession years.
- Price competitiveness has been restored by the exchange rate changes of the past two years. But it takes about two to three years for exports to respond significantly to improved profit opportunities, and those lags may have been lengthened as a result of the relative cyclical behavior of United States and foreign economies.
- Based on current patterns of adjustment, further substantial improvement in United States export volume—on the order of 10 to 15 percent—may be expected over the coming months.

THE EXPORT SLUMP

In 1977 the value of this country's exports was about 18 percent higher than the average during the 1974-76 recession. But, after taking inflation into account, this amounted to an increase in export volume of less than 2 percent, or an average rise of less than 1 percent per year (Chart 1). This performance was poor relative to our own historical experience; export volume had increased about 6½ percent a year throughout the preceding decade. And it was poor by international comparison. Other industrial countries increased their export volume by about 13 percent between 1974-76 and 1977.

An emphasis on export *volume,* rather than on *value,* requires some justification. The choice of a measure of export performance depends on the problem to be examined. Export value is an appropriate broad measure of the impact of trade flows on national income, since an increase in volume brings little economic gain when accompanied by a

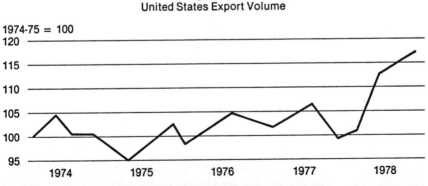

Chart 1
United States Export Volume

1974-75 = 100

Latest plotting is an average for October and November.
Source: United States Department of Commerce

great drop in export prices relative to the general level of prices. Fortunately, the United States does not often find itself in such a situation. Because this country sells a wide range of goods abroad, the average level of our export prices is not much affected by price swings for a few commodities. By the same token, however, this means that, in order to achieve much of a reduction in the United States trade deficit, export volume must increase considerably.

There is another important reason to focus on export volume: it provides a more appropriate measure than export value for comparing the United States performance with that of other countries. Such a comparison is normally made in terms of the share of each country's exports in total world trade. But evaluating performance by value shares has drawbacks. The calculation of value shares requires that all export flows be translated into a common currency at current exchange rates. This immediately reduces the share of a country whose currency has depreciated. Value shares can, therefore, give a misleading indicating of underlying performance. A country's export volume share may actually be improving during a given period in response to a previous depreciation of its currency even as its value share is still declining. For this reason, volume shares are preferred for cross-country comparisons of export performance.

Finally, changes in export volume are the appropriate measure for assessing the impact of foreign sales on domestic employment.

BUSINESS CYCLE EFFECTS

Following the 1974-75 recession, United States exporters faced slower growing export markets than did producers from other major industrial countries (Table 1). By and large, in this period as in the past, a high rate of export volume growth among industrial countries has been associated with relatively faster growing foreign markets. These differences in market growth rates account for only part of the differences in export performance among countries; other factors, such as price competitiveness, are also important. However, the impact is not negligible. For example, had United States export markets grown at the same rate as those for Japan over the period, the rate of increase in foreign sales volume for this country would have more than doubled, even assuming the United States suffered the same loss of relative market share that actually occurred. That would have translated into an extra $3 billion of exports in 1977 (or 2½ percent of the total recorded).

That crude estimate, however, provides only a lower bound to the actual impact on our exports of slower foreign growth. Supply-side influences aggravated the effects on United States export performance of relatively weak demand in foreign markets. If foreign producers who compete directly with United States firms had faced more buoyant markets in their own countries, they might have run into constraints on supplying exports to third markets or they might have competed less aggressively for new business abroad, concentrating instead on meeting demand at home. This would have made it relatively easier for United States producers to compete both in other industrial countries and in the developing countries. Similarly, had the United States economy grown less rapidly than it in fact did, American firms would have found the export market relatively more attractive and competed there with more vigor.

The pattern of global recovery from the 1974-75 recession was particularly adverse for United States exports. Economic expansion in this country was vigorous by any yardstick. The actual rate of growth not only exceeded the economy's longer term potential growth rate, but it also exceeded the average growth rate achieved in recoveries from earlier postwar recessions.

The United States experience contrasts sharply with that of other industrial countries (Table 2). For them, economic recovery from the recession has been weak. Actual growth rates have been below historical recovery rates. And they have even been below longer term potential growth rates. In other words, growth was not fast enough to reduce significantly unemployed resources or to stimulate substantial import demand.

Table 1.—Trade Volume and Market Shares for Selected Countries

Exporting country	Own export volume growth 1974-75 to 1977 (percentage increase)	Rest-of-world import volume growth* 1974-75 to 1977 (percentage increase)	Average market share† 1974-75 (percent)	Average market share† 1977 (percent)	Marginal market share‡ (percent)	Competitiveness ranking measures§ (ratio)
	(1)	(2)	(3)	(4)	(5)	(6)
United States	1.8	13.6	15.1	13.5	2.0	0.1
Canada	17.9	16.1	4.4	4.5	4.9	1.1
Japan	33.6	16.4	7.2	8.3	14.8	2.1
France	14.4	15.5	7.0	6.9	6.5	0.9
Germany	12.7	14.8	12.5	12.3	10.8	0.9
Italy	21.5	15.9	4.4	4.6	5.9	1.3
United Kingdom	15.0	16.6	5.8	5.7	5.3	0.9

*Based on world import volume minues that of the country for which the calculation is made.

†Ratio of each country's export volume index to the rest-of-world volume index.

‡The change in each country's export volume between its 1974-75 average and its 1977 level divided by the change in rest-of-world import volume over the same period.

§Column 5 divided by column 3.

Sources: International Monetary Funds: *International Financial Statistics* and *Direction of Trade.*

Table 2.—Import Volume and Real Domestic Growth

Country	Import volume growth 1974-75 to 1977				Gross national product growth at annual percentage rates			
	Actual (% increases)	Normal* (% increases)	Ratio of own to rest-of-world† (as a %)	Import income elasticity	Growth from 1974-75 to 1977	Actual recovery rate‡	Historic recovery rate	Long-term potential rate
	(1)	(2)	(3)	(4)	(5)	(6)	(7)	(8)
United States	28.2	26.7	31.3	2.6	3.9	5.6	4.4	3.8
Canada.............	4.8	15.2	1.4	1.7	3.5	4.1	6.5	5.2
Japan.............	3.7	16.4	2.5	1.3	4.9	5.3	8.0	6.5
France	16.4	15.9	7.6	1.9	3.2	3.0	6.2	5.5
Germany	23.2	15.5	15.4	2.1	2.9	4.1	6.0	4.8
Italy..............	7.8	10.8	2.5	1.9	2.2	2.4	5.7	4.8
United Kingdom.....	1.8	4.9	0.8	2.1	0.9	2.3	3.3	3.0

*Each country's import income elasticity times its annual growth rate (column 5) compounded over the two and one-half year period from the 1974-75 base to the end of 1977.

†Rest-of-world import volume defined as in Table 1.

‡Actual rates of recovery are calculated from the trough quarter of the recession (which differs for each country) through the fourth quarter of 1977.

Source: Staff estimates, Federal Reserve Bank of New York.

As a result, the United States market was exceptionally attractive to all producers. To foreign producers, the American economy provided nearly one third of the additional demand for "foreign" goods that was provided by the rest of the world combined. To American producers, faced with a buoyant home market and slack markets abroad, the incentives favored sales at home. Export efforts could be retaxed and domestic marketing became easier. Since less than 10 percent of United States gross national product (GNP) is exported, even a small shift in marketing effort by United States producers can have a major impact on exports.

A particular consequence of the slow expansion abroad was a general weakness in world investment demand. Since capital goods form a substantial part of United States exports (30 percent over the past 14 years), weak investment spending had a major adverse effect on our foreign sales during the recovery period. The United States was the only industrial country in which the growth rate of real investment expenditure exceeded real income growth. German investment grew at the same rate as the economy in general. Italy suffered a 5½ percent decline, while real investment spending in the United Kingdom was but ½ percen; above its 1974-75 level by the end of 1977. In Japan, real investment spending rose by 2 percent, compared with cumulative real growth of 13 percent. Under these circumstances, the volume of United States capital goods exports rose less than 1 percent between 1974-75 and the beginning of 1978, compared with an average annual increase of about 8 percent per year over the previous decade.

Another major reason for our weak export performance can be found in the particular sluggishness of imports by Canada and Japan, two of our major markets. Over the last fourteen years, fully 30 percent of United States exports have been sold in Canada and Japan. Those two countries historically tend to increase their imports proportionately less than most industrial countries as their domestic economies expand. In technical terms, their "income elasticities of demand" are relatively low (Table 2). To make matters worse, in this recovery both Canada and Japan drew in far fewer imports than would be expected on the basis of past experience. For these countries, actual import volume growth turned out to be more than 10 percentage points below the growth that would have occurred had the historical relationships between import growth and income growth been maintained. Indeed, a closer look at Japanese import patterns shows an actual decline of about 10 percent in import volume from all industrial countries. United States export volume to Japan fell by a slightly larger proportion. Had Canadian and Japanese import volumes registered normal growth in relation to their income over the period, that alone would have added nearly $4 billion to United States exports in 1977.

DECLINE IN MARKET SHARES

The weakness of United States exports over the recovery period is underscored by the severe drop in our share of foreign markets. The overall market share fell from about 15 percent for the 1974-75 average to under 14 percent in 1977 (Table 1). That means that at the margin less than 2 percent of the increase in world import volume outside the United States was met by American goods.

Comparisons with other countries are instructive. Japan improved its market share dramatically. At the margin, nearly 15 percent of the increase in world import volume outside Japan was met by Japanese goods. As a result, Japan's share of world markets rose from about 7 percent to around 8 percent. For other industrial countries, market shares did not change very much. Italy and Canada experienced small increases, while Germany, France, and the United Kingdom had minor declines in market shares.

These market share comparisons are based on aggregate rest-of-world imnports, but obviously a country may do better or worse in different regional markets. Table 3 provides information on selected regional markets that shows an across-the-board decline in United States market shares. In a number of areas there were even absolute declines in United States export volume. Japan, in contrast, increased its shares in all these areas dramatically. The German performance lies somewhere in between.

Rough orders of magnitude can be attached to the effects of declining market shares on United States export volume. Take the actual rate of foreign market growth faced by the United States and suppose that our market shares had remained constant, rather than falling as they actually did. Under those assumptions, United States export volume growth for the period would have been over 13 percent instead of about 2 percent. Supposing the same price increases that actually occurred, export value for 1977 would have been $14 billion higher. In short, the fall in market shares is the most disturbing aspect of the export slump and accounts for nearly half of the $31 billion merchandise trade deficit in 1977.

PRICES AND EXCHANGE RATES

How much of this market share loss can be attributed to a deterioration in price competitiveness? Conversely, how much reflects the strength of the United States market and the relative weakness of other industrial country markets or the various nonprice influences on overall competitiveness—such factors as delivery delays, inadequate export financing facilities, or the effects of various government policies? Any answers to these questions must be viewed as highly tentative and subject to a considerable margin of uncertainty. Nevertheless, some preliminary estimates can be made.

Price competitiveness of exports depends on both the actual prices of goods produced here and abroad and the exchange rates for the dollar against other currencies. As illustrated in Chart 2, the price competitiveness of United States exports has fluctuated widely over recent years. Chart 3 breaks out the component parts: the ratio of national price levels and the weighted average or "effective" exchange rate of the dollar. It shows that, after exchange rates began to float in March 1973, our price competitiveness initially improved—at first because the dollar depreciated and then because inflation was lower here than abroad. The peak in price competitiveness in this period was reached in the second quarter of 1974. Then an acceleration of United States inflation led to a deterioration of our competitive position through mid-1975. An appreciation of the dollar extended that trend until late that year. By mid-1976, however, the loss of competitiveness was reversing as United States inflation slowed relative to that abroad. This began to restore price competitiveness despite further appreciation of the dollar's weighted average exchange value. The improvement in price competitiveness gathered momentum during 1977 as the dollar fell sharply in the exchange markets. By 1978, domestic inflation had worsened but the dollar's continued depreciation more than compensated for the adverse competitive consequences. Even after the dollar's recovery in the exchange markets after November 1, United States price competitiveness was still around levels comparable to the 1974 peak.

Chart 2
United States Export Competitiveness

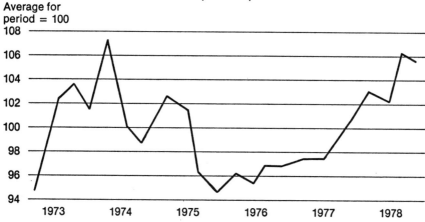

This indicator of changing price competitiveness of United States exports is a ratio of wholesale prices, measured in dollar terms, of the major trade competitors of the United States—Canada, France, Germany, Italy, Japan, and the United Kingdom—to United States wholesale prices. An increase in the ratio suggests an improvement in United States competitivenss, a decline, a worsening. Foreign prices and exchange rates for each country are weighted by the average of the shares derived from, first, 1977 United States bilateral exports to each country and, second, 1977 exports of each country to markets other than the United States.

Chart 3
Components of United States
Export Competitiveness

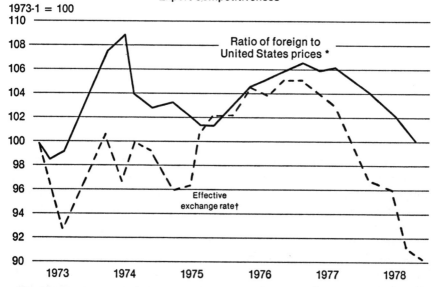

*Prices are wholesale prices. Foreign prices are those of the six countries listed in the footnote to Chart 2 and are weighted in the manner described in that footnote.

†Exchange rates are in terms of foreign currency units per dollar. The effective rate is constructed by weighting dollar exchange rates for the currencies of the six foreign countries in the manner described in the footnote to Chart 2.

The erosion in price competitiveness of United States exports between mid-1974 and early 1976 progressively depressed foreign demand for products made in this country. The adverse effect did not take place all at once, but only gradually as decisions were made at the margin whether to buy goods from the United States or from a competing firm located in another industrial nation. As a result, foreign goods were more frequently chosen whenever price was the determining factor. What is worse, the process continued long after the erosion of price competitiveness had begun to be reversed.

Economists concerned about international trade flows have sought to estimate statistically how and over what time period these factors affect exports. Our results suggest that adjustment lags extending two or three years after a major change in price competitiveness appear to be characteristic of United States exports. In other countries, for which capital goods exports are a less important component of total foreign sales, the time lags seem to be shorter.

By 1977, those lagged effects were having their maximum depressing effect on exports. Over half of the decline in the United States export market share is estimated to have resulted from the erosion in price competitiveness between mid-1974 and early 1976. In other words, for 1977, United States export volume might have been about 8 to 9 percent greater than it was had the erosion not occurred.

To be sure, that leaves much of the decline in market share unexplained. In particular, a large part of that residual may reflect agressive efforts by exporters of some countries to develop and to expand market penetration at a time when domestic growth prospects in their countries looked weak and, at the same time, relative indifference by many American companies to export opportunities.

ADJUSTMENT LAGS

Just as the slump in United States export volume growth took time to materialize, a favorable response of export volume to improved price competitiveness after 1975 also came with a long delay. Before detailing the character of last year's export surge, it is worthwhile to discuss further why the adjustment lags are so long.

Generally, producers in economies that are relatively dependent on exports will be less prone to shift sales patterns between domestic and foreign markets in response to what they feel are transitory factors. When the export sector is large relative to the domestic sector, many producers may find a swift change in sales patterns to be excessively disruptive and undesirable. Therefore, exporters in export-dependent countries have an incentive to maintain their market shares by cutting profit margins. That behavior seems to have had a major effect in slowing adjustment to the changes in price competitiveness as they occurred.

In addition, our statistical analysis suggests that market participants may react fairly quickly to changes in prices of United States goods relative to foreign goods when such changes result from differing domestic inflation rates. But they may react comparatively slowly to changes in prices of United States goods relative to foreign goods when such changes result from movements in exchange rates.

A reason for these differential rates of response may be this. It is likely that domestic exporters and foreign purchasers will not alter their behavior in response to price incentives that they consider to be temporary. Changes in price competitiveness resulting from changes in domestic currency prices of manufactured goods may be viewed as relatively permanent. From experience, firms appear to be uneasy committing themselves to new listed prices only to retract the changes soon thereafter. But exchange rates are known to fluctuate widely over short periods of time. Thus, exporters and importers may take account of exchange rate changes only after rates have appeared to stabilize. That kind of behavior might result in lengthening the observed lag between exchange rate changes and changes in export volume.

The delay in responding may be even longer if exchange market expectations of United States exporters and foreign importers are conflicting. For example, when the dollar began to decline in 1977, United States businesses may have expected an early rebound and may not have taken steps immediately to expand export sales. By contrast, many foreigners might have been willing to purchase United States goods as soon as they became "cheap enough," but held back orders in anticipation of still better prices later on should the dollar decline further.

Another complicating factor tends to lengthen the adjustment lags following an improvement in price competitiveness. Shifting sources of supply involves costs, and buyers may be willing to incur those costs only after they feel a price advantage will be permanent. Take, for example, a commodity like lumber, for which there is a uniform world price. Any depreciation of the dollar makes lumber cheaper to foreign purchasers in terms of their local currency. But lumber purchasers may decide to switch to American lumber only after the depreciation has become large enough to offset whatever adjustment costs are perceived, and the new rate is broadly expected to be sustained.

Suppliers, too, may have to incur additional costs by changing the focus of their sales effort. This is particularly true for products which, unlike lumber, are not uniform in nature, such as industrial machinery or computers. Such products may require a special sales effort because they have distinctive characteristics differing among national producers or because they are built to specification. This may necessitate a substantial marketing expenditure by the producer or the producer's sales agent which, in some cases, may include educating the prospective consumer as to the potential benefits of the product. The existence of these start-up costs when penetrating new markets also explains exporters' reluctance to bear new costs until they are sure that those costs can be recouped.

Finally, the response of exporters and potential exporters to a change in profit incentives to export may be conditioned by the nature of domestic inflationary pressures at the time. An initial improvement in price competitiveness resulting from a depreciation of the dollar may generate substantial foreign orders. For goods already in inventory, both buyer and seller could profit from a quick sale. But for goods that take time to produce, the incentives are more ambiguous if increased inflation is expected to accompany the depreciation. In that case, the exporter, faced with the prospect of higher costs, would tend to raise future delivery prices—and perhaps enough to discourage the potential buyer altogether. It may be that exporters are willing to make firm contracts for future delivery only after the depreciation clearly has gone far enough to compensate for anticipated inflation.

Indeed, a clear increase in sales abroad was delayed until the second quarter of 1978, when it was widely felt that neither a sharp rebound for the dollar nor any likely acceleration in United States inflation would wipe out the existing profit potential to export.

THE EXPORT SURGE

Between January and November of last year, United States foreign sales volume increased at a 25 percent annual rate and the share of our exports in world markets recovered significantly.

The increases occurred across virtually all groupings of commodities sent to all areas of the world. The volume of agricultural exports rose at an annual rate of 18 percent, compared with 27 percent for non-agricultural export volume. Exports to Latin America and other developing countries have rapidly accelerated, in large measure because of exceptionally high agricultural purchases. Consumer goods exports to the nonindustrialized world have also risen substantially. Increased absorption by Western Europe of industrial materials and supplies indicates both the improvement in United States price competitiveness and the somewhat stronger growth of European economies. These changes have also led to mounting purchases of United States capital goods.

Based on our empirical research, about half of the increase in non-agricultural exports can be traced to the improvement in United States price competitiveness since the beginning of 1976 and about half to cyclical developments and other factors. For agricultural commodities, estimating the impact of the dollar's depreciation is more difficult but it certainl contributed to the sudden strength of agricultural export volume early last year.

Relatively favorable price competitiveness can be expected to continue in the months to come, although it will be eroded somewhat to the extent that inflation here is faster than abroad. Nonetheless, a further gain of 10-15 percent in United States export volume is a reasonable anticipation, given an outlook for somewhat stronger growth of demand in foreign countries.

Looking to the longer term prospects for United States exports, one clear challenge is to increase the number of firms that regularly do business abroad. The export promotion package announced by the Administration last September seeks to accomplish that as one of its objectives. The plan envisages increases in Export-Import Bank loan authorizations and expanded efforts to heighten producer awareness of foreign sales opportunities. In addition, it proposes elimination of the requirement that exporters must file environmental impact statements, a move that can help reduce delays in realizing new export opportunities. The extent to which other broad government policies—including those on human rights in foreign countries, on nuclear nonproliferation, on the Arab boycott, and on special business payments to foreign importers—may be impeding the growth of United States exports remains unclear.

Another major challenge is to improve United States productivity, a fundamental determinant of United States comparative advantage, by developing ways to strengthen business capital spending and research and development efforts. The latter, in particular, play an important role in opening up opportunities to export, and in the United States such expenditures have been lagging of late. As a percentage of GNP, United States expenditures on research and development have fallen from 2.7 percent in 1962 to 2.2 percent in 1978. Over approximately the same period such expenditures by Germany and Japan have risen 1 percentage point and ½ percentage point to 2.3 percent and 2.0 percent of GNP, respectively.[1]

Finally, United States export performance is likely to depend crucially on the outlook for world investment spending. The share of investment in GNP has declined in a number of important countries in recent years. A reversal of that trend would provide a significant underpinning for stronger United States exports in the future.

---

[1]National Science Board, *Science Indicators, 1976* (Washington, D.C., National Science Foundation), September 30, 1977.

The Recent U.S. Trade Deficit

No Cause for Panic

Geoffrey E. Wood and Douglas R. Mudd

Alarm has been mounting about the size of the U.S. trade deficit in 1977 and what seems in prospect for the deficit in 1978. The 1977 deficit has been described as the "largest in the Nation's history."[1] It has been implied that the trade surpluses of other countries, which are the counterpart of the U.S. deficits, are in some way harmful.

> There is no reason to believe that this pattern of accumulating surpluses for the oil exporters and chronic deficits for the oil importers will be reversed in the near future. The grim conclusion . . . is that the OPEC countries will continue to pile up excess reserves . . . accumulating some $250-$300 billion in financial assets by 1980.[2]

It has been claimed that the deficit has "produced a loss in jobs."[3]

Perhaps as a consequence of these fears, policy has increasingly come to focus on reducing one component of the trade deficit as a means of halting the decline of the dollar.

But the balance of trade is only one aspect of a country's international economic relations, and there are circumstances when a trade deficit is highly desirable. Further, the fear that a trade deficit will aggravate national unemployment is erroneous. In terms of national economic policy, the recommendation to reduce one component of the deficit so as to strengthen the dollar would not be helpful.

From *Federal Reserve Bank of St. Louis Review,* April 1978, pages 2-7. Reprinted by permission of Federal Reserve Bank of St. Louis.

THE BALANCE OF MERCHANDISE TRADE, THE BALANCE OF TRADE, AND THE BALANCE OF PAYMENTS

A country's exchange rate—that is, the value of its currency in terms of other currencies—will stay unchanged if the quantity of the currency supplied just equals the quantity demanded at the prevailing exchange rate. The exchange rate will rise when the quantity demanded exceeds quantity supplied and will fall when the quantity supplied exceeds quantity demanded.

Broadly speaking, the quantity of U.S. dollars applied to foreign exchange markets in any year is made up of the dollars spent on imports, plus the amount of funds U.S. residents wish to invest outside the United States.[4] The demand for U.S. dollars arises from the reverse of these transactions. Both exports by U.S. residents and the demand by foreigners to invest in the United States require that foreigners acquire dollars to spend in the United States.

Exports and imports comprise both goods (tangible items such as automobiles and wheat) and services (such as banking, insurance, transportation, and investment income). An export of services generates demand for dollars by foreigners just as does an export of goods, and the actual quantities involved in trade in services are very substantial. Net exports of these "invisibles" (as internationally traded services are known) in 1977 were $15.8 billion, having grown fairly steadily from $0.7 billion in 1966.

As shown in Table I, net exports of services by the United States have, over the past few years, turned several deficits in trade in tangible goods into surpluses on total U.S. trade. Further, discussions of the 1977 trade deficit often are in terms of merchandise trade; when invisible trade is taken into account, the total trade deficit is much smaller.

Table 1.—U.S. Balance of Trade
(Millions of Dollars)

	Merchandise Trade Balance	Services Trade Balance	Balance on Goods and Services
1966	$ 3,817	$ 697	$ 4,514
1967	3,800	595	4,395
1968	635	986	1,621
1969	607	395	1,002
1970	2,603	309	2,912
1971	− 2,260	1,920	− 340
1972	− 6,416	328	− 6,088
1973	911	2,609	3,520
1974	− 5,367	7,527	2,160
1975	9,045	7,119	16,164
1976	− 9,320	12,916	3,596
1977	−31,241	15,827	−15,414

Source: U.S. Department of Commerce.

Inflows of foreign funds are required to offset a trade deficit if the foreign exchange value of the dollar is to remain unchanged.[5] It is useful to write that out in the form of an equation, where both exports and imports refer to *total* trade—that is, visibles plus invisibles—and private sector refers to the private sector in *both* the United States and abroad.

$$\text{Exports} + \text{Capital Inflows} = \text{Imports} + \text{Capital Outflows} \quad (1)$$

The left hand side of equation (1) is the private sector demand for dollars; the right hand side is the private sector supply.

Equation (1) can be rearranged in a number of ways; the most useful for the present purpose is as follows:

$$\text{Exports} - \text{Imports} = \text{Capital Outflows} - \text{Capital Inflows} \quad (2)$$

This rearrangement of the equation helps one to see that a trade deficit must, as a matter of arithmetic, be accompanied by a net importation of investment funds, that is, a "capital inflow" in the terminology of balance of payments accounting. *There cannot be one without the other; the United States cannot import funds without running a trade deficit.* The balance of payments must always be in balance.

In the absence of government transactions undertaken with the aim of changing the exchange rate, the exchange rate will adjust until the private sector's supply of U.S. dollars on the exchange market equals the quantity of dollars demanded by the private sector in that market.[6]

The fact that a trade deficit (with an unchanged exchange rate) implies a net capital inflow is vital in seeing the economic significance of the current trade deficit.

TRADE DEFICITS—THE HISTORICAL RECORD

The United States ran a trade deficit for a substantial part of the 19th century. Table II shows ten-year annual averages of U.S. trade deficits, as percentages of Net National Product, for the years 1869 to 1908, and for the years 1967 to 1977 on an annual basis.[7]

A noteworthy feature is that, taken as a percentage of Net National Product, last year's deficit was not markedly large by 19th century standards. Another notable feature of the data in Table II is the shift to a trade surplus that occurred as the century progressed. This implies that the United States was moving from being a substantial net importer of investment funds to being a net exporter.[8] A major reason for this is that in the earlier part of the period, the United States was expanding westwards at a very rapid rate. That created a demand for investment to construct transportation facilities, develop farmlands, and so forth. The rate of return that could be earned on capital in the United States was significantly higher than that which could be earned in the rest of the world. The economy thereby became more industrialized and agriculture more mechanized. Only as the United States became relatively abundant in capital, towards the end of the 19th century, did the situation change and the United States become a capital exporter.

Table II.—U.S. Balance of Trade Relative to Net National Product

Period	Balance on Goods & Services* (Millions of Dollars)	Net National Product* (NNP) (Millions of Dollars)	Balance as Percent of NNP
1869-1878	$− 62	$ 7,667	− 0.8%
1879-1888	− 12	10,601	− 0.1
1889-1898	4	12,049	0.03
1899-1908	353	20,540	1.7
1967	4,395	729,300	0.6
1968	1,621	794,700	0.2
1969	1,002	853,100	0.1
1970	2,912	891,600	0.3
1971	− 340	964,700	− 0.04
1972	− 6,088	1,065,800	− 0.6
1973	3,520	1,188,900	0.3
1974	2,160	1,275,200	0.2
1975	16,164	1,366,300	1.2
1976	3,596	1,527,400	0.2
1977	− 15,414	1,693,100	− 0.9

*Figures for the years 1869-1908 are ten-year averages.

Sources: National Bureau of Economic Research and U.S. Department of Commerce.

THE DEFICIT AND INFLOWS OF FUNDS

As Table II shows, the United States reverted to the position of a net importer of investment funds in 1977. The large increase in oil prices of recent years has provided some oil exporting countries with enormous ability to save out of current incomes. Naturally, they wish to invest these savings. That same increase in oil prices reduced spending power in the United States; people had to spend a larger portion of their incomes on oil, and had therefore less left for other purposes.

This means that it is quite rational for the United States to import investment funds at the present time; in other words, to attempt to borrow funds to pay for the increased imports. These funds allow U.S. consumers to adjust their consumption more smoothly—they are not forced to make a sharp change, which is always unpleasant and can be inefficient since it forces cuts in what is easiest, rather than most desirable.[9]

Further, and ultimately more important, the inflow of funds can make it easier for U.S. firms to invest. The inflow of funds represents an increase in the demand for U.S. securities. Unless the supply of these securities rises by at least the same amount as the increase in demand, the price of U.S. securities is bolstered by this inflow of investment funds, and U.S. interest rates are lower than they would otherwise have been.[10] This increased ease in obtaining funds helps firms to invest, and thus encourages long-run growth in output, which is the only way the decline in U.S. living standards caused by the oil price increase can ultimately be reversed. Without the inflow of funds from the oil exporting countries, living standards would be lower and prospects of raising them bleaker than with the inflow.

THE DEFICIT AND UNEMPLOYMENT

Imports do not cause unemployment. Many imports into the United States are themselves used in U.S. exports. An example is imported steel. Steel can be obtained more cheaply abroad than in the United States, and the prices of U.S. exports which use steel reflect the lower input price. Restrictions designed to raise import prices would also raise U.S. export (and domestic) prices for those goods, as well as directing to the production of steel resources which would more profitably be used elsewhere. The increase in U.S. export prices relative to world market prices would reduce U.S. exports and, hence, U.S. export production and U.S. employment in some exporting industries.

Imports into the United States also create income abroad. If imports were suddenly restricted, U.S. exporters would experience an associated drop in demand. Agriculture, an industry currently eager to export so as to boost income, is an example of an industry highly sensitive to foreign demand for its products.

Hence, imports create some job opportunities as part of the very process by which they reduce others. But, even if the United States used more labor in producing every good than any other country in the world, it would still be possible for the United States to participate in foreign trade, to gain from that trade, and not to suffer unemployment as a result.

That proposition is by no means new. It was demonstrated first in 1817 by the economist and stockbroker David Ricardo. Briefly, the reason why trade cannot permanently cause unemployment is that when workers are displaced from one job by competition from elsewhere, they can move on to another job. It does not matter whether the competition is at home or abroad. If some goods are being produced and sold more cheaply than before, consumers and also producers of these goods, have increased income and thereby increased demand for other products.[11]

That is not of course to say that engaging in international trade cannot cause a temporary fluctuation in unemployment. There can be temporary unemployment as workers move around while some industries expand and others decline.[12] But if trade is restricted to eliminate that type of unemployment, the economy is frozen in a wasteful pattern of production, just as if, when the automobile started to displace the horse and carriage, automobile production had been made illegal to protect the carriage-making industry.[13]

Accordingly, a trade deficit cannot permanently cause unemployment, *if there are no domestic restrictions on labor mobility.* A trade deficit can be accompanied by temporary unemployment as workers move from one job to another, but protecting the old jobs is both unnecessary and harmful to national prosperity. (It is most certainly understandable that workers resist having to move from one job to another; such moving can be expensive and inconvenient. But it is in no one's interest for them not to move.)

THE TRADE DEFICIT AND THE DOLLAR

Eliminating any one part of U.S. imports, even one equal to the deficit, would not do much to prevent the fall in the dollar's foreign exchange value. For example, if the United States suddenly stopped importing oil, it would lose a nearly equivalent dollar inflow from the oil-producing countries, and there would be little net effect on the balance of supply and demand for dollars on the foreign exchange markets.[14]

As a further example, if the United States suddenly stopped importing foreign automobiles, there would be increased demand for domestic automobiles. Thus, resources would be diverted from the production of exports, and income would also of course be reduced abroad, thereby reducing the *demand* for U.S. exports. Again the overall effect on the foreign exchange market is unlikely to be large. Nor would the United States have "gained jobs." There would be an increase in the number of jobs in automobile production, but reduced job opportunities in those industries where foreign demand had fallen. Further, such trade restrictions will divert U.S. resources to activities more productively carried out abroad. Piecemeal attacks on the trade deficit will not achieve an improvement in the balance of payments on any significant scale.

SUMMARY AND CONCLUSIONS

Present concern about the U.S. trade deficit is much greater than the facts justify. When all trade, and not just merchandise trade, is examined, the deficit is, by historical standards, not outstandingly large. Furthermore, the deficit has a most desirable feature. It allows the United States to import investment funds. At the moment this is desirable from the point of view of both the United States and the countries which are supplying those funds.

The deficit has at most a transitory effect on the overall level of employment in the United States. Jobs will be lost in some industries, but gained in others. So long as resources, including labor, can move fairly freely, a trade deficit does not reduce the overall level of employment. Analysis which points to particular activities which are eliminated as a result of engaging in foreign trade, and then concludes that trade has led to a loss of jobs, implicitly assumes that once resources are in place they can never again move. There are instances when artificial barriers restrict these movements, but the problems that arise are due to these barriers and not to the deficit.

Finally, and perhaps most important, measures aimed at eliminating some particular component of the trade deficit would produce wasteful uses of resources, have little effect on the balance of payments, and therefore make little contribution to arresting the slide in the dollar's foreign exchange value. Panic attacks on individual components of the trade deficit will do much harm and little good.

APPENDIX

Merchandise Trade Balance

Exports of goods less imports of goods. Exported agricultural products accounted for about 20 percent of total U.S. merchandise exports in 1977. Imported petroleum accounted for about 30 percent of total U.S. merchandise imports in 1977.

Goods and Services Balance

Merchandise trade balance plus net exports of services. Internationally "traded" services include banking, insurance, transportation, tourism, military purchases and sales, and receipts of earnings on investments abroad. United States exports of services have exceeded imports for the past 16 years.

Current Account Balance

Goods and services balance less unilateral transfers. Unilateral transfers include private gifts to foreigners and government foreign assistance grants but exclude military grants. U.S. unilateral transfers to foreigners have averaged about $4.5 billion per year since 1970.

Capital Account

Includes changes in U.S. investment abroad and changes in foreign investment in the United States. Purchases of foreign (U.S.) government securities and corporate bonds and stocks are examples of U.S. (foreign) investment abroad (in the United States). An increase in U.S. investment abroad represents a capital outflow (entered into balance-of-payments accounts as a negative item). An increase in foreign investment in the United States represents a capital inflow (entered as a positive item). Since changes in U.S. investment abroad, and foreign investment in the United States, include changes in official reserve assets (such as purchases of U.S. Treasury securities by foreign central banks), the capital account and current account must offset each other (a balancing category, "statistical discrepancy," is required to produce an exact offset in the reported data). Thus, with a current account deficit of $20.2 billion in 1977, the United States recorded a net capital inflow of $23.2 billion (and hence a "statistical discrepancy" figure of $ – 3.0 billion).

---

[1]Youssef M. Ibrahim, "$26.7 Billion Trade Deficit, Fed by Oil Imports, Is Nation's Biggest," *New York Times,* January 31, 1978. The revised figure for the 1977 U.S. merchandise trade deficit is $31.2 billion.

[2]U.S. Congress, Senate Committee on Foreign Relations, Subcommittee on Foreign Economic Policy, "International Debt, the Banks, and U.S. Foreign Policy," 95th Congress, 1st session, August 1977, p.33.

[3]U.S. Congress, Joint Economics Committee, Subcommittee on International Economics, "Living With the Trade Deficit," 95th Congress, 1st session, November 18, 1977, p.5.

[4]U.S. importers supply dollars so as to purchase foreign currency to pay for imports, while investment abroad by U.S. residents creates demand for foreign currency because the foreign capital assets purchased—factories, stocks, government bonds, etc.—must be paid for in foreign currency.

[5]An inflow of funds into a country for the purpose of investing there, whether the funds are for investment in bank deposits, securities, or even land, is described as an inflow of capital. An inflow of capital, to the extent that the capital is invested in financial assets, can be thought of as an export of securities. The term "capital inflow" *does not* refer to an inflow of capital goods, although the U.S. resident to whom the funds are lent can of course use them to buy capital goods abroad.

It may appear surprising that an inflow of funds, which can be spent on either consumption or capital goods, is described as an "inflow of capital." But an individual's capital is what can be spent in excess of current income; even if it has been lent to him, the capital is available for current expenditures. An inflow of funds into the United States is the result of foreigners deciding to lend to the

United States, and their doing so lets the United States spend more than its current income, just as when an individual is lent funds he has acquired capital which enables him to spend in excess of current income.

⁶For a discussion of official transactions and a distinction between when they are intended to influence the exchange rate and when they are not, see Douglas R. Mudd, "International Reserves and the Role of Special Drawing Rights," this *Review* (January 1978), pp.10-11.

⁷NNP is used in this comparison as this figure shows much better than GNP (which contains replacement investment) what is happening to national income after maintaining the nation's stock of real capital. Comparing the deficits to NNP, therefore, relates the deficits to what the nation can spend without depleting its accumulated stock of capital goods. (For the purpose of comparison, it may be useful to note that the 1977 deficit, 0.9 percent of NNP, is 0.8 percent of GNP.) Taking deficits as a percentage of NNP both compensates for inflation and relates the deficit to the income which is available to service the change in indebtedness which a deficit implies. Comparisons of deficits as percentages of NNP are therefore the most appropriate form of comparison over long time periods.

⁸These investment funds were, it should be noted, actually used in large part to buy capital goods from abroad in the 19th century.

⁹An example is a family which bought a new automobile just before the oil price increase. The family might want to change to one which used less gas, but initially would be stuck with the car and have to cut back on, say, clothing.

¹⁰It should be emphasized that there is not necessarily a net increase in investment as compared to what would have happened without the oil price increase. There is an increased incentive to invest, as compared to the hypothetical situation where oil prices had increased *but there had been no inflow of funds from abroad.*

¹¹A more detailed demonstration is contained in the screened insert accompanying this article. The demonstration given there is essentially Ricardo's. As his proof considers only the labor which is involved in production, it is particularly well-suited to show the effect of trade on employment. See David Ricardo, *The Principles of Political Economy and Taxation* (London: J. M. Dent & Sons, Ltd., reprinted 1948), pp.77-93.

¹²Workers would also have to move around if a country pegged its exchange rate despite having a higher rate of inflation than its trading partners. They would have to do so because pegging the exchange rate would depress both exporting and import-competing industries. Pegging the exchange rate can therefore cause unemployment, but this, too, would be temporary.

¹³There are very special circumstances when it may be advisable to provide assistance to smooth the decline of an industry; but that assistance should never take the form of trade restriction, and should never aim to actually *prevent* the decline. The arguments for this can be found in Geoffrey E. Wood, "Senile Industry Protection: Comment," *Southern Economic Journal* (January 1975), pp.535-37.

¹⁴At the end of 1977, U.S. banks reported liabilities of about $9 billion to Middle East oil exporting countries. These countries also made net purchases of U.S. corporate stocks and bonds and marketable U.S. Treasury bonds and notes totalling about $7.5 billion during 1977. Further, since these figures omit purchases of land and buildings, they understate the capital inflow. Another large part of OPEC revenue from the United States (some 34 percent) is spent on U.S.

goods. (As noted by Clifton B. Luttrell, "Free Trade: A Major Factor in U.S. Farm Income," this *Review* (March 1977), p.23, agricultural exports rose considerably as a result of OPEC price rises.) Total OPEC spending in the United States is also understated by the amount of U.S. net exports of services to the oil exporting countries. There is good reason for thinking this understatement to be substantial in view of the large jump in U.S. net exports of services after the first major oil price increase. Thus, the simple arithmetic does not support the claim that U.S. imports of oil have produced on foreign exchange markets all the excess supply of dollars which has caused the decline of the dollar's foreign exchange value.

Imports and Jobs

The Observed and the Unobserved

Clifton B. Luttrell

Pleas for liberal trade policies are applauded by the leaders of almost all commercial nations. Nevertheless, free trade among nations may be facing its most serious challenge since the adoption of the Hawley-Smoot Tariff Act of 1930. This Act authorized tariff rate increases on more than 800 items and led to numerous retaliations by other nations. Professor Melvin B. Krauss at New York University stated, "In a scenario all too reminiscent of the beggar-thy-neighbor policies of the 1930s, the United States is now threatening to exceed the recent protectionist measures of certain Western European countries . . . under the dubious theory that caving in to protectionist pressures today is necessary to prevent an even greater cave-in tomorrow."[1] The new "protectionism" has produced such nontariff barriers to trade as industrial and employment subsidies, discriminatory Government purchasing practices and safety standards, "voluntary" export quotas, and "orderly" marketing agreements.[2]

JOB PROTECTION—IMPORTANT OBJECTIVE OF RECENT RESTRICTIONS

An important factor in the move toward greater protection for American products from foreign competition has been the alleged job losses caused by such imports. The alleged job losses have led to a shift in attitude toward foreign trade by the major labor union leaders. Before the late

---

Original version appeared in *Federal Reserve Bank of St. Louis Review,* June 1978, pages 2-10. Revised version that appears in this text reprinted by permission of the author.

1960s the AFL-CIO had strongly supported relatively free trade policies.[3] In 1961 Bert Seidman, economist with the AFL-CIO, contended that unless our country is prepared to pursue a vigorous policy of trade liberalization it may be confronted with three consequences: a decline in our export opportunities, diminished influence in world economic decisions, and a weakening of its political leadership in the free world.[4]

By the late 1960s the attitude of labor leaders on foreign trade policies had changed sharply. Instead of advocating free trade, they had begun to actively oppose tariff reductions, and push for import quotas and other trade restrictive measures. In 1967, for example, labor leaders in the steel industry joined with management in supporting import quotas on steel.[5]

At the hearings on the Trade Reform Act of 1973, labor union opposition to free trade policies was pursued vigorously. AFL-CIO President George Meany, in a lengthy statement before the Senate Committee on Finance, opposed both further imports of goods from abroad and exports of farm products, which, he felt, put the nations of the world in competition with the American consumer for food products.[6] He argued, "The shutdown of manufacturing operations here and their relocation abroad, where low-cost operations are more profitable, depress the whole American economy by the loss of domestic jobs, payrolls, domestic corporate revenues, ... " An AFL-CIO report, included with Meany's statement, argued that "A tide of imports has wiped out more than a million jobs as products and whole industries have been engulfed."[7]

Hence, labor unions have generally shifted from proponents of free trade policies to supporters of protectionist policies during the past two decades. Protectionist policies, they allege, will protect domestic employees from the loss of jobs resulting from rising imports.

Some industry witnesses at the hearings also used the loss-of-jobs argument in addition to the traditional arguments in support of protectionist policies. Representatives of the steel industry, for example, argued that unrestricted imports almost wiped out many product lines in the specialty steel industry in the 1960s and early 1970s and had an adverse impact on jobs.[8]

EMPLOYMENT LOSSES FROM IMPORTS—READILY OBSERVED

The alleged reductions in domestic employment resulting from rising imports are highly visible and readily observed by labor union leaders, workers, and managements of domestic firms which produce goods that are competitive with the imports. The move toward relatively free trade during the 1950s and early 1960s, after a period of protection, had caused some disruptions in the domestic market for a number of goods such as shoes, clothing, and steel mill and blast furnace products where imports are highly competitive with domestic production. Such disruptions cause unemployment for a time and loss of wealth in those industries.

The increases in some major types of goods imported, which are highly competitive with U.S. produced goods, and imports as a percent of total domestic use are shown in Table I. Imports as a percent of use of automobiles, footwear, mineral fuels, and telecommunications apparatus rose sharply from the average for the 1964-65 period to the average for the 1975-76 period. During the latter period average imports for each of the above goods exceeded five percent of total domestic use.

Rough estimates of the direct impact of imports on employment in these industries with sharply rising imports are shown in Table II. Column 1 indicates the average number of employees in the industries during the two years 1964-65. Column 2 indicates the number of employees that would have been employed by these industries in 1975-76 had the ratio of imports to domestic use remained constant, and the level of expenditure on these goods remained unchanged.[9] The third column contains the actual number of domestic employees in the industries in 1975-76, and the fourth column is the estimated loss of employment resulting from imports (Column 2 minus Column 3).

Actual employment in the automobile industry held constant over the eleven-year period 1964-65 to 1975-76, but the industry experienced a sizable loss of potential employment from rising imports, as the ratio of imports to domestic use rose sharply. On the basis of the calculations in Table II, the number employed by domestic automobile manufacturers in 1975-76 would have been about 60,000 higher had the ratio of imports to domestic use remained unchanged. The number of employees would have been about 89,000 higher in mining operations and about 89,000 higher in clothing manufacture had the proportionate rise in these imports not occurred.

These date are readily observable, and to one whose vision is restricted to the production process of these specific industries only, the conclusion follows that the American market must not be opened wide for foreign economic invasion. These data, however, present a highly biased view of the impact of international trade on total domestic employment, overstating the depressive impact. Employment actually declined more than a fraction of a percent in only a few industries which experienced rising competition from imports; namely, iron and steel mill products, clothing, and footwear, but only a portion of the decline in these industries can be attributed to rising imports. In iron and steel mill product industries, for example, total employment declined by 98,000 workers (Table II), but there was only a moderate increase in imports of the products by these industries (from 1.5 percent to 3.8 percent of domestic use). Hence, on the basis of these calculations, only about 18,200 of the decline can be attributed to rising imports. Most of the decline in employment in this industry was the result of such factors as rising efficiency of production or declining domestic demand for iron and steel mill products. Only 58,000 of the total decline of 70,000 workers in footwear can be attributed to the competitive pressure of imports. In the clothing industry all of the decline in employment can be attributed to rising imports, and the loss here was 6 percent of total employment in the industry.

GENERAL EFFECTS OF FOREIGN TRADE ON EMPLOYMENT SAME AS DOMESTIC TRADE

The general effect of foreign trade on employment is no different from that of domestic trade. For example, a reduction in the tariff barriers imposed on new automobiles from Japan will have about the same impact on total employment in the United States as would the emergence of a new, more efficient automobile manufacturing firm in the United States. Assuming no growth in demand for automobiles, suppose, for example, that imports from Japan rise from zero to ten percent of domestic automobile sales. Employment in automobile production in the United States will decline and such employment in Japan will rise. Imports into the United States, however, increase the dollar holdings in Japan which will eventually be spent in the United States. Total demand for U.S. goods and services will thus remain unchanged.[10] Hence, the employment lost through rising imports of automobiles will be gained through rising exports of other goods and services after all adjustments are made to the new demand patterns.

Similarly, if a new automobile manufacturing firm is established in Springfield, Missouri, with new plants in the vicinity manufacturing automobiles which account for ten percent of U.S. sales, the older automobile firms will lose a substantial number of workers as they would in the case of rising imports. The new firm will, in turn, employ new workers, they will spend their incomes, and total employment in the economy will not fall as much as the reported decline at the older automobile manufacturing firms.

UNOBSERVED EMPLOYMENT GAINS OFFSET OBSERVED LOSSES

Offsetting the observed employment losses in some industries attributed to free trade are the sizable gains in sales and employment in other industries which can likewise be attributed to free trade. When foreigners sell us goods and services, they gain purchasing power which eventually leads to a rise in employment in our export industries. Major gains have occurred in employment since 1964-65 in a number of industries as a result of rising exports. Among those industries with a rising proportion of total sales abroad are transport equipment other than automobiles, nonelectrical machinery, chemicals, scientific instruments, and farm products. Exports rose in these industries, both in absolute amounts and relative to domestic production. Net exports (exports less imports) in transport equipment other than automobiles, for example, rose from an average of 4.9 percent of domestic production in 1964-65 to 10 percent in 1975-76 (Table III).

Greatest gains relative to production during the period occurred in the agricultural sector. Total exports of farm products rose from a $6.1 billion average per year for 1964-65 to $22.3 billion for 1975-76 (Chart I). During the period exports of food and live animals rose from 1.7 to 8 percent of domestic sales, and exports of soybeans and textile fibers (largely cotton) rose from 20 to 39 percent. Exports of all farm products rose from an average of 16.4 percent of domestic sales (cash receipts) in 1964-65 to an average of 24.5 percent in 1975-76 (Chart II).

The impact of rising farm exports on farm production cannot be measured with precise accuracy since weather and other factors have a major influence on crop yields. However, the evidence indicates that rising exports have had a major impact on crop prices and production. As indicated in Chart I, crop exports rose moderately in 1971 and 1972 and increased sharply in 1973 and 1974. Crop production generally had been rising at about the same rate as population growth from 1960 through 1970. In 1971, however, the rate of crop production growth accelerated, consistent with the rising exports. Following a temporary decline in 1974 as a result of the worst crop growing weather in three decades, crop output continued up at a rate well above that of population growth (Chart III). During the seven-year period 1970-77 population rose at a compound annual rate of one percent per year while crop production rose four percent per year. By 1977 exports accounted for 60 percent of U.S. soybean production, 55 percent of rice production, 40 or more percent of wheat and cotton production, and about 30 percent of corn, grain sorghum, and tobacco production.[11]

The estimated gain in direct employment resulting from the rise in exports of a selected group of commodities is shown in Table IV. Calculated in the same manner as its counterpart, Table II, this table shows the average actual employment in the respective industries for the years 1964-65 (column 1), the level of 1975-76 employment had exports remained the same percent of production as in the earlier period (column 2), the actual number of employees in 1975-76 (column 3), and the estimated gain in direct employment attributed to the rise in exports (column 4) (see Appendix).

While farm employment during the period actually declined from 4.442 million to 3.339 million, the number of farm employees would have been only 3.106 million in 1975-76 if farm commodity exports had not risen. Hence, about 233,000 workers in this sector can be attributed to the rise in exports.

This increased farm employment as a result of rising farm exports, however, was not observed by some of the nation's labor union leaders. The failure to appreciate the impact of rising farm exports on employment is indicated by the statement by I.W. Abel, President, United Steelworkers of America: "It is most frightening when the Secretary of the Treasury, Secretary of State, and the Administration's Executive Director of International Economic Policy agree before this Committee that our chief export five years from now will be agricultural products. Are we regressing to the status of a developing nation?"[12] This implication, that the highly sophisticated U.S. farm sector is at the same stage of development as the so-called developing nations, fails to comprehend the commercial nature of U.S. agriculture and its impact on the rest of the economy. Much of the farming sector of the developing economies is of the traditional self-sufficient type. Few farm resources are purchased from the nonfarm sector and few nonfarm employees are engaged in the production of capital goods or current inputs used for farm production purposes.

In contrast to the self-sufficient type of agriculture in the developing economies, agriculture in the United States is composed of highly commercial firms. Cash expenditures for hired labor, capital, and operating goods used for farming totaled $82 billion in 1976, more than four-fifths of total farm cash receipts. About $42 billion of the above expenditures were for goods and services produced in the nonfarm sector. These expenditures were for such items as tractors, combines, other farm machinery, farm building materials, fertilizer, and other items the production of which requires nonfarm labor. These purchases resulted in part from the sharp increase in farm commodity exports. Such exports thus had a major indirect impact on nonfarm employment, another unobserved gain from free trade.

Employment increases attributed directly to rising exports, in these selected industries with increases in net export sales during the period from 1964-65 to 1975-76, totaled 367,000 workers. These workers are the "unobserved gains" in employment resulting from the rise in foreign trade. Such unobserved gains in employment at least equaled the losses in other industries observed by the free trade opponents.

UNOBSERVED GAINS IN REAL GOODS—THE ONLY REAL BENEFIT FROM TRADE

Also important is the impact of foreign trade on the quantity and quality of goods available for consumers. Transactions among nations result in gains to both parties in the transactions. The gains occur as a result of the improvement in total output from the greater specialization of resources. The gains can be demonstrated with a simple example using two countries—the United States and Taiwan—and some hypothetical cost of production figures for traded commodities. In the United States the cost of resources used in producing a tractor is, say, $20,000 and the cost of producing a pair of shoes is $25, while in Taiwan the cost of producing a tractor is $25,000 and the cost of producing a pair of shoes is $20. If each nation attempts to produce both 20 tractors and 20,000 pairs of shoes, the tractors and shoes will cost $900,000 in both countries in terms of resources foregone.

Costs of Production

	United States		Taiwan*	
	Cost Per Unit	Total Costs	Cost Per Unit	Total Costs
20 tractors...	$20,000	$400,000	$25,000	$500,000
20,000 pairs of shoes................................	$25	500,000	$20	400,000
TOTAL..		$900,000		$900,000

*Dollar costs at current exchange rates. These calculations assume a constant rate of exchange between U.S. and Taiwan economy.

Through specialization and with the same quantity of resources used in production, more of both types of goods will be available in each nation. This is possible since each nation will be utilizing its resources for the production of the good where it has greatest relative advantage—tractors in the United States and shoes in Taiwan—and exchanging these goods.

Costs of Production

	United States	Taiwan
45 tractors..	$900,000	. . .
45,000 pairs of shoes................................	. . .	$900,000
TOTAL..	$900,000	$900,000

On this basis, U.S. producers of tractors can exchange 22 tractors ($440,000 cost of resources expended) for 22,000 pairs of shoes ($440,000 expended by Taiwan producers). Hence for the $900,000 in resources foregone U.S. producers will have 23 tractors plus 22,000 pairs of shoes.

Taiwan will likewise gain, having available 22 tractors and 23,000 pairs of shoes. Hence, with specialization and trade each nation was able to realize a gain of more than ten percent in real goods available for its use. In other words, with greater specialization and free exchange through foreign trade, each country obtains more goods for a given cost.

The gains from trade may still occur even though one nation has an absolute advantage over another in the production of all goods. Trade between the nations will still be mutually advantageous if one has a greater relative advantage in the production of some particular goods. Both nations will gain by specializing in the production of the goods where they have the greatest relative advantage or least relative disadvantage and exchanging the goods with each other.

SUMMARY

In summary, the job losses in some industries as a result of reduced trade barriers are highly visible. Many of the nation's businessmen and labor union leaders have reported job losses in their sectors from free trade, and concluded that such trade produces a decline in total domestic employment. As a consequence, such leaders have combined forces in the affected industries in opposition to free trade.

Free international trade, however, will not permanently reduce overall employment. Trade is not a unidirectional affair. Movement in the exchange rate between the dollar and other currencies is the balancing mechanism in trade. If U.S. imports rise, we pay for them in dollars which must eventually be used to purchase our exports. Movement in the exchange rates will equalize such payments. If U.S. demand for foreign goods (imports) rises relative to foreign demand for U.S. goods (assuming no change in capital movements), the exchange value of the dollar will decline, making our goods less expensive to foreigners and their goods more expensive to us. Hence, any temporary tendency for industries facing increased foreign competition to reduce employment will likely be offset by the stimulative effects of a falling dollar exchange rate on industries with rising exports.

The data in this analysis illustrate the view that employment gains from freeing up trade have offset the employment losses. Sharp gains have occurred in direct employment in a number of industries having sizable gains in net exports. In other industries, such as agriculture, the number of employees is well above what it would have been without the rise in exports. The rise in farm commodity exports thus prevented a further decline in farm employment. These unobserved increases in employment resulting from freer trade in this analysis have offset the observed losses. Hence, international trade has not contributed to overall unemployment.

Such trade has contributed to major real gains in well-being which are also difficult to observe. The real gains occur through the greater specialization of resources and the larger volume of goods resulting from the use of a given quantity of resources. Through this process of specialized production and exchange, more goods are available to all nations and at less cost than would be available with trade restrictions.

APPENDIX

The calculations presented in Tables II and IV are rough estimates of the effect of international trade on domestic employment in several industries. These estimates are intended to show orders of magnitude.

The estimates presume that changes in spending reflect only changes in *quantity* of output and thus are biased to the extent the prices of domestically produced goods change relative to those of foreign goods. This bias works, however, to give underestimates of both job gains and losses, and thus does not reduce the validity of the analysis.

The measure of loss or gain is given by

$$N^* - N > 0 \quad \text{(job loss)}$$
$$N^* - N < 0 \quad \text{(job gain)}$$

where N is the actual employment in a particular industry in 1975-76, N^* is the employment that would result in that industry in 1975-76 if the proportion of imported output had remained at the ratio of 1964-65 (Column 2 in Tables II and IV).

The correct measure of N^*, given the assumptions used in the article, is given by:

$$(1) \quad N^* = N \cdot \frac{(1 - p_0)}{(1 - p_1)}$$

where p_0 is the proportion of domestic consumption (in *real* terms) accounted for by imports in 1964-65 and p_1 is the proportion for 1975-76. The form used in this study defines these proportions in terms of the ratio of imports to domestic consumption in *nominal* terms.

The bias that is introduced by using nominal variables can be seen by transforming equation (1) to logarithmic form:

Real variables
$$\ln N^* = \ln N + p_0 (q^f - q^d)$$

Nominal variables
$$\ln N^* = \ln N + p_0 (q^f - q^d) + p_0{}' (p^f - p^d)$$

where (q^f) is the rate of change of imported output, (q^d) is the rate change of domestic output, (p^f) is the rate of change of import prices, (p^d) is the rate change of domestic prices, and (p_0') is the ratio of imports to domestic spending in *nominal* terms in 1964-65.

The two results differ only by the term p_0' $(p^f - p^d)$ which is the measure of relative rate of price change of imported vs. domestically produced goods, all in dollar terms.

In the case where domestic prices rise faster than import prices, imports are stimulated and domestic jobs are lost. The term p_0' $(p^f - p^d)$ would then be negative and lead to an underestimate of N* and thus an understatement of the job loss (N* − N).

In the case where foreign prices rise faster than domestic prices, exports are stimulated and domestic employment rises. Thus N will be greater than N*, showing a gain of jobs. However, the term p_0' $(p^f - p^d)$ will be positive, biasing the measure of N* upward and thus giving an underestimate of the difference between N and N*.

---

[1] Melvin B. Krauss, "Stagnation and the New Protectionism," *Challenge* (January/February 1978), p.40.

[2] The United States Department of Agriculture in *National Food Review* (April 1978), p.32, has, for example, just announced more stringent import rules for filberts and "voluntary" meat import restrictions.

[3] Robert E. Baldwin, "The Political Economy of Postwar U.S. Trade Policy," *The Bulletin,* New York University (1976-4), p.23.

[4] U.S., Congress, Joint Economic Committee, Subcommittee on Foreign Economic Policy, *Hearings,* Eighty-seventh Congress, First Session, December 4-14, 1961, p.325.

[5] Baldwin, "The Political Economy of Postwar U.S. Trade Policy," p.24.

[6] U.S., Congress, Senate, Committee on Finance, *Hearings; The Trade Reform Act of 1973,* Ninety-third Congress, Second Session, March 26-April 3, 1974, pp.1136-37 and 1144.

[7] Ibid., pp.1139 and 1168. Other labor leaders making statements in opposition to free trade during the hearings include: I.W. Abel, President of United Steelworkers of America; George Collins of the International Union of Electrical, Radio, and Machine Workers; Leonard Woodcock, President of United Automobile, Aerospace, and Agricultural Implement Workers; and the Communication Workers of America. See Ibid., pp.1329-70, 1686-93, 857-72, and 2919-23, respectively, for their statements.

[8] See statement by Roger S. Ahlbrandt with Allegheny Ludlum Industries, and by Mark Anthony with Kaiser Steel Corporation, *Hearings; The Trade Reform Act of 1973,* pp.1055 and 1058, respectively.

[9] This column is calculated as follows:

$$\left[\frac{E}{1\text{-}P_{1975\text{-}76}}\right] \times [1\text{-}P_{1964\text{-}65}]$$

where E is the average number of domestic employees engaged in the production of the good in 1975-76 and P is net imports as a percent of domestic use.

Since these calculations were designed to show only the order of magnitude, several simplifying assumptions were made. It was assumed that productivity of workers remained constant, that increased volume of international trade did not affect total consumption, and, in particular, that changes in relative prices had minimal effects on labor usage (see Appendix).

[10]Of course, this adjustment is not immediate and a sudden change in the international competitive situation would result in substantial general unemployment which could last for some time. The experience in the United States since the oil embargo is a case in point. This is a problem of adjustment in the labor market which takes time, but is not reflective of a general decrease in demand for U.S. output. For a more comprehensive discussion of the impact of imports on unemployment, see Geoffrey E. Wood and Douglas R. Mudd, "The Recent U.S. Trade Deficit—No Cause for Panic," this *Review* (April 1978), pp. 2-7.

[11]U.S. Department of Agriculture, *1977 Handbook of Agricultural Charts,* Agriculture Handbook No. 524, p.65.

[12]*Hearings; The Trade Reform Act of 1973,* p.1175.

Table I.—Major Industries With Rising Competition from Imports

| | Net Imports[1] | | | |
| | 1964-65 (annual average) | | 1975-76 (annual average) | |
Industry Group	Value (million dollars)	Percent of Domestic use[2]	Value (million dollars)	Percent of Domestic use[2]
Telecommunications apparatus	$ 166	4.61%	$ 2,113	25.08%
Automobiles (new).	−1,100	−2.11	5,800	5.58
Iron and steel mill products	363	1.52	2,129	3.81
Clothing.	497	2.26	3,221	7.79
Footwear.	176	5.63	1,599	27.91
Mineral fuels and related materials.	2,351	7.58	25,888	17.23

[1]Includes estimated rates of duty on imports.

[2]Percentages calculated as follows: telecommunications apparatus—net imports as percent of manufacturers shipments of radio, TV receiving equipment, and musical instruments plus net imports; automobiles—estimated retail value of net automobile imports as percent of personal consumption expenditures for new domestic automobiles, producers durable expenditures for new domestic automobiles, Government purchases, change in business inventories, and net imports marked up to estimated domestic retail value; iron and steel mill products—net imports as percent of manufacturers shipments of blast furnace, basic steel products, and iron and steel foundries plus net imports; clothing—net imports as percent of manufacturers shipments of apparel, other textile products, women's hosiery, except socks, hosiery—not elsewhere classified, knit outerwear mills, knit underwear mills, and women's handbags and purses plus net imports; footwear—net imports as percent of manufacturers shipments of rubber and plastic footwear, and footwear, except rubber plus net imports; and mineral fuelds and related materials—net imports as a percent of domestic consumption of B.T.U.s of coal, crude petroleum, natural gas, and electricity.

Sources: U.S. Department of Commerce, *Statistical Abstract of the United States,* 1976 and 1969; *Business Statistics,* 1975; *The National Income and Product Accounts of the United States, 1929-74; Overseas Business Reports,* "United States Foreign Trade Annual 1970-76," April 1977; *Survey of Current Business,* July 1977; and *Annual Survey of Manufactures,* 1976 and 1964-65; U.S. Department of Energy, *Monthly Energy Review,* June 1978.

Table II.—Number of Employees in Domestic Industries With Rising Competition from Imports and Jobs Lost in These Industries from Rising Imports (thousands)

Industry Group	(1) Actual Number 1964-65 (annual average)	(2) Number Required for 1975-76 Purchases Assuming No Change in Percentages Imported	(3) Actual Number 1975-76 (annual average)	(4) Estimated Loss from Increased Imports[1]
Radio, TV receiving equipment, and musical instruments	149	189.7	149	40.7
Automobiles[2]	743	802.4	742	60.4
Iron and steel mill products[3]	863	783.2	765	18.2
Clothing[4]	1,564	1,574.1	1,485	89.1
Footwear[5]	260	247.4	189	58.4
Mining[6]	633	853.1	764	89.1
Total	4,212	4,449.9	4,094	355.9

[1]Assumes no change in 1964-65 ratio of imports to domestic use and that the number of employees per dollar value of imports are the same as the number per dollar value of domestic production.

[2]Assumes automobile to total transportation employees to be in the same ratio as value of automobile output to manufacturer's sales of all transportation equipment.

[3]Blast furnaces, basic steel products, iron and steel foundries.

[4]Total apparel and other textile products, women's hosiery, except socks, hosiery—NEC, knit outerwear mills, knit underwear mills, and women's handbags and purses.

[5]Rubber and plastic footwear, and footwear, except rubber.

[6]Includes oil and gas extraction plus metal, coal and nonmetallic mining.

Sources: U.S. Department of Commerce, *Statistical Abstract of the United States*, 1965 and 1976; *Employment and Earnings, United States, 1909-75*; *Employment and Earnings*, March 1976 and March 1977; *Survey of Current Business*, July 1977; and *Business Statistics*, 1975.

Table III.—Major Industries With Sizable Gains in Net Exports

	Net Exports			
	1964-65		1975-76	
	Annual Average (million dollars)	Percent of Domestic Production*	Annual Average (million dollars)	Percent of Domestic Production*
Transport equipment other than new automobiles	$2,248	4.9%	$ 8,981	10.0%
Nonelectrical machinery	4,052	10.9	14,693	14.1
Chemicals	1,648	4.6	5,091	5.3
Agriculture	2,042	5.3	12,020	13.2
Professional, scientific, photo, and controlling instruments	240	3.4	1,019	4.3
Textiles other than clothing	− 188	− 1.1	371	1.1

*Basis for domestic production as follows: manufacturers' sales for transport equipment other than new automobiles, nonelectrical machinery, chemicals, professional, scientific, photo, and controlling instruments, and textiles other than clothing; cash receipts from farm marketings for agriculture.

Sources: U.S. Department of Commerce, *Overseas Business Reports*, "United States Foreign Trade Annual 1970-76," April 1977; *Statistical Abstract of the United States*, 1970; *Survey of Current Business*, July 1977; *Business Statistics*, 1975; and *The National Income and Product Accounts of the United States, 1929-74*; U.S. Department of Agriculture, *Agricultural Statistics*, 1977.

Table IV.—Number of Employees in Industries With Sizable Gains in Net Exports
(all employees, thousands)

Industry Group	(1) Actual Number of Employees, 1964-65 (annual average)	(2) Number of Employees in 1975-76 Assuming 1964-65 Levels of Exports	(3) Actual Number of Employees, 1975-76 (annual average)	(4) Estimated Gain in Direct Employment From Increased Exports
Transport equipment other than new automobiles[1]	939	905.0	949	44.0
Nonelectrical machinery	1,674	2,013.9	2,072	58.1
Chemicals	893	1,016.2	1,023	6.8
Agriculture[2]	4,442	3,106.0	3,339	233.0
Professional, scientific, photo, and controlling instruments	379	494.7	499	4.3
Textiles other than clothing	912	913.6	934	20.4
Total	9,239	8,449.4	8,816	366.6

[1]Automobile to total transportation employees assumed to be in same ratio as value of automobile output to manufacturers' sales of transportation equipment.

[2]Total farm employment.

Sources: U.S. Department of Commerce, *Statistical Abstract of the United States,* 1976 and 1965; *Employment and Earnings,* March 1977; *Survey of Current Business,* July 1977; *Business Statistics,* 1975; Council of Economic Advisors, *Economic Report of the President,* 1978.

Towards Integrated Management of International Trade

The U.S. Trade Act of 1974

Kazimierz Grzybowski, Victor Rud, and George Stepanyenko

I. CROSS CURRENTS

a. 1934 and 1974 Acts: Parallels and Analogies

In a number of respects, the efforts made under the 1934 Trade Agreements Act and the 1974 Trade Act to expand American trade were similarly motivated, their basic purpose being to counteract the economic slump in the United States by promoting international trade. These legislative initiatives followed a soul-searching debate which found fault with the policy of economic isolationism into which the United States and the world at large were drifting. However, while the general plan of action and the expected results suggest a similarity of purpose at both periods, the international situation in 1974 differed profoundly from that of 1934.

In 1934 Trade Agreements Act sought to extricate the U.S. economy from the consequences of the Smoot-Hawley Act[1] by mutually agreed tariff concessions. Bilateral negotiations were then the only approach and technique available. Today, the main role in efforts to expand and liberalise trade belongs to multilateral negotiations involving tariffs and non-tariff barriers whose object is to determine the conditions of international trade within the world economic system of which the General

Kazimierz Grzybowski is Professor of Law, Duke Law School; Victor Rud is a member of the New York Bar; George Stepanyenko is Attorney Adv᷑ or Fed᷑ Communications Commission, Washington, D.᷑. Article ᷑rom *International ᷑ Comparative Law Quarterly*, Vol. 26, April, 1977. Reprinted by permission o᷑ British Institute of International and Comparative Law.

Agreement on Tariffs and Trade (GATT) is a part.[2] The 1974 Act takes note of the fact that GATT is an informal international organization supported by a number of international economic institutions such as the International Monetary Fund, the International Bank, the Program of Assistance to Less Developed Countries.[3]

In certain respects, the 1974 Act is a continuation of the 1934 legislation. The basic technique of the 1934 Act by which trade expansion is to be achieved has remained the same. New trade opportunities must be gained by the offer of reciprocity to foreign experts.

> The President whenever he finds as a fact that any existing duties or other import restrictions of the United States or any foreign country are unduly . . . restricting the foreign trade of the United States . . . is authorized from time to time (1) to enter into foreign trade agreements . . . (2) to proclaim such modifications of existing duties and other import restrictions . . . as are required . . . to carry out foreign trade agreements. . . .[4]

This authority was first limited to a three-year period, but was subsequently periodically extended until 1962, when the Congress passed the Trade Expansion Act, and is now again extended by the 1974 Trade Act.

The original (1934) authorised tariff reduction was 50 per cent. of the rates in force in 1934; it was followed by another authorisation of a reduction in tariff of an additional 50 per cent. of the rates in force in 1945[5] under the 1945 Trade Agreements Extension Act. Since 1945 tariff reduction authorisations have been much more modest—15 per cent. under the 1955 Act[6] and 20 per cent. under the 1958[7] Extension of the Trade Agreements Act, a reaction to the formation of the European Common Market with its programme for eliminating tariffs and custom duties among the then six member nations.

In 1962[8] Congress renewed the President's negotiating authority for an additional period of five years. It expired in 1967, leaving the President with no authority to negotiate reciprocal tariff reductions until the 1974 Trade Act was enacted. This lapse of authority and Congressional resistance to further concessions reflect the often declared reluctance to continue the policy of trade liberalisation. In this climate, a new approach had to be worked out, and a new balance between conflicting interests established. There was an unsuccessful effort to enact an interim measure (Trade Act of 1970)[9] which was intended to give the President the power to make minor adjustments in order to compensate a foreign country when it became necessary to raise the duty on a specific article, as the result of "escape clause" action. When the 1974 Trade Act became law, the Administration had been for more than seven years without authority to negotiate, although already, in 1973, members of the GATT were gearing themselves for a new round of negotiations—the Tokyo Round—with a view to taking another step towards the liberalisation of foreign trade.

The 1974 Act and the Tokyo Round (of which more is said later) were a continuation of the policies initiated in 1934, but they were also a move in a new direction. They both raised novel issues: to reform the GATT and to remove, or at least to regulate, non-tariff barriers to trade which had demonstrated convincingly the inadequacy of the then existing arrangements.

b. The Political Climate

The Trade Act of 1974[10] was the capstone on vigorousl competing views about United States trade policy—views which became increasingly strident during the years following the enactment of the 1962 Trade Expansion Act:

> From 1934 until 1962, beginning with the reciprocal Trade Agreements Act and culminating in the "Kennedy" round of tariff reductions (negotiated under the Trade Expansion Act of 1962), United States tariff protection was consistently reduced. The Kennedy round, however, marked the end of an era. During the past ten years there has developed a growing disillusionment with the overall trade policy embodied in the series of tariff reductions produced under the reciprocal trade agreements program. A number of reasons have been given for this trend: increasingly serious balance of payments problems after 1958, intensified competition at home and abroad from the growth of the European Economic Community (EEC) and Japan; disenchantment with the success of economic aid to the lesser developed countries, the increased use by foreign competitors of nontariff protective devices (particularly by the EEC and by Japan), the growth of multinational corporations, and the rapid increase in the level of domestic unemployment since 1970.[11]

The consequent change in the tenor of Congressional debate during this period is conveniently mirrored by the avowed purposes sought to be achieved through enactment of diverse trade Bills.[12] Thus, the Trade Expansion Act of 1962 purported:

> (1) to stimulate the economic growth of the United States and maintain and enlarge foreign markets for the products of United States agriculture, industry, mining and commerce; (2) to strengthen economic relations with foreign countries through the development of open and nondiscriminatory trading in the free world; and (3) to prevent Communist economic penetration.[13]

A decade later, however, the trade reform bills introduced in Congress no longer emphasised "the benefits which might accrue domestically as a consequence of increased international trade levels and trade liberalisation, and [no longer] viewed free trade as an independently valuable gain."[14]

The already mentioned Trade Act of 1970 (also known as the "Mills Bill"), as reported out of the House Committee,[15] was a synthesis of the original Administration proposal[16] and the largely protectionist[17] measures propounded by Chairman Mills.[18] Due to measures introduced through the latter Bill, the Trade Act of 1970 adopted a regressive omnibus approach to trade reform by providing for a variety of changes in then existing U.S. trade laws which, "both in number and in consequence, [were] intended to restrain, and [would] result in the reduction of international trade."[19] The Act proposed absolute import quotas [20] on selected textiles and footwear products, [21] and a significant relaxation of the causation and injury prerequisite to the imposition of import restrictions.[22] Additionally, Executive authority was sharply circumscribed:[23]

> [F]or the first time since the escape clause was originated in 1947, [the Bill] sharply curtailed the President's discretion to accept or reject Tariff Commission findings and recommendations in escape clause cases.[24]

Furthermore, amendments[25] to the Anti-dumping Act of 1921[26] would have required abbreviated inspection and verification procedures on the part of the Treasury Department, thereby effectively serving to promote the premature levying of anti-dumping duties.[27] Finally, the Bill[28] would have liberalised the implementation of the countervailing duty provisions of the Trade Act of 1930.[29]

The Mills Bill, though passed in the House, was effectively blocked in the Senate.[30] On January 21, 1971, it was re-introduced by Chairman Mills in the Second Session of Congress as the Trade Act of 1971.[31] It failed to draw Administration support, however, and was ultimately not reported out of either the House or Senate Committees.

Comparable to the Mills Bill was the Foreign Trade and Investment Act of 1972,[32] otherwise known as the "Burke-Hartke Bill."[53] Introduced in both Houses, the Bill had as its avowed purpose to "discourage American business investment abroad and [to] limit the flow of imports into this country."[34] Impetus for this legislation was concededly grounded on fears generated by the United States balance of payments problems and on the concern of organised labour that domestic jobs were being lost through increased production abroad by United States corporations.[35] According to one of its sponsors:

> [w]ithout it [the Bill] the heavy export of jobs, technology and capital by companies based in this country will continue unabated . . . [T]he technology produced by American genius will be better supervised and controlled, so that American workers are more fully benefitted by these advances.[36]

The Burke-Hartke amendments accordingly proposed to roll back imports through a panoply of measures, including mandatory quotas,[37] the curtailing of certain preferential tariff treatment,[38] reform of the anti-dumping[39] and countervailing duty[40] laws, and amendments to the "escape clause" provisions of the Trade Expansion Act.[41] Exports, for their part, would be curtailed by means of increased taxation of multinational corporate activity[42] and by direct control of exported capital and technology.[43]

In sum, pressures in Congress for protectionist trade legislation such as that contained in the Mills and Burke-Hartke Bills have faithfully reflected changes in the domestic economic situation, as well as changes in the country's relations with the rest of the trading world.

c. The Administration's Proposal

It was against such a background that President Nixon issued his April 10, 1973 message, at the same time as the proposed Trade Reform Act of 1973 was transmitted to Congress:

> [W]hile trade should be more open, it should also be more fair. [This] means that the benefits of trade should be fairly distributed among American workers, farmers, businessmen and consumers alike and that trade should create no undue burdens for any of these groups.[44]

Summarised in its transmittal message, the Administration's proposals contemplated four basic provisions: (i) it would increase Presidential negotiating and executive authority within the context of new international trade agreements; (ii) it would liberalise those standards necessary to the application of import restrictions and implementation of adjustment assistance; (iii) it would afford the President's authority to grant Most Favoured Nation (MFN) treatment to communist countries; (iv) it would allow for preferential tariff treatment for developing countries.[45]

d. Debate in the House

Submitted in anticipation of a new GATT[46] round of multilateral trade negotiations scheduled to commence in Tokyo,[47] H.R. 6767 predictably won less than universal domestic support in respect of the trade liberalisation and increased presidential negotiating authority provisions that were the central feature of that Bill:[48]

> The most important shift in U.S. political constellation on trade policy [was] organized labor's move to the protectionist camp. This shift cannot be explained simply by high unemployment. Labor was becoming more protectionist even as unemployment was dropping steadily after 1962, and

had adopted a completely protectionist stance when unemployment stood at its post-Korea low in early 1969. . . . Organized workers have apparently achieved sufficient income levels that the movement as a whole [had] become more interested in avoiding shifts of geographic location, seniority rights, local interests, etc., than in seeking higher real incomes elsewhere.[49]

Testifying before the House Ways and Means Committee, Leonard Woodcock, President of the United Auto Workers Union, urged Congress largely "to ignore the Administration trade proposal and to fashion new trade legislation. . . . "[50] Paramount concern was expressed over the inadequacy of the provisions for adjustment assistance; while the Bill significantly liberalised the circumscriptive language of the Trade Expansion Act,[51] job security alone was no longer sufficient as a yardstick—health care and insurance protection, pension rights, fringe benefits, and seniority were not to be compromised. Reservations were voiced over "the breathtaking powers to be given to the President, at the further expense of Congress,"[52] and over the tax incentives for overseas investment activity by U.S.-based multinational corporations. As to the latter issue, the UAW was in accord with the Burke-Hartke provisions. Woodcock cautioned, however, that the UAW's "chief deviation from Burke-Hartke is on the use of quotas and the rest, which we think would lead to a retaliatory trade war to the detriment of this and all the other involved countries."[53] In short, the Burke-Hartke approach to trade reform was "not recommended."[54]

Representing the AFL-CIO, I.W. Abel[55] was even more adamant in opposing the Trade Bill, characterising it as "bad legislation, containing confusing and conflicting provisions, wrapped in not-so-plain language. It is a patchwork of yesterday's answers for tomorrow's problems. It ignores the realities of today."[56] In particular, the AFL-CIO opposed that portion of the Bill which drastically changed the relationship between Congress and the Executive in regard to the negotiation and approval of agreements to reduce non-tariff trade barriers (NTBs) such as quotas and markings of country of origin.[57] Representing interests that were threatened by any dilution of such NTBs, the AFL-CIO predictably were apprehensive over the fact that congressional consultation and "approval" of any negotiated reductions in this area were in fact optional and within the discretion of the President.[58] It is no surprise, therefore, that the posture of the AFL-CIO vis-a-vis the Burke-Hartke amendments was in marked contrast to the views espoused by the UAW:

[T]he AFL-CIO supports the Burke-Hartke Foreign Trade and Investment Act of 1973. . . . We believe that H.R. 62 .provides a rational, logical, reasonable framework for attacking the pressing problems we face as a result of our world trade position. These problems are, as we have said, the result of a fundamental change in America's economic position in relation to the rest of the world, and this change requires a fundamental shift in policy. We believe the Burke-Hartke Bill provides this fundamental change. It points the way to getting at the specific problems we see threatening our future economic well being. It is not a protectionist theory, it is a pragmatic approach based on an analysis of the problems for their causes.[59]

On October 10, 1973, the House Ways and Means Committee reported out an amended version of H.R. 6767; the debate had lasted more than five months and had produced in excess of five thousand pages of testimony.[60] Although largely paralleling the Administration's draft proposal, H.R. 10710 contained several important revisions introduced by the Committee,[61] not the least of which was the "Jackson-Vanik Amendment" which would prohibit the extension of Most Favoured Nation treatment to any communist country that denied its citizens the opportunity to emigrate freely.[62]

The Administration had, in effect, won major victories—as against the protectionists—on four of the five major provisions[63] in its original proposal; it clearly lost on the MFN issue.[64] On December 11, 1973, H.R. 10710 was passed by the House and subsequently submitted to the Senate Committee on Finance which began hearing on March 4, 1974.

e. The Senate Revisions

From its introduction in the Senate committee[65] to final ratification by both Houses of Congress took another nine months. The volume of testimony put before the Committee was also considerable. The cast of characters was slightly varied, but the impetus of the dialogue—and often the language itself—differed imperceptibly.[66] In the committee, the Trade Act of 1974, Public Law 93-618, was beginning to take final shape, and as if to justify the Senate's prolonged absorption with it, the changes made in it were many. Substantively, however, the majority of the issues had been predetermined and real revisions were few.

The Public Law 93-618 signed on January 3, 1975, by President Nixon's successor essentially follows the Administration's proposed draft submitted almost two years earlier. Four of the five basic provisions escaped major modification in Congress. Even the MFN provision—though it did not survive in the proffered form—probably incorporates as much of the original as could reasonably have been expected.

II. TOWARDS A NEW REGIME OF INTERNATIONAL TRADE

a. The Thrust of the 1974 Act

The provisions of the 1974 Act fall within two classes. To the first class belong: Title I (Negotiating authority), Title IV (Trade with Countries currently not receiving non-discriminatory Treatment), and Title V (Generalized System of Preferences) dealing with conditions of trade. To the second class belong Title II (Relief from Injury Caused by Import Competition) and Title III (Relief from Unfair Trde Practices). In other words, while trade liberalisation is the main target of the Act's provisions, it also contains techniques and procedures which permit the U.S. Government to correct miscalculations or effects of legitimate or illegitimate competition.

The Act is primarily addressed (Title I) to countries who are partners in trade with the United States and with whom it is desirable to establish a world trade system leading to fair and equitable social and economic relations based on comparative advantage, in the hope that this would promote, to everybody's profit, a more perfect international division of labour.

It is also important that non-market economy countries (Title IV) should be involved in one form or another in the world system of trade. Owing to their structural characteristics, however, a wholesale approach is not possible. Each country must be treated on its merits, and where most favoured nation (MFN) status has been achieved, this is to be respected. The extension of MFN status to other member countries of the socialist bloc depends upon their willingness to meet certain minimal standards in the area of human rights (and in particular freedom of emigration). Special provisions apply to developing countries (Title V) who, as aspirants to full member status in the first group, and because of their backward condition, need economic assistance, protection for their infant industries, and preferential treatment for their export trade, to finance their economic development.

The outline of the international trade policy in Titles I, IV, and V is paralleled by Titles II and III which deal with those adverse effects of trade liberalisation which call for the application of corrective measures, requiring trade competition. A distinction is made between legitimate import competition and unfair trade practices which distort conditions of trade, such as subsidies, grants, remission of taxes, etc. In the first case, the purpose of the measures is to blunt the social effects of import competition. In the second case, the purpose is to deal with unfair trade practices and eliminate sources of competition which cannot produce fair trading based on the comparative advantage to individual nations to be derived from the international division of labour.[67]

The present essay is primarily concerned with the policy of reforming the current international trade mechanism to take account of GATT's new role. This policy does not always appear clearly in the 1974 Act; specific circumstances have affected the final product of the legislative process and clouded the perspective of the Act. The U.S. Government realised that the "policy of trade expansion . . . depends on broad domestic support which suffered . . . considerable erosion" in the 1960s. Important sectors of organised labour and of the business community had reached the conclusion that temporary relief from injurious import competition was virtually inaccessible and that grievances over allegedly unfair import competition would not be given full or timely consideration in Washington.

In order to promote further the policy of trade liberalisation the Trade Act had to make concessions to both labour and business points of view.[68]

b. Disruption of the GATT

At the time when the draft of the Trade Reform Act of 1973 was submitted to the House, the international trade regime which had slowly developed after World War II found itself under considerable stress. Its main instrument was the General Agreement on Tariffs and Trade of 1947 structured round the Most Favoured Nation clause and an obligation to follow the principle of non-discrimination and fair trade practices. It also bound its members to a progressive elimination of trade barriers.[69]

At the moment when GATT came into force, it was joined by 34 States and was dominated by Western industrial nations. Today there are over 100 States associated with the GATT and the developed countries are a minority. The core of the GATT system is the principle of Most Favoured Nation, which rules out discrimination.[70] With the emergence of the Common Market, Latin American Free Trade Area, East African Common Market, the Andean Common Market, and various other trading organisations, GATT lost its original unity and homogeneity, and evolved into a superstructure of trading systems, based upon the formation of a number of foreign trade areas, each of them with its own influences and discriminations. While the capacity of most of these "markets" is generally insignificant, the European Common Market (EEC) represents an important barrier to a unitary system of world trade, particularly in the area of agricultural products; for its Common Agricultural Policy (CAP) and the abolition by it of internal tariffs (customs union) discriminates against non-Common Market countries. In addition, the EEC negotiated preferential agreements with a number of non-Market countries, beginning with Greece and Turkey and ending with a group of some 50 countries which joined the Lome Agreement covering Mediterranean countries, Africa and Latin America, again acting outside the GATT framework.[71]

In 1955 Japan joined the GATT, raising the level of trade competition to an unprecedented level, and causing a number of consequential difficulties. In defence of their interests, members of the GATT resorted to practices hardly compatible with the non-discrimination and most favoured treatment principles which were the foundation of the GATT. Finally, primary materials exporting countries, with OPEC in the lead, established cartels which led to a raising of prices and discrimination against consumer nations. The ultimate effect was the ideological and functional bankruptcy of the GATT and a resort to practices—non-tariff trade barriers—which were at odds with the original vision of the GATT.[72]

With this background in mind, the primary role of the 1974 Act may be seen as authorising the U.S. President to participate in the new round of negotiations aimed at making the GATT once again a useful instrument for the management of international trade in new conditions. In this sense, the 1974 Act was to provide a long-range policy programme.[73]

c. The Tokyo Declaration

The feeling that the legal system of GATT had been outstripped by developments and could no longer provided a useful instrument for the management of world trade was shared by others. The declaration of the Ministers of GATT who met in Tokyo (September 12-14, 1973)[74] outlined a reform programme with an agenda which anticipated the thrust of the 1974 Act. It included the following items: the reduction of tariffs and the removal of non-tariff barriers, or, where that was not altogether feasible, their application on the principle of non-discrimination to all member countries. The Declaration proposed a re-examination of article XIX of the GATT on multilateral safeguards (escape clause) in order to promote further liberalisation of trade, and declared Ministers' support for the principles of the GATT.

Special attention was given to the needs of the developing countries, a problem which did not exist in 1947. In this connection, the Ministers declared themselves in favour of the generalised system of preferences, out of recognition for the need for the protection of internal markets of the developing countries, their weakness in regard to balance of payments problems, and price stability for their products. The declaration contained a promise that agriculture shall be specially considered— an important item in the trade reform outlined in the 1974 Act.

Finally, the Ministers decided to approach the key problem of the world trade system by recognising that—

> The policy of liberalising world trade cannot be carried successfully in the absence of parallel efforts to set up a monetary system which shields the world economy from the shocks and imbalances which have previously occurred. The Ministers will not lose sight of the fact that the efforts which

are to be made in the trade field imply continuing efforts to maintain orderly conditions and to establish durable and equitable monetary systems.

The Ministers declared their support for the principles of the GATT and promised to turn their attention to procedures to enforce them. "Consideration shall be given," the Declaration goes on to say, "to improvements of the international framework for the conduct of world trade. .'.'. " Thus the declaration recognised that there was little wrong with the GATT system, except for procedures which needed improvement and the tendency of groups of states to act on their own, departing from the principle of non-discrimination. As the Ministers stated, negotiations should "reduce or eliminate non-tariff measures or, where this is not appropriate, to reduce or eliminate their trade restricting or distorting effects, and to bring such measures under more effective international discipline." The declaration promised to consider a total reduction of all trade restrictions in selected sectors.

d. Recognition of the GATT

In the long tradition of U.S. foreign trade legislation, the Act of 1974 occupies an exceptional position. For the first time Congress recognised the fact that the United States had become a member of the General Agreement on Tariffs and Trade and that, within its framework, a system of foreign trade was established which included practically all the important trading countries.

Already in the course of the Second World War, the U.S. and Britain had discussed—within the general plan for the world political order—the future regime of foreign trade and of economic co-operation. The outcome of these discussions was the Charter of the International Trade Organisation, which was to include all members of the United Nations and to be a part of the new world order to prevent future wars. In 1946, a conference representing a number of countries assembled in London, appointed a Preparatory Committee to prepare a draft of the Charter of the ITO, which was adopted by the full Conference in Havana on March 24, 1948.[75] ITO was never ratified. Submitted to the Congress in April 1949, it was withdrawn by the State Department in December 1950[76] after it became apparent that it had no chance of approval. With ITO's failure in the United States, it likewise was not ratified by any other country. Of the ITO Charter, only Chapter Five (GATT) containing rules of international trade was adopted, in December 1947 in Geneva, as an interim measure to provide a basis for the operation of the future ITO. It came into force in January 1948, pursuant to a protocol of provisional application.[77] In the United States its authority rested on the 1945 extension of the Trade Agreements Act, and its status was that of an Executive Agreement made pursuant to an earlier Congressional authorisation.[78] In order to meet the conditions of that authorisation, the GATT was not conceived as an international organisation but rather as a multilateral trade agreement. Consequently, it contained no provisions regarding its staff or organisation, the only official organ being the conference of Contracting Parties.[79]

From GATT's inception, the U.S. Congress' attitude was that GATT was a trade policy instrument which was the exclusive responsibility of the Executive, bound by the foreign trade rules as developed by the U.S. internal legislation, and, as such, not a concern for the legislative branch of government. The 1951 Extension of the Trade Agreements Act, section 10, provided that "the enactment of this Act shall not be construed to determine or indicate the approval or disapproval of the Congress of the Executive Agreement known as the General Agreement on Tariffs and Trade."[80]

In 1954-55, the Conference of the Contracting Parties assembled in a Review Session which prepared a Charter of a formal Organisation for Trade Co-operation (OTC) to administer the General Agreement on Tariffs and Trade. However, Congress refused to be moved, and the proposal died.[81]

Although Congress did maintain its hostile attitude toward the GATT, it continued to grant the Administration the negotiating authority needed to participate in the GATT tariff reductions negotiations, and to fund U.S. participation in GATT. The provisions of section 10 continued to appear in subsequent trade agreements legislation, but were omitted from the Trade Expansion Act which authorised the Kennedy Round.

Section 10 returned as section 121 (d) of the 1974 Act. It was however in a new form which bears quotation in full:

> (d) There are authorised to be appropriated annually such sums as may be necessary for the payment by the United States of its share of the expenses of the Contracting Parties to the General Agreement on Tariffs and Trade. This authorisation does not imply the approval or disapproval by the Congress of all articles of the General Agreement on Tariffs and Trade.

The immediate significance of section 121 (d) is that, from now on, U.S. participation in the conference and work of GATT is permanently funded. In those terms the attitude of the Congress to GATT assumes different proportions and reservations voiced in regard to it seem to be directed to special provisions of the General Agreement which make it a less perfect instrument of trade liberalisation policy, particularly in the area of agricultural commodities.[82]

These impressions are strengthened by reference to the rest of section 121, particularly those parts which set a programme of GATT reform which, if realised, would indeed reconstruct GATT as an international organisation for the administration of an international trade code.

One of the most important concessions which Congress has declared its intention of making is that the President shall have power to take action to bring U.S. trade agreements into line with the principles of the open, non-discriminatory and fair world economic system. The Congress reserved the right to approve of changes in such international agreements, should they bring material changes in the Federal law, except when the President acted in pursuance of an already obtained authorisation.[83]

At the same time, section 121 (a) authorises the President to negotiate changes in the GATT structure as regards: (a) the decision-making process (giving the United States a weighted vote reflecting the balance of economic interest); (b) revision of Article XIX (of the GATT) into a strong international safeguard procedure; (c) dispute resolution, including regular consultations and a method of establishing such a system within the GATT agreements dealing with restrictions on imports of specific commodities; development of provisions dealing with import restraints in relation to injurious imports and border adjustments for international taxes (*e.g.* value added tax in the EEC); measures designed in accordance with the GATT articles dealing with balance of payments deficits; and assuring access to supplies of food, raw materials, manufactured and semi-manufactured goods. A special provision proposes the adoption and inclusion in the General Agreement of multilateral procedures with respect to member and non-member countries which deny fair and equitable access to the supply of food and other commodities and which substantially injure the international community. In a special concession to labour interests, Congress said that it would like to see the GATT as a vehicle for the adoption of international fair labour standards and fair trade practices which would remove the handicap of low wages paid to foreign labour and the elimination of unfair trade practices employed in foreign countries.

In the perspective of the GATT reform provisions (section 121 (a)) and of the debate which preceded the enactment of the 1974 Act, another aspect of the general design became apparent. It is particularly visible in the desire expressed in section 121 (a)(4) to achieve "the adoption of international fair labour standards and of public petition and confrontation procedures in the GATT"—a postulate which can hardly be expected to be reached by means of bilateral negotiations. The usual techniques, frequently resorted to by the U.S. Government, are the protection of the labour market by means of tariffs and restrictions denying access to goods produced by countries resorting to cheap labour. This technique cannot be employed in a world economic system as it stands today. The only method reasonably available is a gradual adoption of new standards through the process of economic integration on a world-wide scale.

Title I authorises the President to negotiate new conditions and rules of international trade and at the same time amends U.S. foreign trade legislation as regards the mechanism to be applied to foreign trade management in the United States.

The Act still maintains the fiction that American foreign trade conditions are a matter of bilateral negotiation, which will yield concessions for American exports in other countries.[84] Reform of the GATT and its code of international trade is a separate problem calling for a separate approach.[85] In fact, GATT is an all-embracing trade agreement which replaced most, if not all, of the bilateral agreements made by the United States with individual countries. Trade concessions negotiated by the United States in individual bilateral agreements are now replaced (for the most part) by the schedules attached to the General Agreement. The Act would have gained in clarity if the negotiating authority had dealt primarily with negotiating GATT changes and reform of the code of international trade at which it clearly aims (see s. 2 of the Act and *passim*). It is clear from the circumstances of the Act that its main purpose was to set up the level of concessions the United States delegation to the Tokyo Round would be authorised to make, and this was the prupose of the legislative proposal submitted in 1973 by the Nixon Administration. Its main thrust, as regards the removal of trade barriers, was to negotiate the removal of non-tariff obstacles to trade, offering as a *quid pro quo* the removal of the American Selling Price (ASP) for the purpose of duty valuation.[86]

Parallel to the removal of trade barriers, the purpose of the Act is to restrict, if not to replace altogether, unilateral action to solve imbalances in trade by the GATT members. This is to be done by consultation, agreed adjustment or thirty party adjudication. A typical example of such action which is aimed at here is the case of the U.S. dairy product restrictions, imposed under the Defence Production Act of 1950, which has caused considerable difficulty with U.S. trade partners.[87] It is not quite clear how far the U.S. Congress would go in accepting that aspect of the GATT reform, as it would result in considerable restriction of its power to regulate foreign commerce, but formal authorisation to negotiate a dispute settling is granted.[88]

In spite of the fact that tariff reduction negotiations have been actively pursued since 1934, tariff reductions remain the most important incentive to the expansion of trade and the Act grants the President considerable powers in this area for the next five-year period, including the authority to reduce rates to 40 per cent. of those in force on January 1, 1975. Rates of duty of no more than 5 per cent. *ad valorem* are exempt. The President has power to increase U.S. tariffs, as a result of negotiations, but such increases cannot exceed 50 per cent. of the rate in force on January 1, 1975. No rate of 20 per cent. *ad valorem* may be increased.[89]

The Act adopted three approaches to tariff concessions: those granted on the basis of equality,[90] those extended to developing countries on the basis of preferences,[91] and those made to assure equitable access to supplies.[92] Each of these classes of agreement would call for a different combination of mutual concessions, depending upon the needs and interests of the countries involved. At the same time, section 107 urges that trade agreements made by the U.S. with its partners should provide for internationally agreed rules and procedures providing for the use of temporary measures to ease the adjustment of internal markets to the expanded flow of trade, attributable to the removal or reduction of trade barriers. Such agreements should provide for proper notifications of exporting countries, consultations, joint reviews of the flow of trade, making proper adjustments and mediation of disputes.

Section 102 of the Act speaks of the non-tariff barriers and other distortions of trade, without defining them closely. More specific examples of them may be found in section 121 of the Act which deals with the GATT revision.

Obstacles to the sale of American products abroad fall into two classes.

To the first belong various measures which give advantage to goods either coming from special areas (*e.g.* preferences in the case of Commonwealth countries)[93] and tax or duty devices which lower the price of exported commodities. One example of such a measure is the Common Agricultural Policy of the EEC. Another is value added tax, a turnover tax which is not levied on goods exported abroad and which are therefore sold there at lower prices than in EEC markets. Value added tax (an indirect tax) performs the same function in the EEC as taxes on a manufacturer's profits (direct tax) and therefore discriminates against American manufacturers and places a handicap on American exports. At the same time GATT article XVI prohibits any form of direct subsidising of exports and this is interpreted as a prohibition on the remission of direct taxes to subsidise exports. However, the remission of value added tax is not considered a subsidy.[94]

To the second class of obstacles to the sale of American products abroad belong measures of a social nature such as "fair labour standards" which cannot be settled through the mechanisms of international trade agreements, although low wages may favour exports and disadvantage countries offering high living standards to their workers.

The general programme of trade liberalisation and harmonisation of the international trade code is combined with an effort to regularise procedures dealing with those situations where trade restriction is necessary in order to counteract the adverse effect of increased imports on the economy of the trading partners. The specific example of such a situation arises where the balance of payments is disturbed by the imports. While the Act recognises that the interested State must reserve to itself freedom of action, nevertheless it expressed a desire to have this freedom exercised with moderation on two specific occasions. Of the two alternative techniques open to the interested party—a surcharge and a quota restriction—section 121 (a)(6) lays down that a surcharge is the preferred method "by which industrial countries may handle balance-of-payments deficits in so far as import restraint measures are required." The provisions of section 121 (a)(6) are aimed specifically at article XII of the GATT which deals with this situation.

Section 122 (balance of payments) still, however, uses both techniques of import restriction (import quotas and the surcharge). Resort to these methods is permitted in two situations: first, when there is a serious balance of payments problem and it is necessary to prevent an imminent and significant depreciation of the dollar; and secondly, in order to correct an international balance of payments disequilibrium, even when the American dollar is not threatened. The use of quotas (quantitative restrictions) is reserved only to the case where the use of quotas has been agreed to in an international trade agreement and the problem cannot be corrected by a surcharge.[95]

In a reverse situation, when the U.S. balance of payments is likely to show constant and persistent surplus, or considerable appreciation in the value of the dollar on foreign markets is imminent, the President may encourage imports by lowering custom duties, but by no more than 5 per cent. *ad valorem*. Another measure authorised by the Act is to increase the value of imported articles or temporarily lift restrictions on imports. However, this does not apply in a situation where restriction on the importation of such articles would materially injure firms or workers or endanger national security or otherwise affect the national interest adversely.[96]

Surcharges or quotas may be imposed by the President for a period of no longer than 150 days, but this may be extended by Congress.[97] The Act strongly suggests that the U.S. should make agreements with its partners, that surcharge duties should only be used, and that adjustment liabilities should be shared between the surplus and deficit countries. As a rule, all import controlling measures should apply to all countries without discrimination, except in those exceptional cases when the purpose of balance of payments control may be achieved by action against one or more countries with persistent balance of payments surpluses. In such cases, other countries may be exempt from import restriction measures.[98]

No tariff or non-tariff barrier may be reduced or removed, if the interests of national security come into play.

The general tenor of directives to the Administration is to replace unilateral decisions to protect the balance of payments, national security or the welfare of social groups, firms or communities by previously agreed procedures.

To balance the authority of the Administration to proceed unilaterally in order to protect the American balance of payments, the Act authorises the Administration to compensate possible losses to American trading partners.[99]

Two methods of action are open to the Administration. In the first place, the President may negotiate additional concessions, with partners whose trade may be hurt by escape clause measures. In the second place, the President may unilaterally make such concessions, by reducing tariff rates even below the maximum reduction generally provided for in section 101, or below the rate appropriate to any stage of the process of reduction. The reduced rates may not be less than 70 per cent. of the permissible lowest rates and not more than 30 per cent. of such duty at each stage.[100]

Section 123 (Compensation Authority) follows the pattern outlined by the General Agreement (articles XII and XIX). The emphasis is on agreed action. All emergency measures to prevent or correct damage to balance of payments, or to avoid damage to the national economy, or to avoid adverse effects of increased imports on specific classes of commodities, are to be the result of consultations and negotiations and should provide for compensatory concessions.

In order to give a full presentation of the general drift of the provisions of the 1974 Act in situations in which some restriction of the flow of imports may be necessary (whether within or without the projected reform of the GATT) section 107 of the Act (International Safeguard Procedure) must be referred to. It states that the purpose of the Act is to negotiate international agreements which—

> in the context of the harmonisation, reduction, or reduction of barriers to, and other distortions of international trade, which permit the use of temporary measures to ease adjustment to changes occurring in competitive conditions in the domestic markets. . . .

Such agreements may provide for:

> (1) notification of affected exporting countries: (2) international consultations; (3) international review of changes in trade flows; (4) making adjustments in trade flows . . . ; and (5) international mediation. In addition such agreements may exclude mutual compensation, or retaliation and provide for domestic procedures which may give foreign interests access to internal procedures undertaken under the escape clause.[101]

To round up the description and analysis of the provisions of the 1974

Act aimed at authorising the Administration to participate effectively in the Tokyo Round, two more aspects of the 1974 regime of foreign trade must be mentioned. All actions by the Administration undertaken in order to protect U.S. interests (balance of payments and national security) are temporary, and their extension must involve action by Congress,[102] with all the safeguards of the legislative process. Secondly, the President has the power to retaliate against any party which is in violation of its agreed obligations.

Section 126 imposes upon the President the duty to keep a check on the actual performance of foreign trade partners of the United States, including their implementation of accepted obligations to grant reciprocal trade concessions (duty-free treatment or removal of other import restrictions). This applies, in the first place, to major industrial countries, in the event that any of them fail to make concessions under the 1974 Act providing for competitive opportunities for the commerce of the United States. In such a situation the Act provides that the President shall recommend to Congress appropriate legislative action either for the termination of concessions granted under a trade agreement, or to deny the application to the trade of that country of legislation enacted for the purpose of implementing a trade agreement. The term "major industrial country" covers Canada, the European Economic Community and its members, Japan, and any other foreign country designated by the President.[103]

Directives addressed to the Administration to negotiate further trade concessions and reform the code of international trade were supplemented by an instruction as to how diplomatic processes should be utilised to obtain the best results.

The guiding principle of trade negotiation is to proceed on a sectoral basis, *i.e.* to seek trade concessions on an industry-by-industry basis. According to section 135 the President, before entering into a trade agreement, shall seek advice from the private sector as regards negotiating objectives and bargaining positions. He shall consult the Advisory Committee for Trade Negotiations consisting of representatives of government, labour, industry, agriculture, small business, service industries, retailers, consumer interests and the general public. The President may establish general policy advisory committees for industry, labour and agriculture, and may create and seek advice from sector advisory committees representing individual sectors, industry, labour or agriculture. He may also seek advice from private organisations. The Act thus provides for various channels of information and communication to inform the President on the special problems facing each sector and industrial or labour interests in connection with negotiations in progress. These committees shall also review and report on agreements negotiated by the President or the Congress or the Special Representative for Trade

Negotiations. In sum, the Act assumes that particular interests are effectively represented in trade negotiations, and that their voices are heard.

The same guiding principle is also sustained by section 104 which insists that negotiation of mutual concessions "be conducted on the basis of appropriate product sectors of manufacturing." The basic idea is that mutual trade concessions shall be granted on a sector-by-sector basis and presumably corresponding industrial sectors are to be treated on a basis of reciprocity. This understanding is strengthened by the provisions of subsection (3) of section 104 which states:

> For the purposes of this section . . . the Special Representative for Trade Negotiations together with the Secretary of Commerce, Agriculture, or Labour as appropriate, shall after consultation with the Advisory Committee for Trade Negotiations established under section 135, and after consultations with interested private organisations, identify appropriate product sectors of manufacturing.

At the same time, it is clear that the sectoral approach will not necessarily always be appropriate. For example, one of the problem sectors in the American economy is agriculture, a sector heavily discriminated against in imports to industrial countries. to overcome artificial barriers against agricultural exports, section 103 (Overall Negotiating Objective) visualises that there may have to be departures from the sector principle in that it provides that "to the maximum extent feasible," the harmonisation, reduction, or elimination of agricultural trade barriers and distortions shall be undertaken in conjunction with the harmonisation, reduction, or elimination of industrial trade barriers and distortions.

Another exception to the sectoral approach is included in section 123 (Compensation Authority) which gives the President the power to negotiate compensation in the form of new import concessions to a country affected by quota restrictions on its products, where this is necessary, to remedy large and serious balance of payments deficits. Section 123 suggests that import quota restrictions shall be compensated for by concessions relating to other classes of goods, so as to maintain an overall balance of trade between the United States and that other country. Thus while trade concessions are negotiated on a sectorial basis, the actual progress of the exchange of goods is viewed from the standpoint of maintaining the overall health of the national economy.

The sectoral approach is not an American invention. It reflects the fact that, at this time, the disparity in the competitive position of imports from various countries, to a large degree depending on the disparity in national standards of living, prevents a general removal of trade barriers. Kennedy Round negotiations were saved because it was possible, through the sectoral approach, to agree to concessions affecting sectors rather than the general tariff structure.[104] It is also on the basis of the sectoral approach that the Tokyo Round aims at devising the total removal of trade barriers. The Ministerial Declaration of September 14, 1973, proposed "an examination of the possibilities for the co-ordinated reduction or elimination of all barriers to trade in selected sectors as a complementary technique."[105]

Viewed from a very general point of view, it is clear that on no account can the 1974 Act be considered as the ultimate model for the international trade pattern. Rather, it is a stepping-stone towards liberalised trade among the most important industrial nations, which recognise that free trade ideals are still a possibility.

This understanding of the 1974 Act is strengthened by the terms of section 121 (a)(12) which directs the Administration to seek "to establish within GATT an international agreement on articles (including footwear) including the creation of regular and institutionalised mechanisms for the settlement of disputes and of surveillance body to monitor all international shipments of such articles."

This authorisation has its history. It has been mentioned before[105a] that some time after its inception the GATT system suffered a serious breakdown. In 1955, Japan joined the GATT with its low-wage labour and highly developed industry, ready to flood world markets with its exports and so threatening serious market disruptions. Later on, Japan was joined by other competitors, mostly newly developing countries, which also threatened to invade the markets of the GATT members with cheap commodities (mainly textiles), causing serious economic difficulty. The response of GATT members varied. Some of them refused to grant Japan a Most Favoured Nation treatment. Others—including the United States—forced Japan and textile producers to agree to voluntary quota restrictions, and negotiated a Long Term Textile Agreement.

A full account of these developments is given elsewhere.[106] Here it is sufficient to say that the 1974 Act, with its aim of reforming the GATT, moved to replace unilateral action on the part of individual countries by an agreed international process supervised by GATT, thus legalising in effect a permanent international trade organisation.

III. FUNCTIONAL ANALYSIS

To implement the complicated scheme of negotiation and regulation devised in it, the Trade Act of 1974 provides for a precise interplay between the major functionaries whose actions—pursuant to guidelines established by the Act itself—determine the desired foreign trade policy of the United States. These major functionaries are: the President, Congress, the International Trade Commission (the "revised" Tariff Commission), the Office of the Special Representative for Trade Negotiations, the Secretaries of Labour, Commerce, and the Treasury, and the various advisory and co-ordinating committees established under the Act.

The President

The Chief Executive is the prime mover in effectuating the negotiatory objectives promulgated under Titles I and IV of the Act. The President is empowered by the Act to enter into five basic types of trade agreement: trade agreements aimed at eliminating tariff barriers,[107] trade agreements aimed at eliminating non-tariff barriers and similar distortions;[108] trade agreements aimed at effecting General Agreement on Tariffs and Trade (GATT) revisions;[109] limited commercial agreements extending non-discriminatory (MFN) treatment to countries previously denied such treatment;[110] and orderly marketing agreements[111] (alone or in combination with other, unilateral actions)[112] to provide relief from injury—or the threat thereof—caused by import competition.[113] The section 101, 102, 405, and 203 agreements may be characterised as permissive;[114] the section 121 agreements are mandatory.[115] Presidential authority for effectuating section 101 and 102 agreements is limited to five years from the date of the enactment of the Act,[116] although the section 101 authority may be extended for an additional two years.[117] Until their authority terminates, section 101 trade agreements are to be used to grant new concessions by way of ameliorating the effects of section 203 import relief;[118] thereafter, section 123 provides the authority for such ameliorative relief.[119] In order to carry out section 101 trade agreements, the President may manipulate duties "as . . . required or appropriate."[120]

In the cast of section 102 trade agreements, the President must, "not less than 90 days before the day on which he enters into such trade agreement," notify Congress and promptly thereafter publish notice in the Federal Register of his intention to enter into such a trade agreement. He must enter into consultations concerning its implementation with the Senate Committee on Finance, the House Committee on Ways and Means, "and with each committee of the House and the Senate and each joint committee which has jurisdiction over legislation involving subject-matters which would be affected by such trade agreement."[121] After entering into a section 102 trade agreement, the President must submit to Congress a draft of the implementing Bill and a statement of any proposed administrative action with explanations thereof,[122] as well as a statement of how such an agreement "serves the interests of United States commerce" and why the Bill and administrative action are "required or appropriate to carry out the agreement."[123]

The President is authorised to enter into bilaterial section 101 and 102 trade agreements if he "determines that . . . [such] agreements will more effectively promote the economic growth of, and full employment in, the United States. . . . "[124] If a section 101 or 102 trade agreement will significantly affect "competitive opportunities in one or more product sectors [of manufacturing] . . . ," the President is required to submit to Congress an analysis of the extent to which the section 104 "Sector Negotiating Objective" would be achieved by such an agreement.[125] In negotiating section 101 or 102 trade agreements, the President must reach certain specified negotiating objectives.[126] In addition, he is required "from time to time to publish and furnish the International Trade Commission . . . with lists of articles which may be considered for . . .[127] section 101 trade agreement negotiational purposes."[128] Before making an offer with respect to such trade agreements, the President must have sought[129] and received the advice of the International Trade Commission (ITC), unless the ITC has failed to respond within the statutorily imposed time limit.[130] Moreover, before making an offer with respect to either a section 101 or 102 trade agreement, the President is required to have afforded a public hearing to interested parties and to have received—and apparently reviewed—a summary thereof.[131]

Whenever the implementation of a section 101 trade agreement requires a reduction in duty in excess of ten per cent. of the previous rate, the President is required to implement the reduction by "staging" it at one-year intervals.[132] He is authorised to exceed the relevant per-year limit[133] only for the purpose of "rounding" to "simplify the computation."[134] There is a ten-year staging period limit.[135]

In negotiating section 121 trade agreements, the President is required to promote "the development of an open, non-discriminatory, and fair world economic system."[136] Twelve trade liberalising "principles" are specifically outlined in the Act,[137] but from the directive it is clear that action should not be limited to those specified principles only.[138]

The authority extended by section 121 is really two-fold: the President is required to conform to existing GATT agreements within the trade liberalising principles,[139] and, "to the extent feasible," to enter into new agreements guided by the same principles.[140] Whenever the implementation of a trade agreement entered into pursuant to this section would effect a change in any provision of federal law or administrative procedure, the agreement must be submitted to Congress so that it may pass implementing legislation, unless Congress explicitly delegates such implementing authority.[141]

Title IV of the Trade Act of 1974 begins with a general prohibition against extending non-discriminatory (MFN) treatment to countries which had not previously qualified for such treatment.[142] It then sets out specific categories of non-market economy countries which are ineligible for the extension of MFN treatment.[143] However, these prohibitions are replete with exculpatory provisions. For example, they all apply prospectively, and not retrospectively, so that no country, already enjoying MFN treatment would be denied such a preference;[144] the proscriptions merely enjoin the President from providing new concessions to this class of non-market economy countries.[145] But even new concessions are not totally denied to countries burdened by sections 402 and 409 prohibitions.[146] Should the President decide that a non-market economy country affected by these prohbitions has implemented legislation which would substantiate a finding that it had "mended its ways," he is empowered to enter into commercial agreements with such a country, impeded only by the requirement that he must submit a report to Congress delineating the change of circumstances, both at the outset of the agreement and at six-month intervals thereafter.[146a] The only risk factor is that Congress—by adopting a disapproval resolution in either House within 90 days of the submission of the report[147]—may not only render the commercial agreement thus entered into by the President void, but may preclude his entering into any future agreements "with such country under . . . title [IV] . . . "[148] apparently for the duration of the Act.

In addition, "[d]uring the 18-month period beginning on the date of the enactment of this Act, the President is authorised to waive by Executive order the application of" section 402 (a)[149] and 409 (a)[150] prohibitions, thereby circumventing the risk[151] of proceeding under section 402 (b) or 409 (b) merely by submitting a report to Congress[152] which asserts that " . . . he has determined that such waiver will *substantially* promote the objectives of this section . . . "[153] and that " . . . he has received *assurances* that the emigration practices of that country will henceforth lead *substantially* to the achievement of the objective of this section."[154] The waiver would, of course, free the President to exercise his authority under section 405 to enter into a bilateral commercial agreement with that country.

Waiver authority seems a somewhat superfluous safeguard. It does not grant any independent affirmative action authorisation beyond waiving the proscriptions of section 402 (a) and 402 (b). In other words, should the President wish to accomplish any extension of MFN treatment to a country absolutely denying or imposing economic restrictions on emigration, he would still have to conclude a commercial agreement with that country[155]—an agreement which would take effect *only* if approved by Congress.[156] Notwithstanding this safeguard mechanism, Congress saw fit to promulgate a complicated scheme for subsequent 12-month extensions of waiver authority.[157] This, in effect, states that, following the initial 18-month waiver period, the President may extend waiver authority for any number of successive 12-month periods, provided that the conditions for the initial grant of waiver persist and neither House of Congress has succeeded in blocking the extension by adopting a resolution disapproving it within the statutorily mandated period(s).[158]

In any event, the President may authorise "the entry into force of bilateral commercial agreements providing non-discriminatory treatment to the products of countries heretofore denied such treatment . . . "[159] and "by proclamation extend [such]treatment to the products of a foreign country[160] which has entered into [such] a bilateral commercial agreement. . . . "[161] The President is empowered "at any time [to] suspend or withdraw any extension of non-discriminatory treatment . . . " unilaterally and without the consent, approval, or right to disapproval of Congress.[162] The type of agreement into which the President may enter under the provisions of section 405 is restricted as to parties,[163] and term,[164] and by the mandatory inclusion of various safeguard conditions.[165] Whenever the President takes action under section 404 (a), he must "promptly" transmit to Congress the proclamation, the agreement, and his reasons for so acting.[166] Congress may then approve[167] or disapprove—in the acase of agreements "entered into before the date of the enactment of this Act. . . . "[168]

Finally, the President is authorised to "negotiate orderly marketing agreements"[169]—alone or in combination with other forms of import relief[170]—"limiting the export from foreign countries and the import into the United States of [certain] articles"[171] in order "to prevent or remedy serious injury or the threat thereof to [an] industry . . . and to facilitate the orderly adjustment to new competitive conditions by the industry in question. . . . "[172] It should be mentioned here that the whole panoply of Title II import relief measures may be brought into operation by entirely fair, non-discriminatory, and non-restrictive trade practices which are, unfortunately, successful enough to injure seriously or threaten so to injure a "domestic industry producing an article like or directly competitive with [the] imported article. . . . "[173] In contradistinction, Title III relief is available only pursuant to a determination of unfair, unjustifiable, unreasonable, or discriminatory trade practices,[174] and here the element of competition with a domestic producer is, largely, irrelevant. Moreover, while the initiative for taking action under Titles I, III, IV, and V rests, for the most part, with the President,[175] the preferred initiative for affording Title II import relief is from "an entity . . . which is representative of [the] industry . . . " alleging a need thereof.[176] The President,[177] as well as other officials and agencies,[178] are not, however, precluded from "casting the first stone," in the unlikely eventuality of there being severe import competition and no outcry from the industry concerned.

In determining whether or not to apply the forms of import relief for which he is responsible,[179] the President may negotiate a trade agreement to limit the import into the United States of the offending competitive article.[180] Even after receiving a report containing an affirmative finding by the ITC, under section 201 (b), to the effect "that increased imports have been a substantial cause of serious injury or the threat thereof with respect to an industry," the President may refuse to take action as long as "he determines that provision of such relief is not in the national economic interest of the United States. . . . "[181] However, he must thereupon report his reasons for so deciding to Congress[182] and risk being overruled.[183]

Trade agreements may be negotiated after the imposition of other forms of import relief, in which case they could replace such relief,[184] in whole or in part, or they may be negotiated as preliminary steps in the provision of other forms of import relief.[185] In negotiating section 203 (4) trade agreements, the President must operate within the general premises of the abuses this import relief mechanism was designed to preclude, namely serious injury or threat of serious injury due to *increased* imports of competing articles.[186] The trade agreement, therefore, should not require a decrease in imports below " . . . the quantity or value of such article imported into the United States during the most recent period which . . . is representative of imports of such article."[187] In order to carry out such trade agreements, the President may issue regulations concerning withdrawal from warehouse stocks of articles covered by the agreement.[188] The trade agreements negotiated pursuant to this section are restricted as to their term,[189] but are renewable.[190] Import relief which is to be provided for more than three years must "to the extent feasible" be phased down gradually, with the first reduction occurring no later than the first day of the fourth year in which relief will be provided.[191]

In addition to the authority to enter into trade agreement, the President is empowered by the Trade Act of 1974 to proclaim by executive order four types of unilateral, import-manipulative devices: relief from injury caused by import competition;[192] relief from unfair trade practices;[193] temporary relief from balance-of-payments disequilibria;[194] and duty-free preferences.[195]

The first of these, relief from injury caused by import competition, is basically the same authority allowing the President to conduct the last type of trade agreements examined earlier.[196] The authority commences with an affirmative finding by the ITC "that increased imports have been a substantial cause of serious injury or threat thereof with respect to an industry. . . . "[197] Thereupon, the President may[198] provide four types of relief (excluding the trade agreements discussed earlier): (a) increase or imposition of a duty;[199] (b) imposition of a tariff-rate quota;[200] (c) modification or imposition of a quantitative restriction;[201] or "any combination of such actions," including and in conjunction with a trade agreement.[202] The President, if he intends to proclaim such relief, must act promptly.[203] All the provisions already enumerated with respect to section 203 (a)(4) trade agreements apply to the other forms of relief also.[204]

The President is also empowered to take affirmative action to provide relief from unfair trade practices,[205] defined as (a) tariff or other import restrictions;[206] (b) discriminatory or otherwise unjustifiable or unreasonable acts or policies;[207] (c) subsidies;[208] or (d) unjustifiable or unreasonable restrictions on access to critical supplies.[209] In making his determination, the President is instructed to assess the relationship of his action to the purposes of the Act,[210] namely, to remove impediments which burden or restrict United States commerce, with respect to tariff/import restrictions,211 discriminatory acts/policies,212 and restrictions on access to critical supplies.[213] With respect to subsidies, he is enjoined to consider also (i) whether the Secretary of the Treasury has found that subsidies are being provided;[214] (ii) whether the ITC has found a substantial effect on competitive U.S. product(s);[215] and (iii) whether " . . . the Antidumping Act 1921, and section 303 of the Tariff Act of 1930 are inadequate to deter such practices."[216] Before taking action, the President is required to "provide an opportunity for the presentation of views"[217] and provide for public hearings at the request of *any* interested person,[218] unless "expeditious action" in line with "national interest" require otherwise,[219] in which case the presentation of views and hearings may be postponed until after action is taken.[220] Having made the above determinations and having provided for (or legitimately postponed) the presentation of views and hearings, the President may negate the application or benefits of trade agreements;[221] impose duties, fees or other restrictions;[222] and "take all appropriate and feasible steps . . . to obtain the elimination of such restrictions or subsidies. . . ."[223]

Under "balance-of-payments authority"[224] the President is authorised[225] to proclaim temporary[226] import surcharges[227] or quota limitations,[228] or both,[229] "[w]henever fundamental international payments problems require special import measures"[230] to correct U.S. balance-of-payments deficits,[231] U.S. dollar depreciations,[232] or international balance-of-payments disequilibria.[233] The President is also authorised to act to prevent "fundamental international payments problems" favourable to the United States.[234] However, he may correct only U.S. balance-of-trade surpluses[235] or U.S. dollar appreciations[236] and then only by proclaiming temporary[237] reductions in the relevant rate of duty,[238] in conjunction with quota increases.[239] The Act allows the President to "suspend, modify, or terminate, in whole or in part, any proclamation under this section . . . " at any time.[240]

Finally, the President is authorised to provide, for a period not exceeding ten years,[241] duty-free treatment[242] to certain classes of articles[243] from certain classes of countries, designated "beneficiary developing countries."[244] Subsequently, the President may withdraw, suspend, or modify such preferential treatment,[245] but, by so doing, cannot establish a rate of duty " . . . other than the rate which would apply . . . " under ordinary circumstances.[246] The President is required to withdraw or suspend the "beneficiary developing country" designation[247] upon the occurrence of special changed circumstances,[248] with certain exceptions.[249]

In taking any form of action under the Act, the President is authorised to: (a) terminate, in whole or in part at any time, any proclamation made under the Act;[250] (b) withdraw, suspend, or modify trade agreements and increase duties in retaliation for a unilateral withdrawl, suspension, or modification of trade agreement obligations by a foreign country or instrumentality, without granting adequate compensation;[251] (c) recommend to Congress termination or denial of trade agreement benefits to any "major industrial country" which has failed to reciprocate with substantially equivalent concessions;[252] and (d) to reserve from negotiations articles critical to national security[253] and certain other articles.[254]

The President is also responsible for appointing the Special Representative for Trade Negotiations[255] and his two Deputies,[256] as well as the Commissioners of the ITC.[257] The Act requires the Chief Executive to establish an Advisory Committee for Trade Negotiations.[258] In addition, he may, if necessary, establish general industry, labour, and agriculture policy advisory committees[259] and sector advisory committees.[260]

The Special Representative for Trade Negotiations

The Special Representative for Trade Negotiations heads the Office of the Special Representative for Trade Negotiations[261] within the Executive Office of the President.[262] His primary function is that of chief representative[263] of the U.S. for trade negotiations under Title I (sections 101, 102, 121) and section 301 of the Trade Act of 1974.[264] He is also responsible for advising the President and Congress with respect to matters related to the trade agreements programmes[265] and for chairing the Advisory Committee for Trade Negotiations.[266] The Deputy Special Representatives for Trade Negotiations, of whom there are two,[267] function primarily in conducting trade negotiations[268] under the Act and assisting the Special Representative.[269] One Deputy Special Representative is responsible for chairing the Adjustment Assistance Co-ordinating Committee.[270]

The Special Representative may initiate, on his own authority, section 201 (import competition)[271] and section 406 (market disruption by a Communist country)[272] investigations by the ITC. He is also responsible for conducting the reviews and public hearings concerning unfair trade practices[273] and (in concert with the Secretary of Commerce, Agriculture, or Labour and after consultation with the Advisory Committee for Trade Negotiations) for identifying "appropriate product sectors of manufacturing" to be considered in achieving the "sector negotiating objective" of section 101 and 102 tgrade agreements.[274] Being under the direct control of the President; the Special Negotiator is, of course, "reponsible for such other functions as the President may direct."[275]

The United States International Trade Commission

The ITC is the United States Tariff Commission renamed.[276] The six commissioners are the President's appointees,[277] and they serve, at his discretion, for nine-year terms. Their voting record is a matter of public record,[278] and they may be represented in judicial proceedings by their own staff attorneys or by the Attorney-General of the United States.[279] Like the Special Representative,[280] they perform both in advisory and affirmative capacities; however, while the Special Representative's primary affirmative capacity is negotiational, the ITC performs essentially investigative and decisional (adjudicatory) functions.

In its advisory capacity, the ITC is responsible for conducting various types of investigation,[281] as well as for holding public hearings[282] and advising the President as to the probable economic impact on domestic industries[283] and consumers[284] of any proposed section 101, 123 or 124[285] or 102 trade agreements.[286] The ITC also advises the President on the probable domestic economic impact of extensions of duty-free preferences with respect to certain articles from specified beneficiary countries,[287] and may, if requested to do so, advise the President on the extension, reduction, or termination of section 203 import relief.[288]

Besides rendering purely advisory recommendations, the ITC is directed by the 1974 Act to conduct certain types of investigations and render more binding recommendations, including an independent affirmative action, pursuant to Titles II,[289] III,[290] and IV[291] of the Act. Under Title II, the ITC is required to conduct an investigation[292] and make a determination "whether an article is being imported into the United States in such increased quantities as to be a substantial cause of serious injury, or the threat thereof, to the domestic industry producing an article like or directly competitive with the imported article"[293] It must, in turn, report to the President its findings, the basis therefor, and its recommendations, including dissenting or separate views.[294] A similar provision pertains to market disruption by a Communist country.[295] While the President is impowered to disregard an affirmative finding by the ITC of injury caused by import competition,[296] he cannot provide such relief unless he receives such an affirmative determination by the ITC.[297] Moreover, the commencement of an investigation by the ITC under section 201 invokes action on the part of the Secretary of Labour with respect to adjustment assistance.[298]

Pursuant to authority granted under Title III of the Act,[299] the ITC is required to investigate allegations of unfair trade practices with respect to the levying of anti-dumping duties,[300] contervailing duties,[301] and unfair import competition[302] and to make determinations thereon. The implementation of action based on an affirmative finding by the ITC, however, is reserved to others—except with respect to unfair import competition.[303]

The ITC is also responsible for providing Congress annually with factual information on the operation of the trade agreements programme;[304] establishing, maintaining, and publishing annually a summary of the data collected under the East-West Trade Statistics Monitoring System;[305] and—in concert with the Secretaries of Commerce and the Treasury— collect and publish uniform statistical data on imports, exports, and production.[306]

The Cabinet

The various Cabinet members are authorised under the provisions of the Act to render advisory assistance on trade-related matters.[307] But the more important functions are those performed by the Secretaries of Commerce and Labour under Title II of the Act, and by the Secretary of the Treasury under Title III and V of the Act.[308]

To the Secretary of Labour is delegated the primary responsibility in overseeing and implementing adjustment assistance for workers.[309] He is responsible for receiving petitions for adjustment assistance,[310] publishing notice of their receipt,[311] conducting public hearings thereon,[312] conducting investigations of the allegations therein,[313] making the determination of whether or not adjustment assistance is warranted,[314] and, if it is warranted, certifying the group of workers who are eligible to apply for such assistance.[315] He is also responsible for the general administration of the Adjustment Assistance for Workers Programme.[316]

Likewise, the Secretary of Commerce is primarily responsible for the implementation of the Adjustment Assistance for Firms Programme,[317] and, on consultation with the Secretary of Labour,[318] for the implementation of the Adjustment Assistance for Communities Programme.[319]

Pursuant to authority granted him by Title III of the Trade Act of 1974[320] the Secretary of the Treasury is empowered to investigate, determine the necessity of, assess and collect anti-dumping[321] and countervailing duties.[322] He is also responsible for prescribing regulations necessary to designate articles eligible for Title V duty-free preferences.[323]

Advisory and Co-ordinating Agencies

The Advisory Committee for Trade Negotiations[324] is responsible for providing the President with overall policy advice on sections 101 or 102 trade agreements.[325] The President may choose to establish two additional private-sector advisory committees, as necessary.[326] The Adjustment Assistance Co-ordinating Committee is responsible for the overall co-ordination of the policies, studies, and effective and efficient implementation of the Adjustment Assistance programmes.[327] The East-West Foreign Trade Board is responsible for monitoring "trade between persons and agencies of the United States Government and non-market economy countries or instrumentalities of such countries to insure that such trade will be in the national interest of the United States."[328]

The Congress

The United States Congress reserved for itself the "right of final approval" with respect to most, but not all,[329] of the activities authorised by the 1974 Act. Section 101 ostensibly grants the "basic authority for trade agreements."[330] Immediately section 102 speaks in broad general terms of "any barriers to (or other distortions of) international trade," but is, oddly enough, entitled "non-tariff barriers to and other distortions of trade," and it, apparently, also provides authority for entry "into trade agreements. . . ."[331] Subsequent provisions of the Act refer to both section 101 and 102 trade agreements as if they were discrete entities.[332] Certain negotiational objectives apply to both kinds of agreements,[333] but others to only one kind.[334]

It would appear that three conclusions may be drawn from this substantive gap: (i) that Congress intended that presidential authority under section 101 should be absolute and that trade agreements entered into thereunder needed no implementation; (ii) that Congress intended that an isolated clause in section 121 would suffice to extend its "right of final approval" to section 101 trade agreements; and (iii) that Congress intended section 101 and section 121 agreements to be one and the same. None of the above alternatives makes complete sense; however, it is assumed that a hybrid of the first conclusion pertains: that where section 101 trade agreements are used to effect outcomes provides for under other sections of the Act,[335] the Congressional "right of final approval" pertaining to that section will also govern trade agreements so negotiated, but where a section 101 trade agreement is concluded with respect to a general "basic authority" to remove burdensome and restrictive duties (and other restrictions), if this is possible, no Congressional approval authority exists.

Congress has the authority to approve certain categories of presidential actions, and without such approval they will not take effect. These are (a) section 121 GATT revision trade agreements;[336] (b) extensions— beyond the initial 18-month period[337]—of extensive waiver authority concerning MFN agreements with non-market economy countries;[338] (c) section 102 agreement;[339] and (d) section 405 MFN commercial agreements.[340]

Conversely, Congress has the authority to disapprove: (a) import relief action taken by the President under section 203 (a);[341] (b) action taken by the President under section 301, but only when the action is against "any country . . . other than the country . . . whose restriction, act, policy, or practice was the cause for taking such action . . . ";[342] (c) assessment of countervailing duties;[343] (d) extensions of executive waiver authority concerning MFN agreements with non-market economy countries[344] and (e) section 402 (b) and 409 (b) MFN commercial agreements.[345]

Congress may also, on the recommendation of the President, terminate or deny the benefits of trade agreements[346] and declare section 102 trade agreements implementing legislation [347] void for lack of reciprocal concessions by a "major industrial country."[348] Congress is empowered to select from among its membership[349] ten delegates to serve as official advisors to the U.S. delegation at trade agreement negotiations.[350] Congress also confirms the Special Representative for Trade Negotiations,[351] his two Deputies,[352] and the six ITC Commissioners.[353]

IV. THE PLAN FOR THE INTEGRATED MANAGEMENT

At a time when the Tokyo Round is in its initial stages, the negotiating authority outlined in Title I is only a projection of future trends and developments. There is considerable promise, borne out by the terms of the Tokyo Declaration, that this projection will become a reality, and the GATT will emerge as an international organisation, with its own institutions and techniques of action. It will be able to initiate action to move towards further trade liberalisation, and what is even more important, will be equipped to handle disputes resulting from conflicts of interests and differences of national policy.

Should this happen, international trade regulation will rest importantly in the international domain in the same manner as international civil aviation, international postal or telecommuncations services are in the international domain, on the strength of international conventions and agreements which have established international organisations to take charge of intergovernment co-operation in these areas.

It must be realised that, ever since 1934, when Congress vested the Administration with an authorisation to negotiate trade agreements, the role of tariff legislation has changed materially. From then on tariffs were at least partly dependent upon the outcome of negotiations, and in this area of governmental activity the reins of power were in the hands of the President and his Administration.

Creation of the GATT in 1947 changed the situation materially. Although ignored by Congress, it developed its own legal system and regime of international trade which served its members well until, owing to changes in the international community, simple methods of informal negotiation proved inadequate in the highly complicated situations of modern economic co-operation. Should GATT develop as projected in the 1974 Act and in the Tokyo Declaration, it may regain the ability to handle conflicts resulting from international trade or initiate further progress towards trade liberalisation. It will also contribute significantly towards the solution of international problems connected with the uneven distribution of wealth, uneven economic and political development, and disparities in standards of living among nations.

---

[1]P.L. 361 (1934), 46 Stat 590.

[2]*Cf infra,* text related to p.70.

[3]S. 121 (a).

[4]48 Stat. 360.

[5]59 Stat. 460.

[6]69 Stat. 160.

[7]76 Stat. 872.

[8]72 Stat. 676.

[9]H.R. 1897, 91st Cong. 2nd Sess. (1970).

[10]Trade Act of 1974, s. 101 (a)(1). Public Law 93-618, 88 Stat. 1978 (1975).

[11]*American Enterprise Institute for Public Policy Research: The Burke-Hartke Foreign Trade and Investment Proposal* (1973).

[12]See Ohly, *The Kennedy Round: Estimated Effects and Empirical Evidence Hearings on H.R. 6767 Before the House Comm. on Ways and Means,* 93rd Cong., 1st Sess., Pts. 1-15, at 159 (1973) (hereinafter cited as *House Trade Hearings).*

[13]19 U.S.C., s. 1801 (1962).

[14]Ohly, *supra* n. 12.

[15]H.R. 18970. The most incisive discussion of the "Mill's Bill" is contained in Metzger "The Mill's Bill," 5 J. *World Trade L. 235* (1971).

[16]H.R. 14870, 91st Cong., 1st Sess. (1969), H.R. 14870 largely paralleled the provisions contained in the short-lived H.R. 17551, 90th Cong., 2nd Sess. (1968), introduced by Wilbur Mills at the request of the Johnson Administration.

[17]H.R. 16920, unlike H.R. 14870 (*supra*), did not call for the repeal of the American Selling Price system of valuation.

[18]See Note, "Trade Bill of 1970," 3 *Law & Policy in Int. Bus.* 625 (1971: Rehm, "Proposed Trade Act of 1970: What Direction U.S. Foreign Trade Policy?" 2 *J. Mar. L. & Com.* 289 (1971).

[19]Metzger, *supra* n. 13 at p.235.

[20]"An absolute quota imposes an absolute ceiling on imports beyond which no more imports may enter. A tariff quota, on the other hand, provides that imports may exceed a given ceiling but only by paying a higher duty." Rehm, *supra* n. 16 at p.305, n. 43. See, generally, Note, "Protectionism and the 90th Congress—A Case Study of Steel and Textile Industries," 2 *N.Y.U. J. Int. Law & Politics* 64 (1969).

[21]s. 321.

[22]s. 311.

[23]s. 313.

[24]Metzger, *supra* n. 15 at p.243.

[25]s. 341.

[26]19 U.S.C., ss. 160 *et seq.* :1970). The Anti-Dumping Act of 1921, as amended, provides that when a foreign company dumps merchandise in the United States, the Treasury Department shall levy anti-dumping duties equivalent to the dumping margins. Two requirements are essential for a dumping finding under the U.S. legislation: (i) a Treasury Department "determination of sales at less than fair value," and (ii) a determination of injury by the Tariff Commission. "[S]ales at less than fair value normally takes place when merchandise is sold for less in the United States than in the home market," 1 Commission on International Trade and Investment Policy, Papers 395, in *American Enterprise Institute for Public Policy Research, supra* n. 8 at pp.31-32.

[27]See Metzger, *supra* n. 15 at pp.255-260; Rehm, *supra* n. 16 at p.309.

[28]s. 302.

[29]19 U.S.C., s. 1303. The Countervailing Duty Law was enacted in substantially its present form in 1897. It requires the Secretary of the Treasury to assess a special duty on imported dutiable merchandise, benefiting from the payment or bestowal of a "bounty or grant." The special duty is always equivalent to the "bounty or grant," the purpose of the law being to nullify such benefits. 1 Commision on International Trade and Investment Policy, Papers 409, in *American Enterprise Institute for Public Policy Research, supra* n. 8 at p.33.

[30]"In the face of divided Administration counsel and no leadership from the White House, bi-partisan group of 22 determined Senators . . . blocked this protectionist legislation," *ibid.* at p.235. The Senate Committee on Finance, however, did approve in executive session the basic provisions of the House Bill as an amendment to the Social Security Bill, H.R. 17550, s. 301-378, 91st Cong., 2nd Sess. (1970). See S. Rep. No. 1431, 91st Cong., 2nd Sess., at p.238 (1970).

[31]H.R. 20, S. 4, 92nd Cong., 1st Sess. (1971). See 117 Cong. Rec. 171; Note, "The Trade Act of 1971: A Fundamental Change in United States Foreign Trade Policy," 81 *Yale L.J.* 1418 (1971).

[32]S. 2592, 92nd Cong., 1st Sess. (1971); H.R. 10914, 92nd Cong., 1st Sess. (1971). On January 3, 1973, the Bill was reintroduced in the 93rd Congress, First Session, as S. 151 and H.R. 62. Additionally, on January 18, 1973, Senator Hartke segregated the Bill into eight major parts and introduced each as separate Bills—S. 430, S. 434, S. 435, S. 439, S. 441, S. 442, S. 443 and S. 447.

[33]For its sponsors, Representative James A. Burke (D-Mass.) and Senator Vance Hartke (D-Ind.).

[34]117 Cong. Rec. 33584 (remarks of Senator Hartke).

[35]See *American Enterprise Institute, supra* n. 8, at 5.

[36]117 Cong. Rec. 33583 (remarks of Senator Hartke).

[37]s. 301.

[38]s. 703.

[39]s. 401.

[40]s. 402.

[41]ss. 501 and 502. For many years, the Congress has required that an "escape clause" be included in each trade agreement. The rationale for the "escape clause" has been, and remains, that as barriers to international trade are

lowered, some industries and workers inevitably face serious injury, dislocation and perhaps economic extinction. The "escape clause" is aimed at providing temporary relief for an industry suffering from serious injury, or the threat thereof, so that the industry will have sufficient time to adjust to the freer international competition. . . . By reason of the Congressional requirement, the trade agreements to which the United States is a party contain an escape clause or equivalent provision. Typical and of most general effect is art. XIX.L (a) of the General Agreement on Tariffs and Trade: "If, as a result of unforeseen developments and of the effect of the obligations incurred by a contracting party under this Agreement, including tariff concessions, any product is being imported into the territory of that contracting party in such increased quantities and under such conditions as to cause or threaten serious injury to domestic producers in that territory of like or directly competitive products, the contracting party shall be free, in respect of such product, and to the extent and for such time as may be necessary to prevent or remedy such injury, to suspend the obligation in whole or in part or to withdraw or modify the concession." S. Rep. No. 93-1298, in *U.S. Code Cong. & Admin. News,* 7263, 93rd Cong., 2nd Sess.

⁴²ss. 102 and 103. The result of the present tax provisions is that the American people and the U.S. Treasury pay the bill for economic losses to the U.S. economy due to the expansion of multinational corporations abroad. Because of these tax provisions, American tax-payers will continue to help subsidise the treasuries of foreign countries and the expansion of U.S.-based firms abroad. Despite the fact that U.S. government agencies have now demonstrated the tax advantages of producing abroad instead of in the United States, the new bill fails to recognise this problem: U.S. multinationals paid about 5 per cent. in taxes in 1970; the U.S. corporate tax rate is 48 per cent. Taxes paid to countries whose embargo on oil and threatened stoppages of other needed supplies are credited against the U.S. Treasury—a subsidy to those who jeopardise the American economy by withholding supplies, who add to U.S. inflation by hiking prices, and who provide walls behind which any firm can expand and export to the United Statea and abroad—so that a corporation would gain no net advantage by operating in foreign countries. S. Rep. No. 93-1298 (remarks of Senator Hartke) in 4 U.S. Code Cong. & Admin. News 7366-67, 93rd Cong. 2nd Sess. (1974).

⁴³ss. 601 and 602. For selective treatment of the control of technology transfer, see Mirabito, "The Control of Technology Transfer: The Burke-Hartke Legislation and the Andean Foreign Investment Code; the MNE Faces the Nation," 9 *Int. Law* 215 (1975). *Cf.* Evans, "New Directions in the U.S. Trade Policy," 5 *Law & Policy in Int. Bus.* 1 (1973).

"[T]he bill would deny the nation's consumers freedom of choice in the purchase of goods and boost price levels at least $10 to $15 billion. . . . American workers would be net losers, both as workers and consumers. . . . [M]ore U.S. jobs and higher paying jobs at that, would be lost in the reduction of our exports than will be gained as domestic production substituted for exports. . . . Domestic price rises pressured by the legislation would substantially erode the international competitiveness of the U.S. . . . Foreign nations would retaliate, economically and politically." Statement of Secretary of Commerce Peter G. Peterson to the American Retail Federation, reported in Commerce Today, May 15, 1972, cited in *American Enterprise Institute for Public Policy Research, supra* n. 8, at p.11.

⁴⁴9 Weekly Compilation of Presidential Documents, No. 9, at p.343 (April 16, 1973): H.R. Doc. No. 93-80, 93rd Cong., 1st Sess. (1973).

⁴⁵*Ibid.* See also Davis, "The Trade Reform Act of 1973," 15 *Harv. Int. L.J.* 126 (1974).

⁴⁶The GATT is comprehensively treated in Jackson, *World Trade and the Law of the GATT* (1969). See also Jackson, "The General Agreement on Tariffs and Trade in United States Domestic Law," 66 *Mich. L. Rev.* 249 (1967).

⁴⁷See generally Declaration of the Ministerial Meeting, Tokyo, September 12-14, 1973, GATT Press Release GATT/1134 (Sept. 14, 1973), in 12 *Int. Legal Materials* 1533-35 (1973).

⁴⁸See *e.g. Cong. Rec.* (Dec. 10, 1973) (remarks of Congressman Dent). But see the remarks of Congressman Landrum which were made during the floor debate on whether the Administration's Bill was properly to be considered by the House: "I would say to the members from my region of the country which is concerned primarily with agricultural products and textiles that it is imperative that we have this . . . Bill. Our negotiators today are in Geneva trying to negotiate a renewal of the long-term cotton agreement that expired in September. They are hoping to get into a renewal agreement an understanding that will include man-made fibres as well as cotton, and unless we have this, the textile industry, the agricultural industry, and more than 2 million employees in the apparel and textile industry are going to suffer a serious set-back." Ibid. at 10917-18.

⁴⁹Bergsten "Crisis in U.S. Trade Policy," 49 *Foreign Affairs* 630, 635 (1971). See also the remarks of Congressman Dent wherein he introduced letters from numerous labour organisations calling for defeat of the bill, among them the UAW, the International Union of Electrical Workers, the Amalgamated Meatcutters and Butcher Workmen, the Amalgamated Clothing Workers, 119 *Cong. Rec.* 10, pp.968-970 (Dec. 10, 1973).

⁵⁰*Trade Hearings* 849. In the Senate hearings, Senator Hartke agreed with Woodcock that "the Trade Bill betrays labour."

⁵¹19 U.S.C. sec. 1901 (c)(1), (2) & (3) (1970). The prerequisites for import relief for beleagured domestic industries—which also correspond to those underlying an allowance for adjustment assistance—were construed by the Tariff Commission in Non-rubber Footwear 6 (No. 359, Jan. 1971), noted in "Recent Decisions," 7 *Texas Int. L.J.* 163 (1971). See Bale, "Adjustment Assistance Under the Trade Expansion Act of 1962," 9 *J. Int. L. & Economics* 49 (1974); Robertson, "Adjustment Assistance Under the Trade Expansion Act of 1962: A Will-O'-the Wisp," 33 *Geo. Wash. L. Rev.* 1088 (1965).

⁵²*House Trade Hearings*, p.851.

⁵³*Ibid.* at p.880.

⁵⁴Mr. Woodcock: "[I]f you will forgive me, we are still not standing along with the rest of the labor movement in support of your Bill."
Senator Hartke: "I understand. As long as you come out for the principles for which I stand, you can support anybody you want to. You are for quotas [*sic*] and I am for quotas."
Hearings on H.R. 10710 Before the Senate Comm. on Finance, 93rd Cong., 2nd Sess., at 863 (1974) [hereinafter cited as *Senate Hearings*].

⁵⁵In the Senate, the AFL-CIO was represented by its president, George Meany. By far, he was the most outspoken of all public witnesses in his calling not for merely a revision of U.S. trade policies by "an entire restructuring based on the recognition that the concept of free trade versus protectionism which dominated the thinking of the thirties and forties is badly out of phase with today," *Senate*

Hearings, at p.1136. Meany's testimony characterised the Bill in no uncertain terms as "totally obsolete . . . worse than no Bill at all." *Ibid.* Increasing imports displacing American jobs, as well as vast expansion of agricultural exports, together had redounded to the marked detriment of the American consumer. In particular, Meany attacked the export of sophisticated American technology, which has led to an erosion of America's industrial base. Few words were minced in recommending to the Senate such proposals as a reduction in imports, regulation of multinational firms—including banks—and elimination of U.S. tax advantages and other subsidies. *Ibid.*

⁵⁶*House Trade Hearings,* p.1216.

⁵⁷s. 103 (d).

⁵⁸"The basic change from prior law is the provision for presidential discretion almost without limit, the right to negotiate changes and impose them almost at will, and the authority to act without prior congressional or public approval to impose decisions reached abroad in secret with little of these actions subject to congressional veto. . . . The President's proposal also asks for advance authority from Congress to negotiate the removal of non-tariff barriers. One of these non-tariff barriers is marking of origin. That means that a product imported into this country must carry a stamp showing the country of origin: if it was made in Hong Kong, it must show it was made in Hong Kong. . . . We think this is an important provision in the present trade law that we would want to be made even more definitive. We want to know where the goods and components are coming from, and the American people want to know where they are coming from." *House Trade Hearings,* p.1217.

⁵⁹*Senate Hearings* at pp.1222-1224.

⁶⁰See generally *House Trade Hearings.*

⁶¹See H.R. Rep. No. 93-571, 93rd Cong., 1st Sess. (1973).

⁶²See 199 *Cong. Rec.* 6920-21.

⁶³To recapitulate, see text related to n. 47 *supra.*

⁶⁴See generally *Staff of Senate Comm. on Finance,* 93rd Cong., 2nd Sess., "The Trade Reform Act of 1973" (*Comm. Print* 1974) [Hereinafter cited as *Comm. Print*], in particular, title IV of the Act, s. 401 and 402. By a mind-bogglingly complex procedure, the Committee on Ways and Means attempted to stifle to the utmost the President's authority to grant MFN treatment to communist countries. It chose to do this, however, in such a disguised manner that it wasted fully four pages on unintelligible language which can only cause problems of future construction.

⁶⁵See S. Rep. No. 93-1298, 93rd Cong., 2nd Sess. (1974).

⁶⁶In the Senate—as in the House—while conceding that "what came out of the House was somewhat better than that proposed by the administration," the UAW reiterated its "opposition to the Bill in its totality because of . . . willfully inadequate provisions for adjustment": *Senate Hearings* 858.

Mr. Meany: "I want to remind you, Senator [Hartke], we of the American trade union movement from the time of the Hull reciprocal trade pacts, were free traders. We were free traders right down the line, but we have got a different situation today. In those days we were for lower tariffs. We were dealing with backward European policies where they had the cartel system. But this is a different ballgame today entirely. This is American multinationals. This is American money. This is American technology. This is American know-how, and sitting back here is the American consumer, and I say, that trading with any of these other countries should be dictated by our own self-interests. That is the way they trade. This is the way they do business. They shut the door. You could not go to any of these countries and come in there with some kind of a trade deal that was going to take their jobs away." *Ibid.* at p.1136.

[67]CF. *infra,* text related to n. 108.

[68]Eberle, "U.S. Trade Policy—Appearance and Reality," *N.Y. Times,* Dec. 7, 1975, 14:3).

[69]Cf. Whitney, "The Trade Act of 1974: Coping with Unequal Control Costs," 16 *B.C. Industrial and Commercial L. Rev.* at p.605.

[70]K. Dam, *GATT, Law and International Economic Organisation* (1970); J. Jackson, *World Trade and the Law of the GATT* (1968). See also, "The Trade Act of 1971: A Fundamental Change in United States Foreign Trade Policy," *Y.L.J.,* Vol. 80, 1971, 1418 (78).

[71]Convention ACP-CEE, de Lome (Afrique, Caraibe, Pacifique, Communaute Economique Europeenne), Jan. 31, 1975. *Le Courrier,* No. 31, March 1975.

[72]Committee on Finance, United States Senate, *World Oil Developments and U.S. Oil Import Policies,* A report prepared by the U.S. Tariff Commission, Dec. 12, 1973, U.S. Govt. Printing Office. Cf. Dam. n. 77 at pp.70-71, 265, 297-299, 347-350.

[73]House Rep. No. 91-1435, 21. See also, R.E. Hudec, *The GATT Legal System and World Trade Diplomacy* (1975), pp.200-215.

[74]GATT Press Release 1134, Sept. 14, 1973, XII International Legal Materials 1973, 1533.

[75]Hudec, n. 80, pp.19-43; *Cj.* W.A. Brown, *The United States and the Restoration of World Trade* (1950), pp.89-90.

[76]Hudec, n. 73, at p.50.

[77]55 U.N.T.S. 194.

[78]See n. 5.

[79]Hudec, n. 73, at p.54.

[80]65 Stat. 72. To a certain extent the attitude of the Congress to GATT was the result of the feeling of resentment due to the fact that GATT (a multi-national agreement) was made under the authority of the 1945 Trade Agreements Extension Act which authorised bilateral negotiations only. (Gibson, "The Trade Reform Act at Mid-Passage: A Commentary on H.R. 10710," 5 *Journal of Maritime Law and Commerce* (1374).

[81]Hudec, n. 73, at p. 357, n. 28.

[82]Dam. n. 70, at p.257 *et seq.*

[83]s. 121 (c).

[84]s. 105.

[85]s. 121.

[86]ss 102 and 103 (g)(1). *Cf.* Dam., n. 77, at pp.190-192.

[87]Hudec, n. 73, at pp.165 *et seq.*

[88]s. 121 (a)(9).

[89]s. 101.

[90]s. 105.

[91]s. 106.

[92]s. 108.

[93]s. 121 (a)(10). *Cf.,* Gibson, n. 80, at pp.565-568. *Cf.* Dam. n. 70, at pp. 121-124, 140.

[94]s 121 (a)(5).

[95]s. 122 (a) and (b).

[96]s. 122 (c).

[97]s. 122 (c).

[98]s. 122 (d)(2).

[99]s. 123, Compensation Authority.

[100]*Ibid.*

[101]Title II, ss. 201-203, Import Relief.

[102]See *infra* text related to nn. 329 *et seq.*

[103]s. 126 (d).

[104]Dam, n. 70, at pp.77-78.

[105]N. 81.

[105a]*Cf. supra,* text related to nn. pp.63-71.

[106]Dam, n. 70, at pp.296-315; Hudeck, n. 73, at pp.212-215.

[107]s. 101.

[108]s. 102.

[109]s. 121. At least one commentator has suggested that the s. 101 authority is granted solely in order to execute the GATT revision mandate outlined in s. 121. See, *e.g.* Gibson, n. 87. It would appear, however, that such a restrictive view is unwarranted. First, while that author's views may have been accurate as regards H.R. 10710, the law as enacted has been expanded—together with s. 121. Secondly, subs. (b) of s. 121 may be taken as authorising independent—of s. 101—action by the President "to establish the principles described in [s. 121]." Thirdly, s. 105 expands the presidential authority under s. 101 to bilateral agreements as well, if they would prove to be more effective. And, finally, s. 101 is also to be used in connection with ameliorative compensatory concessions necessitated by the imposition of s. 203 import relief: s. 123 (d).

[110]s. 405.

[111]s. 203 (a)(4).

[112]s. 203 (a)(5).

[113]s. 203 (a).

[114]"[T]he President . . . *may* enter into trade agreements with foreign countries or instrumentalities thereof. . . . " (emphasis added): ss. 101 (a)(1), 102 (b). "[T]he President *may* authorise the entry into force of bilateral commercial agreements providing non-discriminatory treatment. . . . " (emphasis added): s. 405 (a). While the language of s. 203 appears to be mandatory—" . . . the President . . . *shall* . . . negotiate orderly marketing agreements with foreign countries . . . " (emphasis added), any presidential action is predicated on his determination to provide import relief in the first place: s. 203 (a).

[115]"The President *shall* . . . enter into [trade] agreements with foreign countries or instrumentalities. . . . " (emphasis added): s. 121 (b).

[116]ss. 101 (a)(1), 102 (b).

[117]s. 124 (d).

[118]s. 123 (d).

[119]s. 123 (a).

[120]He " . . . may proclaim such modification or continuance of any existing d ty, uch continuance of duty-free or excise treatment, or such additional duties . . . ": s. 101 (a)(2).

[121]s. 102 (c).

[122]s. 102 (e)(2)(A).

[123]s. 102 (e)(2)(B).

[124]s. 105.

[125]s. 104 (a).

[126]s. 101 and 102 objectives: "Overall Negotiating Objective": "obtain more open and equitable market access and the harmonisation, reduction, or elimination of devices which distort trade or commerce."), s. 103: "Sector Negotiating Objective"; s. 104: "Agreements with Developing Countries"; s. 106. S. 102 *only* objectives: "International Safeguard Procedures"; s. 107: "Access to Supplies ['Important to the Economic Requirement of the United States']"; s. 108.

[127]s. 131 (a).

[128]This also concerns s. 123 and 124 trade agreements.

[129]s. 131 (b).

[130]s. 134.

[131]ss. 133 (a)(b), 134.

[132]s. 109 (a).

[133]s. 109 (a)(1).

[134]s. 109 (b).

[135]s. 109 (c)(1).

[136]s. 121 (a).

[137]s. 121 (a)(1)-(a)(12).

[138]s. 121 (a).

[139]*Ibid.*

[140]s. 121 (b).

[141]s. 121 (c).

[142]s. 401.

[143]s. 402 (a) (countries which deny or impose economic restrictions on emigration); s. 403 (a) (countries which do not co-operate with the U.S. in resolving the issue of personnel missing in action in Southeast Asia); s. 409 (a) (countries which deny or impose economic restrictions on their citizens who wish to emigrate to join a "very close" relative in the United States).

[144]ss. 402 (a), 403 (b), 409 (c).

[145]See *e.g.* s. 402 (a): " . . . the President of the United States shall not conclude any commercial agreement with any such country. . . . "

[146]ss 402 (b), 409 (b), and 402 (c).

[146a]ss. 402 (b), 409 (b).

[147]s. 407 (c)(3).

[148]s. 407 (c)(3)(C).

[149]s. 402 (c)(1).

[150]s. 409 (d).

[151]See *supra,* text related to nn. 62-65.

[152]s. 402 (c)(1).

[153]s. 402 (c)(1)(A).

[154]s. 402 (c)(1)(B).

[155]SS. 404, 405.

[156]405 (c)(1).

[157]s. 405 (d)(1)-(d)(5).

[158]Eighteen months, s. 402 (d)(2)(B), plus 60 days, s. 402 (d)(3)(A), plus 45 days, s. 402 (d)(4), in the case of the first extension, and twelve months plus 60 days, s. 402 (d)(5), in the case of succeeding twelve-month periods.

[159]s. 405 (a).

[160]It may be emphasised that the s. 404 and 405 authority extends to all foreign countries, and, as to the countries not characterised as non-market economies practicing discrimination in emigration, the s. 402 (c) & (d) waiver provisions do not apply. That does not, however, mean that this grant of general authority is unencumbered, see *infra,* nn. 88-90.

[161]s. 404 (a).

[162]s. 404 (c).

[163]The agreement must be a bilateral agreement, s. 405 (b).

[164]The agreement is limited to a 3-year initial period, but is renewable for additional 3-year periods, s. 405 (b)(1), if the country has exhibited "good faith" performance of its obligations, see s. 405 (b)(1)(A) & (B).

[165]Suspension or termination for national security reasons; s. 405 (b)(2): consultative, s. 405 (b)(4)(A), and remedial, s. 405 (b)(3)(B), safeguards to prevent market disruption; protection of industrial intellectual property rights for patents and trade marks, s. 405 (b)(4); copyrights, s. 405 (b)(5); and trade secrets, s. 405 (b)(6); dispute settlement mechanism, s. 405 (b)(7); promotion of trade, s. 405 (b)(8); ongoing assessment machinery, s. 405 (b)(9); and any "other arrangements of a commercial nature as will promote the purposes of this Act," s. 405 (b)(10).

[166]s. 407 (a).

[167]s. 407 (c)(1).

[168]s. 407 (c)(2).

[169]s. 203 (a)(4).

[170]s. 203 (a)(5).

[171]s. 203 (a)(4).

[172]s. 203 (a).

[173]Defined, s. 201 (b)(3).

[174]*See generally* s. 301.

[175]*See generally* ss. 101, 102, 121, 301, 404, 405 and 501.

[176]See s. 201, in particular, s. 201 (a)(1).

[177]s. 201 (b)(1).

[178]*Ibid.* Included are the Special Representative for Trade Negotiations, the Committee on Ways and Means (House) and Finance (Senate) and the ITC.

[179]The criteria for presidential action with respect to import relief occasioned by competition are the same regardless of whether the relief is a s. 203 (4) trade agreement or some form of direct import manipulation—which will be discussed more fully in the following paragraphs. For that reason, s. 203 (4) trade agreements were treated last as they provided a perfect transition from the discussion

of the Presidential trade agreement authority to his other, more unilateral, authorities. Since the criteria will be examined here, they will not be repeated later, and the reader is reminded that, although the focus is on trade agreements, the same provisions apply to all the forms envisioned as part and parcel of s. 203 relief. The discussion of the other forms of relief pursuant to this section will, therefore, merely refer back to this treatment of the issues.

[180]s 203 (a)(4).

[181]s. 202 (a)(1)(A). See also sec. 202 (c)(1)-(a) (factors to consider pertaining to "national economic interest").

[182]s. 203 (b)(2).

[183]s. 203 (c). In which case the action recommended by the ITC shall take effect, *ibid.*

[184]s. 203 (e)(2). *Cf.* also s. 203 (a)(4) and (5).

[185]s. 203 (e)(1) & (e)(3).

[186]See s. 201 (b)(1) (emphasis added).

[187]s. 203 (d)(2).

[188]s. 203 (g)(2).

[189]s. 203 (h)(1) (five years from taking effect).

[190]s. 203 (h)(3) (one 3-year period).

[191]s. 203 (h)(2).

[192]s. 203 (a)(1)-(1)(3) & (a)(5).

[193]s. 301 (a).

[194]s. 122.

[195]s. 501.

[196]See text *supra,* related to nn. 94-118.

[197]s. 202 (a). For definitions of the various elements of this multifaceted test, see s. 201 (b)(1)-(b)(6).

[198]The permissive nature of this authority is explained at n. 24, *supra.* A more complete treatment of the entire "presidential determination" process is contained in nn. 104-110, *supra,* and the corresponding text.

[199]s. 203 (a)(1).

[200]s. 203 (a)(2).

[201]s. 203 (a)(3).

[202]s. 203 (a)(5).

[203]s. 203 (3)(1) ("within 15 days after the import relief determination date").

[204]Except, of course, those specifically reserved. See *supra,* text related to nn. 94-118.

[205]s. 301.

[206]s. 301 (a)(1).

[207]s. 301 (a)(2).

[208]s. 301 (a)(3).

[209]s. 301 (a)(4).

[210]s. 301 (b).

[211]s. 301 (a)(1).

[212]s. 301 (a)(2).

[213]s. 301 (a)(4).

[214]s. 301 (c)(1).

[215]s. 301 (c)(2).

[216]s. 301 (c)(3).

[217]s. 301 (d)(1).

[218]s. 301 (e)(2) (emphasis added).

[219]s. 301 (e).

[220]*Ibid.*

[221]s. 301 (a)(A).

[222]s. 301 (a)(B).

[223]s. 301 (a).

[224]s. 122.

[225]It is interesting to note that the language of s. 122 (a) (balance-of-payments deficits and dollar depreciation) is mandatory (" . . . the President *shall* proclaim . . . ") but the standard "contrary to the national interest" (not even "national economic interest"—this may be significant) exception is available, s. 122 (b), *i.e.* it is really permissive. But the language of s. 122 (c) (balance-of-payments surpluses and dollar appreciation) is permissive (" . . . the President is authorised to proclaim . . . ") while the "national interest"—and a few other—exceptions are mandatory, s. 122 (c).

[226]"[N]ot exceeding 150 days (unless such period is extended by Act of Congress) . . . ," s. 122 (a), and substantially the same, " . . . for a period of 150 days (unless such period is extended by Act of Congress) . . . ," s. 122 (c).

[227]s. 122 (a)(A).

[228]s. 122 (a)(B).

[229]s. 122 (a)(C).

[230]s. 122 (a).

[231]s. 122 (a)(1).

[232]s. 122 (a)(2).

[233]s. 122 (a)(3).

[234]s. 122 (c).

[235]s. 122 (c)(1).

[236]s. 122 (c)(2).

[237]See *supra*, n. 140.

[238]s. 122 (c)(A). It is interesting to note that the level of relief—via import surcharge—available to cure unfavourable (to the U.S.) world market fluctuations is up to and including 15 per cent. *ad valorem*, s. 122 (a)(A), while the level of relief—via duty reduction—available to cure favourable (to the U.S.) world market fluctuations is only up to and including 5 per cent. *ad valorem*.

[239]s. 122 (c)(B).

[240]Both during the initial 150-day period and during subsequent extension periods, if applicable, s. 122 (g).

[241]s. 505 (a).

[242]s. 501.

[243]s. 503.

[244]s. 502.

[245]s. 504 (a).

[246]*Ibid.: i.e.* cannot use this title for unauthorized duty manipulations.

[247]s. 504 (b).

[248]s. 504 (c)(1)(A) & (c)(1)(B).

[249]s. 504 (c)(1)(i)-(c)(1)(iii), (d) & (e).

[250]s. 125 (b).

[251]s. 125 (c) and (d).

[252]s. 126.

[253]s. 126 (a).

[254]s. 126 (b).

[255]s. 141 (b)(1).

[256]s. 141 (b)(2).

[257]s. 172 (a).

[258]s. 135 (b)(1).

[259]s. 135 (c)(1).

[260]s. 135 (c)(2).

[261]s. 141 (b)(1).

[262]s. 141 (a).

[263]For which purpose he holds the rank of Ambassador Extraordinary and Plentipotentiary, s. 141 (b)(1).

[264]s. 141 (c)(1)(A).

[265]s. 141 (c)(1)(C).

[266]s. 135 (b)(1).

[267]s. 141 (b)(2).

[268]For which purpose they hold the rank of Ambassador, *ibid.*

[269]s. 141 (c)(2).

[270]s. 281.

[271]s. 201 (b)(1).

[272]406 (a)(1).

[273]s. 301 (d)(2).

[274]s. 104 (c).

[275]s. 141 (c)(1)(B).

[276]s. 171 (a).

[277]s. 172 (a).

[278]s. 173.

[279]s. 174.

[280]See, *supra,* text related to nn. 188-202.

[281]s. 131 (e).

[282]Including labour, agriculture, mining, fishing, and manufacturing, s. 131 (b).

[283]*Ibid.*

[284]*Ibid.*

[285]s. 131 (c).

[286]s. 503 (a).

[287]s. 203 (i)(2).

[288]Under s. 337 of the Tariff Act of 1930, as amended by s. 341 (a) of the Trade Act of 1974, the ITC is empowered to investigate alleged unfair import practices and, upon finding a violation, exclude the offending articles from entry, permit entry only upon the posting of a bond, or issue cease and desist orders to enjoin further violations. The President may, apparently for any reason, disapprove the Commission's action in which case it shall have no force.

[289]s. 201.

[290]ss. 321 (a), 331 (a) and 341 (a).

[291]s. 405 (a)(1).

[292]Based on certain specified criteria: see s. 201 (b)(2)-(b)(6) and (c).

[293]s. 201 (b)(1).

[294]s. 201 (d)(1).

[295]See s. 406 (a)(1).

[296]See, *supra,* text related to nn. 94-102 and 117.

[297]See s. 202 (a).

[298]s. 224.

[299]As it amends ss. 303 and 337 of the Tariff Act of 1930, ss. 331 (a) and 341 (a), respectively, and s. 201 of the Anti-dumping Act, 1921.

[300]s. 321 (a).

[301]s. 331 (a).

[301]s. 331 (a).

[302]s. 341 (a).

[303]See, *supra,* text related to n. 193.

[304]s. 163 (b).

[305]s. 410.

[306]s. 608 (amending and expanding on the authority granted under ss. 484 (e) and 332 (g) of the Tariff Act of 1930).

[307]See, *e.g.* ss. 132 and 431 (a).

[308]Because the implementation of the various forms of Adjustment Assistance is critically examined elsewhere, this portion of the Trade Act of 1974 will only be cursorily described here.

[309]Ch. of Title II. See generally ss. 221-250.

[310]s. 221 (a).

[311]*Ibid.*

[312]s. 221 (b).

[313]ss. 221 (a), 224.

[314]s. 223.

[315]s. 222.

[316]See generally ss. 221-250.

[317]Ch. 3 of Titel II. See generally, ss. 251-264.

[318]s. 271 (e).

[319]Ch. 4 of Title II. See generally ss. 271-274.

[320]As it amends s. 201 of the Antidumping Act, 1921, and S. 303 of the Tariff Act of 1930.

[321]s. 321 (a).

[322]s. 331 (a).

[323]s. 503 (b)(1).

[324]Established by the President, s. 135 (b)(1), and comprising not more than 45 representatives of government, labour, industry, agriculture, small business, service industries, retailers, consumers, and the general public: *ibid.*

[325]s. 235 (b)(1).

[326]s. 135 (c)(1) and (c)(2).

[327]s. 281.

[328]s. 411 (a).

[329]See *e.g.* s. 122 (balance-of-payments authority).

[330]s. 101. Whether this means "all" trade agreements or only some is never explicated. However, the first sentence of subsection (a) refers to "duties or other [presumably similar] import restrictions." In any event, the section grants a 5-year (later expanded by a 2-year residual period: s. 124) authorisation to enter into trade agreements and manipulate duties in order to carry them out.

[331]s. 102 (b).

[332]See *e.g.* s. 104 (d): "If the President determines that competitive opportunities . . . will be significantly affected by a trade agreement concluded under section 101 or 102, he shall . . . " (emphasis added).

[333]See *e.g.* s. 106.

[334]See *e.g.* s. 107.

[335]For example, the President is granted authority under s. 203 (a)(4) to negotiate trade agreements. He is also authorised to do so pursuant to s. 101.

[336]s. 121 (c).

[337]s. 122 (a).

[338]s. 402 (d)(1)-(3). See discussion at nn. 173-181, *supra,* and corresponding text. Most provisions are either "approvable" or "disapprovable." In this instance Congress chose to retain both rights of approval and disapproval: s. 402 (d)(4).

[339]s. 102 (d) and (e)(3).

[340]ss. 405 (c) and 407 (c)(1).

[341]s. 203 (c)(1).

[342]s. 302.

[343]s. 331 (a).

[344]s. 402 (d)(4).

[345]s. 407 (c)(3).

[346]s. 126 (c)(1).

[347]s. 126 (c)(2).

[348]Defined in s. 126 (d).

[349]Five from the House Committee on Ways and Means and five from the Senate Committee on Finance: s. 161 (a).

[350]*Ibid.*

[351]s. 141 (b)(1).

[352]s. 141 (b)(2).

[353]s. 172 (a).

U.S. Role in East-West Trade:

An Appraisal

Irene Lange and James F. Elliott

INTRODUCTION

With the advent of detente and the 1972 Trade Agreement with the USSR, there was great expectation in the early seventies that East-West trade would flourish and that the U.S. would capture a share of the Eastern[1] market that would be commensurate with its size and importance in world trade. To that point it had lagged considerably behind the other major industrialized nations. For the period 1971-1973, the United Nations data, as reported by the Bureau of East-West Trade, show an increase in the U.S. share of Industrialized West (IW)[2] exports to the Eastern bloc: in 1971, the U.S. share was only 4%, in 1972 it had more than doubled to 8.7%, by 1973, it accounted for 14.7% of the Industrialized West exports to the Eastern markets. Import shares for the same years were 1971—2%, 1972—4.5%, and 1973—4%.[3]

The 1972 Trade Agreement with the USSR was the first attempt by the U.S. to establish a general bilateral trade agreement with a communist country; and it included provisions for the granting of Most Favored Nation (MFN) status, for general cooperation and an increase in trade (an anticipated tripling over a three-year period), for payments in a converti-

Dr. Irene Lange is Professor and Chairperson, Department of Marketing at California State University, Fullerton. She served with the Bureau of East-West Trade, U.S. Department of Commerce for two years. James F. Elliott is Assistant Professor of Slavic languages, University of Tennessee. He has recently served as ACE Government Fellow at the Bureau of East-West Trade, U.S. Department of Commerce. This article appeared in the *Journal of International Business Studies,* Fall/Winter 1977. Reprinted by permission of *Journal of International Business Studies* and the authors.

ble currency, and for supervision of the Agreement by the Joint U.S.-USSR Commercial Commission.[4] The Soviets, however, never put the Agreement into effect because the necessary legislation in the U.S. culminated in the Trade Act of 1974, parts of which were unacceptable to the Soviets, particularly Section 402 (Jackson-Vanik Amendment), which links MFN status to the right of free emigration, and Section 613, which places a limit on the aggregate amount of Eximbank credits available to the Soviet Union.

For the 1974-1976 period, the U.S. share of Industrialized West exports to Eastern Europe was as follows: 1974—9%, 1975—10.5%, and 1976—12.4%. Even though the U.S. share of IW exports of manufactured goods is small in comparison to several of its competitors, it has been increasing (sales of U.S. subsidiaries are not reflected in these shares). The U.S. share of imports for the same period was: 1974—6%, 1975—4.7%, and 1976—4.9%. In actual dollars, exports grew from 1.5 billion in 1974 to 3.5 billion in 1976. The share of manufactured goods of total U.S. exports improved for 1974 when it rose from a low 21% in 1973 to 40% in 1974. For 1975, it declined to 35% and for 1976 to 30%. Imports, however, for the same period declined from $900 million in 1974 to $800 million in 1975 and they slightly exceed $800 million in 1976.[5] Thus, it seems that, without a bilateral trade agreement, without Most Favored Nation status (MFN), and with limitations on government credits, U.S. involvement in East-West trade has continued to grow in dollar amount if not in market share. Whether it will continue at its present pace, however, is a matter for speculation.

Soviet Foreign Trade Minister Patolichev recently announced at the July 1977 meeting of the U.S.-USSR Joint Commercial meeting in Washington that Soviet imports of U.S. manufactured goods would be cut by 50 per cent in the coming year.[6] At every opportunity the Soviets have brought up the lack of MFN and government credits as serious obstacles to further development of trade. In the U.S. businessmen have supported the granting of MFN and the expansion of government credits in an attempt to equalize competition since their West European and Japanese competitors already have these advantages in dealing with the East Europeans. Supporters of the Jackson-Vanik amendment, however, suggest that where trade is profitable, it will continue, and, also, that that is the amendment's best justification. Patolichev, on the other hand, points out that a significant decline in trade has not been reflected in the statistics yet because contracts agreed upon in the past are just now being fulfilled. Statistics may in fact already reflect some of the threatened decline in U.S. sales to the Soviet Union, since U.S. data for the first third of 1977 indicate a 6% decrease in U.S. exports of manufactures to the USSR as compared with the first third of 1976. For the same period, U.S. exports of manufactures to the other East European countries declined 11%. Imports, on the other hand, have increased for that period from both the USSR (40%) and the other East European countries (3.5%).[7]

BARRIERS AND INCENTIVES TO TRADE EXPANSION

Structure of Foreign Trade

One of the principal difficulties in assessing the direction and future potential of East-West trade is that policy decisions are frequently based upon political—rather than economic—considerations. This is true to a certain extent for both sides, but especially in the East where it reflects the structure of foreign trade in the East European countries.

In the Soviet Union, foreign trade is a monopoly of the Foreign Trade Ministry, and it is administered through foreign trade organizations (FTOs), each of which is the sole organization that is authorized to import or export products of a given category. At present, most of the FTOs are under the direct control of the Foreign Trade Ministry, but there have been reports of a reorganization that would move some of the organizations out of the Ministry and place them under the control of the industries that they serve. This is viewed in the West as a positive reform, since it would put the officials who purchase equipment in closer touch with the end users.

The dominant feature of the Soviet foreign trade system, as it now operates, is the centralization of the decision-making process. The five-year plan—and its annually amended edition—is formulated by Gosplan (the State Planning Commission), and the Foreign Trade Ministry operates within these parameters, issuing permits for imports and exports and supervising the settlement of the subsequent transactions. The Foreign Trade Bank handles all the necessary banking transactions involved in foreign trade.

The objectives of foreign trade, as set by Gosplan, reflect not only the economic but also the political goals of the Soviet Government. Imports are made for the purpose of supplementing areas of inadequacy in Soviet production as well as for the modernization of Soviet industry. Exports, on the other hand, are not viewed as a possible means of expanding domestic production, but rather, for the purpose of earning hard currency to pay for imports, or to meet bilateral commitments to the Council for Mutual Economic Assistance[8] countries and to developing countries. The latter two are, to a large extent, political objectives.

In discussing the structure of foreign trade in Eastern Europe, the tendency is to deal primarily with the Soviet system, presenting that as a model for the systems in the other countries. This is valid to a point, but there have been significant modifications in some of the more progressive of these countries.

All of the other East European countries have experimented with some form of decentralization of foreign trade, and this may have influenced the reported reorganization of Soviet foreign trade alluded to above. Bulgaria, after rejecting its experiments, remains closest to the Soviet model. East Germany is generally regarded as one of the most rigidly centralized economies, but it permits large enterprises—those involved in export production and sales enterprises attached to industrial associations—to engage in foreign transactions. In addition to this, there are foreign trade enterprises controlled directly by the Ministry of Foreign Trade. Czechoslovakia, like East Germany, permits enterprises whose production is most important for foreign trade to engage in foreign transactions. The central authorities, however, still retain significant control in both East Germany and Czechoslovakia.[9]

The remaining three countries—Poland, Romania, and Hungary—are the leaders in East European economic reform, and this is reflected in their foreign trade systems. Poland permits selected producing enterprises to sell—but not purchase—abroad. This is true for Romania, also, which permits certain industrial combines to conclude agreements directly with foreign firms and to maintain marketing facilities abroad. Hungary has gone further than all the others in that it attempts to conduct foreign trade on a profit-making basis and allows a fairly large number of enterprises to both buy and sell abroad.[10] Romania and Hungary have been participating with Western firms in joint ventures for several years. Poland in 1976 passed similar legislation, but it was more restrictive than that of Romania and Hungary.[11]

Eastern Nontariff Barriers

The structure of the nonmarket economy and the foreign trade system in Eastern Europe are, to a large extent, responsible for creating considerable nontariff barriers to market penetration from the West. Although Eastern tariff structures have not been a significant obstacle to trade from the West, the five-year plans, which have the force of law, determine what can be imported and in what quantity; and they can be viewed, therefore, as import quotas.

As we have observed, the centralization of import decisions necessarily removes them from the end users of the products and puts them in the hands of the central bureaucracy. This situation creates a whole series of problems for the Western businesses, which are accustomed to marketing products or services directly to their customers.

Financing imports is a priority issue for the East Europeans because of the inconvertibility of their own currencies and their chronic shortage of hard currencies. They have found themselves in the crunch between their need to import Western plants, equipment and technology, and their difficulty in exporting sufficient Eastern goods to pay for those imports. The situation is less severe for the Soviets than for most of the other Eastern European countries because, heretofore, they could export energy and other raw materials. If the recent C.I.A. forecast is realized, however, the Soviets could be net importers of oil by the early 1980s,[12] and this would seriously impair their hard currency earning potential.[13]

At least two aspects of this problem act as barriers to trade. The greatest obstacle to trade is the growing pressure on American businesses to engage in countertrade—a financing tool to offset hard currency needs to pay for Western imports by stipulating purchases of Eastern products in the transactions.[14] (Countertrade is discussed in more detail in another section of this paper: "New Forms of Trade.") The other aspect is the Eastern European countries' growing debt to the West.

From 1971 to the present, the total debt of the East European countries has grown from negligible levels to $48.8 billion at the end of 1976.[15] The media attention given to the size of this debt has caused concern in some quarters in the United States, but the total owed to the U.S. banks is only approximately $5 billion. Western European banks, with officially guaranteed credits, account for the largest shares. This may also explain the dominance of Western European countries in this marketplace. In general, both U.S. and Western European bankers consider the East European debt manageable, and they remain ready to extend credit.[16] This appraisal stems from several assumptions: that the Soviet Union with its vast resources is a good credit risk; that the Soviet Union will help out the other Eastern European countries: and, that through central planning the USSR can control its consumption. Poland has the second largest debt, but many analysts see in Poland a great potential for growth in terms of its many resources; many of the loans are used for import substitution or to produce hard currency exportable goods. However, these arrangements and intra-CMEA trade commitments make it difficult to appraise their ability to generate hard currency exports to meet their debts. On a more cautious note, others see that, given the magnitude of debt and the service ratio, some of these loans are used to alleviate balance of payment problems. In addition, certain export-generating projects have not come up on stream and those that did were subject to fluctuating Western demands.

Western Nontariff Barriers

The limit of governmental credits available to communist countries, however, is one of the most frequently cited nontariff barriers to trade on the U.S. side. The Export-Import Bank Amendments of 1974, along with the Trade Act of 1974, make the extension of credits to Eastern Europe (excluding Poland) conditional upon a country's emigration practices as was discussed earlier. The Soviet Union is further singled out: there is a $300 million ceiling on loans for the four-year authorization period; and fossil fuel projects involving $25 million or more in Export-Import Bank's loans would require notification to the Congress before finalization. American businesses in many cases are forced to initiate deals through their subsidiaries in Western Europe in order to take advantage of available government credits in those countries. In view of the growing worldwide scarcity of energy, even the authors of the Jackson-Vanik Amendment to the Trade Act of 1974 have come to the conclusion that it is in the best interests of the United States to facilitate any possible increase in overall energy supplies.[17]

The Export Administration Act of 1969, as amended in 1972, 1974, and 1977, authorizes the Department of Commerce to use export controls to the extent necessary to oversee the export and reexport of commodities and technology transfers deemed of strategic importance. Types of technology, types of transfers, and their control, are key issues for U.S. policy makers and businessmen. In addition to the commodities controlled unilaterally by the United States, all NATO countries (excluding Ireland) and Japan cooperate in the international strategic control system through the Coordinating Committee (COCOM). The export controls, although eased to a considerable extent, still limit certain high technology exports.

Lack of universal standards for health, safety, quality, labeling, and processing act as additional nontariff barriers. A working party of the General Agreement on Tariffs and Trade (GATT) and the United Nations Economic Commission for Europe both have completed drafts on codes of standards definitions which will be used in multilateral trade negotiations.[18] It is a very broad and complex issue, but for our immediate purposes, it is enough to point out that the most problematic area within the broad category is the quality standards of Eastern manufactured goods. Established product standards in the U.S. may make it difficult for Eastern European countries to export certain goods to this country. But, in many respects, the problems are commercial rather than legal. The design, quality, and reputation of their manufactured products often impede access to Western markets and thus impair the potential for Eastern Europe to earn hard currencies. This problem is also one of the reasons that Western businessmen are, on the whole, reluctant to engage in countertrade with Eastern European countries.

Furthermore, the U.S. maintains a number of measures to protect itself from possible dumping or market disruption. These measures include the general escape clause of Title II of the 1974 Trade Act, antidumping provisions in the Anti-Dumping Act of 1921 (amended in Section 321 of the 1974 Trade Act), countervailing duty provisions in the Tariff Act of 1930 (amended in Section 331 of the 1974 Trade Act), and a market disruption provision applied solely to communist countries in Section 406 of the Trade Act of 1974.[19] Application of these measures has not been frequent due to the low level of imports to the U.S. from the East European countries, but it could become significant if this trade flow increases. The centrally planned economies are particularly vulnerable to charges of dumping, however, since the test is whether a given country is selling abroad at a price below cost of production. But it is extremely difficult for the centrally planned economy to establish its cost since costs are not accumulated in the same way as they are in a market economy.

U.S. Tariff Barriers

Although tariff barriers in the East European countries are not a great obstacle for the importation of Western machinery and technology, the reverse cannot be said of U.S. tariffs for Eastern goods.[20] As it was pointed out previously, the 1974 Trade Act made MFN status contingent upon free emigration. Only Poland at that time already had MFN status, and, since then, only Romania has qualified for provisional status, contingent upon its demonstration of continued progress in the area of emigration rights. The failure of most Eastern European countries to receive Most Favored Nation treatment is considered a major obstacle to an increase in exports of a number of products to the American market because it confronts them with the extremely high tariffs of the Smoot-Hawley Act of 1930. A recent study indicates that U.S. imports—especially manufactured goods—from the East European countries would have been 30 to 40 per cent greater if these countries had been receiving MFN tariff treatment from the U.S. in 1974 and 1975. The percentage of increase varied from country to country, running roughly inversely to the value of actual U.S. imports from each. For the Soviet Union, the studies indicate a smaller increase because most of their exports available to the West do not encounter significant tariff discrimination. (The assumptions in the studies, it should be noted, are based on products that have entered East-West trade or that are available for trade.) Demand for specific goods in Western markets is also of major importance. Nevertheless, the studies indicate that a reduction of tariff barriers would probably stimulate both the quantity and composition of imports from Eastern European countries.[21]

Romania is also the only one of the East European countries discussed in this paper which has qualified for the Generalized System of Preferences (GSP). The GSP provides duty free treatment for certain products from developing countries, but the 1974 Trade Act denied this to communist countries, unless, among other conditions, they receive MFN status, are partial to the General Agreement on Tariffs and Trade (GATT), and are members of the International Monetary Fund.[22]

Indicators for Assessing Market Potentials

There is a strong relationship between market potential and central planning. It is not how much the market can absorb, but how much importance is attributed by the central planning officials to that product or industry, which has to be established. However, given the following conditions—that centrally planned economies rely on a system of controlled prices, set for the most part by planners; that prices do not necessarily have a relationship to the relative scarcity of the particular product or to production costs, and that export prices have a general relationship to world market prices, but are adjusted for what the traffic will bear—the analyst is stymied when trying to use the prices for meaningful interpretation.

Since all aspects of investment, growth, production, and development have been tailored by the Government and recorded in comprehensive planning documents, one might suppose that centrally planned economies would offer an easy task to the analyst. It would seem, in other words, that one should need to study only five-year and annual plans to derive import and export plans. However, published plans indicate only the general guidelines for domestic economic growth. The data on total consumption, which would include import and export plans, are not published. In some research studies attempts have been made to extrapolate import needs based on past production data, exports, and imports.[23] This may be useful for vertically integrated industries, but for products or systems where their use is horizontal, this approach is of limited use. Given different nomenclatures in the reports of the end users, the use of statistics further complicates rather than simplifies this assessment.[24]

Published annual plans, reflecting yearly changes in allocations and targets, are more current and detailed than the five-year plan; but inspection of even these reveals that this information is presented in only the broadest terms, making it barely useful for substantive market analysis.[25] However, reviews of annual plans may suggest underfulfillments, which, in turn, may be used to estimate incremental import needs. But even in the case of underfulfillment, the central planners may decide to reduce consumption and avoid importing due to other constraints, including shortages of hard currency or problems in obtaining foreign credit.[26]

"Shopping lists" generated in Eastern Europe have also been used for purposes of analysis. They indicate particular needs and priorities in terms of specific items and technology.[27] These lists may suggest "substitutability" or "complementarity" for other needs, but because of limited disclosures of needs and capacities, the lists may serve as only limited indicators.

Even though there are many discrepancies in reporting of data,[28] a comparison of annual plans with the five-year guidelines may indicate priorities and shortages that may be helpful in estimating potential imports. Along with the annual plans, historical trade composition and patterns may be used for further inferences and modifications of potentials. Lack of normalized relations with Socialist countries and unusually large agricultural shipments have disturbed trade flows in recent years, making historical U.S. trade information of limited value in assessing potentials. Several analytical approaches have been used to circumvent this limitation. Studies have based trade projections upon more normalized conditions, assuming the elimination of major trade and financial restrictions.[29] These studies have followed a market-share approach,[30] using the relationship between U.S. competitiveness in certain product categories and its share of the total imports of the industrialized countries. The inference is that the U.S. should be able to capture similar market shares in Eastern Europe vis-a-vis the other industrialized countries. No adjustment for U.S. subsidiaries is made in this approach.

Balance of trade and payment patterns may be determined from an analysis of trade by product supplier, country, and share of the user sector. Indicators of intent such as various agreements, including countertrade, may also be useful to estimate the future export capabilities.[31] These can also aid Western analysts in assessing potentials for Western participation.

Assessments of these markets also need to be reviewed in terms of CMEA integration activities. Reflecting past performance, Western business cycles, and terms of trade projected economic growth, rates of Eastern European countries are lower in the current five-year plans than in the previous ones. Instead of pursuing integrated economic plans, every country is intent on solving its own regional problems, promoting bilateralism, and establishing trade and financial relations with the West.

Nevertheless, as a result of Western inflation and Eastern Europe's (with the exception of the Soviet Union) dependence on imports of raw materials and energy, some integration is necessary; and so joint projects to supply the area's needs have become important.

Since prices are set differently in each of the countries, plans for multilateral trade with a CMEA and currency convertibility are limited. Under these conditions, bilateral trade is considered both desirable and essential to central planning; thus, it predominates not only in intra-CMEA trade but also with Western countries.

Because of the increased prices for petroleum and other raw materials charged by the Soviet Union to the other CMEA countries, most of these countries have had to increase their exports to the Soviet Union to pay for their imports. This, of course, has put more of a burden on them in their efforts of servicing their Western debts. Since oil exports are the major source of hard currency for the Soviet Union, more pressure will be placed on the other member countries to look for additional sources and to diversify their export base.

Finally, in assessing market potential, an analyst should study decision-making in Socialist countries by identifying key incentives and forces acting upon officials. What targets in the five-year plans, for example, will be most influential in decisions concerning the country or producer from which the product or technology will be purchased? Is there a pattern in decision-making regarding what types of products will be bought from the West instead of CMEA countries? The trend over the last ten years for most East European countries to allocate two-thirds of their trade to the CMEA countries may be a sign that future U.S. trade shares will be fairly consistent in the future;[32] but even this observed behavior has been changing, as evidenced by increasing debt to the West. Trade patterns continue to differ by individual country and by product. Given current trade composition and inflexibility of plans, major shifts may be difficult to attain in the near future. However, with increasing numbers of institutional reforms, industrial cooperation may provide additional opportunities, as will be examined in the next section.[33]

NEW FORMS OF TRADE

The problems experienced by the centrally planned economies of Eastern Europe due to the inconvertibility of their currencies and their chronic shortages of hard currency[34] have resulted in part from the difficulty for their manufactured products to enter Western markets. Several factors have acted as barriers: poor quality controls, lack of marketing expertise, inflexibility to respond to Western demands, and various Western restrictions. These problems are becoming more acute as the level of industrialization of these countries rises, thus increasing their need for Western technology.

A major Eastern European approach to solving the problems of earning hard currency and gaining access to Western markets has been that of industrial cooperation.[35] On the whole, the Eastern perception of industrial cooperation has been that Western firms should supply the basic technology and know-how to assist Eastern enterprises in developing production. The extent of cooperation includes forms of sale of complete production systems or "turnkey" plants, licensing, franchising, coproduction, joint ventures, and other variations.[36] Due to the magnitude of some of these projects, multinational firms have been dominant in this market.[37] In the context of East-West trade, the development of industrial cooperation has been impeded to some extent by the great reluctance of the Eastern Europeans to allow Western equity and real management participation in socialist enterprises located within CMEA. Although joint ventures are now allowed in Romania, Hungary, and Poland, the Eastern partner always retains control, even while allowing Western participation in profits and management.

Usually, at least a portion of the products resulting from industrial cooperation projects in Eastern Europe are to be marketed eventually in the West to pay for the original investment and to earn additional hard currency. Western firms, however, have been reluctant to enter into agreements under which their remuneration, in part or in whole, depends upon the marketing of products in the West, the quality of which they cannot control and which, traditionally, has not met Western standards.

Heretofore, the solution for the USSR has often been that the products marketed in the West have not been manufactured but rather raw or semiprocessed materials for which it is much easier to find buyers. With the possible exception of Poland, this solution, however, has not been possible for the other Eastern Europeans due to their general paucity of raw materials. It is not a satisfactory solution for the Soviet Union either, and in the 1976-80 five-year plan period, all indications are that there will be a strong push for payment arrangements involving manufactured products.[38]

As the use of industrial cooperation as a commercial arrangement has evolved, a financial provision to offset hard currency shortages has been instituted.[39] With the exception of barter, most forms of industrial cooperation between the Eastern European and Western firms require upfront financing via Western credits. Countertrade is the financial proposition which frequently provides a basis for repaying at least part of those credits.

The simplest, but least frequently used form of countertrade, is *barter*. This is a one-time, direct exchange of goods, with no money or credit required and without the involvement of a third party. It was common after World War II when the shortage of convertible currencies was most acute and before more satisfactory marketing channels were reestablished. Pure barter in East-West trade is now quite rare.[40]

Switch financing is another form of East-West countertrade which is sometimes associated with barter. It differs, however, in many significant ways. Switch deals involve at least three parties, usually a Western firm, Eastern Europe, and one of the less developed countries (LDC). The need for switching arises when one party to a bilateral agreement cannot take his full quota of goods, leaving him with a nonconvertible dollar balance which cannot be used for all possible purchases in his partner's country. A third party has to be found who is willing to take the unwanted merchandise and pay hard currency for it, invariably at a considerable discount. Although ten years ago some sources estimated that as much as one-third of East-West trade may have involved a switching, most agree that the use of this complex process is now much less than that and is steadily declining.[41]

Although straight barter and switch financing are no longer significant in East-West trade, most sources agree that *counterpurchase* (also referred to as parallel barter)[42] is currently the most frequently used form of countertrade. In this kind of transaction, two contracts are signed— one in which an Eastern buyer purchases Western products for hard currency (usually supplied by Western credits) and one in which the Western partner agrees to purchase certain goods within a set period (normally no longer than five years). These goods are normally "nonresultant"; that is, they normally are not derived from the first contract.[43]

A variation of counterpurchase occurs when the Western partner receives only partial payment in hard currency and agrees to purchase, for hard currency, Eastern products equal to the remaining value of the contract. This is regarded by many as a poor deal for the Western partner because his full remuneration is deferred until he sells the Eastern goods. As with other forms of countertrade, however, the contract price of the original exports is often set in anticipation of this condition.

Compensation arrangements (also known as buy-back) are regarded as the most rapidly growing form of countertrade, especially with the Soviet Union.[44] The period of the agreement is usually long-term (ten years or longer is not unusual), and the dollar value of the contract is larger than in the other forms of countertrade. Two contracts are signed providing for the Western partner to supply plant, technology, or equipment for hard currency, and in return to purchase, over a period of years, products which most often result from the Western supplied plant or technology. The value of the products purchased over the life of the second contract often equals or exceeds the value of the Western export. A variation of this form permits the Western partner to purchase both resultant and nonresultant Eastern products.

Precise statistics on the proportion of East-West trade which involves some form of countertrade do not exist, but most sources estimate about 20% at present. By 1980 this could be as high as 40%.

Lease financing is another form of East-West trade financing which is now being considered as a possible way to overcome the lending limits of both private U.S. institutions and of the Export-Import Bank. This approach provides for a long-term (10-15 years) lease with fixed payments. Although the lessee enjoys full use of the equipment, ownership is retained by the lessor until the end of the lease period, when it is transferred for a nominal sum. The retention of ownership in the West is paradoxically one of the principal advantages and, at the same time, a disadvantage. It provides the possibility for financing since any loan involved would be exempt from U.S. legal lending limits to communist countries. On the other hand, the centrally planned economies (CPEs) are reluctant to have capital equipment that belongs to a Western company. Some proposals have advanced the possibility that the lessor could be a joint venture with controlling interest held by the CPE, but the question is still unresolved. The Soviets also regard lease financing as a more expensive way to do business, and as long as other sources of financing are available, they probably will not use leasing extensively.

Even with the more conservative five-year plans, future projections seem to suggest that imports of Western technology will continue to be important. Given their large debts, credit limitations, and balance of payment difficulties, countertrade may overcome some of these problems since it may offer entry into Western markets for their products and facilitate technology acquisition and update. The countertrade transactions specify future commitments and are self-liquidating; and these aspects are especially acceptable to central planning. In general, industrial cooperation with the financing and marketing aspects of countertrade encourage bilateral balancing, which is desirable for central planners. However, this puts more financial pressure on Western firms which, in turn, may hamper future growth by creating potential competitors and complicating the task for Western firms of marketing Eastern products.

The use of an industrial cooperation agreement by the Western firm to facilitate entry into other CMEA countries may, however, be limited: Eastern partners often stipulate that resultant products must generate hard currencies. Since most forms of industrial cooperation have a countertrade provision, the price valuation placed on the goods that are accepted as payment is especially critical for the Western partner and his competitors. In the event of low prices, most West European countries and the United States have several measures to protect themselves against any market disruptions. Should pricing in these arrangements present problems, official Western participation in these bilateral arrangements may occur. Even with some of these difficulties, industrial cooperations—which are especially adaptable to large or multinational firms—can facilitate the exchange of goods, the mobility of technology, and the flow of capital and managerial know-how.

CONCLUSIONS AND OUTSTANDING ISSUES

The future development of East-West trade depends most significantly upon Eastern Europe's plans for economic growth and its management of indebtedness to the West. This argument assumes, in turn, flexibility on the part of Eastern European countries to make internal adjustments in the form of institutional changes and economic directives. The U.S. share of this trade is contingent on several other factors: U.S. official policy toward normalization of trade with Eastern Europe; availability of government-supported credit; and willingness of the U.S. firms to participate in industrial cooperation.

An analysis of the new five-year plans of Eastern European countries (1976-80) uncovers several interesting trends in their efforts to solve long-term development problems. Although specifics vary from country to country, some of the key underlying economic trends common to all or most include the following: the plans call for a more balanced overall growth in an attempt to increase the material standard of living of the population, with special attention to energy, technology-utilization, agriculture, and consumer goods production. It is expected that a stronger emphasis on exports will alleviate the increasing trade deficits with the West. Concomitant with this trend is a greater susceptibility to Western market conditions that is unlikely to be reversed. Import strategies will attempt to minimize the fluctuations of Eastern Europe's interdependence with the West. Alternatives to accomplish this include import substitution, long-term trade agreements to smooth out fluctuations, and the upgrading of purchases during favorable periods. Poland, Romania, and Hungary plan to contribute to this effort by continuing the encouragement of Western capital investment through various types of cooperation agreements, including joint ventures.

Reduction in imports, however, does not appear to be an economically or politically viable alternative. Due to continuous problems in economic performance, imports must continue to increase. Adjustments to the debt will have to come, instead, from hard currency generating exports. On the demand side, the accessibility of Western markets is especially critical. Even without any governmental restrictions, the quality, after-sale service, and general marketing approaches are important to the considerations of export expansion. Internally, the ability to satisfy these conditions is contingent on the nation's commitment to the development of Western markets. This consideration also assumes increased flexibility and, perhaps, decentralization in the planning process.

Although a trend toward decentralization is evident in many Eastern European countries, it is not uniformly evident. Because of inconvertible currencies, shortages of hard currency, and balance of payments problems, some forms of control will remain. Bilateral trade agreements will continue to play a large role in foreign trade patterns.

Even though bilateral agreements are the main instruments for facilitating East-West trade, the actual conduct is changing since the concept of industrial cooperation is developing new flows of business. For the Soviet Union, turnkey projects, with long-term agreements for repayment, seem to be most desirable. For the other Eastern European countries, industrial cooperation takes a variety of forms, and, as with the Soviet Union, these arrangements are used to facilitate investment and technological developments. To Eastern Europe, countertrade arrangements are of special importance, both as financial instruments and as a means of access to Western markets and to marketing know-how. The long-term aspects of countertrade agreements are especially suitable to central planning whereas the short, self-liquidating contracts are used to correct specific problems. Industrial cooperation agreements encourage bilateral balancing which is desirable for central planners. Unless alternative forms of financing become available, industrial cooperation agreements and their countertrade components will likely continue to be used to facilitate trade.

For the Eastern Europeans, U.S. firms are especially desirable as partners. U.S. technology is highly respected and recognized as the source of much of the commercial technology currently in use in Europe. Further, in turnkey projects, the U.S. is recognized as perhaps the only logical source of some of the large-scale complexes being sought by the Soviet Union and the other Eastern European countries. The U.S. is also viewed as a rich source of capital and managerial expertise for joint ventures, where these are allowed. To the extent that Eastern European countries see purchasing from the U.S. as necessary or particularly beneficial to their economic development, they appear willing to accept the less than favorable conditions set on such trade.

For the supplier of technology and credit, the ability to assess the returns from such transactions is of great importance. The official U.S. policies—concerning technology transfers, potential dumping, and market disruption problems arising from countertrade—are additional factors that U.S. firms need to consider in the assessment of these new forms of trade.

To supplement the traditional indicators found in their plans, other factors, such as the following, need to be appraised. Several areas are suggested for further research to provide additional analysis of Eastern Europe's long-range economic goals and ability to meet financial obligations.

The composition of loans from the West is of great importance: do they generate new hard currency exports, encourage import substitution, or are they used to alleviate balance of payments problems? Another question concerns the entire aspect of countertrade, especially its share of the total East-West trade and its role in trade with the United States. Both the potential and types of products are important considerations in assessing the impact on the U.S. market. In addition, the overall financial and commodity flows within CMEA and outside may give insight into future trade patterns and forms. Increased dependence on the West may suggest institutional reforms in the planning process and business practices. From a U.S. public policy standpoint, the motivation of U.S. firms to participate in industrial cooperations may be another factor which will affect the position of the United States in East-West trade. Long-term prospects, furthermore, hinge on U.S. foreign policy, which depends upon political as well as economic considerations.

---

[1]For the purposes of this paper, the Eastern market shall include Bulgaria, Czechoslovakia, East Germany, Hungary, Poland, Romania, and the USSR.

[2]Industrialized West in this context shall include Japan.

[3]*The United States Role in East-West Trade: Problems and Prospects,* U.S. Department of Commerce, 1975, p.6. It should also be noted that for these years, agricultural products account for three-fourths to four-fifths of the total exports.

[4]Karen C. Taylor, "The Role of Bilateral Agreements in East-West Trade," in *East-West Trade: Managing Encounter and Accommodations,* an Atlantic Council Policy Paperback (Boulder, Coloraod: Westview Press, 1977), p.76.

[5]*Selected Trade and Economic Data of the Centrally Planned Economies,* U.S. Department of Commerce, Bureau of East-West Trade, 1976; also, *U.S. Trade Status with Communist Countries,* U.S. Department of Commerce, Bureau of East-West Trade, monthly publication.

[6]Soviet purchases of grain are set by the U.S.-USSR bilateral grain agreement of 1975, which provides for between six and eight million metric tons per year. Purchases of more than eight would require special consultation.

[7]See *U.S. Trade Status with Communist Countries.*

[8]Council for Mutual Economic Assistance (CMEA) strives to coordinate the national economic plans and trade flows of the Eastern European countries to achieve integration and growth of the bloc.

[9]Charles H. Movit, "Organization and Conduct of East-West Trade by Non-market Economices," in *East-West Trade: Managing Encounter and Accommodation,* pp.59-60.

[10]Movit, pp.57-58.

[11]Pompilliu Verzariu and Jay Burgess, "The Department of Joint Economic and Industrial Cooperation in East-West Trade," in *East European Economies Post Helsinki,* Joint Economic Committee Compendium of Papers, U.S. Congress, U.S. Government Printing Office, 1977, pp.1225-1242.

[12]"A Discussion Paper on Soviet Petroleum Production," prepared by the C.I.A. and presented at a meeting of the Advisory Committee on East-West Trade, June 29, 1977.

[13]A recent study indicates that in 1975, energy exports accounted for 48 per cent of total Soviet exports to industrialized Western countries. See Alan J. Lenz and Hedija H. Kravalis, "An Analysis of Recent and Potential Soviet and East European Exports to Fifteen Industrialized Western Countries," in *East European Economies Post Helsinki,* pp.1055-1131.

[14]Jenelle Matheson, Paul McCarthy and Steven Flanders, "Countertrade Practices in Eastern Europe," in *East European Economies Post Helsinki,* p.1278.

[15]A recent Chase Manhattan study shows the following breakdown: USSR—$16.2 billion; Poland—$12.6 billion; East Germany—$5.5 billion;

Romania—$2.7 billion; Bulgaria—$2.6 billion; Hungary—$2.5 billion; Czechoslovakia—$1.6 billion; and CMEA banking institutions—$1.9 billion.

[16]"Business Eastern Europe," a publication of Business International, S.A., June 10, 1977, p.177, and *Euromoney,* January 1977.

[17]Summary minutes of the Advisory Committee on East-West Trade, June 29, 1977, p.6.

[18]Karen Taylor, "The Tokyo Round and Nonmarket Economies: A Focus on Nontariff Barriers," in *East-West Trade: Managing Encounter,* pp.139-165; and Karen Taylor, "Import Protection and East-West Trade: A Survey of Industrialized Country Practices," in *East European Economies Post Helsinki,* pp.1132-1175.

[19]Karen Taylor, "Import Protection," p.1162.

[20]Andrew Elias and Marjory Searing, "A Quantitative Assessment of U.S. Restraints on Trade with Eastern Europe and U.S.S.R.," in John Hardt, ed., *Reorientation and Commercial Relations of the Economies of Eastern Europe,* Joint Economic Committee, U.S. Congress, U.S. Government Printing Office, 1974; John E. Jelacic, *Impact of Granting Most Favored National Treatment to the Countries of Eastern Europe and the People's Republic of China,* United States Tariff Commission, 1974; Thomas Wolf, "The Impact of Formal Western Restraints on East-West Trade: An Assessment of Existing Quantitative Research in John Hardt, ed., *Tariff, Legal and Credit Constraints on East-West Commercial Relations* (Institute of Soviet and East European Studies: Carleton University, Canada, 1975).

[21]Helen Raffel, Marc Rubin, and Robert Teal, "The MFN Impact on U.S. Imports from Eastern Europe," *East European Economies Post Helsinki,* pp.1396-1427; *Probable Impact on U.S. Trade of Granting Most-Favored National Treatment to the U.S.S.R.,* Committee on Ways and Means, U.S. Congress, submitted by U.S. International Trade Commission, U.S. Government Printing Office, Washington, D.C., 1977.

[22]Movit, p.66.

[23]Market assessment studies prepared for the Bureau of East-West Trade, U.S. Department of Commerce.

[24]Paul Marer, "Toward a Solution of the Mirror Statistics Puzzle in East-West Commerce," unpublished paper to appear in F. Levick, ed., *Internationale Wirtschaft Vergleich und Interdependenz.*

[25]For a more detailed discussion of planning priorities, market indicators for import, and difficulties in making assessments of market potentials and forecasts, see Christopher Stowell's *Soviet Industrial Import Priorities; with Marketing Considerations for Exporting to the USSR* (New York: Praeger Publishers, 1976).

[26]See John J. Brock and P. Ronald Tarullo, "Estimation of Incremental Import Potentials in the Soviet Union," in this issue.

[27]Prepared by appropriate Foreign Trade Organizations and available through each country's commercial officers.

[28]Paul Marer's unpublished article in footnote 24.

[29]"Normalized conditions" assumed elimination of export controls, reduction of Eximbank restrictions, extension of MFN in some studies. A good summary of major studies concerning Western restraints is in Thomas Wolf, "The Impact of Formal Western Restraints" (see footnote 20), and Thomas Wolfe, "Progress in Removing Barriers to East-West Trade" in Nemschak, ed., *World Economy*

and East-West Trade (New York: Springer-Verlag, 1976).

[30]Thomas A. Wolf, *The Quantitative Impact of Liberalization of United States Unilateral Restrictions on Trade with the Socialist Countries of Eastern Europe,* U.S. Department of State, February 16, 1972.

[31]See Frances W. Rushing and Ann R. Lieberman, "The Role of Imports in the Soviet Growth Strategy for the Seventies," in this issue.

[32]Selected Trade and Economic Data.

[33]Allen J. Lenz and Hedija H. Kravalis, "An Analysis of Recent and Potential Soviet and East European Exports to Fifteen Industrialized Western Countries," in *East European Economies Post-Helsinki,* pp.1055-1132.

[34]John S. Garland, *Financing Foreign Trade in Eastern Europe: Problems of Bilateralism and Currency Inconvertibility,* (New York: Praeger, 1976).

[35]See Marer and Miller, "American Industry in the USSR and Eastern Europe," in this issue.

[36]For definitions of those forms see McMillan, "East-West Industrial Cooperation" in *East European Economies Post-Helsinki,* p.1182.

[37]For more information see, John B. Holt, "New Role for Western Multinationals in Eastern Europe," *Columbia Journal of World Business,* Fall 1973, pp.131-139; and P. Lauter and Paul Dickie, *Multinational Corporations and East European Socialist Economies* (New York: Praeger, 1975).

[38]The degree of difficulty in finding appropriate products for Western markets varies significantly among the other centrally planned economies. For an updated account by country see *Business Eastern Europe* 6, nos. 23-29 (1977), a publication of Business International, S.A.

[39]This next section is drawn from Jenelle Matheson, Paul McCarthy, and Steven Flanders, "Countertrade Practices in Eastern Europe," in *East European Economies Post Helsinki,* pp.1277-1312.

[40]Business International, S.A., a subsidiary of Business International Corporation, New York, *Current Countertrade Policies and Practices in East-West Trade,* a multi-client supported research study, completed November 1976.

[41]For more information see, John P. Morgan, "The Financial Aspects of East-West Trade," Columbia Journal of World Business 8 (Winter 1973), pp.51-56.

[42]A good review article is Jack Kaikati, "The Reincarnation of Barter Trade: A Marketing Tool," *Journal of Marketing,* April 1976.

[43]Jenelle Matheson, et alia., pp.1280-1281.

[44]Jenelle Matheson, et alia., pp.1280-1282.

Technology Exports Can Hurt Us

Jack Baranson

For some time now, it has been the prevailing view that U.S. industry has a self-interest in restricting the release of proprietary technology and that this attitude has safeguarded U.S. national economic interests. Conventional wisdom has argued that, on balance, U.S.-based multinational firms have minimized losses in U.S. income, trade, and employment through judicious investment and licensing in foreign facilities, without which residual earnings for the U.S. economy would have been greatly diminished or entirely lost. It is further argued that manufacturing investments made to serve local markets that are otherwise closed to imports also generate exports of components and equipment for production in overseas facilities, which would otherwise go to foreign suppliers.

This viewpoint is reinforced by assumptions that: (a) American firms enjoy substantial commercial leads in high technology fields; (b) they will continue to invest in research and development (R&D) to maintain these leads; and (c) there is little danger of competition from enterprises in newly industrializing nations (including socialist and resource-rich developing countries) in the foreseeable future.

Contrary to the conventional wisdom, however, U.S. firms may contribute to both the deterioration of the U.S. trade balance and to the loss of U.S. technical leadership by establishing foreign manufacturing affiliates and by licensing their technology to foreign manufacturers. This dissemination of U.S. technology to other economies and the adverse consequences that these transfers may have, have caused considerable

From *Foreign Policy*, Winter 76-77, pages 180-194. Reprinted by persmission.

concern in government circles.[1] A new generation of technology transfer arrangements to non-controlled foreign enterprise[2] gives further cause for concern. The following scenarios illustrate these new arrangements:

General Motors Corporation is negotiating a new agreement with a Polish state-owned automotive manufacturing enterprise (Polmot) that represents a landmark change in U.S. business involvement in overseas markets. Under the proposal, General Motors will design and engineer for volume production (100,000 units a year) in Poland, a new line of vehicles ranging from light pick-up vans to medium trucks in the 5-metric-ton range. General Motors will market, under its trade name, a percentage of the Polish plant's output—15,000 units is the likely number, initially. General Motors will train Polish managers and technicians in their facilities located in England and other parts of Europe, and Polish technicians will participate in the design and engineering of the new truck line. The proposed General Motors agreement takes a significant step beyond the co-production and co-marketing agreements that have been negotiated by American and other foreign enterprises in Eastern Europe, in that it includes the sharing of design and engineering of a new product line for the sophisticated and competitive Western European market.

Cummins Engine Company, a billion dollar corporation, is committed to sharing the production of its newest generation of diesel engine with Komatsu, its licensing affiliate in Japan and a leading tractor and construction equipment manufacturer. Based upon a comparative analysis of capital requirements for future expansion of R&D, marketing, and production capacities, the latter was found to be least efficient in terms of relative rates of return. Cummins' long-range planning seems to point toward a new corporate emphasis on research and development and marketing, rather than on the more traditional manufacturing functions.

In March of 1975, a leading U.S. automobile parts manufacturer completed four years of negotiations with a socialist country for a sizable contract under which the U.S. manufacturer will supply equipment and technical know-how for an automobile parts manufacturing plant. The technology and equipment—including metallurgical, mechanical, electroplating, and casting lines—will be the most sophisticated available and promises to produce an internationally competitive product. The contract was the first one the U.S. manufacturer had negotiated with this country, and the Americans quickly realized that they faced an astute and well-informed bargaining agent. They felt they lacked sufficient backstop commercial and economic intelligence and an understanding of their adversary's tactics in negotiating for and acquiring foreign industrial technology. The major asset that the U.S. firm had was a "cadillac-line" technology, which their client seemed to prefer, and this is what ultimately led to an agreement on the U.S. manufacturer's terms.

Between 1972 and 1975, Fujitsu Ltd., a leading computer manufacturer in Japan, acquired access to highly advanced computer technology developed by the Amdahl Corporation, founded in 1970 by a former IBM design engineer. Amdahl equipment enables users of IBM equipment to double the cost effectiveness of their data processing. In return for successive rounds of finance capital, Fujitsu, backed by Japanese government financing, acquired full patent and manufacturing rights, in Japan, for this advanced computer technology and has since moved the technology to Spain and is negotiating with Siemens in Germany for sharing Amdahl technology. Eighty per cent of Amdahl computer manufacturing requirements have been shifted to Fujitsu in Japan. Fujitsu is now planning to use Amdahl component technology tod esign and manufacture small to medium computers for sale in the U.S.

In 1971, General Electric entered into a joint venture with SNECMA, the French government-controlled manufacturer of military aircraft engines, to design and manufacture 10-to-15-ton civilian prototypes. Under the agreement, General Electric was to provide technology for the "hot-core" (compressor portion) of the jet engine, originally developed for the U.S. long-range B-1 bomber. R&D expense (estimated at near a half a billion dollars—twice General Electric's annual R&D budget) and ownership of the new engine was to be shared by General Electric and SNECMA. General Electric entered into the agreement to maintain its long-standing global position in the civilian aircraft engine market. The agreement represented a marked shift in General Electric's policy toward sharing front-end technology with another commercial group.

In 1972, General Telephone and Electronics signed a $223 million contract with SONELEC/Algeria to build a completely integrated consumer electronics plant, from raw materials through component manufacture (including cathode-ray tubes and semi-conductors) to end products (Tvs, radios, tape recorders, and cassettes). Under the agreement, over 300 Algerian technicians and managers are to be trained in the United States at a cost of $25 million. SONELAC is planning to manage its Sidi-Bel Abbes facility entirely with Algerian nationals within two years.

In 1975, Honeywell entered into a joint venture with CII, the dominant French computer firm, strongly backed by the French government ($280 million in R&D funding and over $400 million in government purchases). Strong inflow of U.S. technology was a condition of Honeywell's entry into the French public sector market.

The foregoing scenarios are excerpts from 25 case studies that Developing World Industry & Technology prepared for the U.S. Department of Labor in five industries—aircraft, automotive, computers, consumer electronics, and chemical engineering. The scenarios cited represent the forefront of a trend revealed in the case material in which U.S. corporations have redefined their "self-interest" such that under some circumstances, they now find attractive the sale of industrial technology to noncontrolled foreign enterprises. The technology sold, in such cases, is increasingly the most sophisticated available, and its release is often under terms that assure the rapid and efficient implantation of an internationally competitive productive capability. This trend represents a radical departure from traditional transfer modes—direct foreign investment and licensing—in which the technology released was, for the most part, based on "mature" product lines and available production techniques.

SOME SIGNIFICANT DISTINCTIONS

The new transfer arrangements shed some revealing light on what is meant by the term "technology transfer" and which modes of transfer (and related conditions and practices) lead to the most rapid, premature, or otherwise disadvantageous erosion of American firms' proprietary technology. It is important to distinguish between relatively innocuous transfers of standardized technology easily available from alternative sources and the more advanced or sophisticated technology which cannot readily be obtained from other U.S. companies or elsewhere in the world. There are also significant distinctions to be drawn between the sale of turnkey plants or process elements and the implantation in the foreign enterprise of the technical know-how to duplicate the technology or to design and engineer new generations of technology from the base acquired under the licensing arrangement. Technology transfer in most of the scenarios described above implies a sustained enterprise-to-enterprise relationship for the purpose of reproducing production capabilities at desired levels of quality and cost efficiency. Experienced technology purchasers realize that the sale of technical information (process sheets, materials specifications, and printed machine-operating instructions) without a sustained enterprise-to-enterprise relationship and the technical support and guidance that accompany such a relationship, does not lead to effective and successful technology acquisition. The amount of sustained effort and the time required to implant transferred technology depend heavily upon the technical sophistication and the absorptive capability of the recipient enterprise and its industrial environment.

The new approach to world marketing and production implicit in the cases cited did not occur overnight nor in response to an isolated event. It is the result of evolutionary trends in the world economy that are changing many corporate viewpoints on foreign involvements and have altered the relative bargaining position of suppliers and purchasers of "operative technology." The proposition that U.S. firms acting in their own self-interest when selling proprietary technology is an adequate safeguard of U.S. national economic interest is also open to question, for other reasons:

1. The technological leads that U.S. industry held following World War II are being progressively challenged and eroded by Japanese and Western European industry. Changing circumstances in the world economy prompted many U.S. corporations to share latest generation technology with foreign enterprises, sometimes as a matter of corporate survival. In addition, enterprises in industrially advanced countries have become alternative suppliers of first-class, operative technology—a result, in part, of the release of design and manufacturing know-how by U.S. firms. Consequently, U.S. firms now argue that if they do not provide the technology, someone else will.

2. The new enterprise-to-enterprise arrangements for transferring late-generation technology and product designs contribute to rapid and extensive implanting of competitive operative technology in enterprises and economies with even modest technical sophistication. The release of proprietary technology is particularly disturbing because of intensified competition from astute and aggressive enterprises of industrially advanced countries. The impetus to release design and manufacturing technology to socialist countries has been reinforced by the U.S. policy of detente. In the case of Eastern European economies, it is contended that technological support leading to internationally competitive industry helps to weaken their political dependence on the Soviet Union. An even stronger argument is put forth regarding the People's Republic of China, where the absorption of advanced technology is viewed as a countervailing force to Soviet power.

3. The case materials provide new evidence of an increasing tendency by U.S. corporations to release technology overseas and a reinforcement of this outward movement by foreign demand. It is no longer merely mature products and standardized technologies that are moving abroad. Certain U.S. firms, for the various reasons outlined, now feel compelled to release to foreign enterprises their most recently developed technology (in terms of product designs, process engineering, and production systems). In some instances, the "product" has become the implanting of design and engineering capabilities which are the spawning grounds of future industrial competitors. Some trade economist scontend that this phenomenon has resulted in the outward shift of comparative advantages from the U.S. economy and that this is occurring at a rate and to an extent that is increasingly threatening and disruptive to the U.S. industrial position in the world economy.[3]

These changes have profound implications for the future competitiveness of U.S.-based industry and its ability to continue to generate production jobs for U.S. labor. It is imperative that we acquire a better understanding of the factors that influence change.

CHANGING CIRCUMSTANCES

The economic consequences of a particular technology transfer depend upon an interrelated set of factors consisting of (a) the motivations, strategies, and capabilities of technology suppliers—conditioned, in part, by government policies and economic conditions; (b) the astuteness, bargaining power, and absorptive capabilities of recipient enterprises—as reinforced or conditioned by government action and economic policies; and (c) the nature, quantum, and complexity of technology transferred.

Insofar as corporate strategies are concerned, the willingness to release proprietary technology to noncontrolled enterprises has stemmed from a variety of motivations and conditions. The motivations range from acute capital shortages (as in the Amdahl-Fujitsu case) to sale of technology that is no longer central to company business. The shift from equity position and managerial control of overseas production facilities to management service contracts (General Motors-Polmot and General Telephone and Electronics-SONELEC) is, in part, due to a major change in corporate attitudes toward overseas capital investments in plant and equipment. A growing number of U.S. firms have now decided that the economic uncertainties and political risks associated with capital investments in overseas plants have become too high for realized rates of return.

Aside from the political uncertainties in a widening area of the world, there are economic vicissitudes brought on by world inflation, exchange rate revaluations, and recessionary cycles, all of which have added to the risks of locking into fixed investments. These conditions have been compounded by the fragmentation of world markets resulting from import substitution behind tariff barriers and regional trading blocks, done to partially offset the inefficiencies of protected national economies. Additional financial burdens have resulted from expanded R&D costs in response to emerging demands for fuel economy, emission controls, and more stringent safety standards, coupled with more exacting demands for model changes and variations due to intensified worldwide competition.

This recent phenomenon, however, cannot be fully explained by an examination of the factors and conditions that motivate U.S. corporations alone; equally important, if not more important, is the shift in the nature of foreign demands for technology and in the bargaining power of the purchasers. It is useful here to distinguish among three distinct recipient environments: (1) industrially advanced economies (Japan and Western Europe); (2) socialist countries (the Soviet Union, the People's Republic of China, and Eastern Europe); and (3) oil-rich developing nations (Algeria and Venezuela) and/or those with a relatively advanced industrial base (Brazil and Iran). There are substantial differences among and within these groups in terms of (a) government policies; (b) bargaining power (in terms of financial resources, astuteness in orchestrating contract negotiations, and access to alternative technology sources); and (c) technical absorptive capabilities (at the enterprise level and among supporting industrial sectors).

It is the official policy of several Western European governments and the Japanese government that national enterprises should acquire certain advanced technologies—particularly in the fields of computers, the aircraft, and certain automotive and electronic components—in order to develop internationally competitive industries. An increasingly popular mode of transfer in these cases is the formation of a joint venture between a U.S. firm and a foreign firm, or consortium of firms, in which the former provides the technology and the latter, with government financing, provides venture capital and R&D and production-tooling funds or the means by which nontariff barriers to market entry are circumvented or offset requirements met. To a U.S. firm suffering severe capital constraints and feeling excluded from important markets, these can be extremely attractive terms on which to negotiate a joint venture. Amdahl-Fujitsu in the computer field and General Electric-SNECMA in jet aircraft are two cases in point. The firms in this grouping have demonstrated, on numerous occasions, a high absorptive capacity and the ability not only to duplicate and to improve upon U.S. industrial technology, but to more successfully commercialize and market the improved technology.

The technology transfer agreements with the socialist countries have been state-negotiated and are aimed at technological self-sufficiency. This group (Poland and Rumania, in particular) has spearheaded the drive to negotiate the new generation of technology transfer agreements that involve the implanting of internationally competitive technology and production systems (high-volume, cost-efficient, and quality-controlled products). This is the case in the General Motors-Polmot negotiations and in several other transactions with Eastern European economies involving Control Data (computer peripherals), Clark (heavy equipment axles), and International Harvester (specially designed, heavy-duty trailers and chassis).

These agreements generally include: (a) fast and efficient enterprise-to-enterprise implantation of production capabilities; (b) patent and trademark rights; (c) marketing of end-products outside socialist country markets to earn the foreign exchange needed to pay for the acquired technology, and (d) sometimes—as in General Motors-Polmot—the design and engineering of a new or improved product line to compete in world markets. Some U.S. firms have argued—sometimes self-deceptively—that this type of involvement obviates the purchaser's need to develop his own production designs and thereby locks associated enterprises into a continuing technological dependence.

The bargaining position of Eastern European and other socialist countries is considerably enhanced by the fact that in most cases they are dealing in technologies for which there are usually several sources. If General Motors had turned down the Polmot deal, Mercedes-Benz (Germany) or Volvo (Sweden) undoubtedly would have been equally competent and willing to consummate a similar arrangement. Another strong bargaining factor is that the socialist governments are prepared to provide investment capital and pay for design and engineering costs, thus obviating the need for capital expenditures by the U.S. firm, which can still earn highly attractive returns on its management and technology assets.

The third group of purchasers—the resource-rich developing countries—is characterized by government policies of rapid industrialization, based on foreign technology, to process their raw materials for world markets. The Fluor Corporation, a leading U.S. chemical engineering company, has $4 billion in new contracts in Saudi Arabia alone. In other oil-rich countries, demands are for management and control of lead-sector industrial facilities. Behind the SONELEC and General Telephone and Electronics agreement are Algerian motivations to lay the base for an internationally competitive industry and for expanded self-reliance in designing and engineering future generations of production systems adapted to Algeria's needs and industrial capabilities. Two other considerations in contract relations involving the design and construction of industrial facilities are: (a) the training of technicians and engineers to duplicate and innovate, and (b) the development of domestic capital goods industries and related supplier plants as contributions to overall industrial growth and development. Resource-rich developing countries, while low in absorptive capabilities, have resources to purchase the best technology available.

NEW PROBLEMS

Enhanced bargaining power on the part of foreign purchasers coupled with changing circumstances that prompt corporations to share technology with foreign enterprises, have given rise to a new set of problems and issues that warrant more intensive scrutiny. Based on the 25 case study findings, the following implications for the U.S. economy can be drawn:

1. The new generation of management service contracts, coupled with evolving corporate strategies for maximizing returns on technology assets, may result in a further erosion of U.S. production jobs in such key industries as automobiles, aircraft, consumer electronics, and chemicals. Design engineering and capital equipment industries will

benefit from the first-round effects of foreign plant construction, but where the transfers result in internationally competitive facilities, U.S. production and employment could be threatened.

2. These technological displacements could prove particularly troublesome: (a) under adverse domestic economic conditions (low growth rate, high unemployment, inflation, declining productivity, and balance-of-payments difficulties); (b) in the absence of substantial improvement in labor market adjustment mechanisms (to relocate and retrain displaced production workers); and (c) in an economy where technologically dynamic industries (or services) are not expanding at a rate sufficient to absorb labor displacement from declining industrial sectors. The shift from the low-skill range of production jobs to higher-skill technical support requirements poses additional manpower adjustment problems.

3. A permissive posture in the release of front-end technology to commercially astute and aggressive foreign enterprises can prove to have especially damaging consequences for other U.S. producers in that industry. Not only can there be anticipated an erosion in the U.S. market share in newly developing regions, but also in the most industrially advanced export markets. The Amdahl-Fujitsu joint venture is an excellent case in point. It has been estimated that the infusion of Amdahl's technology has allowed Fujitsu to close approximately a three-to-five-year technological gap between it and the U.S. industry. By 1980, the Amdahl-Fujitsu joint venture can sell a sufficiently large number of 150 systems in North America, Western Europe, and Japan to displace more than $500 million in revenue to IBM. Furthermore, Fujitsu is now negotiating with several German computer firms to establish joint ventures to enter European markets.

4. There is some evidence that certain U.S. firms are beginning to falter in their will and determination to produce industrial systems that can continue to compete aggressively in U.S. and world markets, given the relatively high level of U.S. wages and the faltering rate of productivity advances. In the Cummins Engine-Komatsu case, the corporate decision was to allocate major manufacturing responsibility for its most advanced engine line to a strong, successful Japanese firm (formerly a licensee), because of the faltering proficiency of production and the difficulty of raising expansion capital in the United States. The dearth of venture capital was a determinant factor in the substantial release of front-end technology in the Amdahl-Fujitsu case.

5. The proliferation of internationally competitive, industrial technology in Japan, Western Europe, and socialist economies may be weakening the bargaining position of U.S. firms in negotiations on supplying technology to newly industrializing countries and in trade negotiations with these countries. Japan has become a technological intermediary for many countries of the developing world, having absorbed and adapted

segments of U.S. technology. The socialist countries may follow suit in time, depending on the volume of transfers and the efficacy of implantation. These trends make it even more necessary for U.S. industry to maintain technological leads through investments in R&D and the commercialization of technical innovation *within the U.S. production system* (as distinct from the tendency to move abroad as it becomes difficult to maintain production competitiveness in the U.S. economy).

6. Technological partnerships with industrial enterprises in developing countries (such as Algeria and Brazil) could be mutually beneficial. Until such time as the technology and managerial gaps are considerably narrowed, U.S. enterprise can continue to export U.S.-manufactured goods, engineering services, and capital equipment. In a changing world economy in which developing countries play an expanding role in producing manufactured good, the United States will continue to shift to the capital-intensive range of manufacturing, relinquishing the more labor-intensive segments of production to lower-wage countries. These shifts, however, place an added burden on U.S. labor-market adjustment mechanisms.

GUIDELINES FOR CHANGE

The time has clearly come to reconsider national technology policies and their effect on the international operations of U.S. corporations. The impact of economic changes on the future competitiveness of U.S. industry warrants comprehensive examination. In particular, consideration should be given to the shift in international trade patterns from direct investment to the new generation of management services and co-production agreements. Policy recommendations are beyond the scope of this paper. Nonetheless, certain guidelines do emerge:

1. Sector analyses should be undertaken to determine if the incidence of technological erosion found in the case studies cited is indicative of a trend in particular industries leading to a decline in competitiveness and in productive employment. Sector surveys should include an examination of countervailing forces, such as the R&D of new generations of technology, that would obviate such concerns. If sector analyses show marked shifts in international trade patterns away from direct investment and toward management services and co-production agreements—in the absence of countervailing forces—medicinal measures must be considered. The exercise of preparing the sector analyses may itself serve as an effective early warning of technology erosion and would allow for timely adjustments *before* major economic disruptions and dislocations occur. These adjustments may take the form of (a) preventive controls (an extension of current export control procedures); or (b) positive reinforce-

ment of fiscal measures and other incentives (or subsidies) to encourage innovation and its commercialization in the United States and to discourage U.S. technology assets from moving abroad to the detriment of U.S. employment (or at least remove any fiscal incentives for this).

2. There are at present no interagency mechanisms or procedures, aside from the East-West Export Control Board, to provide government agencies with an analysis of the economic impact of major technology transfer agreements. The East-West Export Control Board focuses its attention on the political and strategic dimensions of technology transfer, largely ignoring the longer-term economic effects, as outlined in this article. Even the narrow sampling of cases cited would indicate the need to re-examine interagency review of "major" technolory transfer agreements and the need to develop a framework for evaluating the economic impact of these agreements. American firms applying for export licenses, or benefiting from government financing (through the Export-Import Bank or possibly through the Overseas Private Investment Corporation) should be subject to such review and be required to furnish necessary details on the technology transfer agreements.

---

[1]See U.S. Defense Science Board Task Force on Export of U.S. Technology, *An Analysis of Export Control of U.S. Technology—A DOD Perspective;* February 1976. See also U.S. General Accounting Office, *The Government's Role in East-West Trade—Problems and Issues,* February 1976.

[2]Noncontrolled foreign enterprise refers to a foreign company in which the U.S. firm holds no equity and over which it has no managerial control.

[3]See, for example, Harry G. Johnson, "Technological Change and Comparative Advantage: An Advanced Country's Viewpoint," *Journal of World Trade Law,* January-February 1975, pp.1-14.

Cartels, Combines, Commodity Agreements and International Law

Stanley D. Metzger

I. INTRODUCTION

Some twenty-eight years ago at Havana, in March 1948, the world's leading trading nations almost succeeded in creating a framework of law and institutions to regulate cartels, combines and commodity agreements. Chapter V—"Restrictive Business Practices"—and Chapter VI—"Inter-Governmental Commodity Agreements"—of the International Trade Organization Charter[1] would have established some substantive and procedural rules to govern their operation as well as an institution to administer them. The ITO Charter, however, never entered into force, and to this day we have nothing which can be called an international regulatory system in these areas of international economic activity.

An examination of the ITO Charter provisions can be more than an historical exercise if it sheds light upon present problems in this area. That light might be helpful even if it only points to those changes in circumstances during the past quarter century which today make generalized solutions to the twin problems of industrial and raw material cartels difficult to achieve. It is also a convenient starting point for a look at the present international legal ambience of both private and public restrictive business practices affecting international trade.

The Charter's provisions on cartels, combines and commodity agreements cannot be viewed apart from its chapter on commercial policy.[2] The basic construct of the Charter was to free international trade from

This paper was first presented at the Conference on Transnational Economic Boycotts and Coercion held February 19-20, 1976 at the University of Texas School of Law, Austin. The article appeared in *Texas International Law Journal*, Vol. II, Summer 1976, pages 527-539. 11 TEX. INT'L. L.J. 527 (1976). Reprinted with permission.

artificial restrictions. The commercial policy chapter—which became the GATT in 1947 and was to be reinserted in the Charter after it entered into force—was an institutionalized effort to organize trade upon fundamental free trade principles—trade on the basis of comparative advantage in the production and distribution of goods.[3] The principal artificialities in the commercial policy area were high tariffs and quantitative restrictions, but numerous other governmental measures also were employed to restrain trade in the interest of protecting domestic industry. The overall objective of the Charter was the most efficient economic allocation of the world's resources in the interest of industrial and general economic development, steadily growing real income, and equal terms of access to markets, products, and productive facilities. The freer trade system envisioned in the commercial policy chapter was the centerpiece of the ITO effort.

It was easily seen, however, that it would do little good to make marked progress in dismantling governmental restraints on trade while mechanisms by which commercial enterprises limited international trade through artificial means—cartels and combines—were left untouched.

II. CARTELS AND COMBINES

The framers of the ITO Charter attempted to meet this problem by establishing an agreed principle, by elaborating on that principle through specific prohibitory rules, and by creating a procedural system for the enforcement and supplementation of those rules.

Each member of the Organization to be established by the Charter was obliged to take appropriate measures and to cooperate with the Organization. The aim was to prevent private or public commercial enterprises from engaging in business practices that affect international trade and that restrain competition, limit access to markets, or foster monopolistic control, whenever such practices have harmful effects on the expansion of production or trade and interfere with the achievement of any of the other objectives set forth in article 1.[4]

The restrictive practices thus generally described were particularized in article 46(3). Several were specifically identified: price-fixing with regard to any product; territorial allocation or division of markets, including allocation of customers or fixing of sales or purchase quotas; discriminating against particular enterprises; limiting production or fixing production quotas; preventing development or application of technology or invention, patented or unpatented; and extending the use of patents, trademarks, or copyrights to matters not within the scope of such grants.[5] The Organization by a two-thirds majority vote, on a "one country, one vote" basis, could also declare "any similar practices" to be restrictive business practices.[6]

The procedure to be followed in applying the prohibitory rule merits description, since it indicates the limitations as well as the scope of the system of control that was envisaged. To enable the Organization to decide in a particular instance "whether a practice has or is about to have the effect" that was deemed harmful, complaints concerning any of the specified practices (*i.e.,* price-fixing, territorial division of markets) had to be made to the Organization.[7] The Organization would have to be satisfied that the practice was engaged in or made effective by one or more private or public commercial enterprises or by any combination, agreement or other arrangement between them, and that those enterprises "individually or collectively," possess "effective control of trade among a number of countries in one or more products."[8]

Several noteworthy features mark this procedure. First, "monopolistic control" (combines) is in principle covered along with the familiar cartel arrangements among independent enterprises, but the control over monopolies is limited to the situation in which monopolistic control eventuates in an abuse of power. That is, combines must engage in one or more specifically prohibited practices, not merely possess the market power to do so. It follows that mergers or other combinations which result only in the acquisition of market power are not controlled. Secondly, since commercial enterprises, which individually or collectively engage in such practices, must also "possess effective control of trade among a number of countries in one or more products,"[9] a purely national monopoly or combine or a purely national export cartel, such as a Webb-Pomerene export association of American phosphate producers,[10] could not be the subject of a complaint to, and control by, the Organization. Third, even where the monopoly or cartel qualifies for Organization investigation and control, it must be found not only to have committed the offense of price-fixing or territorial market division, but that offense must be found to have or be about to have "harmful effects on the expansion of production or trade" as well as to be interfering with the achievement of "any other of the objectives" of the Charter, *i.e.,* industrial and general economic development.[11] Thus, the *per se* rule of American antitrust law, whereby such practices as price-fixing and territorial market division are conclusively presumed to be unreasonable,[12] found no place in the Charter scheme. Each complaint could be the occasion of an inquiry into the "reasonableness" of the practice engaged in by the monopoly or cartel in terms of the extremely broad Charter objectives.

If the complaint met the above requirements, it would be the subject of an investigation by and a hearing before the Organization,[13] and a decision would be rendered which recommended remedial measures to be carried out by the offending member country in accordance with its laws and procedures.[14] If the complaint related to the conduct of a public commercial enterprise acting independently of any other enterprise, the complaining country would have to proceed first with bilateral consultation with the offending country.[15] In other cases the Organization could arrange for such consultation if requested and if it considered the request justified.[16]

It can thus be seen that the ITO effort to create law and an institutional enforcement structure in the cartels and combines field was a modest one. Only international cartel practices and monopolistic abuses of power found to be harmful to international trade and without compensating redeeming economic features could be the subject of investigation, findings, and suggested remedies. Mergers, oligopolies, and national export cartels were left untouched.

Nonetheless, it was a fair beginning. To establish as an agreed international principle, even with substantive and procedural limitations, that cartels and combines should be subjected to scrutiny and cooperative remedial measures when found to be harmful to international trade was no mean achievement, especially when considered in light of the role they played in the economies both of the richer and poorer countries. For, at the close of World War II, cartels, combines, and oligopolies occupied not only the commanding heights, but also most of the foothills and a large area of the plains as well of the economies of most of the industrialized, richer countries, large and small, and of practically all of the less developed, poorer nations. The fact that governments signed the ITO Charter, and thereby indicated a willingness to move in the direction of controlling foreign combines and cartels adversely affecting their econ mies did not mean that they were prepared to undertake a restructurin, f their own economies. It did, however, signify that antitrust was enteri, heir thinking even in that respect.

We not know what might have been had the ITO Charter come into being, instead of falling in the United States Congress under the combined attack of protectionists, firms that were fearful of being targets of international investigation, such as the large oil companies, and others. Nor can we know what would have happened if the Draft Restrictive Business Practices Convention[17] supported by the United States in the Economic and Social Council of the United Nations in 1951-52 had been pushed to completion instead of being abandoned by the United States in 1953, primarily because of oil company opposition. That Convention, patterned after Chapter V of the ITO Charter, would also have established an Organization that would have conducted studies, investigate complaints, and recommend remedial action.

Perhaps the cartel and combines landscape would not have been much altered. Countries might well have been quite reticent about acting as plaintiffs before the international body against foreign cartels and combines harming their international trade, for they might soon have been defendants themselves if they were not in control of the activities of their own cartels and combines that were restraining or monopolizing the trade of other countries.

It is noteworthy, on this score, that the United States and approximately twenty other countries are parties to the postwar bilateral Friendship, Commerce, and Navigation (FCN) treaties, which contain "antitrust" articles. For example, article XVIII (1) of the U.S.-Japanese FCN treaty of 1953[18] states:

> The two parties agree that business practices which restrain competition, limit access to markets or foster monopolistic control, and which are engaged in or made effective by one or more private or public commercial enterprises or by combination, agreement or other arrangement among such enterprises, may have harmful effects upon commerce between their respective territories. Accordingly, each Party agrees upon the request of the other Party to consult with respect to any such practices and to take such measures as it deems appropriate with a view to eliminating such harmful effects.

This provision is, of course, no epitome of strength. The obligation to consult, with remedial measures to be taken only as the offending part deems appropriate, is extremely modest. Yet the provision can be utilized as a formal means of representation. Indeed, it is not too much to say that there would at least be a probability of securing some relief if the case is strong enough to produce agreement that harm has been caused by the restrictive practice. To my knowledge, article XVIII (1) and its counterparts have never been utilized by the United States or by its FCN treaty partners during all the postwar years in which the articles have been included in FCN treaties.

T'·.· disuse of the FCN treaties, while not conclusive, tends to indicate that ιhe organization administering the ITO or the Restrictive Business Practicos Convention would not have been inundated with complaints.

These failed efforts to create a system of law affecting cartels, combines, and oligopolies in the immediate post-war years were not a prologue to later more successful efforts. There has been nothing since 1953 resembling the serious effort displayed in devising the ITO Charter or the Convention. In the industrial goods sector, there have been national efforts to create meaningful antitrust laws in the Federal Republic of Germany, in the European Community's Treaty of Rome, and in Britain, Canada, and some other developed countries.[19] These were all designed to free, to varying degrees, the internal economies of those countries and areas from restraints of trade, the German and European Community efforts being more intensive than the others. Though none adopted the *per se* approach of American antitrust law with respect to cartels, and all were markedly weaker in interdicting mergers, they represented serious first-time efforts, at least on the national level, and, in the case of the European Community, on a multinational level. None of these efforts, however, addressed itself seriously to the problems of oligopolies or of freeing the "world economy" from the harmful effects of cartels and combines.

Indeed, the record of the past two decades shows considerable retrogression in the sphere of preventing or remedying restraints of trade affecting the so-called world economy. Countries the world over have taken no action to prevent their nationals from restraining the trade of others through cartels and combines. There has been a permanent floating "open season" for restraining the trade of foreigners. Some of the most important trading countries, such as the United States, have given serious thought to encouraging this trend further.

The 1974 Report on "Export Cartels" produced by the Committee of Experts of the Organization for Economic Cooperation and Development provides some of the most depressing reading that has been made available in some time.[20] Basing their conclusions on responses to requests for information—responses which the OECD experts themselves have characterized as fragmentary—the Committee reported the existence of no fewer than 590 "national" and "international" export cartels operating in six OECD member countries—Federal Republic of Germany, Japan, Netherlands, Spain, United Kingdom and United States.[21] Undoubtedly this figure would be significantly greater if the cartels operating in France, Belgium, Canada, and other states that did not respond were added into the total. National cartels are those whose members consist solely of corporations of the country specified; international cartels include those of two or more corporate nationalities.[22] All the reported cartels appeared to be lawful, according to the OECD's examination of the laws of the countries involved. At the very least, these cartels had not been made the subject of adverse legal action by those countries.

One of the more complete responses to the OECD request for information came from the United Kingdom.[23] As of 1970, the United Kingdom reported 227 national export cartels comprising 2,606 firms and 61 international agreements, composed of 469 United Kingdom and 518 foreign firms.[24] As to types of restraints, 87 percent of the national cartels contained agreed prices, 14 percent established quotas for firms, and 41 percent contained agreed payment terms.[25] As might be imagined, the agreements covered a wide range of goods, from electric cables to locomotives, from woollens and worsteds to glycerine, to name a few. Their geographic coverage was usually worldwide.

The OECD experts deplored the development of this pervasive network of cartels, the true extent of which was only suggested by their information. They found that national cartels "maintained or created barriers to trade by forcing customers to pay high, non-competitive prices or by limiting the quantity of exports" and "lead to a deliberalisation of international trade, which jeopardizes important economic policy goals, such as increasing economic efficiency and the optimum supply of commodities to consumers."[26] This is true "irrespective of the fact whether (national) export cartels aim at increasing or at decreasing the participants' international ability to compete."[27] The Committee addressed this last remark to those who have contended that national export cartels may be beneficial because they enable small or medium-sized firms to engage in international trade. The OECD experts noted, "the typical firm benefitting from the exemption from domestic antitrust laws for export cartels in the United States and in Germany was not the small or medium-sized firm."[28]

The OECD experts further pointed ut: (1) that "experience has shown that legal authorization of national cartels by one country is often an incentive for other countries," *e.g.,* the U.S. Webb-Pomerene exception adopted in 1918 was justified in part as a response to the permitted existence of German cartels; (2) that actions taken under those exemptions have the effect of inducing export cartelization in other countries; and (3) that those firms which form export cartels to fix prices and divide markets territorially are likely to engage in such conduct at home as well.[29] It is a rare swimmer whose breathing is different depending upon whether he swims in an ocean or a river.

The anti-competitive effects of international cartels are "even more serious": they "virtually always create barriers to international trade" and most "contain explicit provisions for home market protection which sometimes remove all import competition."[30] The OECD experts asked "whether private profits, which result from a deliberalisation of world trade through international cartelisation, have any social or economic value in the market economies of Member countries."[31]

The 1967 Federal Trade Commission report on 50 years of Webb-Pomerene associations[32] said much the same, and there have been many recommendations for repeal. Unfortunately, the American Williams Commission in 1971, without any indication that it was even aware of the excellent FTC report, recommended expansion of this export cartel exemption from American antitrust laws.[33] It advocated statutorily broadening the permitted activities of such cartels, thereby redefining the limitations which had been staunchly upheld in several Supreme Court decisions.[34] The Commission further recommended the extension of the exemption's scope from the export of goods to the export of various services as well.[35] In April 1973, the Nixon Administration secured the introduction of legislation to achieve these effects.[36] These backward steps, which have been indicated but not yet taken and which hopefully will be rejected definitively, are disheartening. For, by attempting to foster additional cartelization, they undercut efforts, such as that of the OECD experts, to establish at the least a launching pad for a new effort to create an international legal system to control cartels and combines.

There re additional and broader effects of the pervasive cartelization of international trade in industrial goods and the failure of the richer, industrialized countries to take effective action to control its further extension. One important consequence is that the poorer, less developed countries treat as a blatant exercise in hypocrisy the complaints of the richer countries directed against their own cartelization efforts in the raw materials area. Another is that the less developed countries note carefully the continued diplomatic support offered by the richer nations to their own enterprises that engage in the cartelization and monopolization of the economies of the poorer countries. In the face of this record can the poorer countries realistically be expected to respond to pleas by the richer, industrialized countries concerning the health of a "world economy of interdependent countries and peoples" by refraining from attempts to emulate the "success" of OPEC intergovernmental cartel for those raw materials for which they are able to muster the cohesion and strength to "manage" international trade?[37]

This leads to a consideration of the state of the legal art respecting the cartelization of raw materials, in recent years generally considered under the rubric, "Intergovernmental Commodity Agreements."

III. COMMODITY AGREEMENTS

While Chapter V of the ITO Charter, "Restrictive Business Practices,"[38] covered "any product," this phrase must be read in light of the immediately succeeding Chapter VI concerning "Inter-Governmental Commodity Agreements," which purported to establish a different regime for "primary commodities," defined as "any product of farm, forest or fishery or any mineral, in its natural form or which has undergone such processing as is customarily required to prepare it for marketing in substantial volume in international trade."[39]

The difference in the ITO Charter treatment of raw material cartels as compared with those for industrial products resulted from the view of the majority of countries that the difficulties of a "free market" for primary commodities outweighed its virtues, particularly where very wide price fluctuations could have serious social repercussions in the "one or two crop countries" that made up most of what we now call the "developing countries." Greater tolerance of "monopolistic combinations of the cartel type"[40] was to be shown in this area, despite the wide recognition that the prewar private cartels in tin, rubber, and tea had been far from happy ventures from the viewpoint of the consumer and, indeed, from the viewpoint of many producer countries.[41]

The Havana Charter reflected this tolerance while simultaneously seeking to mitigate the degree of divergence from free trade principles that it connoted. Recognizing that reasonable stability of prices "about the current long-period trend" and "reasonably appropriate and stable incomes to primary producers"[42] were desirable, the Charter nonetheless required that a "burdensome surplus"[43] or "widespread unemployment or underemployment"[44] occur or be expected to develop before a commodity control agreement could be countenanced. Even in these circumstances, such agreements—regulating the production or quantitative control of exports or imports or regulating prices—must be among governments, not private parties;[45] must offer membership to consuming as well as producing countries;[46] must provide each, as a group, equal weight in decision-making under the agreement;[47] and must be limited to five years duration so that a reassessment as to the necessity for continuation of the agreement would be taken at relatively short intervals.[48] The Charter provided for only these procedural limitations with each commodity agreement's substantive obligations left to negotiation on a commodity-by-commodity bass, depending upon the vagaries of trade in the particular commodity.

Although the Charter never came into effect, the procedures of Chapter VI were retained in an attenuated legal form—an Economic and Social Council resolution in 1947 recommending that governments be guided by the Chapter's provisions.[49] Some of the prewar cartel members, such as the tin producers in Malaya, Indonesia, and Bolivia, grumbled at having to work through governments, but in view of the changed circumstances, they were prepared to endure the inconvenience to achieve what they saw as the revival of the old cartels. The existence of a huge American tin stockpile that could be used at any time to break the price forced those countries to be prepared to operate under a milder cartel regime in which prices and quotas were set at levels at least within the tolerance of important consuming countries. The wheat, sugar, coffee, and cocoa agreements comported with the procedural guidelines of Chapter VI of the Havana Charter for similar reasons. These were relatively modest requirements, since the producers had the ultimate whiphand in price and quota decisions under the agreements, and consuming countries were "captive" enough (*e.g.,* United Kingdom and Malaya on tin) to vote with the producing country, or were so numerous as to be an unwieldy opposing group.[50] Also, the same political interest tht led the consuming countries to be prepared to raise the price of the commodity for themselves was likely to continue after the first five year period, provided that the cartel did not raise the price outrageously or restrict exports too severely.

The real problems in negotiating the commodity control agreements were not these requirements. The more troublesome difficulties related to the levels of prices and the devices, principally the quota, used to enforce these price levels. The principle of stabilization of prices over the long term was never really accepted by those who wanted to restore the old cartels. They wanted price levels stabilized at levels that protected the marginal producers and that were, thus, by definition, substantially higher than the "free market" long-term trend. This asked a great deal of consuming countries—too much unless their political interests were very strong indeed, and even then difficult because it meant a profit squeeze for important producer interests within the consuming country. Thus, the steel industry of the United States opposed American membership in the tin agreement, and the chocolate manufacturers have been less than enamored of the cocoa agreement which the United States has recently decided not to join.

Later, however, after UNCTAD was organized in 1964, things became even more difficult. The concept of "stabilization" was changed to one of outright price augmentation in order to secure higher levels of export earnings for developing countries as a whole than they would receive were prices to be stabilized on the basis of the long period trend, even as modified to protect the marginal producer. Consuming countries that had found it difficult enough to justify raising prices to themselves were now being asked for more of the same, not as a means of stabilization but as a supplementary form of foreign aid.[51] That meant that relatively poorer groups in both developing and developed countries were being asked to subsidize the estimated 5 percent of the population in the producing countries that was already relatively affluent.[52]

There were important practical problems as well. There have been two fundamental difficulties connected with the formation of commodity cartels, with or without consuming country participation. One is the ability of consumers to substitute or otherwise do without the commodity or with substantially less of it. No rubber cartel was formed after the war because of synthetic rubber; no cotton agreement was formed because of man-made fibres. Parties to the tin agreement have proceeded with care because of the American stockpile of tin and because of the widespread use of aluminum. The second difficulty is achieving an equitable division of the market (depending, in part, on price agreement) among producers, for example, Latin America versus Africa in coffee and Southern Asia versus Africa in tea. It is tempting to say that had it not been for the nice groundwork long laid by the private international oil cartel, it would have been very difficult for the various OPEC countries to overcome this obstacle, and it is still not clear that a depressed market will not have an effect upon continued harmony in OPEC's ranks. Nonetheless, OPEC's current success has induced the bauxite, banana, and other cartel candidates to strive, with varying degress of success, to achieve similar results, and there seems to be little doubt that this effort will continue.

Too much depends on future rates of economic growth, unemployment, and inflation within major consuming countries to agree now with those who seem confident that there will be a proliferation of commodity cartels or with those who gainsay such a possibility. The slower and more uneven the economic recovery, the harder it will be for the cartels to form.

It is not too soon, however, to predict that the present disarray over raw material cartel principles will be with us for a very long time, and that the chances are nonexistent for creating at any time in the near future a general legal regime—procedural or substantive, or both. The difficulties of negotiating individual commodity agreements, including whether under given circumstances they are desirable, and the dual problems of price and distribution of market shares, to say nothing of procedural problems, have become apparent. The question raised in seeking to establish some generalized approach to future commodity agreements is whether these "conflicts of interest, difficult enough to resolve in a single commodity agreement," can be "reconciled through broad agreement on over-all or common interest"?[53] The UNCTAD Secretariat, raising this question in July 1975, believed that if these problems could be resolved it would necessarily be "at the highest political level if impetus is to be given to an integrted programme."[54] It was quick to add, however, that any such programme had to assume "more concrete and detailed shape" than any hitherto put forward.[55] Meanwhile, however, "governmental and international clarification of the issues and facts of the situation that would influence final attitudes to adoption of the programme" should not be precluded. No one in his right mind should oppose clarification of the issues and facts of this or any other proposition, and likely no one will. Indeed, I would expect, as I believe UNCTAD anticipates, that this process will be going on for the next several decades.

CONCLUSION

Where does this leave us, insofar as the relationship between law and industrial and raw materials cartels, combines, and commodity agreements is concerned? The current confusions will be a very long time straightening out. The conflicts of interest are too sharp, the interactions too complex, and the perceptions of the desirable too disparate, to expect law and institutions to develop soon. Moralistic posturing is clearly out of order. If employed in the future, as in the recent past, it will most likely hinder whatever cooperative measures may be possible.

I would offer a few general propositions that seem to comport with events. The richer, industrialized countries will have no success in restricting the agenda for discussion and negotiation to raw material cartels. They must be prepared to deal seriously with their own export cartels if they are to expect any degree of cooperation from the poorer countries. While many would urge that this cooperation should aim at suppressing both types of cartels, this idea seems unrealistic for the foreseeable future. Short of that, countries could aim in the direction of establishing a regime which might at least control the operations of those cartels decided to be tolerated, in order to minimize the adverse effects of cartels upon international trade. Unfortunately, it is more reasonable to expect a mutual tolerance of industrial and raw material cartels regardless of their overall economic costs.

---

[1]Havana Charter for an International Trade Organization, in *United States Dept. of State, Havana Charter for an International Trade Organization,* 23-140 (1948).

[2]Havana Charter, ch. IV, *supra* note 1, at 45-85. The ITO Charter's commercial policy chapter became in large part the rules of the General Agreement on Tariffs and Trade (GATT).

[3]*Id.*

[4]*Id.* art. 46(1), at 86.

[5]*Id.* art. 46(3), at 86-87.

[6]*Id.* art. 46(3)(9), at 87.

[7]*Id.* art. 46(2), at 86.

[8]*Id.* art. 46(2)(b), (c), at 86.

[9]*Id.* art. 46(2)(c), at 86.

[10]The Export Trade Act (Webb-Pomerene Act), 15 U.S.C. § 61 (1970, exempts from antitrust laws export associations of American firms, provided their exports of goods do not result in restraints upon the domestic economy or import trade of the United States.

[11]Havana Charter, art. 46(1), *supra* note 1, at 86.

[12]See Turner, *Principles of American Antitrust Law,* 12 INT'L & COMP. L.Q. 1 (1963); reprinted in 2 S. METZGER, LAW OF INTERNATIONAL TRADE 1379-80 (1966).

[13]Havana Charter, art. 48(1)-(6), *supra* note 1, at 87-88.

[14]*Id.* art. 48(7), at 88.

[15]*Id.* art. 48(1), at 87.

[16]*Id.* art. 47, at 87.

[17]*Ad Hoc* Committee on Restrictive Trade Practices, *Restrictive Business Practices,* 16 U.N. ECOSOC, Supp. 11, at 12-18, U.N. Doc. E/2380 (1953); reprinted in METZGER, *supra* note 12 at 1500-15.

[18]Treaty of Friendship, Commerce, and Navigation with Japan, April 2, 1953, art. XVIII(1), [1953] 4 U.S.T. 2063, T.I.A.S. No. 2863, 206 U.N.T.S. 143 (effective October 30, 1953).

[19]Articles 85 and 86, Treaty Establishing the European Economic Community,

done March 25, 1957, 298 U.N.T.S. 11 (effective Jan. 1, 1958), represent the principal effort. See H. STEINER & D. VAGTS, TRANSNATIONAL LEGAL PROBLEMS 1342-49 (2d ed. 1976).

[20]ORGANIZATION FOR ECONOMIC COOPERATION AND DEVELOPMENT, COMMITTEE OF EXPERTS ON RESTRICTIVE BUSINESS PRACTICES, EXPORT CARTELS (1974), [hereinafter cited as OECD Report].

[21]*Id.*

[22]*Id.* at 7.

[23]*Id.* at 73-77.

[24]*Id.*

[25]*Id.*

[26]*Id.* at 50.

[27]*Id.*

[28]*Id.*

[29]*Id.* at 49-50.

[30]*Id.*

[31]*Id.* at 51.

[32]FEDERAL TRADE COMMISSION, WEBB-POMERENE ASSOCIATIONS: A 50-YEAR REVIEW (1967).

[33]COMMISSION ON INTERNATIONAL TRADE AND INVESTMENT POLICY, UNITED STATES INTERNATIONAL ECONOMIC POLICY IN A INTERDEPENDENT WORLD 120, 126 (1971). Albert Williams was chairman of the commission.

[34]*Id.* at 126.

[35]*Id.* at 120, 126.

[36]OECD Report, *supra* note 20, at 48.

[37]*Id.*

[38]Havana Charter, ch. V, *supra* note 1, at 86-92.

[39]*Id.* art. 56(1), at 92.

[40]ROWE, PRIMARY COMMODITIES IN INTERNATIONAL TRADE 121 (1965).

[41]*Id.* at 120-55.

[42]*Id.* at 157.

[43]Havana Charter, art. 62(a), *supra* note 1, at 97.

[44]*Id.* art. 62(b), at 97.

[45]*Id.* art. 61, at 95-96.

[46]*Id.* art. 60(1)(d), at 95.

[47]*Id.* art. 63(b), 64(2), at 98.

[48]*Id.* art. 65(1), at 99.

[49]ECOSOC Res. 30(IV), U.N. Doc. E/473, at 3 (1947).

[50]See Metzger, *Intergovernmental Commodity Agreements: The Actuality* in 2 METZGER, *supra* note 12, at 1208.

[51]See Metzger, *UNCTAD,* 61 AM. J. INT'L L. 756, 762-63 (1967).

[52]See Wasserman, *Key Issues in Development,* 10 J. WORLD TRADE L. 17, 22 (1976).

[53]United Nations Conference on Trade and Development, Trade and Development Board, Committee on Commodities, An Integrated Programme for Commodities: The Impact on Imports, Particularly of Developing Countries, U.N. Doc. TO/B/c.1/189, at 1 (1975).

[54]*Id.*

[55]*Id.* at 2.

Public Law 480, American Agriculture and World Food Demand

David Helscher

Famine and mass starvation are possibilities which the world must fact in the coming decades. Despite all the advances and increased in grain production, the world situation regarding to food supplies is at a precarious stage. Supplies and surpluses of grain have been sufficient to meet world demand, but this may change within the decade. The progression of growth of food supplies and population predicted by Malthus[1] may reach critical levels.

A cursory examination of American agriculture reveals that is is of great importance to the United States and the world. Agriculture is a major industry for many American states and is also the largest single industry in the United States.[2]

Agricultural exports are an important factor in the American balance of trade, balancing in part the huge deficits created by imports of foreign oil.[3] Exports are also an issue when dealing with trade agreements and foreign imports by some of America's closest allies, especially Japan, due to the quantities of grain imported by these countries.[4] The United States is the largest grain exporter in the world.[5] Holding such a position in the world market, domestic issues and programs acquire major importance for importers of American grain.

During the 1950's, the United States Congress passed the Agricultural Trade Development and Assistance Act of 1954, which has become known as P.L. 480.[6] The Act provides for food assistance on cash or credit terms to nations in need. There are also provisions for emergency

From *Case Western Reserve Journal International Law,* Volume 10, Number 3, Summer 1978, pages 739-760. 10 Case W. Res. J. Int'l L. 739 (1978). Reprinted by permission.

aid when nations are faced with extraordinary needs or natural disasters.

The recent actions of American government officials have come under attack as manifesting the exercise of too much discretion.[7] This criticism and the current dissent voiced by American producers calls for a major reevaluation of American farm policy and foreign trade. This paper shall consider these factors and the continued viability of P.L. 480. As a part of American farm policy, P.L. 480 must be evaluated in the context of world population, exports and imports, and the needs of American producers. With more food needed to feed more people, the economic vitality of food producers is imperative. The price paid by American customers for food must be part of any economic formula of farm policy. As the breadbasket for the world, the United States has a moral obligation to prevent the starvation of millions of fellow inhabitants of this planet. In an age of increasing interdependence of nations, a total view of world markets is necessary for the study and evaluation of agricultural legislation. These factors shall be considered in the context of P.L. 480.

I. PUBLIC LAW 480

The Agricultural Trade Development and Assistance Act of 1954[8] (P.L. 480) authorizes the President to expand current international trade, to develop new foreign markets, to increase domestic productivity, to combat hunger and malnutrition with emphasis on improving agricultural techniques, and generally to promote the foreign policy of the United States.[9] Title I of the Act authorizes the sale of agricultural goods for cash or credit to friendly countries.[10] A friendly country is defined as one which is not Communist or controlled by a world Communist movement, or is not an aggressor against countries which have diplomatic relations with the United States.[11] Further, assistance can be provided to friendly countries to resist Communist domination.[12] In exercising his authority under Title I, the President is charged to consider efforts by nations to improve their agriculture, to reduce population growth, to take precautions not to greatly disrupt world prices or trade, and to achieve terms favorable to the United States.[13] The largest recipient of Title I aid for 1974 was East Asia (Vietnam and Cambodia) followed by the Near East (Israel) and South Asia (Pakistan and Bangladesh).[14]

The humanitarian slant of P.L. 480 becomes more apparent under Title II. Under that title, the President is authorized to make aid available to meet extraordinary relief needs, such as famine. One million tons of food aid is to be distributed through nonprofit agencies and the world food program.[15] Efforts are to be made to encourage other nations to contribute to world food programs and to aid in the alleviation of emergency situations.[16]

Titles III and IV are minor provisions of P.L. 480. Title III empowers the Secretary of Agriculture to exchange commodities for goods used in other foreign assistance programs or for goods not sufficiently produced to meet domestic demands.[17] Under Title IV, the Secretary is prevented from using agricultural products for P.L. 480 programs if domestic supplies fall below demand.[18] This section of Title IV has never been used. To promote the national interest of the United States, the President shall seek to increase farmer to farmer contacts, to increase available commodity research and educational opportunities, and to seek the establishment of an agricultural reserve system to meet world emergencies.[19]

P.L. 480 was due to terminate at the end of 1977. The United States Congress, by amending P.L. 480, has extended its provisions for an additional four years.[20] Congress, by amending the legislation, has made the determination that P.L. 480 is still valid in the 1970's. However, since its original enactment in 1954, many factors affecting American agricultural policy have changed. In light of these changes, P.L. 480 must be compared with the current world situation.

II. EXISTING WORLD MARKETS

A. Historical Perspective

The present world population of four billion is expected to double early in the next century.[21] An increase in population means a greater demand for food, especially in those nations with the highest rates of population growth. This is important to exporters of grain, such as the United States, in regard to production, price structure, selection of importers, and communication between the developed and undeveloped nations.

The United States has been a net exporter of agricultural products throughout its history, but the "North American Breadbasket" has become increasingly important in recent years. The United States is responsible for thirty-five percent of world wheat exports since World War II, seventy-five percent of soybean exports since 1949, and has been the largest exporter of feed grains since 1951.[22] The developed countries have served as the major markets for American grain exports.[23] Among the Third World countries, there are importers which are hard-pressed to buy the necessary foodstuffs, while other nations are readily able to pay for what they import.[24] The major competitors for these wheat markets are Canada and Australia.[25] In 1976, the United States, Canada, and Australia supplied seventy-three percent of the world import needs for wheat.[26] The dominant American position in agriculture is even greater in the area of feed grains, with Argentina and Western Europe being the closest competitors.[27] Brazil, the most significant Third World exporter,[28] and the People's Republic of China are America's major competitors for soybean products.[29]

It is possible to speculate that three countries, the United States, Canada, and Australia, could form a food cartel, as they control sizable portions of food exports. There are three situations, however, which make such a possibility unlikely. First, none of the countries has made an effort in this direction. Such an initiative would have to include the United States because of its dominant position in this area, although the United States alone does not have sufficient control of the world market to alter prices at will. Second, the countries that would suffer the most serious impact are those of the Third World, already hard-pressed to purchase grain. Strained political relations between the cartel members and purchasers of grain would almost certainly result. Finally, the major American customers are Japan and Western Europe, both able to afford higher prices, but they are also importers of American non-agricultural products as well as exporters of finished products to the United States. The major importers of American wheat are Asian countries (especially Japan) and Latin American nations; Japan and Western Europe are the largest soybean importers.[30] The European Economic Community (EEC) and Japan are the largest importers of feed grains, but within the last five years, the Soviet Union has entered the American market and has made very significant purchases.[31]

Several of the developed countries have taken measures to reduce their dependence on grain imports from the United States. Member nations of the EEC have replaced soybeans with lowfat dry milk as a feed supplement and the United States has alleged that this is a violation of the General Agreement on Tariffs and Trade.[32] The Japanese have made plans to buy American grain when available in order to buffer against price fluctuations. In 1975, the United States assured Japan of top priority access to American crops.[33] The Soviet Union, for the period 1976-80, plans to reduce expansion of livestock production and to increase grain production.[34] These three examples, in several of the major American markets, demonstrate the potential economic effects on both sides if a cartel is formed. A reduction in agricultural trade, trade protectionism, and a trading war may result in the event a cartel is formed.[35]

It has been anticipated that the United States role as exporter will continue as the dependence of lower income countries on American exports increases.[36] Since the mid-1950's, agricultural production by the Third World countries has increased by fifty percent, but rapidly expanding populations will eliminate any gain in production.[37] Among the developed countries, the People's Republic of China recently has turned to the United States for grain imports.[38] There also has been an increasing demand for meat, which incorporates a large consumption of cereal. This relationship is shown dramatically in the case of the Soviet Union when livestock production programs, initiated in the late 1960's, led to purchases of American grain in the 1970's.[39]

All of these events have increased the value of exports. For 1974, these exports amounted to $21 billion.[40] However, despite the growing volume of agricultural commodities, the quantity of products going to food aid programs, specifically through P.L. 480 programs, has decreased dramatically to levels near those of 1954, the year P.L. 480 was enacted.[41] The average value of P.L. 480 programs has stabilized near $1 billion, peaking between 1960-64, but by 1974, the value of the aid was at its lowest point since enactment. The aid has been increased since 1974, by recent estimates, to near its previous level of $1 billion.[42]

Funding for Title I programs generally is three to five times that of Title II. The decrease in funding in the early 1970's was a result of a decrease in Title I funding while funds available for Title II programs have been steadily increasing since 1954.[43]

The most important agricultural product used in P.L. 480 is wheat. Wheat is generally used for direct human consumption while feed grains are fed to another animal before human consumption. A total of 187 million metric tons of wheat has been shipped under P.L. 480 and the present annual aid averages at 4.3 million tons. Feed grain shipments have been reduced to an annual average of 0.4 million metric tons. Other products shipped under P.O. 480 total 34.7 million tons. Almost all of the above grain has been shipped under Title I.[44]

Worldwide production of grain has been increasing over the past twenty years. Increased demand would lead to an increased supply when possible. Implementation of modern farming techniques by less developed countries and exposure to new agricultural ideas may lead to an increase in production by Third World countries. The advancement of technology, increased production, irrigation of once under productive or barren land, and introduction of new types of hybrid grains have all contributed to better harvests and the availability of more grain for export. Still, despite all of the advances and increases in grain production, the world food situation is at a precarious stage. Many of the developed countries of Western Europe and Asia have come to realize the importance of controlled population and their economic structure has allowed them to control their rate of growth. Countries, like those of OPEC, have the technological knowledge or the ability to purchase the necessary technology, information, and equipment to feed their populations. These countries are also in a position to be able to afford gradual increases in the price of foodstuffs although a sharp increase in the prices may create havoc in the international economic structure.

At the other end of the economic scale, there are many countries which are poor due to a lack of marketable resources or because their population consumes more than the country can produce. Many of these countries have no means of feeding themselves without massive foreign aid. The key to any planned program of food consumption must be birth control. This is one of the stated purposes of P.L. 480,[45] but such efforts may be frustrated by centuries-old social and religious beliefs.

It is also clear that the food aid programs are endangered by a number of factors. The Soviet Union has bought grain from the United States in recent years and it is possible that such purchases will increase if the Soviets attempt to expand livestock production beyond their own grain supply. The People's Republic of China is also interested in foreign grain purchases. The possible entrance of this huge market may greatly decrease the amount of grain available for food aid programs.[46] In addition, other measures taken by some of the developed countries may reduce their demand for American imports and make available grain for food aid programs or for export to other markets.[47]

B. Recent Foreign Influence

The dominant position of the United States has been demonstrated in wheat, feed grains, and soybeans. This position allows for the exertion of a strong influence on world markets and subjects American products to market price fluctuations.

Many of the lesser developed nations are able to satisfy their needs by trade with the United States in years of low production. Such demands are often unreliable in terms of long range planning and, separately, the requirements of such nations are small and can be met by government programs, such as P.L. 480. The developed countries are more likely to engage in long term planning and consequently their needs are more predictable. The requirements of large-scale livestock production and the funds available for storage facilities allow for this predictability. Because developed nations with industrial economies are the largest purchasers of American agricultural products, they often exercise the strongest influence on the American, as well as the world, market.

It was predicted in the fall of 1977 that on a worldwide basis, many good harvests were expected for 1977. Such harvests would mean a lowering of grain imports and, in some cases, an increase in grain for export. However, several countries were expected to import American grain, including the Soviet Union, Italy, Japan and other Asian countries which have been steady American customers.[48] For 1977, Japan was expected to have a better than average harvest with general production up five to six percent.[49] However, the future may not be as bright as these figures indicate. The United States has expressed concern about a Japanese trade surplus, half of which is a result of trade with the United

States.[50] A dispute arose between the two countries and as a result of negotiations a trade pact was announced in early January of 1978. Japan agreed to undertake efforts to reduce an $8.5 billion trade surplus beginning in April 1979 and to allow more imports of American agricultural products.[51] When asked in an interview what was the greatest economic problem for Japan, the Minister for External Economic Affairs and chief Japanese negotiator of the trade agreement, Nobuhiko Ushiba replied:

> Of course, agriculture. Our agriculture is really in a difficult situation because we have an accumulated rice surplus of nearly 4 million tons, and we have been pushing farmers to switch to livestock or other crops such as fruit. If we open up the country to a flood of oranges and beef—as the U.S. demands—our farmers would lose confidence in our agricultural policy, which could be fatal to the rule of the pro-American, free trade Liberal Democratic Party.[52]

Although the agricultural concessions made by the Japanese will have little impact on American producers, it has been viewed as a willingness on the part of the Japanese to cut back on exports and increase imports, contrary to traditional Japanese trade policy. It is hoped that by 1980 the Japanese trade surplus will be reduced to zero.[53]

The American response to the Japanese trade surplus may be repeated in dealings with other countries which have a favorable balance of trade with the United States. There have been no indications of this coming about but if trade protectionism is the current mood of Congress and the Administration, an increase in agricultural exports may be in store.

In Western Europe, Britain and Italy enjoyed record harvests while French and German production also increased.[54] The excellent harvest could mean a decrease in the demand for grain imports from the United States. Members of the EEC had begun plans in 1976 to decrease American grain imports by replacing soybeans with dry milk in feed grains. The expected result of this plan is the eventual reduction of soybean imports by 300,000 to 400,000 tons with an estimated damage of $136 million to American producers.[55] A resolution was introduced in the House of Representatives, co-sponsored by forty-two representatives, to seek elimination of the EEC practices and to seek compensation for injuries under Article 23 of the General Agreement on Tariffs and Trade.[56]

For Asia, 1977 was a mixed year. The Japanese expected a better than average harvest but agreed with the United States to allow more agricultural imports, as discussed above. South Korea, Taiwan, and India were expected to have good harvests.[57] For 1978, it is expected that India will have a record crop due to favorable weather and improved technology,[58] but India's storage facilities will be inadequate to meet the demand imposed by this output. The World Bank, the United States, Canada, and Australia plan to aid India in creating storage facilities.[59] It has been reported that there is a possibility that Bangladesh could become self-sufficient by 1985.[60]

The People's Republic of China generally does not purchase American grain, but rather imports from Canada and Australia which recognize the Peking government as the legitimate government of China.[61] However, Peking has turned to the United States at times in order to obtain immediate delivery. In March and November of 1977, the Chinese purchased American soybeans after experiencing delivery problems with Brazil.[62]

As a whole, the Asian market has been and will continue to be an attractive market for the American producer. Sales of wheat to Asia have averaged $900 million a year with annual increases of five to twenty percent expected for several years.

C. Soviet Grain Purchases

The Soviet Union is a major example of a market which has become available to American producers in the 1970's. In part, the increase in Soviet demand has been created by expanding consumption rates and a decreased supply in years of smaller than expected harvests.

For 1976, the Soviet Union had a record grain harvest of 223.8 million tons. The harvest for 1977 had been predicted to reach 215 milion tons but bad weather before and during the harvest resulted in a revision to 194 million tons, the fourth largest ever, but far below that of 1976.[64] The Soviets turned to the West to make up the difference. Under a 1975 trade agreement, Moscow was required to purchase six million tons of American grain, and if the needed grain should rise above eight million tons, Washington was to be informed. However, the Agriculture Department and the Central Intelligence Agency (CIA) had forecast the Soviet harvest at 215 million tons. When Soviet President Leonid Brezhnev announced that the Soviet harvest would be less than expected in November of 1977, the statement took both American agencies by surprise. The Soviets would be required to buy ten to fifteen million tons more than expected.[65] To complicate the situation, much of the grain required by the Soviet Union had already been purchased. During the summer and fall of 1977, grain prices were depressed in the United States. The Soviets then purchased large amounts from European subsidiaries of American companies and other traders.[66] The Soviets had been able to exploit a loophole in the Soviet-American trade agreement by the use of orders of "optional origin grain."[67] In early October, a Soviet trade delegation had come to the United States and was offered the right to purchase up to fifteen million tons of grain in order to reduce American surpluses.[68] By November 2, the date of Mr. Brezhnev's announcement, the Soviets had contracts for eighteen to twenty million tons from Australia, Canada, India, and the United States.[69]

There had been several signs that the Soviets were making grain purchases. In July, the Soviets were contracting for ships to carry grain and in an effort to keep secret this intention, the bills of lading were altered at sea in order to disguise the ultimate destination of the ships. World freight rates climbed by fifteen percent and in October, Chicago commodity traders had heard of Soviet purchases, and American wheat and corn prices moved slightly upward from August to October. Through this process, the Soviets were able to save $100 million.[70]

Despite the Soviet savings, the American producer may be able to recoup part of the lost revenue. The Soviet purchases have reduced surpluses and have helped to raise prices.[71] The Soviets are expected to purchase another fifteen million tons of grain, which they had contracted for in November.[72] Other major exporters have sold most of their available grain for export leaving the United States as the only exporter with large supplies on hand.[73] If the Chinese or another importer should need sizable imports they would have to buy from the United States.[74]

A crisis, like those of 1973 and 1975, was averted due to record harvests and the resulting low prices.[75] The CIA and the Department of AGriculture were blamed for faulty intelligence gathering and the possible grain shortages which could have resulted.[76] Secretary of Agriculture, Bob Bergland, attempted to explain the inaccurate forecasts of Soviet production as due to conflicting reports.[77]

The reasons for the Soviet grain purchases are multiple. Since 1971, the Soviet Union, historically an exporter, has become a net importer.[78] The 1977 Soviet production figures were the result of bad weather.[79] The 1973 soybean embargo had its beginnings in the fall of 1972, when world demand for soybeans was high, and in February of 1973, when the dollar was devalued for a second time.[80] The Chicago Board of Trade limited the trading of soybean futures on June 22, 1973.[81] Secretary of Commerce, Frederick Dent, and Secretary of Agriculture, Earl Butz, imposed an embargo on soybean exports when faced with an insufficient supply for domestic use and anticipated exports, on June 27,[82] but this was replaced on July 2 with an export licensing control.[83] In June, soybean prices had been high but at the time the export controls were lifted, on September 21, the price had fallen.[84]

In 1975, the Soviets turned to the West again when June production figures were revised downward,[85] which continued until it was announced that Soviet grain production would total only 170 million tons.[86] On August 11, 1975, the Secretary of AGriculture requested export dealers to suspend sales to the Soviets until grain figures were available.[87] In response to possible domestic food price increases, the maritime unions on the Atlantic Coast, the Gulf of Mexico, and the Great Lakes refused to load Soviet grain.[88] The situation was relieved by record wheat and corn harvests.[89] Negotiations between the United States and the Soviet Union culminated in a five year grain agreement and an end to the sales restraints.[90] Under this agreement the Soviet Union agreed to purchase six million metric tons of wheat and corn annually for five years. They could also purchase another two million tons without government consultation, but if purchases should exceed eight million tons, consultation with the United States Government would be required. The United States is allowed to restrict Soviet purchases to less than six million tons if American grain production should fall below 225 million tons in any year.[91]

The Soviet Union has had to turn to the West in order to meet demand created by domestic consumption and increased livestock production. Further, there are significant political ramifications tied to poor Soviet harvests.

> The Soviets have already moved into marginal and submarginal areas for the grain production to meet commitments they have made to their people to upgrade the Russian diet, by increasing the percentage of protein in the form of meat.
> This has created a condition in which they will be inevitably dependent upon foreign sources. Where they have been exporting up to 8 million tons of grain a year to Eastern Europe, that is phasing out rapidly and Eastern Europe is now looking to us for their supplemental grain requirements.[92]

The Nixon and Ford administrations came under heavy pressure for the actions taken in 1973 and 1975. During 1975 and 1976, several bills were introduced in the Senate to curtail government export restrictions and to prevent actions to seek the "voluntary restraint" of exports.[93] Mr. Rueben Johnson, then Director of Legislative Services of the National Farmers Union, testified before the House International Relations Committee in 1976, stating:

> In 1973 and in 1974 and again in 1975 the Government has intervened and is now interfering to prevent farmers from selling their crops freely.
> Because this was done without any guidelines, without any link to a policy of food abundance, this has been the worst possible form of export control. It has exposed farmers, American consumers, and our export consumers alike to the capricious, irresponsible, and incompetent whim of politicians in the executive branch, acting unpredictably and arbitrarily under the pressures, the hysteria, and the political motives of the moment.[94]

Counsel for the National Association of Wheat Growers felt that there was a possibility that President Ford had acted unconstitutionally in seeking voluntary restraints of trade and that there may have been antitrust violations by the grain companies which went along with the voluntary restraints.[95] Mr. Tony Denchant, President of the National Farmers

Union and President of the International Federation of Agriculture Producers, felt that the trade limitations of 1975 had reduced American crop values by $2 million.[96]

The Ford administration took the position that the trade controls were necessary to protect American markets.

> As a major exporter of raw materials, we wish to improve our access to other countries' markets for our exports and convince other countries that we are a dependable supplier. Excessively volatile price fluctuations are a matter of concern both to the developing and to the developed countries.[97]

The examples of 1973 and 1975 show that there is the potential for *raiding* American supplies by foreign purchasers. In years of high demand, inadequate supplies could result in prices which only developed countries could afford, proving disastrous to undeveloped nations. Demand for grain will increase as animal production and increased populations place greater strains on anticipated grain production. To avoid worldwide disaster, supplies must be maintained and increased.

III. DISSENT AMONG AMERICAN PRODUCERS

Despite what may appear as a bright future for grain exporters, American producers have not been able to reap the maximum benefits from the productivity. The plight facing American farmers has reached a crisis stage for some. Prices for their products have come down in recent years so that income from farming has reached a forty year low. At the same time, expenses for seed, labor, and fertilizer have been steadily increasing.[98] Net farm income has fallen from an average of $9950 in 1973 to $5300 in 1977.[99] The total net farm income has also fallen between the years 1973 and 1975.[100] Many foreclosures have been prevented only by the rising value of land. Based on what has been on what has been paid for farm land, the value has increased by 114% in the last five years. The rise in value may become a thing of the past as a 1.2% decrease in land prices was reported for the third quarter of 1977. Farmers' debt has doubled since 1970, and now exceeds $100 billion.[101]

By way of reaction to these conditions some of the producers banded together calling for a nationwide strike, that began on December 14, 1977, and now plan to continue the strike until they receive 100% of parity.[102] The striking farmers have rallied around an organization called American Agriculture, which claims the support of forty percent of the nation's farmers. This claim may be unfounded as many of the established agricultural groups, such as the American Farm Bureau Federation, and producers of perishable goods, are not taking part.[103] In any event, any increase in parity will certainly be passed on to the consumer.

For 1978, food prices are expected to rise four to six percent but if 100% of parity is achieved, the rise could be by as much as twenty to twenty-five percent.[104]

The Secretary of Agriculture, Bob Bergland, sees the problem as one of overproduction in that the American farmer is producing thirty to forty million tons over market demands.[105] He finds the majority of large producers need no government help and does not intend to give them any.[106] A plan to set aside twenty percent of wheat acreage and ten percent of corn and other feed grains has been established for 1978.[107] Other recommendations have been made to cope with over-production.

> We recommend that supply management programs be voluntary. In order to facilitate crop-acreage changes to meet market demands of the future and to encourage the growing of crops in the most efficient areas for those crops, we recommend that acreage allotments and marketing quotas be made negotiable or transferable. In the case of voluntary programs, the historical bases could be made transferable.[108]

In 1977, Congress passed the Food and Agriculture Act of 1977, amending P.L. 480.[109] There are three basic additions to the legislation. First, items for purchase under Title I are to be advertised so as to provide for public bids. Second, the funding for Title II programs has been increased from $600 million to $750 million. Finally, P.L. 480 has been extended to 1981.[110] The Food and Agriculture Act of 1977 also makes provisions for setting aside acreage for crops, and encourages the President to seek development of an international food reserve.[111] President Carter has acted upon this legislation. In his 1978 State of the Union address, President Carter stated that the United States would propose contributing six million metric tons of food products to the international grain reserve.[112]

IV. P.L. 480 IN PERSPECTIVE

Countries which historically have been exporters, such as the Soviet Union, and countries which have been reluctant to seek imports, like China, have increasingly turned to exporters, especially the United States, to meet their needs. Some nations have been able to overcome large imports and have begun to export grain, but in the case of India, the most notable example, this situation may be short-lived if the weather does not cooperate. The demands of the Third World countries have been met by aid from the developed countries, through P.L. 480, and more recently through the establishment of the International Grain Reserve.

The balance between world agricultural supply and demand and the delicacy of this balance was brought home to American producers, consumers, and government officials in 1973 and 1975. It has already been predicted that between 1980 and 1985 food aid needs will exceed the availability of American grain to meet those needs.[113] If this does come about, it will leave exporters with two basic choices, increase the amount of food available through food aid programs, or leave those nations dependent on food aid to their own resources. To complicate this condition, some scientists have predicted a radical change in weather patterns. Although climatologists warn that the data has been compiled over too short a timespan for concrete conclusions, they feel that the earth is warming up.[114] The destruction of forests on a worldwide basis may also be reponsible for the increase of carbon dioxide in the atmosphere.[115]

In light of future expectations of world demand, policy decisions may have to be made regarding the amount and type of food aid that will be provided to lesser developed countries. The International Grain Reserve appears to duplicate the functions of Title II of P.L. 480. A worldwide effort of contributing to this reserve and the sharing of its products may prove to be the most effective means of distributing food aid from the United States. The United States, as the world's largest exporter, should take the lead in this development and should be one of the largest contributors to the reserve, as should be other nations with sizable exports.

As the International Grain Reserve duplicates much of the Title II programs, Title II may no longer be necessary. Part of the purpose of P.L. 480 is to serve humanitarian goals and to promote the foreign policy of the United States. A program under international control, by chance or the influence of the United States, may achieve the same ends, but the furtherance of American foreign policy goals cannot be guaranteed. This would seem to be the sole justification for continuing Title II programs rather than increasing contributions to the grain reserve.

The grain that was originally earmarked for Title II could be included in the contribution destined for the grain reserve. Before the 1977 amendments to P.L. 480, the President was authorized to make available, under Title II, a minimum of 1.3 million tons or $600 million annually in aid.[116] President Carter's proposal calls for a contribution of six million tons to the International Grain Reserve.[117] For the period 1955 to 1977, the average annual aid donated under Title II was 1.9 million tons.[118] In 1962, 2.9 million tons was exported under Title II, the single largest aid package in one year.[119]

The appropriation of a minimum of $750 million for Title II programs, increased in 1977, can be used for other purposes. Any nation which imports or produces grain must have storage facilities until the food is ready for distribution or consumption. If the grain is not properly stored, it could rot or spoil before distribution. Aid from the United States and other countries, and loans from international financing institutions, such as the World Bank, could provide the necessary funds.

The construction of storage facilities may produce the added benefit of grain purchases from exporters when there are surpluses and lower prices. In addition, funds made available through Title II could be used to curtail birth rates. The funds could be put to use in distributing birth control information adaptable to the customs and religious beliefs of the native culture.

Inherent in programs similar to P.L. 480 is the economic effect on local markets. These programs introduce foodstuffs at a time when supply is low. This basically has the same effect as a good harvest for the recipient country. Local producers thus receive lower prices for their product at times of high demand. The effect will be to further increase the dependence of the recipient country on American grain, thus increasing the market for American producers, but devastating to the local farmers. Emphasis on agreements running over a period of years, rather than the current annual basis, creates more certainty and predictability for recognizing demand in years of less than favorable harvests by providing a minimal level of requirements and the ability to meet obligations and needs in other markets.

Unreliability of supplies can also harm American markets in developed countries. In a year of short supply, the United States could hardly turn its back on those countries dependent on American grain in favor of more profitable markets. If the United States is unable to meet the needs of the developed countries, they will turn to another, more reliable supplier. Despite the importance of the above considerations, primary emphasis should still be given to the American producer and consumer. Under long-term supply contracts, which the American producer can rely on to predict demand, he will be able to produce according to this demand and to avoid surpluses and depression of the farm market.

Any government program to aid the American producer, whether in the form of a direct subsidy or through manipulation of natural market forces to decrease the supply in times of overproduction, will increase food prices. Controlling production by forecasting demand can ease the consumer burden, while allowing for steady increases in prices for the producers.

In light of the extensive Soviet purchases, the requirement of P.L. 480, that the recipient country be classified as a friendly and non-communist nation, no longer seems to be valid. The Chinese have attached part of the past to their trade dealings with the West, but faced with the realities of food supply, even they have turned to the United States. Because of these realities, the Chinese may be the next market to open up for the American producer. With a population of nearly one billion people, the People's Republic of China has the potential of becoming one of the world's largest markets for grain and foodstuffs. The Chinese have placed conditions on the establishment of large scale trade relations with the United States, principally the recognition of the Peking Government.

A major responsibility for the distribution of information to the producers must fall with the major agricultural organizations. They can prove invaluable inproviding information of expected foreign and domestic demand. Such information will enable sole producers and producer cooperatives to plant accordingly, allowing for some surplus to meet higher demand and compensate for future years when production is low or demand is high.

Continued expansion of demand for American agricultural products is inevitable in light of world consumption and population factors. Population growth, increased livestock production, and diversification of diets all mean a greater demand for foodstuffs and grain. The Soviet Union is one example of a nation expanding one segment of their agricultural economy while another segment is unable to provide the needed supply. Lesser developed countries suffer from rapidly expanding populations and already inadequate food supplies. All of these factors are placing increased demand on producer nations.

The type of aid that may prove most effective in the long run is that which is designed to increase production in recipient countries. The providing of food to nations which production near demand may have the effect of depressing the local agricultural markets and discouraging increased production due to lower prices. The effect may be the dumping of surplus American grain in these countries and the perpetuation of a market for imports. Aid in the form of information, seed, and machinery can encourage nations to become self-sufficient for their food needs.

The Carter administration has indicated that it is interested in changing the approach of the United States to food aid programs, aiding those countries most seriously affected by food shortages. The Carter approach is basically three pronged: (1) to increase the aid provided by private organizations and participation by a larger number of organizations; (2) to increase congressional funding for government agencies that are providing food aid; and (3) to seek greater coordination with agencies of the United Nations in aiding countries to increase production.[120] This proposal begins to solve a complex problem but it is only a start. A comprehensive evaluation of all phases of agriculture may be necessary. Coordination between foreign exports and domestic production is needed to insure supplies and to meet demand in the future. An economically advantageous climate must be established for American farmers to operate in, and to profit from their labors. At the same time, market prices must be such that the farmers can profit and foreign purchasers, especially undeveloped nations, can readily purchase the commodities produced.

V. CONCLUSION

The outlook for American agriculture is economically good while the world situation is facing grave pressures. All efforts must be made to insure the continued viability of American agriculture as a valued source of foreign exchange, to balance American imports, to provide a livelihood for those involved in American agriculture, and to promote the foreign policy of the United States.

It is not inconceivable that at some point within this century millions could starve. It is even possible that there will be food available but insufficient granary facilities would make necessary the storage of grain in the open, subject to natural elements. Thus, P.L. 480 is an important program for achieving the stated purposes of American agriculture and the Carter plans for food aid. Its importance surely will increase within the next decade as the world's food deficiency becomes more apparent and American production of grain becomes more essential.

---

[1] T. MALTHUS, FIRST ESSAY ON POPULATION 25 (A. Kelley, ed., 1965).

[2] *The Tractor Rebellion,* NEWSWEEK, Dec. 19, 1977, at 57.

[3] N.Y. Times, Jan. 31, 1978, at 1, col. 1.

[4] *Use of U.S. Food Resources for Diplomatic Purposes—An Examination of the Issues: Hearings Before the House Comm. on International Relations,* 94th Cong., 2d Sess. 79, 81 (1977) [hereinafter cited as *Food Resources*].

[5] *Id.* at 74.

[6] Agricultural Trade Development and Assistance Act of 1954, as amended by 7 U.S.C. §§ 1691-1736 (1976) [hereinafter cited as P.L. 480].

[7] S. 950, 94th Cong., 1st Sess. (1975); S. 2739, 94th Cong., 1st Sess. (1975); S. 2993, 94th Cong., 2d Sess. (1976).

[8] P.L. 480, as amended by Food and Agriculture Act of 1977, Pub. L. No. 95-113, 91 Stat. 913 (1977) [hereinafter amendment cited as Food and Agriculture Act].

[9] P.L. 480, § 2. To enforce these provisions, special emphasis is to be given to nations with serious food shortages. Domestic price and supply situations are to be taken into account in determining the commodities exported.

[10] *Id.* § 101. This requirement is evidence of the legislative purpose when the legislation was enacted, at the height of the Cold War.

[11] *Id.* §§ 102, 103(d). Cuba and Vietnam are specifically excluded from Title I programs. The United Arab Republic is excluded unless inclusion would be in the national interest. The President can waive any of these exclusions if it is determined to be in the national interest. Egypt is presently receiving large shipments of grain under Title I.

[12] *Id.* § 103(j).

[13] *Id.* §§ 103(a), 106(a). Section 111 places restrictions on sales to countries with *per capita* gross national product in excess of $300. The President also may provide emergency assistance worth up to $5 million. *Id.* § 104(d).

¹⁴*American Foreign Food Assistance: Public Law 480 and Related Materials: Hearings Before the Senate Comm. on Agricultural and Forestry,* 94th Cong., 2d Sess. 37-41 (1976) [hereinafter cited as *American Foreign Food Assistance*]. Only estimates of 1975 and 1976 aid were available but the pattern of 1974 continued. The only major difference was an increase in aid to Latin America. Under the 1974 Title II programs, the principal recipients were India, Morocco, Columbia, Brazil, Mali, Niger, Sudan, and Tanzania.

¹⁵P.L. 480, §§ 201(a),(b), 204. The aid ceiling was increased from $600 million to $750 million in 1977. President Carter has also expressed interest in contributing more aid through the World Food Program in 1978.

¹⁶*Id.* § 205.

¹⁷*Id.* § 303.

¹⁸*Id.* § 401. Tobacco and alcoholic beverages are excluded from P.L. 480 regulations. *Id.* § 402.

¹⁹*Id.* §§ 404, 406(a), 412. It is this reserve system which President Carter plans to encourage under a world food program.

²⁰Food and Agriculture Act, *supra* note 8.

²¹T. FEJKA, THE FUTURE OF POPULATION GROWTH 192 (1973).

²²*Food Resources, supra* note 4, at 79, 81. The United States has supplied 50% of world feed grain exports since 1973.

²³*Id.* at 8, 9, 11. Japan is the single largest export market. Western Europe also imports a sizable portion of American grain. Japan imports 90% of its soybeans, 70% of its feed grains, and 67% of its wheat from the United States. Western Europe imported 25% of the total American agricultural exports in 1975.

²⁴*Id.* at 18. The OPEC nations, South Korea, and Taiwan have economies which allow for sizable imports, while Bangladesh and the Philippines are unable, at times, to purchase the necessary food. India has begun to export grain in recent years due to good rains.

²⁵*Id.* at 19, 74. Since 1951, the United States has supplied 35% of wheat exports; Canada, 23%; Australia, 10%; Western Europe, 10%; the Soviet Union, 8%; and Argentina, 5%. These same countries produce 50% of the world's wheat. South Africa, Thailand, Argentina, Western Europe, Canada, and Australia produce 17% of the world's feed grains and supply 33% of the exports.

²⁶*Id.* at 74.

²⁷*Id.* at 80. Since 1951, the United States has exported an average of 42% of world exports, 48% since 1970. Since 1951, Argentina has contributed 11% of world exports, Western Europe, 10%.

²⁸*Id.* at 18. Brazil supplies 20% of world's soybean exports. Other grain exporters include Kenya, Rhodesia, Thailand, Burma, and Mexico.

²⁹*Id.* at 19, 74. Brazil and China did have difficulties in 1977, resulting in China purchasing grain from the United States.

³⁰U.S. DEPT OF COMMERCE, BUREAU OF CENSUS, FOREIGN TRADE DIVISION, UNITED STATES EXPORTS, 1976, at 30 (1977).

³¹*Food Resources, supra* note 4, at 81.

³²*Id.* at 16.

³³*Id.*

[34]*Id.*

[35]*Id.* at 77.

[36]Schertz, *World Food: Prices and the Poor,* 52 FOREIGN AFF. 511, 518 (1974).

[37]*Id.* at 515.

[38]*Id.* at 526.

[39]*Id.* at 513-14.

[40]*Id.* at 511. *Food Resources, supra* note 4, at 77. The average annual value of American exports for 1967-72 was $6.7 billion; for 1972, $9.4 billion; and for 1973, $18 billion.

[41]*Food Resources, supra* note 4, at 76. For 1965 to 1959, the average value of wheat exports was $701 million with $489 million, or 68.6% of total wheat exports going to food aid programs. For 1970 to 1974, only 24.8% of wheat exports was earmarked for food aid, or $340 million.

During 1955 to 1959, 22.5%, or $104 million, of feed grain exports went to food aid programs, but this has dropped to only 4.8% or $80 million for 1970 to 74.

This proportion of total soybean exports that is devoted to food aid has decreased from 85% in 1955 to 1959 to 49% for 1970 to 1974.

[42]*American Foreign Food Assistance, supra* note 14, at 33.

[43]*Id.*

[44]*Id.* at 34-36. At the height of P.L. 480 programs an annual average of 12.5 million tons of wheat and 2.5 million tons of feed grains was shipped. Total feed grain exports has been 44.3 million metric tons.

Of the total amount of P.L. 480 aid, 159 million metric tons of wheat, 34.7 million tons of feed grains, and 25.9 million tons of other grains were shipped through Title I. Title II programs have totaled 27.7 million tons of wheat, 9.6 million tons of feed grains, and 8.8 million tons of other grains have been transported. These other grains include rice, vegetable oil, and nonfat dry milk.

[45]P.L. 480.

[46]Schertz, *supra* note 36, at 513-14.

[47]*Food Resources, supra* note 4, at 16.

[48]U.S. NEWS & WORLD REPORT, Nov. 21, 1977, at 57.

[49]*Id.* Rice production was expected to be up 10%, fruit up 6%, and vegetables near normal.

[50]*Japan Agrees to Slice the Surplus,* TIME, Jan. 23, 1978, at 63.

[51]Chicago Tribune, Jan. 13, 1978, at 1, col. 3. These include beef and citrus products.

[52]*Ushiba: Maneuvering Room,* NEWSWEEK, Jan. 9, 1978, at 32.

[53]TIME, *supra* note 50.

[54]U.S. NEWS & WORLD REPORT, *supra* note 48.

[55]*ECC Imports Deposits on Vegetable Protein Products: Hearings Before the House Comm. on Agriculture, Sub-Comm. on Oilseeds and Rice,* 94th Cong., 2d Sess. 2 (1976).

[56]H.R. Con. Res. 60, 94th Cong., 2d Sess. (1976).

[57]U.S. NEWS & WORLD REPORT, *supra* note 48.

[58]N.Y. Times, Oct. 30, 1977, at 3, col. 1. The use of hybrid seeds, water

storage and irrigation, and the use of natural fertilizers have contributed to increases of 30% in production in some areas.

[59]U.S. NEWS & WORLD REPORT, Jan. 23, 1978, at 46.

[60]N.Y. Times, Oct. 20, 1977, at 27, col. 1.

[61]U.S. NEWS & WORLD REPORT, Nov. 7, 1977, at 54. N.Y. Times, Nov. 18, 1977, at D2, col. 6. Peking purchased 142 million bushels in March and 900,000 bushels in November.

[62]*Id.* at 53.

[63]N.Y. Times, oct. 30, 1977, at 3, col. 4. Senegal, Gambia, Mauritania, and the Cape Verde Islands had requested 500,000 tons of food. See also N.Y. Times, Nov. 17, 1977, at D1, col. 1. The Libyans have made overtures to American producers to purchase $60 million of grain. The Libyans have decided to deal directly with producers rather than the United States government because Washington previously had blocked the sale of cargo planes.

[64]U.S. NEWS & WORLD REPORT, *supra* note 48.

[65]*Another Soviet Grain Sting,* TIME, Nov. 28, 1977, at 88. See also U.S. NEWS & WORLD REPORT, *supra* note 48, at 29. The announcement on November 2nd was 10% below the CIA and USDA forecasts and 19 million tons below the Soviet goal.

[66]U.S. NEWS & WORLD REPORT, *supra* note 48, at 29.

[67]N.Y. Times, Nov. 21, 1977, at 53M, col. 5. Normally, exporters know the final destination of the products and thus the United States would have known of the purchases by the Soviet Union but the orders were made in a category known as "optional origin grain," in which the exporter does not know the final destination or plans to fill the order in another country.

[68]U.S. NEWS & WORLD REPORT, *supra* note 48, at 29.

[69]TIME, *supra* note 65.

[70]*Id.* at 89. The destination was altered from Rotterdam to the Soviet Union with trans-shipment by way of Rotterdam.

[71]*Id.*

[72]N.Y. Times, Nov. 21, 1977, at 33M, col. 5; N.Y. Times, Nov. 18, 1977, at D2, col. 6.

[73]TIME, *supra* note 65.

[74]*Id.*

[75]*Why Farmers Are Up in Arms,* U.S. NEWS & WORLD REPORT, Oct. 31, 1977, at 60.

[76]Safire, *Against the Grain,* N.Y. Times, Nov. 10, 1977, at 37, col. 3. William Safire questioned the ability of the CIA, in light of the inaccurate information, to be able to provide the necessary intelligence needed during a military crisis.

[77]U.S. NEWS & WORLD REPORT, *supra* note 75. The reports were based on satellite photos and actual observation.

[78]*Id.*

[79]*Id.* Weather conditions included a mid-summer drought and heavy rains at harvest time.

[80]N.Y. Times, Feb. 13, 1973, at 1, col. 8. The devaluation of the dollar made American products more attractive to foreign purchasers.

[81]N.Y. Times, June 22, 1973, at 43, col. 8.

[82]N.Y. Times, June 28, 1973, at 1, col. 3.

[83]N.Y. Times, July 3, 1973, at 31, col. 5.

[84]N.Y. Times, Sept. 22, 1973, at 39, col. 5.

[85]N.Y. Times, June 11, 1975, at 73, col. 4. The USDA revised the Soviet harvest figures downward, from 210 million to 200 million tons.

[86]N.Y. Times, Oct. 6, 1975, at 32, col. 5. This figure was 45 million tons short of the Soviet goal.

[87]N.Y. Times, Aug. 12, 1975, at 1, col. 6.

[88]N.Y. Times, Aug. 19, 1975, at 1, col. 5.

[89]N.Y. Times, Oct. 11, 1975, at 1, col. 5.

[90]N.Y. Times, Oct. 21, 1975, at 1, col. 1.

[91]*Grain Sales to Russia: Hearings Before the House Comm. on Agriculture,* 94th Cong., 1st Sess. 2 (1975) (Statement of Undersecretary of State for Economic Affairs, Charles Robinson).

[92]*Id.* at 8.

[93]S. 950, 94th Cong., 1st Sess. (1975); S. 2739, 94th Cong., 1st Sess. (1975); S. 2993, 94th Cong., 2d Sess. (1976).

[94]*Extension of the Export Administration Act of 1969: Hearings Before the House Comm. on International Relations,* 94th Cong., 2d Sess. 269 (1976) (Statement of the Director of Legislative Services, National Farmers Union, Rueben Johnson).

[95]*United States Foreign Trade Policy: Hearings Before the Senate Comm. on Finance,* 94th Cong., 2d Sess. at 286-87 (1976).

[96]*Id.* at 304.

[97]*Id.* at 72.

[98]U.S. NEWS & WORLD REPORT, Dec. 26, 1977, at 69.

[99]*The Tractor Rebellion,* NEWSWEEK, Dec. 19, 1977, at 57.

[100]N.Y. Times, oct. 13, 1977, at D1, col. 4. Total farm income for 1973 was $29.9 billion, a record year. For 1977, farm income totaled $20.1 billion; for 1976, $21.9 billion.

[101]U.S. NEWS & WORLD REPORT, *supra* note 98.

[102]N.Y. Times, Oct. 3, 1977, at 18, col. 1. For a discussion of parity, see *supra* note 98, at 70. Basically, parity is giving the farmer the same purchasing power for his crop as that of the period 1910 to 1914. In the fall of 1977, farmers were receiving 66% of parity.

[103]U.S. NEWS & WORLD REPORT, *supra* note 98, at 70.

[104]*Id.*

[105]*Why Farmers Are Up in Arms,* U.S. NEWS & WORLD REPORT, Oct. 31, 1977, at 57.

[106]*Id.* at 58.

[107]Food and Agriculture Act, *supra* note 8.

[108]National Advisory Commission of Food and Fiber, CO-OP GRAIN Q., reprinted in AGRICULTURAL POLICY IN AN AFFLUENT SOCIETY 141 (V. Rutton, A. Waldo, J. Hoock, eds. 1969).

[109]Food and Agriculture Act, *supra* note 8.

[110]*Id.*

[111]*Id.*

[112]N.Y. Times, Jan. 20, 1978, at A12, col. 4.

[113]A. Montgomery and E. Weeks, *Implications of Export Policy: Choices for American Agriculture,* reprinted in FOOD GOALS, FUTURE STRUCTURAL CHANGES, AND AGRICULTURAL POLICY: A NATIONAL BASEBOOK 301 (1969).

[114]*Long-Term Forecast,* NEWSWEEK, Jan. 23, 1976, at 34. By the year 2050, it is predicted that the atmosphere will be three degrees Celsius warmer. If this is the case, it could turn the majority of the American Midwest into an arid plain.

[115]*The Carbon Dioxide Question,* SCIENTIFIC AM., Jan. 1978, at 34.

[116]*American Foreign Food Assistance, supra* note 14.

[117]N.Y. Times, *supra* note 112.

[118]*American Foreign Food Assistance, supra* note 14, at 33.

[119]*Id.*

[120]Jones and Southerland, *Carter Plans Assault on World Hunger,* Christian Science Monitor, Oct. 18, 1977, at 1, col. 1.

United States Nuclear Export Policy:

Developing the Peaceful Atom as a Commodity in International Trade

Michael A. Bauser

Nuclear export policy has aroused increasing interest and, during the 94th Congress, was the subject of numerous bills and resolutions.[1] Unfortunately, little progress was made toward developing a policy which controls the risks of nuclear weapons proliferation associated with the widespread distribution of nuclear facilities, technology and materials while improving the competitive status of United States suppliers on the world market. This article seeks to place issues related to nuclear export policy in historical, legal, political, and commercial perspective and analyzes pertinent legislation enacted by the 94th Congress. It also examines the provisions of certain unenacted measures which raised problems with which the 95th Congress will have to deal in its consideration of the reform of United States nuclear export policy.

BACKGROUND

Atoms for Peace and Nuclear Exports in General

On December 8, 1953, President Eisenhower proposed a bold course before the United Nations General Assembly in his Atoms for Peace speech.[2] The address marked the beginning of a worldwide effort to reshape the awesome power of the atom from a destructive sword into a useful plowshare.[3] The Atoms for Peace program comprised a plan to

From *Harvard International Law Journal,* Vol. 18, Spring 1977, pages 227-264. Reprinted with permission of the Harvard International Law Journal Association.

reduce the threat of nuclear weapons by channeling fissionable material into an international pool to be used for peaceful purposes, and by creating an International Atomic Energy Agency (IAEA) with extraordinary powers of inspection.[4]

Shortly thereafter, the President sent to Congress a message calling for broad international cooperation in the development of nuclear energy for peaceful purposes.[5] The Congress shared the Administration's view that atomic energy was capable of important peaceful applications and enacted the Atomic Energy Act of 1954 (Act).[6] The Act provided, for the first time, legislative authorization of and mechanisms for a broad program of international cooperation in the peaceful, as well as the military, uses of atomic energy.

In the score and four years which have elapsed since President Eisenhower's Atoms for Peace speech, nuclear power has passed through research and development, experimental, and demonstration stages and the initiation of large scale commercial utilization.[7] The Atomic Energy Commission (AEC)[8] spent about $1.5 billion in developing the light-water reactor (LWR).[9] In addition, $2 billion was spent on the United States Navy's LWR development program which was of major benefit to civilian nuclear power.[10] Largely due to the technology thus developed, the LWR has become widely adopted, both domestically[11] and abroad.[12]

During the remainder of this century the nuclear energy market, probably dominated by LWRs,[13] is projected to grow dramatically. In the year 2000 domestic installed nuclear capacity has been conservatively estimated at 380 GWe,[14] with foreign, non-Eastern bloc, capacity at about two to three times that level.[15] The world demand for nuclear fuel and fuel services is also projected to grow accordingly.[16] In terms of balance of trade impact alone, annual United States nuclear power export revenues are projected to range between $3-$4 billion by 1985 and to increase to between $8-$10 billion annually by the year 2000.[17] The stakes are high indeed.

Control of United States Nuclear Exports and Safeguards

The Atomic Energy Act of 1954 provides, *inter alia*, for the control of important commodities and technology used in atomic energy programs and for undertaking international cooperation in the peaceful uses of atomic energy. These purposes are reconciled in United States regulations and policy, particularly those of the Energy Research and Development Administration (ERDA) and the Nuclear Regulatory Commission (NRC). National policy and security implications are reviewed by these agencies and the Department of State plus, as appropriate, other agencies and offices including the Department of Defense, Department of Commerce, and the Arms Control and Disarmament Agency.[18] Controls are prescribed over, among other things, production and utilization facilities as well as source, by-product, and special nuclear material.[19]

Prominent among the mechanisms for achieving the dual objectives of export promotion and export control is the Agreement for Cooperation which the United States has made on a bilateral basis with some 30 countries. Pursuant to section 123 of the Act,[20] the export of civil production and utilization facilities may be licensed only pursuant to the terms of an Agreement for Cooperation, as defined in section 11.b.[21] Likewise, special nuclear material, with the exception of such material exempted from this requirement pursuant to section 54.b of the Act,[22] may be distributed abroad or licensed for export only pursuant to an Agreement for Cooperation.[23]

Section 123 requires that Agreements for Cooperation contain, among other things, (1) a guarantee by the cooperating party that security safeguards and standards as set forth in the Agreement will be maintained; (2) except for Agreements in the military uses of atomic energy, a guarantee by the cooperating party that any material to be transferred pursuant to such Agreement will not be used for atomic weapons, or for research on or development of atomic weapons or for any other military purpose; and (3) a guarantee by the cooperating party that any material to be transferred pursuant to the Agreement for Cooperation will not be transferred to unauthorized persons or beyond the jurisdiction of the cooperating party, except as specified in the Agreement.[24] All Agreements for Cooperation must be approved by the President, who is required to authorize their execution and determine in writing that performance of the Agreement "will promote and will not constitute an unreasonable risk to the common defense and security."[25] Thereafter, depending on the extent of cooperation to be undertaken, a civil Agreement for Cooperation must lie before various congressional committees specified in the rules of the House and Senate for 30 days, or before the Congress for 60 days while it is in session, before becoming effective. Agreements involving significant cooperative activities may be prevented from becoming effective if the Congress, by concurrent resolution, expresses disapproval during the 60 day waiting period.[26]

A somewhat different regime applies to source and by-product material which may be distributed abroad either pursuant to an Agreement for Cooperation or upon a statutory determination as provided for in sections 64 and 82.b of the Act.[27] In addition, the Department of Commerce licenses the export of nuclear reactor equipment and components not constituting a utilization facility and certain materials unique to the fabrication of nuclear reactors. These responsibilities, once conducted pursuant to the Export Administration Act of 1969,[28] were maintained by executive order when the export legislation expired at the end of the last session of Congress.[29]

In addition to this panoply of regulatory controls on the export of nuclear materials and facilities, controls called "safeguards" are applied to monitor the use of United States-origin materials and facilities once exported.[30] Over the course of the past two decades, such safeguards have been implemented pursuant to a variety of different schemes. Since no international safeguards systems existed at the time the United States initiated its export activities, the United States initially assumed safeguards responsibilities for materials and equipment supplied through its bilateral agreements.[31]

When the United States ratified the IAEA Statute,[32] agency safeguards were looked upon as an inevitable and necessary replacement for United States bilateral safeguards since multilateral safeguards were felt to be more credible to the world at large and more efficient than numerous bilateral safeguards arrangements applied by different supplier nations.[33] Accordingly, as a matter of United States policy, bilateral safeguards have been largely suspended in favor of international safeguards.[34]

One mechanism for effecting this transfer of safeguards responsibility to the IAEA was the trilateral agreement concluded among the IAEA, the United States, and the recipient country. In 1963 responsibilities for implementing safeguards under the United States-Japan Agreement for Cooperation were assumed by the IAEA pursuant to the first such trilateral agreement.[35] Since that time, the United States has strongly encouraged its bilateral partners to accept IAEA safeguards procedures on material and equipment supplied under bilateral Agreements for Cooperation.[36]

Significant additional responsibilities for the application of safeguards have also devolved upon the IAEA in consequence of the provisions of the Treaty on the Non-Proliferation of Nuclear Weapons (NPT).[37] Under the terms of the NPT non-nuclear-weapon States party to the treaty forswear the right to manufacture or acquire nuclear weapons or other nuclear explosives[38] and undertake to accept safeguards on all peaceful nuclear activities within their territories as set forth in agreements with the IAEA for the purpose of verifying the fulfillment of obligations under the treaty.[39] All States party to the treaty are similarly obliged by the NPT not to export source or special nuclear material to any non-nuclear-weapon State unless such materials are safeguarded by the IAEA.[40]

THE 94TH CONGRESS — POLICY CONTEXT AND LEGISLATIVE ACTION

As the foregoing review indicates, Congress has actively participated in the formulation of nuclear export policy since its genesis in the Atoms for Peace program.[41] Even so, the 94th Congress is notable for the amount and intensity of effort devoted to the reformation of United States policy in this area. While only one piece of legislation specifically concerned with nuclear export policy was actually enacted,[42] consideration of the experience of the 94th Congress is useful in view of the certainty that major attention will be devoted to the same subject during the current Congress.[43]

The Policy Context

The coalescence of three factors in the period just prior to and during the 94th Congress made the reformation of United States nuclear export policy both necessary and difficult. First, the threat of nuclear proliferation became much more palpable. Second, the competitive position of the United States in the nuclear export market was visibly eroded, entailing diminished United States control over events in the international nuclear trade. Finally, a variety of domestic legal developments began to impair the capacity of the United States to respond aggressively to this loss of control.

To date, five nations have successfully tested nuclear weapons: the United States, the Soviet Union, the United Kingdom, France, and the People's Republic of China. On May 18, 1974, India detonated a nuclear device in the desert of Rajasthan which, it has insisted, was designed for peaceful purposes.[44] The nuclear weapons club had expanded.

The following month, on June 14, 1974, the President of the United States, Richard Nixon, announced his intention to enter into a cooperative nuclear power agreement with Egypt; three days later, he announced that negotiation of a similar arrangement with Israel was planned.[45] Still later, Germany and Brazil entered into an agreement providing for the development of an entire nuclear industry in the latter country[46] and, in a similar move, France agreed to provide Pakistan with a reprocessing plant which would allow the processing and separating of fissionable material from the spent fuel produced by Pakistan's reactor.[47] In addition, reports have also circulated that Taiwan was secretly reprocessing spent nuclear fuel.[48] The diffusion of enrichment and reprocessing facilities was forging a link between civilian power programs and military capabilities.

With respect to reactors alone, nuclear power plant commitments outside of the United States soared by 17% from 1975 to 1976.[49] Moreover, the number of countries committed to employing nuclear energy for the production of electricity rose to 41 from 38 in 1975 and 32 in 1974.[50] In 1976, Argentina announced that the first Latin American heavy-water plant would be constructed there to serve its power plant needs.[51] With the widespread adoption of nuclear power throughout the world, plutonium production figures were published and circulated indicating the quantities of the material which would be produced. The impact of these figures was sometimes enhanced by equating the results of calculations to "minimum-bombs-equivalent," thus further emphasizing the safeguards implications of the worldwide utilization of nuclear power.[52]

Amid the dramatic developments, however, the more subtle patterns of nuclear proliferation began to emerge and take on detail. Policymakers became increasingly aware that emphasis on the role of nuclear exports in relation to proliferation had obscured the existence of an additional route to nuclear weapons, at once more simple and politically less risky than the use of material derived from imported civil facilities pledged to peaceful uses under safeguards.[53] That route is the construction of facilities on a purely national basis, unassisted by imported equipment or technology save that available in the public domain.[54]

The near monopoly position and corresponding influence the United States once enjoyed in the international nuclear trade is a thing of the past. Several countries other than the United States are now in a position to export enrichment technology, reprocessing technology and facilities, and light-water reactors. The economics of the domestic energy industries in most of these countries makes it almost imperative that companies secure foreign sales in order to supplement domestic markets for nuclear power.[55] One measure of the fact that the nuclear export market has become highly competitive is the dramatic decline in the market share of the United States. From 1956 through 1973 the United States captured almost 80% of the reactor export market. From 1974 through 1975, however, the United States share of a 24-reactor export market was only 13 reactors, or slightly more than 50%.[56]

The deterioration of the United States market position is compounded by the lagging rate of technology implementation and development. For example, while a number of fuel reprocessing plants serving power plant reactors are in operation throughout the world, there are no such facilities operating in the United States and none are expected in the near future.[57] In regard to enrichment, there are three United States government-owned plants which have historically provided nearly all of the domestic and foreign demands for enriched uranium. Although limited additions to capacity are planned,[58] the entire output of the present plants is currently committed by contract,[59] thus precluding further contracting in support of additional nuclear capacity.

Other countries, however, are moving aggressively in the enrichment field. An international consortium composed of France, Belgium, Spain, Italy, and Iran called EURODIF is building a large gaseous diffusion enrichment plant in southern France utilizing French technology.[60] Another international consortium composed of West Germany, the Netherlands, and the United Kingdom, and known as URENCO, is building enrichment facilities based on an advanced gas centrifuge technology and currently operates pilot plants in England and in Holland.[61] Canada is independently considering the construction of a gaseous diffusion plant as part of its policy of exporting uranium in the most highly processed form; South Africa, which has just announced the successful start-up of its pilot enrichment plant (based on a not fully disclosed process), may adopt a policy similar to Canada's.[62] Australia, with its large reserves of uranium, may follow suit.[63] Preliminary studies have also been made on the siting of enrichment plants in the Republic of Zaire and in Papua, New Guinea. The Republic of Zaire has large reserves of uranium and undeveloped hydro resources which could provide the large amounts of electricity required to run a diffusion plant. Papua, in New Guinea, also has undeveloped hydro resources that could provide very inexpensive electricity for a diffusion plant.[64] Finally, the People's Republic of China and the Soviet Union both have enrichment plants. Although their capacity, technology, and location have not been published, the Soviet Union is, in fact, offering to sell enrichment services. Certain nations have already availed themselves of the offer.[65]

It is perhaps in the area of advanced reactors, however—and fast breeders in particular—that the demise of United States technolog .l leadership is most apparent. Outside of the United States five nations either have operating now, or are expected to have operating around 1980, demonstration fast breeder reactors. An optimistic guess concerning the United States demonstration plant at Clinch River in Tennessee would put the commencement of operation in 1983 or 1984. The 250 MWe French Phenix fast breeder reactor has been operating with excellent results since 1973. The United Kingdom's 250 MWe PFR began operation in 1974, while the Soviet Union's 350 MWe BN-350 has been operating since 1972.[66]

Some of these countries are also moving quickly into the construction of large, commercial-sized breeder reactors. The French are planning a 1,300 MWe Super-Phenix project which will be conducted as a joint venture by French, German, and Italian utilities.[67] The Soviet Union's 600 MWe fast breeder is already nearing completion. Both the United Kingdom and France have expressed interest in exporting reactors, and the French have even offered a 450 MWe export version of the Phenix for sale.[68]

Domestic legal and administrative developments, too, are likely to complicate and impair the orderly development and implementation of a sound and reasoned nuclear export policy. On May 26, 1976, the Second Circuit enjoined[69] the NRC from issuing any licenses—even on an interim basis—for commercial "mixed oxide fuel related activities"[70] pending the completion of proceedings associated with the Generic Environmental Statement on the Use of Recycle Plutonium in Mixed Oxide Fuel in Light Water Reactors (GESMO).[71] This decision, if permitted to stand, will prevent the operation of any domestic commercial fuel reprocessing plant until after the completion of a lengthy hearing process which could stretch for years.[72]

More recently, on July 21, 1976, the United States Court of Appeals for the District of Columbia Circuit held, *inter alia*, that the NRC had improperly considered certain environmental impacts associated with the domestic licensing of individual nuclear power plants.[73] As a result, a moratorium was imposed on the issuance of all construction permits, full power operating licenses, and related authorizations until remedial action could be taken.[74]

Finally, the nuclear export licensing process itself is not conducive either to the efficient administration of policy or confidence in the reliability of the United States as a suppplier on the world market. The *Edlow* case[75] provides an indication of the difficulties which have arisen thus far and what the future may hold in store. *Edlow* involves applications for special nuclear material export licenses covering fuel (slightly enriched uranium) for the Tarapur Atomic Power Station (TAPS). The station is owned by the Government of India and managed by the Atomic Power Authority.[76] The Sierra Club, the Natural Resources Defense Council, Inc. (NRDC) and the Union of Concerned Scientists filed petitions to intervene in the export licensing proceeding which, had they been granted, would have resulted in an adjudicatory, or trial-type, hearing.[77] The petitioners' interest in the proceeding was alleged to be based on concern over maintaining "a healthy and safe environment" for their individual members[78] and the possibility that the Commission would fail to "carry out relevant analyses of the risks posed by the pending licenses" and thereby impair the "petitioners' ability to fulfill their information and educational functions."[79] Although the Commission found that the petitioners lacked standing to intervene as a matter of right and demand a fullblown adjudicatory hearing,[80] it did decide to exercise its discretion and conduct a legislative-type hearing on the basis of a determination that a public proceeding to consider issues bearing on the license applications would be in the public interest.[81] That decision in the *Edlow* case, however, may make it difficult, if not impossible, for the Commission to exercise its discretion differently in other cases when a hearing is requested.[82]

The oral hearing process itself, even the legislative variety, is not a mechanism geared to controlled, timely decision-making. Even in informal proceedings, the right of each party to participate must be protected in ways which sometimes may be difficult to foresee.[83] This, in turn, not only hampers the agency in controlling the timing, course, and scope of such proceedings,[84] but also makes it difficult for any party to rely on the agency's determination until after all opportunity for appeal and judicial review has been exhausted—a process which often takes several years.[85] Coupled with other recent developments in the licensing process,[86] the *Edlow* decision casts doubt on the ability of the NRC to administer effectively export policy.

In sum, the international nuclear export environment today is far different than that which existed only a short time ago. It is within this overall factual and legal setting that recent congressional activities must be reviewed.

Legislative Action

The Symington Amendment

The single piece of legislation specifically concerned with nuclear export policy which did become law was a generally positive response to the problems presented by the new policy context. In enacting the International Security Assistance and Arms Export Control Act of 1976,[87] Congress provided, in section 305,[88] for an amendment of the Foreign Assistance Act of 1961[89] serving to restrict United States aid to any country either delivering or receiving sensitive nuclear materials, equipment or technology except under specified conditions and controls.

The nuclear transfer section had its genesis in a Senate provision initially offered by Senator Symington[90]. The Senate bill, as considered by the commmittee of conference on the disagreeing votes of the two Houses, would not have allowed economic assistance (except for certain aid in the event of natural disasters or to meet other urgent relief requirements) or any form of military assistance to any country supplying or receiving nuclear enrichment or reprocessing equipment, materials, or technology unless: (1) the supplier and recipient agreed to place all transferred equipment, material, and technology under multilateral auspices and management, when available, and (2) the recipient agreed to IAEA safeguards on everything transferred and on all nuclear fuels and facilities in the recipient country. The House bill contained no similar provision.[91] However, after discussing the Senate provision and receiving the views of the Executive branch, the committee of the conference agreed to the Senate provision, subject to amendment.[92]

The basic thrust of the original Symington proposal was preserved in the International Security Assistance and Arms Control Act. However, as a result of the committee of conference amendment, the President may, by executive order effective in not less than 30 days, permit deliveries to a country to which the denial of aid provision would otherwise apply if he: (1) determines that the termination of assistance would have a serious adverse effect on vital United States interests, and (2) certifies that he has received reliable assurance that the country in question will not acquire or develop nuclear weapons or assist other nations to do so. Such determination and certification would be transmitted to the Congress with specific supporting reasons. In the event that the President issued an executive order permitting delivery and transmitted the requisite determination and certifications, the Congress could still terminate or restrict assistance to the countries in question by a joint resolution introduced within 30 days of the President's transmittal, with the joint resolution being considered in the Senate under expedited procedures.[93]

The adoption of the Symington proposal is an important and noteworthy step. First, it is and has been United States policy not to export either uranium enrichment or fuel reprocessing facilities.[94] In view of the extreme sensitivity of such facilities—especially the latter—this policy makes good sense. It is to be hoped that the Symington provision will encourage other nuclear supplier nations to adopt[95] and maintain similar policies by demonstrating the deep concern with which this country views the establishment, anywhere in the world, of nuclear fuel facilities without adequate protection against weapons-related activity.[96]

Second, the Symington proposal operates in such a way as to be effective without placing United States suppliers at a competitive disadvantage. By providing sanctions applicable to any supplier or recipient, the goal of limiting the export of sensitive nuclear equipment, materials, and technology is advanced without, at the same time, additionally burdening the sales of the United States nuclear industry.

Third, the provisions of the Symington proposal reflect the type of cooperation between the Congress and the Executive branch in developing nuclear policy that is vital to effective policy. The tensions which exist between Congress and the Executive under our system of separation of powers are a source of creativity as well as frustration. The Presidential certification provisions of the Act and the drafting process which led to their inclusion exemplify a cooperative attitude on the part of both branches—reflecting an understanding and appreciation by each of the concerns and perspective of the other—which is essential to progress.

The Symington provision, of course, is not beyond refinement. The requirement that, to avoid sanctions, the supplying country and the receiving country must have agreed "to place all such equipment, materials, and technology . . . under multinational auspices and management when available" is troublesome. The report of the Senate Committee on Foreign Relations states that "Since no multilateral auspices and management exist at present, the Members agreed, upon the motion of Senator Javits, that such arrangements should be required 'when available.' "[97] It then goes on to discuss ways in which "multilateral auspices and management" might come about and encourages their development.[98] Confusion remains, however, and, during floor debate, Senator Glenn simply equated "when available" with "right now, today."[99]

Multinational fuel facilities may well prove to be desirable and should be considered very closely. However, studies of their technical, economic, and political aspects are still underway[100] and more information should be considered before expressing approval or disapproval of the concept and its adoption. This is particularly true since such an endorsement might be read as supporting the proposition that *all* nuclear fuel production facilities—domestic and foreign alike—should be placed under multinational control.[101]

Unenacted Legislative Proposals

The 94th Congress produced a variety of well-intentioned legislative initiatives to deal with various aspects of nuclear export policy. But the dominant features of the various schemes to control nuclear weapons proliferation evidenced little concern for their own consequences or, indeed, for striking at the real source of the problem. Study of the shortcomings of these measures is necessary if progress is to be made in the current Congress.

The significant legislative proposals developed in the 94th Congress—aside from the Symington proposal, which was the only one enacted—were embodied in the Export Reorganization Act (S. 1439);[102] provisions of legislation extending the Export Administration Act of 1969[103] (H.R. 15377);[104] provisions of ERDA authorization legislation for fiscal year 1977 (H.R. 13350 and S. 3105);[105] and various versions of the Nuclear Explosive Proliferation Act of 1976—S. 3770 (H.R. 15273 identical)[106] and H.R. 15419[107] in particular.[108]

The seminal legislative initiative dealing with nuclear export policy was the Export Reorganization Bill, S. 1439. The initial version of S. 1439 was introduced on April 15, 1975, by Senators Percy, Ribicoff, and Glenn in order to correct what were perceived as deficiencies in the nuclear export licensing process.[109] In its original form the bill centralized nuclear export licensing in the Department of Commerce while, at the same time, providing the NRC with additional authority and resources to enable it to make independent safeguards certifications.[110] As the bill was redrafted in 1976, emphasis shifted toward consolidating nuclear export licensing functions in the NRC rather than in the Department of Commerce.[111]

The consolidation did not always mean the NRC was given greater authority than it had had before. Section 6(c)(1) of S. 1439[112] made issuance of a nuclear export license conditional upon the written approval of the Secretary of State. For exports of major production and utilization facilities, at least, State Department approval is in effect required by the present system of obtaining Executive branch views and analysis of such exports pursuant to Executive Order 11902.[113] In contrast, when the State Department favored an export but the Commission did not, sections 6(c)(3) and (4) of the bill would have established a novel procedure for esolution of the disagreement by the Congress. Under the proposed procedure, the license was to be referred to Congress which could pass a concurrent resolution disapproving the license within 60 days of the referral. If no such resolution were passed, the NRC was required to grant the license at the conclusion of the 60-day period.[114] The net effect was to place the NRC in a position where all it could do with final effect was to agree with the State Department. If the Secretary of State did not favor an export, the matter was ended. If the Secretary favored an export but the Commission did not, the question was automatically referred to Congress for final decision.[115]

The bill was reported unanimously by the Senate Government Operations Committee in May 1976[116] and referred to the Senate Foreign Relations Committee and the Joint Committee on Atomic Energy.[117] The Foreign Relations Committee concluded its consideration by, in effect, offering as a substitute, a version of the Nuclear Explosive Proliferation Control Act,[118] while the Joint Committee on Atomic Energy recommended against passage.[119]

Although S. 1439 received the ministrations of both the Congress and the Executive branch,[120] the bill as reported by the Senate Government Operations Committee failed to win the support of the administration.[121] To be sure, the bill was complex, and opposition to it was based on a variety of factors.[122] Most opposition, however, was rooted in concern that passage of the bill would likely have had a detrimental effect on the ability of the United States to function as a reliable supplier in a highly competitive market.[123]

One provision, not atypical, justifying such concern directed the preparation of Nuclear Proliferation Assessment Statements (NPAS) by the Arms Control and Disarmament Agency (ACDA). Section 7 would have required the preparation of these assessments and their submission to the NRC, the Secretary of State, and the Congress for all major United States governmental nuclear export activities.[124] According to the Government Operations Committee report, the purpose of the statements was simple: "to require hard headed thinking by an independent agency of the potential effect of new or modified agreements and major actions taken under them."[125]

The propriety of procedures requiring ACDA, an agency of the Executive branch, to submit directly to Congress the advice it gives the Secretary of State and other agencies is doubtful.[126] In addition, such statements, in view of their stated purpose of informing the public,[127] would have been an open invitation to lengthy proceedings and contentious hearings with prolonged exposure to judicial review.[128] It is problematic, in fact, whether United States suppliers, so hobbled, could compete effectively on the world market. Consumer nations cannot be expected to choose an uncertain source of supply over a more reliable one, other factors being roughly equal. Even though one of the express concerns of the Senate Government Operations Committee was to strengthen the role of ACDA,[129] it is surprising that such an inflexible provision would be included in S. 1439, which professedly was intended to control proliferation by enhancing the reliability of the United States as a world supplier of nuclear goods.[130]

When it became apparent that S. 1439 could not achieve passage because of agency opposition, the Nuclear Explosive Proliferation Control Act of 1976 (NEPCA) was offered by the Senate Foreign Relations Committee as a substitute for S. 1439.[131] The bill was also introduced as S. 3770 (H.R. 15273)[132] as a result of consideration of S. 1439 by the Joint Committee on Atomic Energy.[133] Due to the reservations expressed by some members of the Joint Committee to which the bill, along with H.R. 15273, had been referred, a hearing was held on the final day of August.[134] As a result, a revised version was introduced in the House as H.R. 15419 by Congressmen Price and Anderson on September 2, 1976.[135] Subsequently, the Joint Committee met on September 14, 1976, and voted to report H.R. 15419 to the House with amendments suggested by ERDA Administrator Dr. Robert Seamans,[136] apparently as spokesman for the administration.[137] Although the amendments received less than close scrutiny in the crush accompanying the waning hours of the session,[138] they were adopted essentially *in toto*. The committee action thus produced, albeit in somewhat haphazard fashion, the first and only nuclear export bill apparently acceptable to the Ford Administration.

The bill contained provisions calling for the submission of ACDA views on Agreements for Cooperation to the President along with the proposed Agreements as negotiated by the Secretary of State,[139] and the preferential treatment of foreign fuel-service customers committed to certain policies designed to prevent the spread of nuclear explosives.[140] The provisions of NEPCA which received the most attention, however, were those containing export licensing criteria.

The concept of criteria had been developed in sections 14 and 15 of S. 3770. These would have added a new section 112 to the Atomic Energy Act of 1954 providing for six criteria governing peaceful nuclear exports. In essence, two separate sets of binding criteria would have been established. The first set, contained in section 14, would have taken effect immediately. The second, more stringent, set, contained in section 15, would have come into force 18 months later.[141].

The licensing criteria themselves dealt with IAEA safeguards, nuclear explosives, physical security, retransfer, and reprocessing. The new section 112(a)(1) would have required the application of IAEA safeguards, or their equivalent, to all United States nuclear exports. Section 112(a)(2) would have required assurance that no United States nuclear exports would be used in any nuclear explosive device, or for research on or development of such a device. The third criterion was that adequate physical security measures would apply to United States nuclear exports. Section 112(a)(4) prohibited the grant of any license in the absence of assurances that no United States nuclear export would be retransferred to a third country without prior United States approval. The United States could only approve such transfer if the receiving nation or group of nations had agreed to accept all applicable conditions imposed by the United States on the original transfer. Assurance that nuclear fuels exported by the United States or produced using United States exports would not be removed from a reactor and altered in form or content, *e.g.*, for reprocessing, without prior United States approval would have been required by section 112(a)(5). All of the above sections applied to material produced in United States-origin facilities or derived from United States-origin fuel as well as to the exported items themselves. Finally, section 112(a)(6) required an assurance that any item developed utilizing material or information of United States-origin would be subject to the restrictions enumerated in sections (a)(1)-(a)(5).[142]

These criteria were to be replaced by more stringent and far-reaching criteria at the end of a short period, in the S. 3770-H.R. 15273 version, eighteen months. Basically, after eighteen months any recipient nation would have to guarantee that the above safeguards applied to all of its nuclear activities, whether indigenous or derived from United States exports. The 18-month criteria did not impose a requirement of prior United States approval on retransfer of indigenous items.[143]

The criteria in S. 3770 were probably sufficient to have removed the United States, as a supplier, from the nuclear export market.[144] The amended version of NEPCA, H.R. 15419, recognized and bounded the disastrous sweep of the criteria, however. It refashioned the criteria into a set of "principles governing United States nuclear exports"[145] and target criteria for the conduct of "international nuclear trade which would be of significance for nuclear explosive purposes."[146]

The "principles governing United States exports" contained in section 14 of H.R. 15419 were intended to have immediate effect. The "principles" themselves were extractions from the initially effective criteria of S. 3770.[147] Strict, literal compliance with the criteria would not have been required,[148] for the intent of the provision was to establish basic policy while preserving flexibility. The principles could probably have been applied in practice with net salutary effect inmany cases. The broader 18-month criteria of S. 3770 were also re-established, but this time as "objectives for negotiation,"[149] to be applied eventually in the conduct of international nuclear trade.[150] The President was directed to take immediate steps to assure that maximum effort was made to negotiate an agreement committing all nuclear suppliers and recipients to the application of the same criteria.[151] In contrast to S. 3770, however, there was no requirement for the utilization of the criteria by the United States prior to the effective date of such international arrangements and undertakings.[152]

It is unfortunate that H.R. 15419 never reached a vote. The bill offered a workable first step toward comprehensive reform of nuclear export policy. While the bill was not without deficiencies,[153] it emphasized positive intiatives[154] and avoided action likely to isolate the United States from the international nuclear community at a critical time. It evidenced an admirable congressional concern tempered with a sense of perspective.[155]

At the same time that H.R. 15419 was being considered, another nuclear export related measure was developed as an amendment to legislation extending the Export Administration Act of 1969.[156] This amendment, often called the Zablocki Amendment,[157] required the inclusion of certain provisions in new Agreements for Cooperation. Any new Agreement had to extend the restrictions on reprocessing normally applicable to fuel supplied by the United States to all material produced using reactors supplied by the United States.[158] In addition, the recipient nation under any new Agreement would have had to have agreed to allow the IAEA to report to the United States the status of all inventories of plutonium, uranium 233, and highly enriched uranium.[159] The Secretary of State was also directed to seek inclusion of similar provisions in all current Agreements for Cooperation.[160]

The Zablocki Amendment also dealt with the problem of peaceful nuclear explosives. It prohibited the issuance of any export license until the recipient country had agreed that no item received under the relevant Agreement for Cooperation would be used to develop any nuclear explosive device.[161] The amendment also set forth a standard to be used by the Secretary of State when making a determination approving the reprocessing of fuel. Under Agreements providing for such reprocessing only when effective safeguards can be applied,[162] the Secretary of State would have been required to find "that the reliable detection of any diversion and the timely warning to the United States of such diversion will occur well in advance of the time at which that party could transform strategic quantities of diverted nuclear material into explosive nuclear devices."[163]

The report of the International Relations Committee reveals a deep and serious concern over the problem of nuclear weapons proliferation.[164] As a means of addressing this problem, however, the Amendment was clearly inadequate and served to illustrate, in fact, the pitfalls of a piecemeal approach to nuclear export policy reform. For example, the "timely warning" criterion imposed on the Secretary of State's evaluation of safeguards prior to approval of reprocessing could not be met currently. This was clearly reflected in the report of the International Relations Committee.[165] The intent of the Committee was to encourage the development of technologies which would eventually allow the standard to be satisfied.[166] Unfortunately, the "timely warning" criterion might have accomplished just the opposite result by casting doubt on the propriety of conducting any reprocessing operation at the present time. The possibility that application of the standard would have discouraged implementation of multinational reprocessing facilities even on a demonstration basis is particularly disturbing.

The IAEA reporting provision was another unfortunate aspect of the Amendment. Access to information on recipient country inventories of all special nuclear materials—whether supplied by the United States or not—may be desirable from the perspective of insuring the adequacy of IAEA safeguards.[167] Nevertheless, attempting to achieve this objective by conditioning United States exports upon such access is heavy-handed. Moreover, disclosure of this information conflicts with existing IAEA mandates and commitments in Agency bilateral and multilateral agreements.[168] The measure could have dissuaded nations wishing to keep their inventories of special nuclear material confidential from becoming parties to the NPT, since under that treaty they are obliged to accept IAEA safeguards.[169] The Amendment's provision on nuclear explosives is also curious. Present United States policy requires such a pledge.[170] The Amendment's provision, however, would not have become effective until one year after enactment of the section.[171]

Although a number of these deficiencies were identified on the floor of the House, both during debate on the rule under which the bill was considered[172] and in debate on the bill itself,[173] H.R. 15377 was eventually approved in the House of Representatives by a vote of 318 to 63.[174] During floor debate, however, there was a serious clash over the propriety of approving legislation taking a piecemeal approach and which had never been considered by the Joint Committee on Atomic Energy, rather than awaiting that Committee's comprehensive export policy legislation, H.R. 15419.[175]

House passage of H.R. 15377 ultimately came to naught; almost one month earlier the Senate had approved extension of the Export Administration Act of 1969 through the adoption of a different measure: S. 3084.[176] When it came time to consider the differing versions in a committee of conference, the tough foreign boycott provisions of the Senate bill[177] made extension of the Export Administration Act of 1969 too hot a political potato to handle shortly before a Presidential election, and conferees were never appointed.[178]

Another nuclear export policy measure to receive active consideration in the 94th Congress was a provision contained in legislation authorizing appropriations for ERDA fiscal year 1977. On May 20, 1976, the House adopted an amendment to its ERDA authoriation bill, H.R. 13350.[179] It prohibited the use of ERDA funds for the production of fuel to be exported under Agreements for Cooperation which had not been approved by Congress under the revised 1974 procedure,[180] unless the first license for export of reactors or fuel pursuant to such Agreement after the effective date of the amendment had undergone congressional scrutiny. The restriction did not, however, apply if the purchaser of the ERDA services was an NPT party.[181]

A similar restriction was imposed the following month in the Senate's ERDA authorization legislation, S. 3105.[182] The Senate amendment differed from that adopted by the House in two respects. First, it provided for the termination of fuel exports to affected countries, absent Congressional review, regardless of the use of ERDA funds. Second, it exempted exports to nuclear-weapon States from further congressional review procedures.[183]

The two varying provisions were considered in conference with the committee apparently agreeing to a modified version of the Senate amendment.[184] The modification contained an exemption provision that would have permitted further exports under existing Agreements for Cooperation without congressional review under two conditions.[185] First, it was necessary for the State Department and other concerned agencies of the Executive branch to certify that the proposed export would not be inimical to the national security interests of the United States.[186] Second, the NRC had to find that the recipient nation or group of nations would apply non-proliferation measures to the export similar to the section 14 "criteria" of S. 3770.[187] The House agreed to the conference report on the last full day of the session.[188] However, the Senate failed to act[189] and, as a result, the entire measure died.[190]

The 94th Congress might be judged a failure in advancing the policies of non-proliferation. Only one effective measure, the Symington proposal, was adopted. Much of what was otherwise proposed would likely have proved counterproductive in practice. Nevertheless, the attention focused on the subject has provided an impetus for reconsideration of United States foreign policy within the Executive branch.[191] In this and other ways, the work and deliberations of the 94th Congress have helped immeasurably in putting relevant issues in full and complete perspective and making possible a synoptic view.

CONCLUSION

Controlling the proliferation of nuclear weapons is not and cannot be the only goal of United States international nuclear policy. It must be considered along with (1) distributing the benefits available from the application of peaceful nuclear technology; and (2) securing for the United States a fair share of the international nuclear export market. Over the last twenty years, the atom has become an international commodity of equal interest to a growing number of nuclear materials exporters and importers for whom nuclear power may be the key to energy independence.

In proper perspective, the pursuit of each of these goals facilitates the achievement of the others. The amount of influence the United States will ultimately be able to exert turns on the strength of its competitive position, and on the leadership it displays in effectuating internationally acceptable controls.[192] It should also be recognized that a single-minded approach is counterproductive. For example, exporting nuclear fuel free from any safeguards provisions might enhance the competitive position of the United States, but it would not contribute to limiting the spread of nuclear weapons.

The recent legislative activity of the 94th Congress dealing with reform of nuclear export policy failed to adequately reflect an appreciation of the relationship between the maintenance of the United States competitive position in the nuclear export market and United States nonproliferation objectives. The reliability and credibility of United States supply arrangements have been cornerstones of United States nonproliferation policy. If reliability and credibility are impaired by cumbersome administrative procedures and unduly restrictive licensing criteria, the United States may lose all influence on the evolution of international nuclear weapons non-proliferation policy. This result, however, is not yet inevitable. If it is to be avoided, a new course must be charted at once.

The prompt adoption of an aggressive competitive posture on the international nuclear export market is a necessity. It should be coupled with initiatives intended to bring about agreements among supplier nations to limit and control the export of nuclear facilities, materials, and technology. In particular, the United States should actively encourage agreement among supplier nations to halt—at least for the present—the sale of enrichment and reprocessing facilities. Because they form the critical interface between the peaceful atom and potential weapons capability, their spread should be restricted to the maximum possible extent. In this regard, the recent activities of the London Nuclear Suppliers Conference are heartening and should be encouraged.[193] Renegotiation of existing Agreements for Cooperation may in some cases be appropriate. To the extent that revision for non-proliferation purposes is desirable, it should be undertaken with extreme care and sensitivity, so as to avoid casting doubt upon the credibility of the United States as a reliable supplier of nuclear goods and services.[194]

Ultimately, the acquisition of a nuclear explosives capability must be identified as a course of conduct no longer acceptable to the world community. The United States must adopt an activist role to bring about that perception, and to arrive at a consensus on the nature of sanctions to be applied. The foundation for establishing a norm is already in place in the form of the NPT.[195] What now remains is to build upon it a lasting structure,[196] a structure which can only be erected by determined effort on the international plane.

---

[1]See, *e.g.,* Export Reorganization Act of 1975, S. 1439, 94th Cong., 1st Sess., 121 CONG. REC. S5960 (daily ed. Apr. 15, 1975), reprinted in *The Export Reorganization Act—1975: Hearings on S. 1439 Before the Senate Comm. on Gov't Operations,* 94th Cong., 1st Sess. 499 (1975); Export Reorganization Act of 1976, S. 1429, 94th Cong., 2d Sess., reprinted in *Export Reorganization Act of 1976, Hearings on S. 1439 Before the Senate Comm. on Go't Operations,* 94th Cong. 2d Sess. 1255 (1976), modified version reprinted in *S. 1439: Export Reorganization Act of 1976: Hearings on S. 1439 Before the Joint Comm. on Atomic Energy,* 94th Cong., 2d Sess. 68 (1976); Nuclear Explosive Proliferation Control Act of 1976, H.R. 15419, 94th Cong., 2d Sess., 122 CONG. REC. H9491 (daily ed. Sept. 2, 1976); Nuclear Explosive Proliferation Control Act of 1976, H.R. 15273, 94th Cong., 2d Sess., 122 CONG. REC. H9083 (daily ed. Aug. 25, 1976); S. Res. 415, 94th Cong., 2d Sess., 122 CONG. REC. S4384 (daily ed. Mar. 26, 1976); H.R. Res. 1076, 94th Cong., 2d Sess., 122 CONG. REC. H1678 (daily ed. Mar. 4, 1976); notes 104-08 and accompanying text *infra.*

[2]Address by President Dwight D. Eisenhower before the General Assembly of the United Nations on the Peaceful Uses of Atomic Energy, Dec. 8, 1953, 1953 PUB. PAPERS OF PRESIDENT DWIGHT DAVID EISENHOWER 813 [hereinafter Atoms for Peace Address].

[3]It is a common misconception regarding the origin of the program for international cooperation in the peaceful use of nuclear energy that the United States held the lead, and took the initiative, in the development and export of nuclear power facilities. Such was not the case. The United Kingdom, by 1955, already had under construction its first nuclear power plants, based on the natural uranium, gas-cooled graphite system. The first demonstration unit was completed in 1956. The first two nuclear power reactors sold in international commerce were British reactors of this type, purchased by Italy and Japan. Although this kind of reactor has failed to be economically competitive, the units built both in the U.K. and in two countries which made early purchases continue in reliable operation to this day. Kratzer, *Nuclear Cooperation and Non-Proliferation,* 17 ATOM. ENERGY L.J. 250, 254-55 (1976).

[4]Atoms for Peace Address, *supra* note 2.

[5]See H.R. Doc. No. 328, 83d Cong., 2d Sess. (1954).

[6]42 U.S.C. §§ 2011-2021, 2033-2039, 2051-2053, 2061-2064, 2071-2078, 2091-2099, 2111-2112, 2121-2122, 2131-2140, 2151-2154, 2161-2166, 2181-2190,

2201-2210, 2221-2224, 2231-2242, 2251-2257, 2271-2282, 2291-2296 (1970 & Supp. V 1975).

[7]Today nuclear power accounts for about 43 Gigawatts electric (GWe) domestically (about eight percent of total installed capacity) and 36 GWe foreign. See NATIONAL ELECTRIC RELIABILITY COUNCIL, SIXTH ANNUAL REVIEW OF OVERALL RELIABILITY AND ADEQUACY OF THE NORTH AMERICAN BULK POWER SYSTEMS, Appendix C (1976); NUCLEAR ENGINEERING INT'L, July 1976, at 9.

[8]The Atomic Energy Commission was abolished and its responsibilities divided between the Energy Research and Development Administration and the Nuclear Regulatory Commission pursuant to the Energy Reorganization Act of 1974, 5 U.S.C. §§ 5313-5316 (Supp. V 1975); 42 U.S.C. §§ 5801, 5811-5820, 5841-5849, 5871-5879, 5891 (Supp. V 1975).

[9]A basic description of the LWR fuel cycle is presented in Appendix I.

[10]1 U.S. ENERGY RESEARCH AND DEVELOPMENT ADMINISTRATION, FINAL ENVIRONMENTAL STATEMENT ON U.S. NUCLEAR POWER EXPORT ACTIVITIES, 3-91 (ERDA-1542 1976) [hereinafter 1 EXPORT FES].

[11]See, *e.g.,* U.S. ATOMIC ENERGY COMM'N, NUCLEAR POWER GROWTH 1974-2000, at 12 (WASH-1139, 1974); E. Hanrahan, R. Williamson & R. Bown, United States Uranium Requirements 7 (Oct. 19, 1976) (unpublished paper presented at The Uranium Industry Seminar and available from the author).

[12]1 EXPORT FES, *supra* note 10, at 3-91.

[13]See, *e.g.,* U.S. ATOMIC ENERGY COMM'N, *supra* note 11, at 12-17, 21.

[14]See E. Hanrahan, R. Williamson & R. Bown, *supra* note 11, at 5.

[15]See, *e.g.,* E. Hanrahan, R. Williamson & R. Bown, World Requirements and Supply of Uranium 7-8 (Sept. 14, 1976) (unpublished paper presented at the Atomic Industrial Forum International Conference on Uranium) (available from the author).

[16]*Id.*

[17]See 1 EXPORT FES, *supra* note 10, at 4-15.

[18]Executive branch review procedures are contained in Exec. Order No. 11,902, 3 C.F.R. 4877 (1976), reprinted in 42 U.S.C. § 5841 note (Supp. V 1975), and reproduced in Appendix II.

[19]These terms are defined under the Act by the NRC as follows:

"Production facility" means: (1) Any nuclear reactor designed or used primarily for the formation of plutonium or uranium-233; or (2) Any facility designed or used for the separation of the isotopes of uranium or the isotopes of plutonium, except laboratory scale facilities designed or used for experimental or analytical purposes only; or (3) Any facility designed or used for the processing of irradiated materials containing special nuclear material, except (i) laboratory scale facilities designed or used for experimental or analytical purposes, (ii) facilities in which the only special nuclear materials contained in teh irradiated material to be processed are uranium enriched in the isotope U-235 and plutonium produced by the irradiation, if the material processed contains not more than 10^{-6} grams of plutonium per gram of U-235 and has fission product activity not in excess of 0.25 millicuries of fission products per gram of U-235, and (iii) facilities in which processing is conducted pursuant to a license issued under Parts 30 and 70 of this chapter, or equivalent regulations of an Agreement State, for the receipt, possession, use, and transfer of irradiated special nuclear material, which authorizes the processing of the irradiated material on a batch basis for the separation of selected fission products and limits the process batch to not more than 100 grams of uranium enriched in the isotope 235 and not more than 15 grams of any other special nuclear material.

"Utilization facility" means any nuclear reactor other than one designed or used primarily for the formation of plutonium or U-233.

NOTE: Pursuant to subsections IIv. and 11cc., respectively, of the Act, the Commission may from time to time add to, or otherwise alter, the foregoing definitions of production and utilization facility. It may also include as a facility an important component part especially designed for a facility, but has not at this time included any component parts in the definitions.

"Source Material" means (1) uranium or thorium, or any combination thereof, in any physical or chemical form or (2) ores which contain by weight one-twentieth of one percent (0.05%) or more of (i) uranium, (ii) thorium or (iii) any combination thereof. Source material does not include special nuclear material.

"Byproduct material" means any radioactive material (except special nuclear material) yielded in or made radioactive by exposure to the radiation incident to the process of producing or utilizing special nuclear material.

"Special nuclear material" means (1) plutonium, uranium-233, uranium enriched in the isotope 233 or in the isotope 235, and any other material which the Commission, pursuant to the provisions of section 51 of the act, determines to be special nuclear material, but does not include source material; or (2) any material artifically enriched by any of the foregoing but does not include source material.

10 C.F.R. §§ 50.2(a), 50.2(b), 40.4(h), 30.4(d), 70.4(m) (1976).

[20]42 U.S.C. § 2153 (1970 & Supp. V 1975).

[21]*Id.* § 2014(b) (1970). An LWR is a utilization facility. Enrichment facilities and reprocessing plants are production facilities. See note 19 *supra*. From a proliferation standpoint, enrichment facilities and reprocessing plants are particularly sensitive because they are required in order to produce the special nuclear material suitable for weapons use. See generally Appendix I *infra*.

[22]42 U.S.S. § 2074(b) (Supp. V 1975). Under section 54.b of the Act, the Commission is authorized to permit the export of certain special nuclear material in the absence of an Agreement for Cooperation upon a determination that the export would not be inimical to the common defense and security of the United States. Section 54.b permits the export of special nuclear material in classes or quantities or for classes of users or users exempted pursuant to section 57.d of the Act, *id.* § 2077(d), and plutonium containing 80 percent or more by weight of plutonium-238 in the absence of an Agreement for Cooperation. These sections provide, among other things, for the use of plutonium-238 as a power source in cardiac pacemakers.

[23]42 U.S.C. § 2153 (1970 & Supp. V 1975). In connection with the transfer of technology, section 57.b of the Act prohibits any "person" as defined by section 11.s, *id.* § 2014(s) (1970), from engaging, directly or indirectly, in the production of any special nuclear material outside of the United States except: (1) under an Agreement for Cooperation made pursuant to section 2153, or (2) upon authorization by the Commission after a determination that such activity will not be inimical to the interests of the United States. *Id.* § 2077(b). This prohibition extends to the furnishing of atomic energy-related information to foreign re-

cipients for use abroad as well as to activities associated with the furnishing of plants and equipment. 10 C.F.R. § 810 (1976) implements the provisions of section 57.b Section 810.7 (1976) of the regulations sets forth a general authorization to engage in those activities prohibited by section 57.b of the Act outside of specified Communist-bloc countries, subject to certain exceptions. Outside of the Communist-bloc countries the general authorization specifically excludes activities pertaining to the design, construction, fabrication, and operation of facilities for (a) the chemical processing of irradiated special nuclear material; (b) the production of heavy-water; and (c) the separation of isotopes of uranium, or equipment or components especially designed for any of these facilities. ro C.F.R. § 810.7(a)(2) (1976). These activities require specific authorization if undertaken anywhere outside of the United States. United States policy has been to avoid the export of sensitive reprocessing, heavy-water production, and enrichment technologies. *Export Reorganization Act of 1976, Hearings on S. 1439 Before the Senate Comm. on Gov't Operations,* 94th Cong., 2d Sess. 772 (1976) (testimony of Secretary of State Henry A. Kissinger).

[24]42 U.S.C. § 2153(a) (1970).

[25]*Id.* § 2153(b).

[26]*Id.* §§ 2153(c), 2153(d) (1970 & Supp. V 1975). The full congressional review procedure pertains to proposed Agreements for Cooperation dealing with nuclear reactors capable of producing more than five megawatts of thermal energy or fuel for such reactors. *Id.* § 2153(d). This procedure first became law in 1974, Act of Oct. 26, 1974, Pub. L. No. 93-485, 88 Stat. 1460, and Agreements entered into before that date have not, consequently, been subjected to this full congressional review. See notes 179-83 and accompanying text *infra.* In addition it should be noted that while section 123 of the Act refers to Joint Committee on Atomic Energy jurisdiction over Agreements for Cooperation, such jurisdiction was modified earlier this year by amendments to the rules of the House and Senate. H.R. Res. 5, 95th Cong., 1st Sess., 123 CONG. REC. H22 (daily ed. Jan. 4, 1977); S. Res. 4, 95th Cong., 1st Sess., 123 CONG. REC. 52307 (daily ed. Feb. 4, 1977).

[27]42 U.S.C. §§ 2094, 2112(b), (1970). A number of such determinations to permit the issuance of general licenses for the export of source and by-product material have been made. 10 C.F.R. §§ 30.01-30.71, §§ 40.20-40.24 (1976).

[28]50 U.S.C. app. §§ 2401-2413 (1970 & Supp. V 1975).

[29]Exec. Order No. 11,940, 41 Fed. Reg. 43,707 (1976), reprinted in 42 U.S.C. § 5841 note (Suppl. V 1975).

[30]The term "safeguards," in the context of international nuclear cooperation, refers to a system for detecting—and thereby deterring—the diversion of nuclear material from its authorized use. The basic measures available to a safeguarding authority are mterials accountability, surveillance, and containment. Kratzer, *supra* note 3, at 258-70.

[31]Under the Act, Agreements for Cooperation must contain a guarantee by the cooperating party that any material transferred will not be used for atomic weapons or for research on or development of such weapons or for any other military purposes. 42 U.S.C. § 2153(a)(3) (1970). For elaboration of the meaning of this clause, see note 44 *infra.* Safeguard rights reserved by the United States in bilateral Agreements for Cooperation were the basis for the bilateral safeguards program. During this period of developing international safeguards, countries other than the United States implemented bilateral safeguards programs. Such bilateral safeguards have been applied by the United Kingdom in its

civilian nuclear export program discussed at note 3 *supra*. These safeguards have been fully honored by the purchasers. For discussion of the special problems presented by natural uranium reactors from a non-proliferation standpoint, see Appendix I.

[32]Statute of the International Atomic Energy Agency, opened for signature Oct. 26, 1956, 8 U.S.T. 1093, T.I.A.S. No. 3873, 276 U.N.T.S.3.

[33]Even when bilateral arrangements were recommended in the early 1950's as a means of expediting the availability of peaceful atomic power, the ultimate desirability of international safeguards was recognized. See 1 PANEL ON THE IMPACT OF THE PEACEFUL USES OF ATOMIC ENERGY, 84TH CONG., 2D SESS., REPORT ON THE PEACEFUL USES OF ATOMIC ENERGY TO THE JOINT COMM. ON ATOMIC ENERGY 93-98 (Comm. Print 1956).

[34]See Kratzer, *supra* note 3, at 278-81.

[35]Agreement on the Application of Safeguards by the IAEA, Sept. 23, 1963, United States-Japan-IAEA, 14 U.S.T. 1265, T.I.A.S. No. 5429. See 1 EXPORT FES, *supra* note 10, at 6-22.

[36]See Kratzer, *supra* note 3, at 278-81. Somewhat surprisingly, the transfer to international safeguards has not proven easy. The majority of nations initially preferred safeguards, including inspections on their own territory, to be applied by the United States rather than by an international organization of which they themselves were members. *Id.* at 278-79. (Membership in the IAEA does not, by itself, obligate a country to accept IAEA safeguards except on projects undertaken with IAEA assistance.) The difficulties notwithstanding, United States bilateral safeguards have now been suspended in lieu of IAEA safeguards except for isolated cases in France and Italy. 1 EXPORT FES, *supra* note 10, at 6-22.

United States nuclear cooperation with the nations of Western Europe is unique in a number of respects. A major part of this cooperation has been undertaken directly with the European Atomic Energy Community (EURATOM). Agreement for Cooperation with the European Atomic Energy Community (EURATOM) Concerning Peaceful Uses of Atomic Energy, Nov. 8, 1958, 10 U.S.T. 75, T.I.A.S. No. 4173. All EURATOM member countries (France, Belgium, Luxemburg, Germany (FRG), Netherlands, Italy, Ireland, Denmark, and the United Kingdom), except France, are parties to the Treaty on the Non-proliferation of Nuclear Weapons (NPT). See Appendix III. In a novel development the IAEA and the non-nuclear-weapon States of EURATOM have negotiated an NPT safeguards agreement which takes into account the multinational character and the considerable experience of the EURATOM safeguards program. Under the agreement, the IAEA will rely on the EURATOM safeguards system but will also be able to carry out independent verification of EURATOM safeguards findings. Although a nuclear-weapon State, the United Kingdom has made a voluntary offer to accept IAEA safeguards. 1 EXPORT FES, *supra* note 10, at 6-23.

The United States has also entered into an Agreement for Cooperation with the IAEA itself. See generally *id.* at 3-119 to -123. Agreement for Cooperation in the Civil Uses of Atomic Energy, May 11, 1959, United States-IAEA, 10 U.S.T. 1424, T.I.A.S. No. 4291, extended and amended Feb. 12, 1974, 25 U.S.T. 1199, T.I.A.S. No. 7852.

[37]Treaty on the Non-proliferation of Nuclear Weapons, opened for signature July 1, 1968, 21 U.S.T. 483, T.I.A.S. No. 6839, 729 U.N.T.S. 161 [hereinafter NPT].

[38]*Id.* art. II.

[39]*Id.* art. III, para. 1.

[40]*Id.* art. III, para. 2. Thus, IAEA safeguards apply to United States-origin materials and facilities pursuant to two different schemes which differ in significant respects. Most importantly, safeguards pursuant to the trilaterals apply only to United States-origin materials and facilities whereas those under an NPT safeguards agreement apply to "all peaceful nuclear activities" within the territory of the recipient NPT party. This distinction sets up what some have called "reverse NPT discrimination." When the United States exports nuclear materials and facilities to a non-party to the NPT, the safeguards regime is less stringent than that imposed upon an NPT party, in effect establishing a disincentive to NPT accession. See generally, *e.g.,* 1 EXPORT FES, *supra* note 10, at 3-98 to -124.

[41]See text at notes 6 and 26 *supra.* For a comprehensive overview and authoritative analysis of congressional involvement in nuclear matters over most of the past thirty years, see McCormack, *U.S. Congressional Attitudes and Policies Affecting Nuclear Power Development in the World,* 17 ATOM. ENERGY L.J. 289 (1976).

[42]The International Security Assistance and Arms Control Export Act of 1976, Pub. L. No. 94-329, § 301, 90 Stat. 755 (1976).

[43]Indeed, the 94th Congress even took measures to assure that nuclear export policy would continue to receive scrutiny. For example, provisions were made for a special Senate delegation to visit the Middle East, Europe and other areas to study United States security and foreign policy interests involved with the widespread utilization of nuclear reactors. S. Res. 523, 94th Cong., 2d Sess., 122 CONG. REC. S14,580 (daily ed. Aug. 26, 1976). While in the Middle East, the delegation was reportedly barred from inspecting Israel's research facilities in the Negev Desert at Dimona. Washington Post, Nov. 9, 1976, § A, at 1, col. 4. In addition, numerous bills dealing with nuclear export policy have already been introduced. See, *e.g.,* H.R. 4409, 95th Cong., 1st Sess. (1977); S. 897, 95th Cong., 1st Sess. (1977); H.R. 1561, 95th Cong., 1st Sess. (1977); S. 69, 95th Cong., 1st Sess. (1977).

[44]Agreements for Cooperation are generally silent concerning the development of so-called peaceful nuclear explosives (PNEs). Although Agreements provide that nations will use transferred items solely for civil purposes, and will not use them for atomic weapons, or research on or development of atomic weapons, or for other military purposes, there is often no explicit prohibition on PNEs. See generally LIBRARY OF CONGRESS CONGRESSIONAL RESEARCH SERVICE, 94TH CONG., 2D SESS., UNITED STATES AGREEMENTS FOR COOPERATION IN ATOMIC ENERGY: AN ANALYSIS FOR THE SENATE COMM. ON GOV'T OPERATIONS CRS-18 to -19 (Comm. Print 1976). Since PNEs and atomic weapons are technically indistinguishable, development of PNEs may be prohibited since it is impossible to develop a PNE without having done research on or development of atomic weapons. Statement of Ambassador Joseph Martin Jr. before the Conference of the Committee on Disarmament (Mar. 4, 1975), excerpted in E. McDOWELL, 1975 DIGEST OF UNITED STATES PRACTICE IN INTERNATIONAL LAW 842-43 (1976). The United States has made this interpretation known to its bilateral partners by means of a series of *aide-memoires* and exchanges of notes. See, *e.g.,* Agreement Extending the Agreement for Cooperation of July 12, 1955, Jan. 13, 1975, United States-Israel [Related Notes], 26 U.S.T. 127, T.I.A.S. No. 8019. United States opposition to the development of peaceful nuclear explosives by non-nuclear-weapon

States, moreover, is well known. It has been suggested that development of such a device, indicating a serious difference of opinion with the United States as to what constitutes a peaceful purpose, could bring into play the rule of *rebus sic stantibus* under which a substantial change in the state of facts which existed at the time an Agreement became effective would suspend the obligations of the parties under the Agreement. See generally, *e.g.,* A. Fisher, U.S. Commitments to Supply Nuclear Materials to Other States (unpublished memorandum), reprinted in *Export Reorganization Act of 1976, Hearings on S. 1439 Before the Senate Comm. on Gov't Operations,* 94th Cong., 2d Sess. 1402-04. See als note 161 *infra* and accompanying text.

[45]See S. REP. NO. 964, 93d Cong., 2d Sess. 1 (1974).

[46]See NUCLEAR ENGINEERING INT'L, Apr./May 1976, at 10.

[47]*Id.* France also negotiated with South Korea for the sale of a nuclear fuel reprocessing pilot plant. However, plans were shelved at least partly as a result of pressure from the United States. NUCLEAR ENGINEERING INT'L, Mar. 1976, at 5.

[48]Taiwan agreed to halt nuclear fuel reprocessing although it did not admit that any secret reprocessing had been accomplished despite alleged United States intelligence reports to the contrary. NUCLEAR ENGINEERING INT'L, Oct. 1976, at 12.

[49]NUCLEAR ENGINEERING INT'L, July 1976, at 9.

[50]*Id.*

[51]NUCLEAR ENGINEERING INT'L, June 1976, at 9. The nuclear power station at Atucha—the first to operate in Argentina—obtains heavy-water from Canada at present. *Id.*

[52]The result of one calculation, for example, was that 46 countries would produce sufficient plutonium by 1990 to produce 3,002 small nuclear explosives annually. RICHARD J. BARBER ASSOCIATES, REPORT ON LDC NUCLEAR POWER PROSPECTS, 1975-1990: COMMERCIAL, ECONOMIC & SECURITY IMPLICATIONS, at V-5 to -12 (ERDA-52 1975).

[53]In fact, no nation has employed safeguarded material derived from nuclear power production facilities to produce its first nuclear explosive. See Kratzer, *supra* note 3, at 274-75.

[54]Many small and/or developing nations could probably build a reactor capable of producing about 10 kilograms of plutonium per year for about $13 to $26 million. The necessary design information is available in the open literature, and all necessary components and materials are available. See J. LAMARSH, ON THE CONSTRUCTION OF PLUTONIUM-PRODUCING REACTORS BY SMALL AND/OR DEVELOPING NATIONS (1976) (report prepared for the Congressional Research Service of the Library of Congress), reprinted in *Export Reorganization Act of 1976, Hearings on S. 1439 Before the Senate Comm. on Gov't Operations,* 94th Cong., 2d Sess. 1326 (1976).

[55]See, *e.g.,* Joskow, *The International Nuclear Industry Today,* 54 FOREIGN AFF. 788, 791-98 (1976).

[56]See FORTUNE, Dec. 1975, at 145. The mobility of buyers on the market was again recently emphasized by South Africa. After difficulties arose in a deal for two reactors which had been negotiated with· a consortium led by General Electric, South Africa backed out and awarded the contract to a French consortium led by Framatome. See NUCLEAR ENGINEERING INT'L, July 1976, at 8. Iran, likewise, abandoned efforts to obtain nuclear components for its

facilities from the United States, as have other countries. See Doub & Fidell, *International Relations and Nuclear Commerce: Developments in United States Policy,* 8 LAW & POL'Y INT'L BUS. 913, 917-19 (1976).

[57] See Rippon, *Reprocessing—What Went Wrong],* NUCLEAR ENGINEER- ING INT'L, Feb. 1976, at 21-27. Facilities at La Hague in France—the first to offer substantial new capacity for the commercial reprocessing of highly ir- radiated oxide fuels—came into operation in May 1976 and are expected to reach 50 percent of full capacity in 1977. NUCLEAR ENGINEERING INT'L, July 1976, at 8. In the United States, however, the outgoing Ford Administration an- nounced a new policy calling for a halt in reprocessing plans pending further evaluation. See President's Statement, 12 WEEKLY COMP. OF PRES. DOC. 1624, 1626 (Nov. 1, 1976). In establishing the new policy, the President called for international cooperation in undertaking the evaluation program and stated that "While the decision to delay reprocessing is significant, it will not prevent us from increasing our use of nuclear energy." *Id.* The new policy represents a sharp break with past plans, however, and its full development and effects are likely yet to be seen.

[58] See, *e.g.,* U.S. ENERGY RESEARCH AND DEVELOPMENT AD- MINISTRATION, DRAFT ENVIRONMENTAL STATEMENT ON PORTS- MOUTH GASEOUS DIFFUSION PLANT EXPANSION (ERDA-1549 1976).

[59] See 1. EXPORT FES, *supra* note 10, at 1-10.

[60] Joskow, *supra* note 55, at 795. An independent company called COREDIF, of which EURODIF is a 51% shareholder, has also been formed to build a se- cond gaseous diffusion enrichment plant. See Rougeau, *Uranium Enrichment by Eurodif and Coredif,* NUCLEAR ENGINEERING INT'L, Nov. 1976, at 62.

[61] Joskow, *supra* note 55, at 796. URENCO is actually comprised of two in- dustrial companies (URENCO Ltd. and CENTEC GmbH) and is often now referred to as "Urenco-Centec." Its first commercial delivery of enriched uranium was made in 1975. See van Dijk & Abraham, *Urenco-Centec Centrifuge Enrichmend Producing Now and a Secure Future,* NUCLEAR ENGINEERING INT'L, Nov. 1976, at 52-53.

[62] See 1 EXPORT FES, *supra* note 10, at 3-69.

[63] *Id.* Japan, in addition to engaging in centrifuge research and development, has held discussions with Australia concerning the construction of an enrichment plant in the latter country. *Id.* See also NUCLEAR ENGINEERING INT'L, Nov. 1976, at 9.

[64] 1 EXPORT FES, *supra* note 10, at 3-69.

[65] *Id.* It has been reported that, because of its large hydro plants which provide inexpensive electricity, the Soviet Union's enrichment services have been offered at less than United States costs. *Id.*

[66] Joskow, *supra* note 55, at 797. Even the 1983-1984 start-up date for the Clinch River plant may be too optimistic in view of the Carter Administration's decision to, at least, reduce program funding for fiscal year 1978. [1977] EN. USERS REP. (BNA) 4 (Feb. 24, 1977).

[67] *Id.* Dutch utilities are also expected to take a share in the Super-Phenix proj- ect. NUCLEAR ENGINEERING INT'L, Nov. 1976, at 12.

[68] Joskow, *supra* note 55, at 797. In fact, the United States breeder program is now so far behind that of other countries that it may never catch up, a possi- bility that prompted the following observation: "With the U.S. fast reactor pro- gramme slipping far behind Europe, there is clearly an interest on both sides of

the Atlantic in laying foundations for possible future license agreements which for once might be in an east-west direction." 20 NUCLEAR ENGINEERING INT'L 895 (1975).

[69]Natural Resources Defense Council, Inc. v. NRC, 539 F. 2d 824 (2d Cir. 1976), cert. granted, 45 U.S.L.W. 647 (U.S. Mar. 28, 1977) (No. 76-653).

[70]539 F. 2d at 846. "Mixed oxide fuel" refers to that nuclear fuel which is composed of a mixture of recycled plutonium oxide and uranium oxide. The plutonium, of course, is obtained through the reprocessing of spent reactor fuel. See Appendix I.

[71]The GESMO is a generic environmental impact statement being prepared by the NRC pursuant to the National Environmental Policy Act of 1969 (NEPA), 42 U.S.C. §§ 4321-4347 (1970 & Supp. V 1975). The NRC announced the preparation of GESMO in February 1974. See 39 Fed. Reg. 5356 (1974). However, the task is not yet complete.

[72]The NRC announced that public hearings would be held on the GESMO in December 1974. 39 Fed. Reg. 43,101 (1976). Based on developments thus far, prospects for an expeditious proceeding are poor indeed. The Second Circuit's decision may operate to limit modification of the new policy on reprocessing announced by President Ford. See *supra* note 57.

[73]Natural Resources Defense Council v. NRC, [1976] 9 ENVIR. REP. (BNA) 1149, cert. granted, 45 U.S.L.W. 3554 (U.S. Feb. 22, 1977) (No. 76-419). The environmental effects involved were those associated with fuel reprocessing and the disposal of high level radioactive wastes as ascribed by the NRC to the operation of individual reactors. *Id.* A related case was decided by the court on the same day. Aeschliman v. NRC, [1976] 9 ENVIR. REP. (BNA) 1289, cert. granted, 45 U.S.L.W. 3554 (U.S. Feb. 22, 1977) (No. 76-528). See generally Lloyd Harbor Study Group, Inc. v. NRC, No. 73-2266 (D.C. Cir. Nov. 9, 1976) (per curiam), petition for cert. filed, 45 U.S.L.W. 3435 (U.S. Nov. 9, 1976) (No. 76-745).

[74]The issuance of full power operating licenses, construction permits, and limited work authorizations for nuclear plants was halted by the Commission in August following the two decisions. On November 5, 1976, the Commission announced that—primarily on the basis of an October 8 pronouncement by the court apparently providing for conditional licensing pending the outcome of remanded proceedings, and the issuance of a proposed interim rule responsive to the court's concerns—operating licenses, construction permits, and limited work authorizations could be issued subject to specified conditions. NRC Press Release No. 76-245 (Nov. 5, 1976).

[75]*Edlow Int'l Co.* (Agent for the Government of India on Application to Export Special Nuclear Material), to be reported in 3 N.R.C.———(1976), II NUCLEAR REG. REP. (CCH) ¶ 30,069 (May 7, 1976) [hereinafter all references to the *Edlow* case will be to the NUCLEAR REG. REP.].

[76]*Id.* ¶ 30,069.02.

[77]In the words of the Commission: "The petitions to intervene filed on behalf of these organizations, if granted, would require the holding of an adjudicatory, or trial-type hearing subject to appropriate modifications made in accordance with the Administrative Procedure Act's "foreign policy" exception. 5 U.S.C. § 554(a)(4)." *Id.* ¶ 30,069.03. The prefatory language to the quoted section of the Administrative Procedure Act, however, provides for adjudicatory proceedings only in cases which—unlike those arising under the Atomic Energy Act of 1954—are "required by statute to be determined *on the record* after opportunity

for an agency hearing." Emphasis added. *Compare* Administrative Procedure Act § 5, 5 U.S.C. § 554(a) (1970) *with* Atomic Energy Act of 1954 § 189a, 42 U.S.C. § 2239(a) (1970). This at least opens to debate the question as to whether any type of formal, trial-tyPE hearings—"foreign affairs" variety or otherwise— are required in connection with export license cases. See United States v. Florida East Coast Ry., 410 U.S. 224 (11973); United States v. Allegheny-Ludlum Steel Corp., 406 U.S. 742 (1972).

Prior to the *Edlow* case no request for intervention or a hearing on a nuclear export license had been received by the NRC or its predecessor, the AEC. II NUCLEAR REG. REP. ¶ 30,069.03.

⁷⁸*Id.* ¶ 30,069.05.

⁷⁹*Id.* ¶ 30,069.04.

⁸⁰*Id.* ¶ 30,069.02. This determination on the part of the Commission has since been appealed *sub nom.* Natural Resources Defense Council, Inc., v. NRC, No. 76-1525 (D.C. Cir. filed June 11, 1976).

⁸¹II NUCLEAR REG. REP. ¶ 30,069.02; *id.* ¶ 30,069.13.

⁸²For additional discussion of the *Edlow* case and other pertinent NRC activities see Doub & Fidell, *supra* note 56, at 945-51.

⁸³See the cases cited in notes 69 and 73 *supra;* Mobil Oil Corp. v. FPC, 483 F.2d 1238 (D.C. Cir. 1973); Int'l Harvester v. Ruckelshaus, 478 F.2d 615 (D.C. Cir. 1974). *But cf.* United States v. Florida East Coast Ry., 410 U.S. 224 (1973); United States v. Allegheny-Ludlum Steel Corp., 406 U.S. 742 (1972) (indicating that where adjudicatory proceedings are not mandated by statutory prescription relatively informal procedures are adequate).

⁸⁴This particular problem was implicitly recognized in the *Edlow* decision itself. In providing for a hearing, the Commission stated:

> Because of the generic character of the issues raised, the Commission may act on one or both of these applications prior to the conclusion of the hearings if it finds that a need for greater expedition in acting on these issues has been shown. The hearings would then be continued for the purpose of assisting the Commission in its determination of subsequent licenses for the Tarapur facility.

II NUCLEAR REG. REP. ¶ 30,069.13. While the Commission may, thus, have succeeded in defining an approach, it has not solved the problem.

⁸⁵Whatever the potential benefits to be derived from special interest group participation in export license proceedings, it is less than apparent that the cost would be commensurate with any gain. Even Commissioner Gilinsky, who has praised intervention in domestic reactor licensing cases, see, *e.g.,* 41 Fed. Reg. 50,836-38 (1976) (dissenting from a statement of consideration associated with the termination-of rule-making concerning financial assistance to participants in Commission proceedings) joined in the unanimous *Edlow* decision.

⁸⁶About one month after the Commission's May 7, 1976, *Edlow* intervention decision, NRC Commissioner Gilinsky cast the first dissenting vote ever in an export licensing case involving the shipment of a reactor to Spain. *Westinghouse Electric Cor.* (Application for the Export of Pressurized Water Reactor to Association Nuclear ASCO II, Barcelona, Spain), to be reported in 3 N.R.C.———(1976), reprinted in II NUCLEAR REG. REP. ¶ 30,080.10 (June 21, 1976) (Gilinsky, Commn'r, dissenting). The following month, Commissioner Gilinsky again dissented, this time in connection with a decision in the *Edlow* case allowing the shipment of a certain amount of fuel to India because of the "urgency with which this license is required by the Government of India and the

need to avoid, on the part of the United States, undue adverse impact on United States foreign policy interests." *Edlow Int'l Co.* (Agent for the Government of India on Application to Export Special Nuclear Material), to be reported in 4 N.R.C.————(1976), reprinted in II NUCLEAR REG. REP. ¶ 30,085.01 (July 1, 1976) (Gilinsky, Commn'r, dissenting).

⁸⁷Pub. L. No. 94-329, 90 Stat. 729 (1976) (to be codified in scattered sections of 22 U.S.C.).

⁸⁸Section 305 'of the International Security Assistance and Arms Export Control Act of 1976 reads as follows:

Chapter 3 of part III of the Foreign Assistance Act of 1961 is amended by adding at the end thereof the following new section:

"Sec. 669. *Nuclear Transfers—*

"(a) (except as provided in subsection (b), no funds authorized to be appropriated by this Act or the Arms Export Control Act may be used for the purpose of—

"(1) providing economic assistance;

"(2) providing military or security supporting assistance or grant military education and training; or

"(3) extending military credits or making guarantees; to any country which—

"(A) delivers nuclear reprocessing or enrichment equipment, materials, or technology to any other country; or

"(B) receives such equipment, materials or technology from any other country; unless before such delivery—

"(i) the supplying country and receiving country have reached agreement to place all such equipment, materials, and technology, upon delivery, under multilateral auspices and management when available; and

"(ii) the recipient country has entered into an agreement with the International Atomic Energy Agency to place all such equipment, materials, technology, and all nuclear fuel and facilities in such country under the safeguards system of such Agency.

"(b) (1) Notwithstanding the provisions of subsection (a) of this section, the President may, by Executive order effective not less than 30 days following its date of promulgation, furnish assistance which would otherwise be prohibited under paragraph (1), (2), or (3) of such subsection if he determines and certifies in writing to the Speaker of the House of Representatives and the Committee on Foreign Relations of the Senate that—

"(A) the termination of such assistance would have a serious adverse effect on vital United States interest; and

"(B) he has received reliable assurances that the country in question will not acquire or develop nuclear weapons or assist other nations in doing so.

Such certification shall set forth the reasons supporting such determination in each particular case.

"(2) (A) The Congress may by joint resolution terminate or restrict assistance described in paragraphs (1) through (3) of subsection (a) with respect to a country to which the prohibition in such subsection applies or take any other action with respect to such assistance for such country as it deems appropriate.

"(B) Any such joint resolution with respect to a country shall, if introduced within 30 days after the transmittal of a certification under

paragraph (1) with respect to such country, be considered in the Senate in accordance with the provisions of section 601(b) of the International Security Assistance and Arms Export Control Act of 1976."
Id. § 305, at 755.

[89] Foreign Assistance Act of 1961, 75 Stat. 424 (codified in scattered sections of 22 U.S.C.).

[90] See, *e.g.,* 122 CONG. REC. S9041 (daily ed. June 11, 1976) (remarks of Sen. Glenn); 122 CONG. REC. S11,784 (daily ed. July 19, 1976) (remarks of Sen. Symington).

[91] See H.R. REP. NO. 1272, 94th Cong., 2d Sess. 53-54, reprinted in [1976] U.S. CODE CONG. & AD. NEWS 2182, 2189-90.

[92] *Id.* at 54.

[93] Quoted in note 88 *supra.* The requirement tht any joint resolution terminating or limiting assistance be introduced within 30 days of the President's transmittal is not precisely stated in the statutory language but is clearly specified in the committee of conference report. See H.R. REP. NO. 1272, 94th Cong., 2d Sess. 54 (1976). In any case, a joint-resolution is, of course, subject to veto by the President. See H. ZINN, HOW OUR LAWS ARE MADE, H.R. Doc. No. 323, 92d Cong., 2d Sess. 7 (1972).

[94] See note 23 *supra.*

[95] France and West Germany both announced recently that they would no longer export nuclear reprocessing plants. Washington Post, Dec. 17, 1976, § A, at 34, col. 1; Washington Post, Dec. 21, 1976, § A, at 1, col. 4. There must be some question as to whether or not these policy shifts were motivated by the Symington provision since they do not affect the French and German deals with Pakistan and Brazil, respectively. *Id.* See note 96 *infra.* See also notes 46 & 47 *supra* and accompanying text.

[96] It appears, at the present time, that only Pakistan and Brazil may attract sanctions under the Symington provision since they are the only countries liable to receive United States economic or military assistance which are likely to also be engaged in the type of transactions covered. 122 CONG. REC. S9043 (daily ed. June 11, 1976).
It should also be noted, however, that the propriety of attempting to legislate not only the domestic policy of another nation, but its relations with others as well, has not gone unquestioned. See Doubt & Fidell, *supra* note 56, at 926-27.

[97] S. REP. No. 876, 94th Cong., 2d Sess. 52 (1976).

[98] *Id.* at 52-53.

[99] 122 CONG. REC. S9041 (daily ed. June 11, 1976) (remarks of Sen. Glenn).

[100] See, *e.g.,* IAEA STUDY PROJECT ON REGIONAL NUCLEAR FUEL CYCLE CENTRES STATUS REPORT, SEPTEMBER 1976 (EAEA-RFCC/3).

[101] Another ambiguity in the Symington provision is contained in the clause concerning IAEA safeguards. Section (3)(B)(ii), quoted in note 88, *supra.* It is not clear if the provision would be satisfied if each facility constructed in a country were placed under safeguards pursuant to a separate agreement, or whether a single, comprehensive agreement—along the lines of the safeguards commitment contemplated by the NPT for non-nuclear-weapon states—is required. See notes 37-40 *supra* and accompanying text. In addition, because sanctions are imposed only on countries receiving United States aid, there could be a tendency to read the Symington measure as at least tacit approval of the transfer of sensitive nuclear equipment, materials, or technology among countries that

are not recipients of United States assistance since they would remain unaffected. Although such a reading would be a tortured one at best, there is no reason why general disapproval of such transfers could not be explicitly embodies in the statutory language of the amendment.

¹⁰²S. 1439, 94th Cong., 1st Sess., 121 CONG. REC. S5960 (daily ed. Apr. 15, 1975); reprinted in *The Export Reorganization Act—1975: Hearings on S. 1439 Before the Senate Comm. on Gov't Operations,* 94th Cong., 1st Sess. 499 (1975); S. 1439, 94th Cong., 2d Sess. (1976), reprinted in *The Export Reorganization Act of 1976, Hearings on S. 1439 Before the Senate Comm. on Gov't Operations,* 94th Cong., 2d Sess. 1255 (1976), modified version reprinted in *S. 1439: Export Reorganization Act of 1976: Hearings on S. 1439 Before the Joint Comm. on Atomic Energy,* 94th Cong., 2d Sess. 68 (1976) [hereinafter all references to S. 1439 will be to the 1976 Joint Committee version unless otherwise specified].

¹⁰³50 U.S.C. app. §§ 2401-2413 (1970 & Supp. V 1975).

¹⁰⁴H.R. 15377, 94th Cong., 2d Sess., 122 CONG. REC. H9398 (daily ed. Sept. 1, 1976).

¹⁰⁵H.R. 13350, 94th Cong., 2d Sess., 122 CONG. REC. H3494 (daily ed. Apr 26, 1976); S. 3105, 94th Cong., 2d Sess., 122 CONG. REC. S5842 (daily ed. Mar. 9, 1976).

¹⁰⁶H.R. 15273, 94th Cong., 2d Sess., 122 CONG. REC. S14481 (daily ed. Aug. 25, 1976); 94th Cong., 2d Sess., 122 CONG. REC. H9083 (daily ed. Aug. 25, 1976).

¹⁰⁷H.R. 15419, 94th Cong., 2d Sess., 122 CONG. REC. H9491 (daily ed. Sept. 2, 1976).

¹⁰⁸Aspects of these proposals are also considered in Doub & Fidell, *supra* note 56, at 929-45.

¹⁰⁹See S. Rep. No. 875, 94th Cong., 2d Sess. 3 (1976) for the drafting history of the bill. The 1975 version of the bill is reprinted in *The Export Reorganization Act—1975: Hearings on S. 1439 Before the Senate Comm. on Gov't Operations,* 94th Cong., 1st Sess. 499 (1975).

¹¹⁰See S. REP. No. 875, 94th Cong., 2d Sess. 3 (1976).

¹¹¹*Id.* at 5.

¹¹²S. 1439, 94th Cong., 2d Sess. § 6(c)(1) (1976).

¹¹³See note 18 *supra*.

¹¹⁴S. 1439, 94th Cong., 2d Sess. § 6(c)(3)-(c)(4) (1976).

¹¹⁵Congressional arbitration of disputes arising between the State Department and the Nuclear Regulatory Commission was strongly opposed by both parties on constituional as well as other grounds. See, *e.g.,* S. *1439: Export Reorganization Act of 1976: Hearings on S. 1439 Before the Joint Comm. on Atomic Energy,* 94th Cong., 2d Sess. 45-46, 166 (1976). In additiona, the motivation for the procedure itself was less than completely clear. According to the Senate Government Operations Committee report, the basic concern was that "the lack of adequate procedures to resolve internal conflicts regarding the . . . licensing of major nuclear exports could make the United States appear to be an unreliable supplier of nuclear fuels and services on the world market." S. REP. No. 875, 94th Cong., 2d Sess. 7-8 (1976). However, as the report itself recognized, the odds of a stalemate actually occurring are not very great. *Id.* at 9-10. Perhaps a truer reflection of basic motives was the statement in the analysis part of the report pertaining to section 6(c)(3) that "A fundamental assumption

underlying this provision is the Committee's judgment that should an application raise issues which the NRC and the Secretary of State cannot settle, then the issues are likely to be important enough to require direct Congressional attention and action." *Id.* at 18.

[116]*Id.* at 6.

[117]S. REP. No. 1193, 94th Cong., 2d Sess. 4 (1976).

[118]See text at notes 131-55 *infra.*

[119]S. REP. No. 1193, 94th Cong., 2d Sess. 1 (1976).

[120]The bill was clearly a closely considered one, developed over a period of more than one year. Seven days of hearings were held. Witnesses included the Secretary of State, Director of the Arms Control and Disarmament Agency, the Chairman of the NRC, the Administrator of ERDA, and the United States Representative to the IAEA. See S. REP. No. 875, 94th Cong., 2d Sess. 4-6 (1976).

[121]*Id.* at 6.

[122]The Senate Government Operations Committee summarized administration opposition to S. 1439 as based on the assessment that current nuclear export procedures are sound; that further reorganization and additional regulation would weaken United States influence on the international nuclear market; and that it was necessary to avoid giving the impression that United States policy is in flux. *Id.* A letter from Robert J. McCloskey, on behalf of the Department of State, to Senator John Sparkman (June 23, 1976), reprinted in S. REP. No. 1193, 94th Cong., 2d Sess. 45-56 (1976), mentioned these criticisms and others. The administration was concerned about the constitutional issues involved in congressional intrusion into Executive branch responsibilities. Beyond the separation of powers question, S. 1439 addressed initiatives which the administration had already undertaken and would have restricted flexibility in negotiation. For more detailed criticisms, see generally *S. 1439: Export Reorganization Act of 1976: Hearings on S. 1439 Before the Joint Comm. on Atomic Energy,* 94th Cong., 2d Sess. (1976).

[123]*E.g.*

With reference to the Bill's implications for our non-proliferation policy, the encumbrances its various provisions would add to our export licensing procedures would materially diminish the credibility of the United States as a stable and reliable supplier of nuclear equipment and materials. This credibility has been an essential element in our non-proliferation policy for over twenty years. This policy has been predicated on the belief that active U.S. cooperation in the nuclear export field has enabled us to exert a positive non-proliferation influence on the nuclear programs of countries with which we have agreement for cooperation. . . .

The role we have played in securing restraint against the spread of nuclear weapons capabilities is directly related to and heavily dependent on how reliable we are perceived by other to be as suppliers. Several of the provisions of S. 1439 would raise the most serious questions in the eyes of our nuclear partners as to the promptness and final outcome of every export license application. The inevitable result would be consumer nations either turning to suppliers other than the U.S. for their nuclear needs or accelerating their own capability toward independent nuclear development.

Letter from Robert J. McCloskey to Senator John Sparkman, *supra* note 122.

[124]The section applied to all new or modified agreements for nuclear coopera-

tion, to subsequent arrangements of strategic significance, and to applications for export of nuclear facilities, components, or materials of strategic significance. The NRC was to make the determination of strategic significance, in effect allowing it at times to request an NPAS. Subsection 7(c) also authorized the Director of ACDA to "prepare such a statement at his own discretion." S. 1439, 94th Cong., 2d Sess. § 7 (1976).

[125]S. REP. No. 875, 94th Cong., 2d Sess. 19-20 (1976). The report continued:
The requirement that Congress shall directly receive such statements, at the same time that they are provided to the NRC and to the Secretary of State, gives some assurance that the assessments will not be stopped or intercepted within the Executive Branch. In addition this will ensure that as much of this information as possible will be available to the public.
Id. at 20.

[126]This matter was raised by ACDA Director Ikle himself. See *S. 1439: Export Reorganization Act of 1976: Hearings on S. 1439 Before the Joint Comm. on Atomic Energy,* 94th Cong., 2d Sess. 65 (1976).

[127]See note 125 *supra.*

[128]Section 6(b) specifically addressed the question of public hearings in connection with "applications for licenses for export of atomic energy facilities, components, and materials for use for nonmilitary purposes and applications for approval for export of nonmilitary atomic energy technology." S. 1439, 94th Cong., 2d Sess. § 6(b) (1976). While not itself mandating public hearings, the section required "the NRC to establish clear procedures for as great a degree of public participation in the licensing process as is feasible." S. REP. No. 875, 94th Cong., 2d Sess. 17 (1976).

[129]*Id.* at 8-9.

[130]*Id.* at 9-10 (expressing concern that lack of an adequate procedure to resolve differences between the NRC and the Department of State would affect United States reliability as a supplier).

[131]See note 118 *supra* and accompanying text.

[132]S. 3770, 94th Cong., 2d Sess., 122 CONG. REC. S14,481 (daily ed. Aug. 25, 1976). Senator Pastore sponsored S. 3770. H.R. 15273, 94th Cong., 2d Sess., 122 CONG. REC. H9083 (daily ed. Aug. 25, 1976), was co-yponsored by Congressmen Price and Anderson. All were membegs of thehJoint Committee on Atomic Energy. S. 3770 and H.R.h15273hwere, in substance, identical to the revised version of S. 1439 reported by the Senate Foreign Relations Committee.

[133]See H.R. REP. No. 1613, 94th Cong., 2d Sess. 18-19 (1976).

[134]H.R. REP. No. 1613, 94th Cong., 2d Sess. 19 (1976).

[135]*Id.*

[136]*Id.* at 20-23.

[137]*Id.* at 20.

[138]The consideration given to the amendments was related by Congressman Brown in his dissenting views.
During the two hour mark-up session the Joimt Committee staff read the "technical" amendments also provided by ERDA, and explained them. The members spent the entire two hours discussing the "technical" amendments, and frequently amended these proposals on the advice of staff and their own good judgement. It was only at the very last 60 seconds of the meeting that the "substantive" amendments of "policy significance" were considered. They were adopted by voice vote, without being read, without staff

explanation, and without an opportunity for members, such as myself to object. It should be noted that, like myself, the staff of the Joint Committee only received these ERDA amendments the morning of the vote.
Id. at 57.

[139]H.R. 15419, 94th Cong., 2d Sess. § 8, 122 CONG. REC. H9491 (daily ed. Sept. 2, 1976). Provisions in the H.R. 15419 bill for Nuclear Proliferation Assessment Statements were dropped. Section 11 of S. 3770, 94th Cong., 2d Sess. § 11, 122 CONG. REC. S14481 (daily ed. Aug. 25, 1976), had contained an NPAS provision but its section 14 limited potential procedural delays by providing, "No court shall have any jurisdiction to compel the performance of, or to review the adequacy of the performance of, any Nuclear Proliferation Assessment Statement called for in this section and elsewhere in this Act." *Id.* § 14.

[140]H.R. 15419, 94th Cong., 2d Sess. § 4, 122 CONG. REC. H9491 (daily ed. Sept. 2, 1976); H.R. REP. No. 1613, 94th Cong., 2d Sess. 35 (1976).

[141]S. 3770, 94th Cong., 2d Sess. §§ 14, 15, 122 CONG. REC. S14,481 (daily ed. Aug. 25, 1976). The concept of criteria was also responsive to comments which had been raised in connection with S. 1439 to the effect that, instead of setting itself up as a referee in disputes between the State Department and the NRC, Congress should concern itself with legislating general standards to govern the granting of export licenses. See, *e.g., S. 1439: Export Reorganization Act of 1976: Hearings on S. 1439 Before the Joint Comm. on Atomic Energy,* 94th Cong., 2d Sess. 45-46, 166 (1976).

[142]S 3770, 94th Cong., 2d Sess. § 14, 122 CONG. REC. S14,481 (daily ed. Aug. 25, 1976).

[143]*Id.* § 15.

[144]Section 15(b) provided a narrow mechanism for postponing the effective date of the 18-month criteria by delaying their application to a particular country in 12-month increments. *Id.* § 15(b). However, even the immediately effective criteria would likely have been difficult, if not impossible, to have met *in toto.*

[145]H.R. 15419, 94th Cong., 2d Sess. § 14, 122 CONG. REC. H9491 (daily ed. Sept. 2, 1976).

[146]*Id.* § 15.

[147]See generally notes 141-43 *supra* and accompanying text. One change of substance occurred. Prior United States approval for reprocessing was not required if the reprocessing occurred under "conditions which will enhance the United States non-proliferation objective of discouraging the further spread of national reprocessing facilities." H.R. 15419, 94th Cong., 2d Sess. § 14(5), 122 CONG. REC. H9491 (daily ed. Sept. 2, 1976).

[148]"[T]he Commission need not find that there has been a commitment by the recipient nation to adhere to the precise wording of the principles if, in the Commission's judgment, some other commitment on the part of the recipient is the functional equivalent of the principle in question." H.R. REP. No. 1613, 94th Cong., 2d Sess. 42-43 (1976). Despite the Committee's intention that the Commission apply the principles "in addition to other applicable requirements under law," *id.* at 42, the legal force of the principles is unclear.

[149]*Id.* at 43.

[150]*Id.* The six criteria were not transferred *in haec verba* from S. 3770 to H.R. 15419, but most of the essentials were preserved. A provision forbidding nations from stockpiling any weapons-grade material was added. H.R. 15419, 94th Cong., 2d Sess. § 15(6), 122 CONG. REC. H9491 (daily ed. Sept. 2, 1976). In

addition, the requirement of renouncing any national reprocessing was substantially modified. *Id.* § 15(5). Instead of a series of specific requirements which in effect ruled out reprocessing, the new criteria were satisfied if, in the judgement of the exporting nation in a particular transaction, safeguards adequate for nonproliferation objectives had been provided. For instance, United States exports to Brazil after the purchase of reprocessing facilities by Brazil from West Germany, for example, would not offend the criteria so long as West Germany was satisfied with the safeguards to which Brazil had agreed. The provision thus made room for the eventual development of an international consensus on proliferation, replacing the earlier attempt to impose standards articulated by Congress on transactions to which the United States was not a party.

[151]*Id.* § 15.

[152]H.R. REP. No. 1613, 94th Cong., 2d Sess. 43-44 (1976).

[153]One of the notable shortcomings of the bill was its failure to simplify and consolidate the overall nuclear export regulatory scheme. Another was its failure to specifically address the problems likely to arise as a result of the imposition of new conditions—notably the "principles governing United States exports"—in connection with valid, existing international agreements.

[154]For example, section 7 provided for the establishment of an international safeguards and security training program. H.R. 15419, 94th Cong., 2d Sess. § 7, 122 CONG. REC. H9491 (daily ed. Sept. 2, 1976). Section 4 undertook to enhance the ability of the United States to function as a reliable supplier of nucler fuel services. *Id.* § 4. Section 15, of course, mandated a "maximum effort" by the United States to obtain an international commitment to a strict set of nuclear trade critera. *Id.* § 15. Some of these innovations had appeared in the earlier legislative proposals. Both the 1976 version of S. 1439 and S. 3770 contained provisions to establish international safeguards schools. S. 1439, 94th Cong., 2d Sess. § 8, (1976); S. 3770, 94th Cong., 2d Sess. § 7, 122 CONG. REC. S14,481 (daily ed. Aug. 25, 1976). Likewise, both of these bills directed Presidential negotiations and provided detailed negotiation objectives. S. 1439 *supra* §§ 12(a)-12(b); S. 3770 *supra* § 5.

[155]The extreme haste surrounding the report of H.R. 15419 by the Joint Committee was unfortunate. See note 138 *supra*. It suggests, however, that, with additional time, the cooperative efforts of the Congress and administration might have been even more productive.

[156]The bill, H.R. 15377, 94th Cong., 2d Sess., 122 CONG. REC. H9398 (daily ed. Sept. 1, 1976) was amended in the House International Relations Committee to provide for the addition of a new section 17 to the Export Administration Act of 1969. See H.R. REP. No. 1469, 94th Cong., 2d Sess. 1-3 (1976).

[157]The bill was named for Rep. Clement Zablocki of Wisconsin.

[158]H.R. 15377, 94th Cong., 2d Sess. § 18, 122 CONG. REC. H9398 (daily ed. Sept. 1, 1976).

[159]*Id.*

[160]*Id.*

[161]*Id.* This was also known as the "Indian provision." It was inserted to deal with the problem raised by India's use of a research reactor and heavy-water supplied by Canada and the United States in the manufacture of an explosive device. See 122 CONG. REC. H10,820 (daily ed. Sept. 22, 1976) (remarks of Rep. Anderson). The heavy-water was not subject to any safeguards, as that term is now understood, but the supply contract did include an undertaking that the material would be used "only in India by the Government in connection with

research into and the use of atomic energy for peaceful purposes." India apparently took the position subsequent to the execution of the contract, however, that the development of a nuclear explosive device was not inconsistent with the peaceful uses undertaking. See *S. 1439: Export Reorganiation Act of 1976: Hearings on S. 1439 Before the Joint Comm. on Atomic Energy,* 94th Cong., 2d Sess. 11-19 (1976).

[162]See, *e.g.,* Agreement on Atomic Energy: Cooperation for Civil Uses, Mar. 20, 1974, United States-Spain, art. VIIIc, 25 U.S.T. 1063, T.I.A.S. No. 7841. This agreement employs the standard formulation in United States Agreements for Cooperation. It requires that "reprocessing or alteration shall be performed in facilities acceptable to both Parties upon a joint determination that the provisions [of the agreement relating to safeguards] may be effectively applied." *Id.*

[163]H.R. 15377, 94th Cong., 2d Sess. § 18, 122 CONG. REC. H9398 (daily. ed. Sept. 1, 1976).

[164]See H.R. REP. No. 1469, 94th Cong., 2d Sess. 6, 22 (1976).

[165]*Id.* at 24-25.

[166]*Id.*

[167]In the words of the International Relations Committee report: "The committee believes that the information obtained from the IAEA is necessary to aid in assessing the intentions and capabilities with respect to the development of nuclear weapons of nations receiving U.S. nuclear exports." H.R. REP. No. 1469, 94th Cong., 2d Sess. 24 (1976). In addition, the adequacy of IAEA safeguards has been the subject of criticism. See, *e.g.,* COMPTROLLER GENERAL OF THE UNITED STATES, GENERAL ACCOUNTING OFFICE, ROLE OF THE INTERNATIONAL ATOMIC ENERGY AGENCY IN SAFEGUARDING NUCLEAR MATERIAL (1975). See also COMPTROLLER GENERAL OF THE UNITED STATES, GENERAL ACCOUNTING OFFICE, ASSESSMENT OF U.S. AND INTERNATIONAL CONTROLS OVER THE PEACEFUL USES OF ATOMIC ENERGY 38-45 (1976). But criticism should be viewed from a broad perspective which accounts for the difficulties and benefits associated with international safeguards. See generally Szasx, *International Atomic Energy Agency Safeguards,* in INTERNATIONAL SAFEGUARDS AND NUCLEAR INDUSTRY 73 (M. Willrich ed. 1973). See also M. WILLRICH, NON-PROLIFERATION TREATY: FRAMEWORK FOR NUCLEAR ARMS CONTROL 99-126 (1969).

[168]See, *e.g.,* Agreement for the Application of Safeguards in Connection with the Treaty on the Non-Proliferation of Nuclear Weapons, Mar. 7, 1972, IAEA-German Democratic Republic, art. 5, 895 U.N.T.S. 4.

[169]NPT, *supra* note 37, art. III, para. 1. Such a result would have been especially ironic in view of the concern expressed in the Amendment over the "undermining [of] the principles of nuclear nonproliferation agreed to by the United States as a signatory to the NPT." H.R. REP. No. 1469, 94th Cong., 2d Sess. 1 (1976).

[172]H. Res. 1549, 94th Cong., 2d Sess. (1974). See generally 122 CONG. REC. H10,815-23 (daily ed. Sept. 22, 1976). During consideration of H. Res. 15419, a sharp jurisdictional dispute broke out between members of the Joint Committee on Atomic Energy and members of the House Committee on International Relations, with the former group charging the latter with a violation of House rules by virtue of the presence of the Zablocki Amendment. *Id.* at H10,819-22.

[173]122 CONG. REC. H10,823-68 (daily ed. Sept. 22, 1976).

[174]*Id.* at H10,864. As adopted, H.R. 15377 also contained an amendment offered by Congressman Fraser which would have directed the President to "conduct an in-depth study of whether, or the extent to which, the education and training of foreign nationals within the United States in nuclear engineering and related fields contributes to the proliferation of explosive nuclear devices or the development of a capability of producing explosive nuclear devices" and to report to the Congress within six months. *Id.* at H10,855-56.

[175]*Id.* at H10,835-36 (remarks of Rep. Bingham), H10,852-53 (remarks of Rep. Anderson; remarks of Rep. Long). See note 172 *supra*.

[176]S. 3084, 94th Cong., 2d Sess., 122 CONG. REC. S14,864 (daily ed. Aug. 27, 1976). The Senate bill also contained a provision, offered by Senator Stevenson, dealing with nuclear export policy. It was a more moderate measure than the Zablocki Amendment, however, expressing the "sense of the Congress that the President should actively seek, and by the earliest possible date secure" a number of arrangements aimed at strengthening international cooperation in the nuclear export area, and that he report his progress to the Congress within one year. *Id.* at S14,857-59.

[177]*Id.* at S14,866-67 (daily ed. Aug. 27, 1976).

[178]See notes 28 & 29 *supra* and accompanying text.

[179]H.R. 13350, 94th Cong., 2d Sess. 122 CONG. REC. H3494 (daily ed. Apr. 26, 1976); 122 CONG. REC. H4706-08 (daily ed. May 20, 1976).

[180]See note 26 *supra* and accompanying text.

[181]The procedure for congressional approval of export license applications was to be the same as that for new Agreements for Cooperation. H.R. 13350, 94th Cong., 2d Sess., 122 CONG. REC. H3494 (daily ed. Apr. 26, 1976); 122 CONG. REC. H4706-08 (daily ed. May 20, 1976).

[182]S. 3105, 94th Cong., 2d Sess., 122 CONG. REC. S5842 (daily ed. Mar. 9, 1976).

[183]See 122 CONG. REC. S10,582-85 (daily ed. June 25, 1976). This second facet of the Senate amendment made eminently more sense than the House provision which would have subjected exports to a nuclear-weapon State, particularly France, a non-NPT party, to congressional review procedures.

[184]See H.R. REP. No. 1718, 94th Cong., 2d Sess. 13-14, 56-58 (1976). Unfortunately, the conference report was less than a model of clarity in that it also presented, as section 201 of the reproted legislation, the House provision. *Id.* at 9. Confusion was compounded when, during subsequent consideration of the report, House conferees stated that, in case of any conflict between the conference report provision and section 201, "section 201, the House provision, is the prevailing provision." 122 CONG. REC. H11,949 (daily ed. Sept. 30, 1976).

[185]H.R. REP. No. 1718, 94th Cong., 2d Sess. 13-14, 56-58 (1976).

[186]This was not a new requirement but a restatement of existing Executive branch policy. See generally Appendix II *infra*.

[187]See note 141 *supra* and accompanying text.

[188]122 CONG. REC. H11,946-59 (daily ed. Sept. 30, 1976).

[189]In the final hours of the 94th Congress a dramatic clash occurred in the Senate Chamber between Senators Jackson and Gravel over appointments to the Joint Committee on Atomic Energy. When Senator Gravel threatened to call for a reading of the entire conference report if Senator Jackson would not agree to his appointment to the Joint Committee, angry words were exchanged, and the bill was withdrawn. See 122 CONG. REC. S17,755-56 (daily ed. Oct. 1, 1976).

[190]Funds for ERDA were provided by means of a continuing resolution. H.R.J. Res. 1105, 94th Cong., 2d Sess., 122 CONG. REC. H12,156-57, S17,557-58 (daily ed. Oct. 1, 1976).

[191]During the closing weeks of the Session Senator Percy, Robert Fri, Deputy Administrator of ERDA, and Charles Robinson, Deputy Secretary of State, worked feverishly to develop a consensus over a final, comprehensive piece of legislation. Although the effort failed, agreement was apparently reached concerning strict guidelines to govern future international negotiations. See 122 CONG. REC. S18,062-63 (daily ed. Oct. 1, 1976).

[192]The importance of assuming a leadership role cannot be overstated. It is vital, for example, that every effort be made to reduce any motivation for customer nations to acquire their own, independent uranium enrichment and fuel reprocessing plants as well as mixed oxide fuel fabrication facilities. Aside from its obligations under the NPT, *supra* note 37, art. IV, the United States should act promptly to dvelop and provide—independently or, if appropriate, in association with others—competitively priced and reliable enrichment, reprocessing, and relted fuel services to user nations. In this area, however, the United States is at a particular disadvantage, with neither enrichment capacity nor reprocessing and related fuel cycle services available. In the absence of the availability of such capacities from supplier countries, however, the odds in favor of their development elsewhere increase substantially, to the great detriment of the non-proliferation cause. Then-candidate Carter emphasized the need for positive action in each of these areas in his United Nations speech. See Address by Jimmy Carter at the United Nations, May 13, 1976, reprinted in 122 CONG. REC. S8541, S8543-44 (daily ed. June 4, 1976). Hopefully, the bulk of the work involved with utalizing the peaceful atom will fall to private industry. However, action is now crucial. Where the private sector is not currently able to meet all of the demands for planning and action, the federal government should take the initiative, but in partnership with private industry whenever possible. See also, Letter from Rep. Melvin Price, Chmn. House Armed Services Comm., to Joseph S. Nye, Deputy to Under Secretary of State for Security Assistance (Feb. 22, 1977), (available from Rep. Price) (emphasizing the need for the United States to aggressively develop nuclear energy as a domestic energy resource and a base for renewed leadership in the development of international nuclear trade policy).

[193]See, *e.g.*, note 95 *supra*. The Conference is an informal association of countries, including Great Britain, Canada, France, the United States, the Soviet Union, Japan, East and West Germany, Belgium, Czechoslovakia, Italy, the Netherlands, Poland, Sweden, and Switzerland, engaged in developing mechanisms for controlling weapons proliferation. The Conference itself might be viewed as an outgrowht of the Zangger List consultations which led to the development of a list of product triggering safeguards under the NPT. See generally Doub & Fidell, *supra* note 56, at 951-58.

[194]Any renegotiations will call for the nicest sense of diplomacy to avoid pyrrhic victories in the larger non-proliferation war. Just recently, for example, the Soviet Union was reported to have agreed to supply India with 200 tons (or about a six-year supply) of heavy-water for its nuclear power program. See NUCLEAR ENGINEERING INT'L, Jan. 1977, at 13. Earlier Canada had unilaterally cut off supplies when India refused to provide assurances that it would not detonate additional nuclear explosives.

[195]The seeds of such a norm are also in other international agreements and treaties, such as those establishing nuclear free zones. See, *e.g.*, Treaty for the

Prohibition of Nuclear Weapons in Latin America, opened for signature Feb. 14, 1967, 634 U.N.T.S. 281. To the extent that non-nuclear weapon countries might seek to take advantage of the peaceful applications of nuclear explosives, article V of the NPT specifically provides:

> Each Party to the Treaty undertakes to take appropriate measures to ensure that, in accordance with this Treaty, under appropriate international observation and through appropriate international procedures, potential benefits from any peaceful applications of nuclear explosions will be made available to non-nuclear weapon States Party to the Treaty on a nondiscriminatory basis and that the charge to such Parties for the explosive devices used will be as low as possible and exclude any charge for research and development.

NPT, *supra* note 37, art. V.

[196]For an interesting discussion of nuclear non-proliferation as an international norm, see Comment, *Legal Implications of Indian Nuclear Development,* 4 DENVER J. INT'L L. & POLICY 237 (1974).

U.S. Export Policy: Recommendations

Subcommittee on International Finance

The United States is awakening slowly to the fact that U.S. competitiveness in world markets is slipping. Not only Japan and the Western European countries, but also the developing countries of Latin America, Asia and Africa, are becoming strong competitors for U.S. producers across the full range of industrial and agricultural products and services.

Floating exchange rates alone cannot restore U.S. trade competitiveness. Nor can the United States afford to permit the international value of the dollar to erode indefinitely; the cost in domestic inflation, capital outflow, OPEC oil price increases and declining international confidence in the United States would be intolerable. As long as the dollar is the sole reserve currency and its value is uncertain, levels of international trade will be diminished. A strong national export policy is needed to strengthen the dollar as well as reduce the trade deficit.

The Subcommittee recommends the following actions: (1) organize the Executive branch to conduct a co-ordinated, forceful U.S. export policy: (2) facilitate organization by U.S. industry and agriculture to expand exports; (3) redirect and expand existing export promotion programs; (4) provide efficient tax and non-tax incentives for research and development and innovation, as well as exports, by U.S. industry and agriculture; (5) expand export financing to meet foreign competition; (6) negotiate reductions in foreign barriers to U.S. exports; and (7) reduce U.S. Government restrictions and disincentives imposed on U.S. exports.

From *U.S. Export Policy: A Report Submitted by the Subcommittee on International Finance to the Committee on Banking, Housing, and Urban Affairs, United States Senate,* February, 1979, U.S. Government Printing Office.

EXECUTIVE BRANCH ORGANIZATION TO SUPPORT EXPORTS

The United States alone among the major trading countries has no single government agency with authority and responsibility to advance its trading interests. Other countries rely upon trade ministries to help their exporters investigate markets abroad, develop new export products, co-ordinate export bidding, arrange subsidized financing, insurance and shipping and bargain with foreign governments to assure market access.

Two approaches are possible to organizing the Federal Government to support exports. A new Department of Trade incorporating most trade-related government activities could be established, or an Office of International Trade could be established in the White House with authority to orchestrate the trade-related actions of all government agencies.

Creation of a Department of Trade need not entail additional Cabinet posts nor additional expenditures. The Office of Special Trade Representative, a Cabinet office, could be merged with the trade functions of the Departments of Agriculture, Commerce, State and Treasury to create a new department which could absorb the International Trade Commission and Export-Import Bank as well.

An alternative would be to expand upon the STR's Office, giving it authority not only over trade negotiations, but also to coordinate export promotion and trade disputes. The unhappy experience of the Council on International Economic Policy may have unduly discouraged consideration of this laternative. What CIEP lacked in statutory authority and support from the President are not defects inherent in the concept of a White House office to manage international trade policy.

The International Finance Subcommittee has not held hearings on possible reform of executive branch organization to support exports, but its export policy hearings do point clearly to the need for U.S. exporters to receive more centrally co-ordinated U.S. Government support. It would appear particularly useful to merge the system of commercial officers provided by the Department of State with the system of export promotion operated by the Department of Commerce. A career service in international trade should be established even if no other reorganization steps are taken. International trade specialists of the highest caliber are more likely to be attracted and retained by a career service which offers rotating assignments abroad, in Washington, and in U.S. field offices.

ORGANIZING U.S. INDUSTRY AND AGRICULTURE TO EXPORT

United States policy has long been inconsistent toward organizing U.S. industry and agriculture to meet competition in foreign markets. U.S.

anti-trust law applies beyond U.S. borders to prevent combinations which could restrain trade within the United States. The Webb-Pomerene Act of 1918, authorized the formation of export trade associations so long as they did not reduce competition within the United States. The purpose of Webb-Pomerene was to enable U.S. exporters to compete more effectively against foreign cartels. However, the vague wording of the Act and narrow interpretations by the Justice Department, the Federal Trade Commission, and U.S. Courts have discouraged formation of export trade associations.

The Webb-Pomerene Act could be revised to expand the scope of permissible activities by export trade associations; services such as engineering, construction, insurance and finance, could be included. The Justice Department could be requried to issue clear guidelines and offer advisory opinions on interpretation of the Act. The Commerce Department could be directed to assist and encourage the formation of export trade associations. U.S. exporters could be explicitly permitted to form consortia to bid on major foreign projects abroad, as their foreign competitors are permitted to do.

But Webb-Pomerene may be too weak a reed on which to rely reliance for organizing U.S. exporters. The United States needs trading companies able to organize the exporting efforts of small and inexperienced U.S. firms, to conduct marketing on a global basis and absorb exchange rate fluctuations, just as Japanese and Korean trading companies do. Anti-trust law should be modified as necessary to permit formation of such trading companies. Informal interpretation of anti-trust law will not suffice—most firms will not take even a small risk of incurring criminal penalties, nor should they. Grey areas in anti-trust law are minefields for the unwary: clearly demarcated boundaries are needed.

Export trading companies should be free to market goods and services around the globe and their profits should be eligible for tax deferral, that is, not be taxed until distributed in the United States. Only with such freedom of maneuver can U.S. producers take on the Japanese trading companies and bidding consortia organized by European governments. The United States should continue international efforts to reach agreements restricting export cartels, but U.S. exporters and the U.S. economy can no longer afford to bear the full cost of foreign recalcitrance on anti-trust practice.

REDIRECTING AND EXPANDING U.S. EXPORT PROMOTION PROGRAMS

The Commerce Department has recognized that its export promotion efforts need to be targeted more toward new-to-export and new-to-market firms.[24] Smaller, less experienced firms would be major beneficiaries of improved export promotion services because such firms have less access to private sector exporting information services and less opportunity to travel abroad and to meet potential foreign buyers. Commerce has developed a strategy for redirecting its services to better meet such objectives, but funding levels are inadequate at present to permit significant improvement in export promotion activities. Congress should appropriate sufficient funds to the Commerce Department for fiscal year 1980 to enable the Department to carry out an expanded and reoriented export promotion program. Commerce should give greater attention to exports of services, which promise to be a growing portion of U.S. exports. U.S. serice industries have special needs by way of export support, and Commerce should be organized to meet those needs. Commerce should provide loans to small firms and export wssociations to cover initial marketing costs in new export markets and for new-to-export companies. Repayment would be based upon export sales. The Commerce Department should work more effectively within the United States through its District Offices and State and local trade and economic development offices to reach companies with export potential but lacking export experience. Both at home and overseas Commerce should concentrate its efforts on new exporters and new, rapidly growing markets.

Business has a responsibility to provide for self-education, as well. The professional business associations have given little attention to export education for their members. Experienced industrial firms and banks should conduct programs through their subsidaries and correspondent banks to deliver exporting assistance to firms outside the major cities. If relatrions between Government and business were more cooperative, instead of adversarial, the Commerce Department, Export-Import Bank, Treasury Department and Federal Reserve Board would join with the business associations in fostering and conducting an export expansion drive.

PROVIDING EFFICIENT INCENTIVES FOR R. & D. INNOVATION AND EXPORTS

Tax incentives should be used to stimulate higher levels of research and development than would otherwise occur in our "maturing" economy, and to encourage producers to make the extra effort required to enter foreign markets. Tax incentives may also be justifiable to enable U.S. producers to match European and Japanese competition in third country markets as long as competing countries continue to provide significant tax incentives to their exporters.

The United States has three tax policies which encourage exports: DISC, deferral on foreign corporate earnings, and Section 911 tax relief for certain personal income earned abroad. DISC may not be a particularly efficient incentive but exporters believe DISC is essential to profitable exporting. Removal of DISC without providing a superior tax alternative could lead to a large reduction in U.S. exports. Accordingly, DISC should be retained until another, more efficient tax incentive can be put into effect.

The export benefits of DISC could be expanded in two ways. Smaller companies not directly involved in exporting but supplying parts and components used in exports can set up DICs to sell to the exporting firms. In this way the benefits can trickle down to smaller businesses. Use of DISC in this way is permissible at present, but has received little encouragement from the Government. Small firms may be unaware of this opportunity and may also be discouraged by the requirement that DISCs be formally incorporated. The incorporation requirement seems a needless expense for firms to incur.

Second, the money flowing into DISCs could be recycled to finance additional exports if it would be re-lent to other firms or foreign purchasers. The Export-Import Bank could use its resources in parallel with DISC funds to multiply the export punch of the DISC incentive.

DISC violates GATT rules and may come under further pressure as a result of the subsidies code being drafted in the Tokyo Round. If DISC is barred, Congress should study alternatives, including a value-added tax with rebates for exports. The VAT system is widely used abroad, is consistent with GATT rules and could be used to fund a portion of social security benefits. VAT is often criticized as being inflationary as well as regressive in impact; however, these effects could be mitigated if VAT were adopted in conjunction with other tax changes. Many foreign countries have adopted VAT systems within the past two decades and their experience should help Congress determine what costs and benefits VAT would entail for the United States.

Another alternative to DISC would be to defer taxation of export sales abroad attributed to an export sales subsidiary. At present the United States attempts to restrict use of such "tax haven" arrangements by requiring such income to be reported as current earnings. The U.S. practice reduces the export incentive effect of the general deferral of taxation on income earned abroad, contrary to the practice of other governments. To be most effective, U.S. policy should encourage the formation and use of export sales subsidiaries by consortia of U.S. firms.

Section 911 of the Internal Revenue Act provides exemption for some forms of personal income and expenses by U.S. citizens working abroad. Favorable tax treatment is an important export incentive in the engineering and construction industries, which in turn stimulate additional U.S.

goods exports. The effect of Section 911 on U.S. exports requires careful examination and the tax incentive should not be reduced prematurely.

Over the long term, the most significant way to promote exports is to improve U.S. industrial competitiveness by encouraging innovation and productivity growth. The important circularity of causation between trade and domestic industrial growth should be more widely recognized, and U.S. industrial and export policies should be correspondingly integrated. The President's annual Economic Report should contain a section specifically reviewing developments in capital formation and research and development, with evaluation of the export implication of such developments.

In particular, the pivotal importance of innovative small businesses and research-intensive industries should be acknowledged. Tax policies and securities regulations which have seriously affected the rate of formation of new ventures need reconsideration, and incentives used in a number of foreign countries to stimulate R. & D. should be investigated.

For example, several Western countries, including Canada and West Germany, allow immediate write-off of research-related capital investments. The West Germans also permit R. & D. venture companies to depreciate up to three times the original investment in the venture before being subject to corporate income taxation.

An investment tax credit for research and development expenditures on "intangibles" could stimulate higher levels of R. & D. Another possibility would be to increase the existing investment tax credit for capital expenditures that are research-related. Alternative incentives could involve accelerated depreciation for capital equipment embodying new technology or capital with research and development uses.

Industrial innovation is hampered by barriers to cooperative research imposed by the government in the name of competition. The extent to which current antitrust restrictions and Justice Department policies inhibit industry from collaborating to make optimal use of R. & D. resources should be reassessed. Indeed, it is time to move beyond the traditional adversarial government industry relationship and examine the possible gains from cooperative research institutes, funded by business and government, with university participation. Such three-way cooperation has been successful in basic research efforts in the past; work in a broader range of areas, including the development of commercial technologies, should be explored.

More effective commercialization of existing federal research would also be beneficial for exports. Greater industry involvement in the selection and management of government funded projects could help insure that the results are commercially viable. Restrictive agency patent policies, conflict of interest rules and other impediments to innovators working on federal contracts demand reconsideration.

Finally, the United States must awaken to the fact that technology transfer is no longer a one-way street. In an age where two-thirds of all research and development takes place outside the United States, our channels for acquiring foreign technologies and scientific information are woefully inadequate. The United States has, relatively, far fewer science attaches abroad than do European countries, Japan and the U.S.S.R. Moreover, the activities of U.S. science attaches are largely oriented to the administration of science agreements rather than the search for foreign-developed advanced technologies. The links between science attaches and U.S. firms operating abroad are weak, where they could be immensely valuable. There is little sense of the potential commercial gains from encouraging and assisting U.S. firms to obtain foreign technologies. Bolstering the commercial awareness of science attaches and strengthening the technological awareness of commercial attaches in order to improve the two-way flow of technology are far more promising strategies than trying to limit the outflow of American technology.

EXPANDING EXPORT FINANCING

The Export-Import Bank and the Commodity Credit Corporation are the primary U.S. government institutions providing financing for U.S. manufactured and agricultural commodity exports respectively. Both face political as well as economic constraints on funds and the markets in which they can operate—constraints not faced by corresponding institutions in competing countries.

Eximbank is required to obtain approval in an appropriations Act each year for its level of direct lending. The Office of Management and Budget has tended to regard Eximbank as a drain on the Federal budget despite the Bank's essential role in expanding U.S. exports, and thereby, profits, employment and Federal tax revenue. The budget proposed for fiscal year 1980 would permit the Bank to provide only one-third of the direct loans for U.S. exports expected to be requested from the Bank. Because Bank support is the determining factor in two-thirds of the export sales it supports, and because the value of the exports supported averages twice the value of the Bank's direct loans, as much as 10 to 15 billion dollars in U.S. exports may be foregone duje to the ceiling imposed on Eximbank activity in fiscal year 1980 by OMB.[25] Congress should increase Eximbank's direct loan authority for fiscal year 1980 to 12 billion dollars from the 4 billion level approved by OMB. Congress should also review the budgetary treatment of the Bank to determine whether such treatment accurately reflects the fiscal impact of Bank activities.

Eximbank policies should also be changed to increase the support it can provide for U.S. exports. The Bank should end its practice of returning an annual "dividend" to the U.S. Treasury. No public purpose is served by shuffling U.S. Government funds from one account to the other. Eximbank need not perpetuate a fictional financial independence. All the Bank "profits" should be added to Bank reserves available to meet possible default by foreign purchasers.

Eximbank should also consider adopting some of the export-supporting programs offered by foreign official credit agencies: performance bond guarantees, financing for prefeasibility studies and increased local and foreign content financing. The Bank should abandon its 5 million dollar threshold for direct credits and financial guarantees, because the threshold limits access to the Bank by small exporters. The Bank should consider joint export financing activities together with counterpart institutions in other exporting countries.

Congress hould make Eximbank and CCC support available, subject to periodic review, to all countries with which it is U.S. policy to encourage trade. Large potential markets for U.S. goods and services are being conceded to foreign competitors because Eximbank and CCC cannot assist U.S. exports to certain countries.

Another area of growing competitiveness is the provision of low-interest, long-term loans to poorer developing countries for capital goods imports. Except in rare instances, Eximbank cannot afford to match foreign credits to developing countries which combine concessional development support with export financing, so-called "mixed credits." In addition, many developing countries would like to purchase goods and services from the U.S., but cannot meet the Bank's normal credit standards.

To meet this dual challenge, Congress should authorize a new Bank program to provide export financing for sales to countries with per capita income below $1,000. Financing could be provided on normal Bank terms; however, the Bank could offer such terms as necessary to match foreign competition. An initial authorization and appropriation of $500 million in capital should be provided for the program.

Private financing of U.S. exports will be assisted by changes incorporated in the International Banking Act of 1978 which liberalize usage of Edge Act Corporations for export financing. The Federal Reserve Board should promptly issue revised regulations putting the new Edge provisions into effect, and the Commerce Department together with the Treasury Department and the Federal Reserve Board should launch a program to educate U.S. businesses in the formation and use of Edge corporations to finance exports.

NEGOTIATING REDUCTIONS IN FOREIGN BARRIERS TO U.S. EXPORTS

The export implications of the trade agreements negotiated at Geneva should be reviewed thoroughly by the Congress. The Subcommittee on International Finance will hold hearings on the agreements later this year.

Many of the non-tariff barriers which thwart U.S. exports will not be removed automatically by adoption of the trade agreements and the accompanying codes of behavior. A continuing effort to compel implementation of the codes will be required, and many disputes will arise which can only be resolved through bilateral negotiation. Congress should give particular attention to the mechanisms for implementing the trade agreements and insuring compliance with the codes.

Agriculture is the sector which sufers most from foreign non-tariff barriers and has the greatest long-term promise for U.S. export growth. The United States Government should increase its pressure on foreign governments to admit U.S. agricultural products, if necessary, by linking U.S. action on manufactured goods imports to foreign actions affecting U.S. agricultural exports.

Congress should re-examine agricultural policy to consider replacing a system of price supports and set-asides which pays farmers not to produce with a system of target prices and cash payments which encourages food production, holds down food prices, and stimulates agricultural exports. Meat is the most efficient means for the United States to provide protein to the rest of the world. Grain-fed meat exports would benefit from lower feed costs under a target-price system, and so would U.S. consumers.

The Commodity Credit Corporation should be authorized and directed to serve as U.S. agent in grain sales to non-market economies. CCC could match the deals arranged by the Canadian and Australian wheat boards.

When the Tokyo Round of trade negotiations is finally concluded, it will be time for another. The Tokyo Round negotiations open the doors to a series of new negotiations. Non-GATT members have trade barriers, too, which should be tackled in multilateral negotiations. Special trade facilitation committees may be needed to clear trade complaints arising under the proposed GATT codes. U.S. export incenives have a vital role both in helping U.S. industry and agriculture to fulfill the promise of the MTN package, and in insuring that other countries keep their part of the promise.

Congress should adopt a package of export-stimulating measures to accompany the trade agreements. United States producers should be given maximum encouragement to exploit the export opportunities expected to result from the reduction of tariff and non-tariff riers.

REDUCING U.S. GOVERNMENT DISINCENTIVES TO EXPORT

Exporters assert that the biggest incentive the United States Government could provide to exports would be to reduce the many export restrictions and disincentives it imposes. U.S. exporters face export controls, anti-trust, anti-bribery, human rights, environmental review and other restrictions not faced by their competitors. Congress should resist the impulse to restrict exports to countries whose internal or external policies do not meet U.S. standards and objectives, when restrictions would prove ineffective.

Testimony received by the Banking Committee suggested that unilateral efforts by the United States to exert economic leverage on foreign governments through export restrictions have genrally been unsuccessful.[26] In many cases other countries have captured the export business and it is questionable whether U.S. foreign policy objectives have been advanced.

Congress should review the statutory and regulatory resrictions on U.S. exports to determine whether such restrictions accomplish purposes outweighing their economic cost. In many cases it may prove possible to design alternative approaches which serve U.S. moral and foreign policy concerns without sacrificing market opportunities. A place to begin is with revision in 1979 of the Export Administration Act.

Delays in export licensi g decisions pursuant to the Act are a significant cause of U.S. export loss. Exporters should be informed of the speci ic reasons for license delays or rejections. Because U.S. licensing policy is often unclear, foreign purihasers come to regard the U.S. as an unreliable . In areas of rapidly expanding technology, the control levels should be revised more frequently. Too often the Commerce Department responds to a rapidly evolving state of the art around the world only when deluged by license applications which should not have been required in the first ilace. If the Executive departments will not devise a more efficient way to provide essential monitoring and control without excessive disruption of U.S. exports, Congress must.

The restrictions in the Trade Act of 1974 and the Export-Import Bank Act on granting nondiscriminatory trade treatment and credits to communist countries should be amended o permit expanded trade and credits sueject o periodic review by Congress and the President of relations with such countries.

The President's Executive Order requiring environmental reviews of many U.S. exports threatens to discourage exports without encouraging environmental protection. Regulations to be issued pursuant to the executive order should be subject to careful public scrutiny as provided in the Administrative Procedure Act. Agencies should pursue international efforts to encourage environmental protection to the maximum extent feasible rather than imposing unilateral environmental reviews. The President should revise his order to authorize U.S. government review of the environmental effect in a foreign country of U.S. exports only upon the request of the foreign government, and to require consideration of foreign availability and the reputation of the U.S. as a supplier before proceeding with any environmental review pursuant to the order.

INTERNATIONAL FINANCE AND U.S. EXPORTS

Competitiveness will avail the United States little if the world is insolvent. The problem of financing economic growth throughout the world is beyond the scope of this study, but not beyond the scope of this subcommittee's interest. Global institutions of finance and trade are needed as urgently as a U.S. export policy. The Bretton Woods system has been seriously undermined, but the world awaits U.S. leadership to develop a replacement. The world monetary order should be expanded, as well as stabilized. In addition, the United States should lead in the creation of new global institutions to deal with the resource problems of an interdependent world and the economic development of the poorest countries.

These objectives intertwine. Developing countries today purchase more of the U.S. capital goods than do Europe, Japan and the East Bloc combined. These countries also represent our fastest growing export markets. An increased commitment to development assistance and international scientific and technological cooperation should be made, not out of a sense of short-term political expediency, but with the conviction that these directions unchallengeably advance the long-term economic and political interests of the United States. The potential is clear, but the U.S. response is not. We must act before these goals are preempted by policies too narrowly conceived to serve an interdependent world.

---

[24]See "Export Protection Strategy and Programs," pp.198-129 of *Export Policy* hearings, 6.

[25]Ten billion dollars in lost exports would represent 20 billion dollars in lost GNP, 4 billion dollars in lost tax revenue, and 400,000 lost jobs.

[26]See hearings on the *Use of Export Credits and Controls for Foreign Policy Purposes*, Committee on Banking, Housing and Urban Affairs, October 10 and 11, 1978.

II
U.S. Arms Policy:
Is the U.S. a
Merchant of Death?

Controlling Arms Transfers:

An Instrument of U.S. Foreign Policy

Lucy Wilson Benson

It is commonplace to acknowledge that science and technology are among the dominant influences of this mad and magnificent century. But far too little has been done to act upon that recognition and integrate the considerations of technology into either long-range planning or everyday operations of foreign policymaking. It is now my job to try to improve that situation.

There are a great many issues involved—painful, familiar to us all, and global in nature: Population growth, food supply, air and water pollution, the arms race, nuclear proliferation, energy insecurity, health care, competition for resources, the widening development gap.

Secretary Vance has given my office broad purview over these matters, with the intention of providing coordination among the many responsible bureaus and elevating the level of attention given to these issues. Generally speaking, I divide my attention into three main areas: science and technology as they relate to foreign policy, the transfer of conventional arms, and the control of nuclear technology.

We could talk about any one of these subjects for the whole afternoon, but I would like to concentrate on arms transfers; that is, the export of conventional, as distinct from nuclear, weapons.

I choose it for four reasons: It is controversial, it is complex, it is very important, and we do have a brand new policy. Let me begin with a few facts for background:

Address delivered before the Woman's National Democratic Club June 27, 1977 by Lucy Wilson Benson, Under Secretary for Security Assistance, Science and Technology. Text from *Department of State Bulletin,* August 1, 1977.

—About half the international trade in military arms and services in the last five years has been conducted by the U.S. Government.
—Last year we did more than $9 billion worth of arms business with 68 countries.
—More than 60 percent of this traffic was with the Middle East, specifically with three countries—Israel, Iran, and Saudi Arabia. About a third of the trade was with NATO and our major Asian allies—Korea and Japan. About 40 percent of the total was weapons and ammunition. The rest was services, spare parts, and supporting equipment.

For over a quarter of a century arms transfers have been a useful instrument of U.S. foreign policy. We have used them:

—To strengthen our collective defense arrangements and to encourage allies to assume a stronger self-defense role, as for example, in NATO;
—To maintain regional balances, as in the Middle East;
—To secure base and operating rights for U.S. forces, as in Spain, Turkey, and the Philippines;
—To limit Soviet influence or to enhance our own influence in specific regions or with particular governments; and
—To offset or compensate for the withdrawal of U.S. forces, as in Korea.

These are, and will remain, legitimate objectives of our arms transfer actions.

Over the past few years, however, there has developed a growing concern that, however laudable the ends, the huge export of arms and our own prominent position as "chief trafficker" carries with it serious liabilities. In the last five years our annual sales of military arms and services has grown fourfold—from just under $2 billion to well over $9 billion. This growth hs focused public, congressional, and executive attention on a number of awkward questions.

—Have we been encouraging competition in arms?
—Have we been heightening local tensions or involving ourselves in local conflicts in which we have no legitimate interest?
—Have we been compromising our technological advantage not only over potential opponents but also over the allies who are our commercial competitors?
—Have we been distorting the allocations of scarce resources, particularly in the underdeveloped world?
—Have we been associating ourselves too closely, and where our national security interests are not really involved, with authoritarian and repressive regimes? Are we perhaps even reinforcing them?

It would be easy if we could answer yes to all of those questions. Arms transfer policy then would be only a question of withdrawing from the market and either refusing to deal in arms at all or doing so only with a few close friends.

However, as you all are seasoned politicians, you know there are no yes-no answers to these questions. You also will recognize that there are some important but conflicting interests involved in our international arms trade that go to the very heart of our national security interests. The fact that we are the largest arms seller in the world is not due solely to the energy of our salesmen or our price and credit terms. Indeed other suppliers of arms; that is, other countries, are often more competitive in these areas than the United States.

Our predominance as an exporter of arms has come about because both our government and U.S. industry have together a reputation as a reliable supplier of the best equipment and service and because there exists between ourselves and our major customers a basic congruence of interests and objectives. The governments which buy our weapons have defense requirements which they view as urgent and legitimate as our own.

No simple, narrowly focused policy can possibly reconcile all the contradictions that are imbedded in this complicated subject. Let me give you two examples. Severe reductions of arms sales to unstable areas would seem, logically, to be a practical and desirable policy guideline. Yet in some areas access to arms may be necessary to avoid creating a tempting imbalance in military strength, as in Israel, Jordan, and Korea.

ARMS TRANSFERS AND HUMAN RIGHTS

President Carter, Secretary of State Vance, and the Congress have repeatedly emphasized the importance of human rights in foreign policy, and that obviously includes arms transfer policy. But how do we apply our concern in this area, since human rights are not just the right to vote or the right to a fair trial or freedom from fear of torture? Human rights also include the right to safety from terrorism and from external threat. We used to call this "freedom from fear" 30-odd years ago. What do we do, therefore, about Korea, which has an authoritarian government, but which also has an implacable and well-armed enemy across the demilitarized zone? How do we accommodate these conflicting objectives, and if we cannot, how do we decide which rights to give priority?

There are no easy answers. As is always the case, facts have to be weighed and judgments made. Patt Derian [Patricia M. Derian], former Democratic National Committeewoman from Mississippi, who, as you know is the President's Coordinator for Human Rights [and Humanitarian Affairs in the Office of the Deputy Secretary of State], says it is very discouraging to hear the same arguments and rationales *for not doing things* as we used to hear in the days of civil rights activism. And, I might add, it is discouraging to hear those same old arguments ad nauseam in these days of struggling for equal rights for women. At the same time, as Ms. Derian said recently, cutting off military sales or economic assistance to a country is not a very effective way to show our dissatisfaction with human rights conditions in a particular country. And so we are left with the age-old problem in politics and public policy— trade-offs, often among unsuitable or at least unattractive alternatives.

All of this is by way of saying that the new arms transfer policy described by the President in mid-May represents an effort to recognize and deal with these contradictions.[2] It also sets a challenging goal—to reduce the worldwide trade in arms and to reduce our own dependence on this trade as a foreign policy instrument.

In his May statement the President stated that arms transfers would henceforth be considered an exceptional policy instrument. That means it will be used only where it can be clearly shown that the transfer contributes to our national security interest. Moreover, the burden of proof will rest with the proponents of a sale, not with the advocates of restraint.

THE APPLICATION OF CONTROLS

President Carter specified a number of new controls—new controls to be applied to all transfers and to all countries except those with whom we have longstanding commitments, such as Israel, or with whom we have major defense treaties (NATO, Japan, Australia, and New Zealand).

The controls are:

—We will reduce the dollar-volume of new commitments to sell weapons and weapons-related items beginning in 1978;
—We will not be the first to introduce into a region advanced weapons that create new or higher combat capability;
—We will not sell weapons that are not in the inventory of our own armed forces;
—We will not develop advanced weapons solely for export;
—We will sharply curtail the production of U.S. weapons and components by foreign governments;
—We will rigorously discourage the reexport of U.S. equipment to third countries; and
—We will strengthen the regulations governing business and government sales activities abroad.

The message of these controls is obvious: *discipline and restraint.*

It is the objective of this Administration to sell less and to sell with discrimination. The test of U.S. national security interest will be the starting point for considering a sale, a test that too often has been neglected in the past.

So much for the policy. It is very straightforward. Now, let me say a few words about implementation and impact.

IMPLEMENTATION AND IMPACT OF POLICY

Decisionmaking in the arms transfer business is extraordinarily complicated. Most of the major agencies of our government have important interests at stake and must be involved in the decision process. The State Department must worry about relations with foreign governments; Defense about military capabilities; Labor, Commerce, and Treasury about jobs, the economy, and the balance of payments; and the Agency for International Development about allocation of resources. Questions of arms control, human rights, domestic jobs, and compromise of our technological lead also must be dealt with.

To help me advise the Secretary of State, we have organized an interagency Arms Export Control Board to bring together the experts on these matters. Nine separate agencies are represented, and no meeting takes place with less than 15 people at the table. The process is thorough and it guarantees full exposure and a fair hearing to all the contending interests.

Nothing, however, can obscure the fact that the effects of decisions made under this new policy are going to be widely felt by everyone from the aircraft and electronics workers in Dallas and Boston to the Korean soldiers on the demilitarized zone. We fully recognized this when we were developing the new policy, and we designed the controls to insure that they do not drive policy beyond common sense. For example, when the President stated that we will apply the test of our national security interests, he also made explicit one particular test—that we will continue to fully uphold our treaty obligations and our historic responsibility "to assure the security of the State of Israel."

We are fully conscious that for much of the free world the ability to deter attack, to prevent coercion, and to defend against aggression rests on a nation's ability to acquire modern arms. Our policy does not challenge this fact; on the contrary, it accepts it as a given.

With respect to domestic effects, they have been meticulously examined. We believe the impact will be manageable. Some jobs will be lost, some industries will suffer; but it is our judgment that the aggregate effect will be modest.

More worrisome is the likely concentration of the effects on a few industries—aircraft, electronics, and ordinance—in a few states. But even here, there are ameliorating factors.

There is a very large backlog—over $30 billion—of unfilled orders for which signed contracts exist. This Administration considers these obligations to be good-faith commitments, and it will not interfere with the completion of existing contracts. The new policy applies to new orders, not old ones. Thus the backlog will take some years to work through, and there will be time for the government and the defense industries involved to adjust to the future.

Moreover, it is important to remember that U.S. defense industries have never, in the aggregate, depended on foreign sales for their survival. Their big customers are and will remain our own military services and our close friends and allies with whom we will continue our defense cooperation.

SETTING AN EXAMPLE OF SELF-RESTRAINT

A second big problem with which we have to deal is to persuade other sellers of arms—that is, France, Germany, Britain, and the Soviet Union—not to fill the void we create.

Many people argue that self-restraint is an open invitation for the competition to move in and that when the competition does move in, the United States will lose not only jobs but also leverage, influence, and control. They cite the historical example of Latin America, where we have exercised restraint over the last 10 or 15 years with the result that the Europeans now have 70 percent of the Latin American arms market.

It is a tough argument, and there is some truth in it. But to accept uncritically the proposition "if we don't sell, others will" is to accept a slogan, not a policy. We propose to deal with the problem in two ways.

First, we will set an example of restraint by demonstrating that the United States will not rush into every possible market. In so doing, we will try to alter the intensity of the competitive atmosphere surrounding the arms trade. To some extent, of course, if we don't sell, buyers won't buy. We will try to encourage that atmosphere.

The other approach will focus on sellers. We will seek their active cooperation and try to convince both allies and adversaries that restraint is in everyone's interest.

The President, the Vice President, and Secretary Vance have raised the matter in their trips to Europe, the Middle East, and the Soviet Union. In addition, the United States and the Soviet Union have established a joint working group on conventional arms transfers, and we will hold discussions with our European allies.

Our hope is that our own restraint will attract the support of buyers and sellers alike over a period of time. It is very important to recognize that progress is likely to be slow. We will aim, with both suppliers and buyers, for a code of behavior—perhaps by regions, perhaps globally— that will be adopted because of mutual interest. Our initial emphasis might well be on such obvious and troublesome problems as:

—Arms sales to unstable regions;
—Sales of sensitive weapons and technology, such as long-range surface-to-surface missiles;

—Sales of equipment particularly attractive to terrorists, such as hand-carried anti-aircraft missiles; and
—Sales of highly and indiscriminately lethal weapons.

We don't underestimate the difficulties. Still less do we ignore the fact that without cooperation from both suppliers and buyers a policy of self-denial will be ineffective. Obviously, however, we must try: Unrestrained competition is madness.

DECISIONS TO FILL OR REFUSE REQUESTS

Finally, there is the question of how we as an exporter decide which requests to fill and which to refuse. How do we impose our views of what is necessary and affordable on sovereign states whose perception of their own needs may be quite different from our own?

To this I can only say that the new policy involves the very essence of diplomacy. In the last couple of weeks you have seen this Administrationmake two very difficult decisions. We turned down Pakistan's request to purchase A-7 aircraft on the grounds that the sale would introduce a significantly greater military capability into one side of the South Asian military balance.

We have also refused to authorize at this time the sale to Iran of the F-18L, a new lightweight fighter, because it is not now scheduled to be in the inventory of the U.S. military services.

Both of these decisions were direct expressions of the new policy. Both involved our relations with friendly foreign governments. Both involved the prosperity of important American industrial firms and the job prospects of their highly skilled workers. Both involved loss of economic benefits to our economy, to the private sector, and to the Treasury. But both also involved the broadest and most fundamental national and global interests.

Either we apply the policy—thoughtfully and with scrupulous attention to the costs and benefits—or we don't. But if we take the latter course and duck the tough decisions, then we lay ourselves open to charges of political expediency and diplomatic impotence. It is not for such behavior that this Administration or this country intends to be remembered.

---

[2]For the text of President Carter's statement of May 19, see BULLETIN of June 13, 1977, p.625.

Arms Transfers by the United States:

Merchant of Death or Arsenal of Democracy

Archibald S. Alexander

I. INTRODUCTION

Controversial events of the last few years have presented the American public with the question whether arms transfers by the United States have gotten out of hand. Has our country become the chief "merchant of death," as believed by many at the time of Senator Nye's investigation soon after World War I, or is it the "arsenal of democracy," as generally believed during and after World War II? This article deals with transfers of all kinds of non-nuclear arms from or by the United States, and it examines all types of transfers including grants, transfers on credit, government to government sales, and commercial transactions in which the seller is part of the private sector of the United States. There is an analysis of statutory law and applicable international agreements, followed by a description of the machinery that the United States Government uses to make decisions regarding transfers. The statistics are then discussed, focusing primarily on the current programs, but seeking to discern trends. There is a discussion of United States foreign affairs and military policy involved in arms transfers and a consideration of economic factors. In conclusion there are some comments about the future.

From *Vanderbilt Journal of Transnational Law,* Volume 10, Spring 1977, Number 2. Copyright © 1978 by the Vanderbilt University School of Law. Reprinted by permission of the *Vanderbilt Journal of Transnational Law,* Nashville, Tennessee.

II. THE LEGAL FRAMEWORK

A. International Agreements

Of the numerous international arms control agreements, treaties, and protocols, only some have been effective; others have been disregarded by nations considering it in their national interest to do so. The agreements that have been wholly or partially effective include: the Antarctic Treaty, effective in 1961; the Treaty of Tlatelolco, effective in 1971, forbidding nuclear weapons in most of Latin America; the Limited Test Ban Treaty of 1963, which entered into force in 1963 and prohibited nuclear testing in the atmosphere, outer space, or under water; the Non-Proliferation Treaty, effective in 1970, designed to prevent the spread of nuclear weapons; various strategic arms limitation agreements between the United States and the U.S.S.R.; the Geneva Protocol of 1925, which was probably disregarded in World War II, adhered to by the United States in 1975; subsequent bacteriological and chemical warfare treaties prohibiting use or manufacture of these types of weapons; and the Seabed Arms Control Treaty, which entered into force in 1972.

International agreements that have been honored primarily in the breach include several relating to the arming of countries in Southeast Asia and the Western embargo against the People's Republic of China (PRC) during the Korean War. An embargo on Rhodesia, imposed by the United Nations Organization in 1968, and an embargo on Cuba, imposed by most of the countries of North and South America, were increasingly disregarded by many nations. Soon after the establishment of the State of Israel, the United Kingdom, France, and the United States reached a relatively informal understanding designed to limit arms transfers to the Middle East. This understanding was effective for several years, until about 1956, when Egypt nationalized the Suez Canal. The British, French, and Israelis attempted to capture the Canal, and Egypt and other Middle Eastern countries turned to the Soviet Union for arms.

B. Domestic Legislation

The law of arms transfers has recently been evolving more rapidly as Congress and the public become increasingly aware of the magnitude of the United States arms trade. The latest comprehensive congressional legislation is the International Security Assistance and Arms Export Control Act of 1976.[1] This act carries forward the trends present in earlier amendments to the Foreign Assistance Act of 1961[2] and related statutes.

An important document is the 1974 Committee Print of the House Committee on Foreign Affairs entitled "The International Transfer of Conventional Arms." This document, which consists of a report to the

Congress by the Arms Control and Disarmament Agency (ACDA)[4] describing the period from 1961 through 1971, was submitted to the Congress in response to the Roth Amendment to the Foreign Relations Authorization Act of 1972.[5] As an Appendix, the Print contained valuable and sometimes critical comments on the ACDA report by Charles R. Gellner of the Congressional Research Service.

After Congress, the news media, and at least certain sectors of the United States public had had the oportunity to analyze the 1974 ACDA report, there followed hearings and a report by the Senate Committee on Foreign Relations.[6] Although legislation embodying the recommendations of the Committee was vetoed by President Ford, the report is of special interest because its Appendix contains an "index of legislative veto provisions." One of the issues presented by recent congressional action in the arms transfer field is the constitutionality of the "legislative veto" authorized by Sections 211 and 305 of the International Security Assistance and Arms Export Control Act of 1976,[7] which became effective on July 1, 1976.

The foregoing summary of recent legislative action gives some idea of the complex evolution of the present law. This evolution exemplifies the changing nature of the roles of the executive and legislative branches of the United States Government. The formation of the North Atlantic Treaty Organization (NATO) and the commencement of the Korean War triggered the development of broad policies on foreign military assistance and detailed plans for arms transfers by the executive branch. During the 1950s and 1960s the Congress generally approved the policy determinations of the executive branch and provided the necessary funding. In the 1960s Congress continued to allow large transfers of arms and credits to the government of South Vietnam and to other countries in the Far East. The hostilities in the Middle East in 1967 and 1973, the oil embargo of 1973, and the later oil price increases by the Organization of Petroleum Exporting Countries (OPEC) were also reasons for continued congressional acquiescence in the executive branch actions. The following summary of the International Security Assistance and Arms Export Control Act of 1976 will provide a basis for understanding the present statutory setting for arms transfers.[8]

III. INTERNATIONAL SECURITY ASSISTANCE & ARMS EXPORT CONTROL ACT OF 1976

A. Title I: Military Assistance Program

1. *Authorization.*—Appropriation of $196 million is authorized for 1976, and $177 million for 1977, for limited military assistance *grants* for

limited purposes, together with smaller amounts for "administrative and other related purposes" (section 101). There is a limitation on the amounts (which aggregate more than the totals authorized) that may be allocated to eight individual countries out of the foregoing total amounts. Two of these countries are Greece and Turkey, and the others are in Asia or the Middle East.

2. *Special Authority.*—The Act permits the President to order articles and "defense services" from the Department of Defense, provided he first determines and reports to Congress: (1) "that an unforeseen emergency exists which requires immediate military assistance to a foreign country or international organization"; (2) "that a failure to respond immediately to that emergency will result in serious harm to vital United States security interests"; and (3) that there is no other provision of law under which the emergency can be met (section 102). For any fiscal year, the total value of articles and services under this section may not exceed $67.5 million.

3. *Stockpiling of Defense Articles for Foreign Countries.*—Section 103 provides for planned stockpiling of defense articles for foreign countries up to an aggregate value of $93.75 million for the period July 1, 1975, to September 30, 1976, and $125 million for the 1977 fiscal year.

4. *Termination of Military Assistance Advisory Groups and Missions.*—Section 104 forbids the creation of any foreign military assistance advisory group or similar organization after September 30, 1977, unless specifically approved by Congress. In addition, not more than three members of the United States armed forces may be assigned to the head of each United States diplomatic mission in connection with "international military education and training."

5. *Termination of Authority to Furnish Military Assistance.*—Section 105 partially terminates the furnishing of military assistance by grants—*i.e.,* for little or no consideration—as of September 30, 1977, and completely terminates such grants as of September 30, 1980.

6. *International Military Education and Training.*—Section 106 authorizes the appropriation of $27 million for fiscal year 1976 and $30.2 million for fiscal year 1977 for military education and training of foreigners through attendance at military educational and training facilities or special courses of instruction in observation and orientation, whether in the United States or abroad. Overseas military education and training are authorized only when "reported and justified" by the President to Congress.

B. Title II: Arms Export Controls

1. *Arms Sales Policy.*—Section 201 changes the title of "The Foreign Military Sales Act" to "Arms Export Control Act." Section 202 strikes

out the last paragraph in the congressional statement of policy in the Foreign Military Sales Act, which had advocated an increased commercial role and less United States Government participation in arms and defense service transfers. Instead, the following two paragraphs were substituted:

> It shall be the policy of the United States to exert leadership in the world community to bring about arrangements for reducing the international trade in implements of war and to lessen the danger of outbreak of regional conflict and the burdens of armaments. United States programs for or procedures governing the export, sale, and grant of defense articles and defense services to foreign countries and international organizations shall be administered in a manner which will carry out this policy.
>
> It is the sense of the Congress that the President should seek to initiate multilateral discussions for the purpose of reaching agreements among the principal arms suppliers and arms purchasers and other countries with respect to the control of the international trade in armaments. It is further the sense of Congress that the President should work actively with all nations to check and control the international sale and distribution of conventional weapons of death and destruction and to encourage regional arms control arrangements. In furtherance of this policy, the President should undertake a concerted effort to convene an international conference of major arms-supplying and arms-purchasing nations which shall consider measures to limit conventional arms transfers in the interest of international peace and stability.

Earlier passages in the statement of policy objectives reiterate language in the Arms Control and Disarmament Act providing that "an ultimate goal of the United States continues to be a world which is free from the scourge of war and the dangers and burdens of armaments," and assert that regional arms control and the dangers and disarmament agreements are to be encouraged and arms races discouraged. These passages also provide that sales and guaranties are not to be approved if "they would have the effect of arming military dictators who are denying the growth of fundamental rights or social progress to their own people," though this limitation may be waived by the President if "he determines it would be important to the security of the United States and promptly so reports" to the Congress.

In this section Congress indicates the direction which the whole statutory scheme for arms transfers is now taking. It should, however, be read in conjunction with part of the Foreign Assistance Act, 22 U.S.C. § 2301.[9] The troublesome ambivalence of the national objectives appears clearly when these two sections are contrasted. The two inconsistent objectives are the reduction of the risk of war, the encouragement of "regional arms control and disarmament agreements," and the discouragement of "arms races," on the one hand, and the support of alliances, particularly NATO, the encouragement of democracy and free enterprise abroad, and the protection of other countries against "international Communism" on the other. Many of the difficulties and inconsistencies of the arms transfer program arise when these differing policies are implemented.

2. *Transfer of Defense Services.*—Section 203 requires the President to justify any transaction involving training and "defense services" by a finding that the transaction "will strengthen the security of the United States and promote world peace."

3. *Approval for Transfer of Defense Articles.*—Section 204 adds new provisions requiring the President, before consenting to transfer of "a defense article, or related training or other defense service," whether by sale or grant, to give 30-day notice to Congress, describing what is to be transferred, the recipient, the reasons for the transfer, and the intended date thereof.

4. *Sales From Stocks.*—Section 205 deals with sales of defense articles and services *for U.S. dollars* from Department of Defense stocks "to any eligible country or international organization." It provides that after September 30, 1976, there may be included in the price of defense articles or services charges for administrative services and "a proportionate amount of any non-recurring costs of research, development, and production of major defense equipment." Section 206 prohibits sales of defense articles and services that have a significant adverse effect on the combat readiness of the armed forces of the United States. The President is required to transmit to the Congress a statement including "a full description of the impact which the proposed sale will have on the armed forces of the United States."

5. *Annual Estimate and Justification for Sales Program.*—Section 209 requires the President to transmit to Congress an annual estimate of anticipated sales to each country and an explanation of the foreign policy and national security considerations involved. In addition, he must transmit for each recipient country "an arms control impact statement," which must include "an analysis of the relationship between expected sales to each country and arms control efforts relating to that country" and "the impact of such expected sales on the stability of the region" where the recipient is located. This section also requires the President to submit additional information requested by the Senate Committee on Foreign Relations or the House Committee on International Relations within 30 days of receipt of the request; and the President is required "to make every effort" to treat information submitted as unclassified.

6. *Military Sales Authorization.*—Section 210 limits foreign military sales to not more than $1,039,000,000 for fiscal year 1976 and $740 million for fiscal year 1977. It also permits credit sales of not more than $2,374,700,000 for fiscal year 1976, "of which not less than $1,500,000,000 shall be available only for Israel," and "of not more

than $2,022,100,000 shall be available only for Israel." Half of the amounts due from Israel on these credit sales need not be repaid, and repayment of the balance is to be "in not less than twenty years, following a grace period of ten years."

7. *Reports on Commercial and Governmental Military Exports.*—Section 211 requires quarterly reports, unclassified, with certain exceptions, by the President to the Congress, listing all letters of offers to sell and all export "licenses and approvals" for commercially sold articles of "any major defense equipment" for $1 million or more. Before issuance of letters of offer "to sell any defense articles or services under this Act for $25,000,000 or more, or any major defense equipment for $7,000,000 or more" information thereon must be submitted by the President to the Congress, including, if requested by Congress, "an analysis of the arms control impact pertinent to such offer to sell, prepared in consultation with the Secretary of Defense."[10] Within 30 calendar days after receiving this information, the Congress may adopt a concurrent resolution objecting to the sale, which is thereby prohibited unless the President states that an emergency exists. A similar provision governs sales by corporations or individuals, but it lacks the concurrent resolution "veto power." Information regarding American personnel—military or civilian—who would be involved in a foreign country in connection with or as a result of the sale must be contained in the information provided to the Congress.

8. *Miscellaneous.*—Sections 212 through 215 contain provisions for: (1) controls of licenses of both exports and imports of arms by Americans in the private sector; (2) cancellation of contracts "if the national interest so requires"; (3) inclusion of administrative expenses of the United States Government "primarily for the benefit of any foreign country," in the sales prices; and (4) reports on foreign sales including "excess defense articles." Section 216 contains definitions.

C. Title III: General Limitations

1. *Human Rights.*—Section 301 articulates the policy of the United States favoring "respect for human rights and fundamental freedoms for all without distinction as to race, sex, language, or religion." This policy is made applicable to security assistance programs. Upon receipt of requested information from the executive branch, the Congress may adopt a joint resolution "terminating, restricting, or continuing security assistance" for any particular country. "[T]orture or cruel, inhuman, or degrading treatment or punishment" and "prolonged detention without charges and trial" are among the human rights violations to which this section applies.

Section 302 is aimed at any foreign country which prevents "any

United States person . . . from participating in the furnishing of defense articles or defense services . . . on the basis of race, religion, national origin, or sex." Upon receipt of information from the executive branch, the Congress may adopt a joint resolution terminating or restricting a transaction or sale.

Section 303 requires the President to terminate the foreign assistance or arms transfer program to any government "which aids or abets, by granting sanctuary from prosecution to, any individual or group which has committed an act of international terrorism," except in cases in which the President justifies to Congress that the national security of the United States requires otherwise.

2. *Ineligibility.*—Section 304 makes any country that breaks an arms transfer agreement limiting the use of arms or services to particular purposes ineligible for assistance. Among the breaches resulting in ineligibility are (1) the unauthorized use of arms or services, (2) the transfer of arms or services to the control of others without the consent of the President, and (3) the failure to keep the articles received secure.

Section 305 prohibits economic or military assistance to any country that "delivers nuclear reprocessing or enrichment equipment, materials, or technology to any other country," or receives the same, unless multilateral or International Atomic Energy safeguards are agreed to. Again, the Congress may terminate or restrict assistance to any country in violation of section 305 by joint resolution.

D. Title IV: Provisions Relating to Specific Regions or Countries

1. *The Middle East.*—Congress expects that the United States will determine "Middle East Policy as circumstances may require," so that nothing agreed to in connection with the Early Warning System in Sinai or under the present Act is to be construed as a commitment beyond the limited area of the Sinai system (section 401).

2. *Cyprus.*—The authorization for aid to Cyprian refugees has been increased from $30 million to $40 million (section 402).

3. *Turkey.*—The President may, for fiscal years 1976 and 1977, suspend provisions that forbid the transfer of defense articles and defense services to Turkey to the extent he determines necessary "to enable Turkey to fulfill her defense responsibilities" as a member of NATO. No more than $125 million worth of transfers may be authorized for each of the fiscal years. The President's suspension power exists only if Turkey "observes the cease-fire on Cyprus, does not increase its military forces or its civilian population on Cyprus, and does not transfer to Cyprus any United States supplied arms, ammunition, or implements of war" (section 403).

4. *Angola.*—Assistance which would help "any nation, group,

organization, movement, or individual to conduct military or paramilitary operations in Angola" is forbidden (section 404). Congress believes that Soviet intervention in Angola, including the support of Cuban armed forces there, is inconsistent with "detente," the 1975 Helsinki Agreement, and "the spirit of recent bilateral agreements" between the Soviet Union and the United States (section 405).

5. *Chile.*—Section 406 forbids the furnishing of arms, military assistance, credits, military education, or training to Chile. Provision is made, however, for economic assistance of $27.5 million for the period from July 1, 1976, through September 30, 1977. This amount may be doubled if the President certifies in writing to the Congress that Chile does not engage in "a consistent pattern of gross violations of internationally recognized human rights, including torture or cruel, inhuman, or degrading treatment or punishment, prolonged detention without charges or trial, or other flagrant denials of the right to life, liberty, or security of the person," has permitted unimpeded investigation by "internationally recognized commissions on human rights," and "has taken steps to inform the families of prisoners of the condition of and charges against such prisoners."

6. *The Indian Ocean.*—Section 407 states "that the President should undertake to enter into negotiations with the Soviet Union intended to achieve an agreement limiting the deployment of naval, air, and land forces" of the two countries "in the Indian Ocean and littoral countries."

7. *Mexico.*—Section 408 calls upon the President to try to insure that international cooperation "to restrict traffic in dangerous drugs" is consistent with respect for fundamental human rights. Reference is made to concern "over treatment of United States citizens detained in Mexico."

8. *Portugal.*—Section 409 recommends that the President act to alleviate the emergency food needs in Portugal.

9. *Lebanon.*—Section 410 deplores the situation in Lebanon, including the possibility that it will be exploited to the detriment of Israel. Sections 414 and 416 authorize $15 millin for housing reconstruction in Lebanon and $20 million for the "relief and rehabilitation of refugees and other needy people in Lebanon."

10. *Korea.*—Section 411 asks the President to transmit to Congress a report reviewing the Korean progress in modernizing its armed forces "so as to achieve military self-sufficiency by 1980," the role of the United States "in mutual security efforts" in Korea, and the prospects of "phased reduction of United States Armed Forces assigned to duty" in Korea. Section 412 reads as follows:

> The Congress views with distress the erosion of important civil liberties in the Republic of Korea and requests that the President communicate this

concern in forceful terms to the Government of the Republic of Korea within sixty days after enactment.

11. *Indochina.*—Existing law dealing with assistance to Indochina, except for provisions regarding contracts funded or approved for funding by the Agency for International Development prior to June 30, 1975, has been repealed (section 413).

12. *Italy.*—Section 415 authorizes an appropriation of $25 million for fiscal year 1976 to furnish assistance "for the relief and rehabilitation of the people who have been victimized by the recent earthquake in Italy.

E. Title V: Miscellaneous Authorizations

1. *Security Supporting Assistance.*—Section 501 authorizes appropriation by the President of $1,766,200,000 for fiscal year 1976 and $1,860,000,000 for fiscal year 1977 for security supporting assistance. Of the 1976 amount, not less than $65 million is available only for Greece, $730 million is available only for Israel, and $705 million is available only for Egypt. Of the total $1.86 billion for fiscal year 1977, not less than the following amounts are available: Israel, $785 million; Egypt, $750 million; Zambia, $27.5 million; and Zaire, $27.5 million. In the case of Zambia and Zaire, no funds may be used for "mlitary, guerrilla or paramilitary activities in either such country or in any other country."

2. *Middle East Special Requirement Fund.*—Section 502 authorizes $50 million for fiscal year 1976 and $35 million for fiscal year 1977 for the Middle East Special Requirement Fund, available to assist Egypt and Israel in connection with carrying out and paying for the Sinai Early Warning System, and for United States contributions of $12 million in each of those years towards the deficit of the United Nations Relief and Works Agency for Palestine refugees in the Middle East. Except section 507, which authorizes "such sums as may be necessary for the fiscal year 1977 to carry out international agreements or other arrangements for the use by United States Armed Forces of military facilities in Spain, Greece, or Turkey," the other sections of Title V do not directly relate to arms transfers.

F. Title VI: Miscellaneous Provisions

Section 601 deals with expedited procedure in the Senate in case a joint, concurrent, or other resolution regarding arms transfers is considered. Section 604 requires the President to report in considerable detail, "each payment, contribution, gift, commission, or fee" in connection with government-to-government sales of defense articles or services, and also in connection with commercial sales thereof.

Section 607 requires the President to submit to Congress a report on "information which substantiates that officials of a foreign country receiving international security assistance" accepted "illegal or otherwise improper payments" from an American corporation in return for a contract to buy defense articles or services, or extorted or tried to extort something of value for granting a permit to do business in that country. The report must recommend whether the United States should continue the assistance program for that country.

IV. PROCEDURE FOR ARMS TRANSFERS

A complex process precedes any particular arms transfer by or from the United States. In most cases, the process begins with three participants: the manufacturer or owner of the article, the foreign government, and the American military personnel assigned to the particular country as members of the Military Assistance Advisory Group. If the transfer includes "defense services," an American corporation may not be involved, although frequently the services involve training, maintenance, or spare parts in connection with weapons, such as aircraft, tanks or naval vessels, originating in the United States.

A. Present Procedure

In the case of weapons sales, the American manufacturer seeking to increase sales often provides the chief initial stimulus for the negotiation of a weapons transfer. Also participating at a fairly early stage are the regional bureaus and country desks at the State Department and the military assistance group members serving overseas.

When agreement has been reached between the purchasing country and the American manufacturer on the details of a particular transfer, the transfer must be approved by the United States Government. Although the determination of overall policy and the final decision on a particular transfer are made by the Secretary of State, the Secretary of Defense is responsible for fitting the weapon to the need. Recently, Congress has added the requirement of statements as to the impact on arms control and disarmament, which are the responsibility of the State Department and the Arms Control and Disarmament Agency, but which must be "prepared in consultation with the Secretary of Defense." In addition, in the case of "any major defense equipment sold under a contract in the amount of $7,000,000 or more," and in the case of "defense articles or defense services sold under a contract in an amount of $25,000,000 or more" there must be advance notice to the Speaker of the House and to the Chairman of the Senate Committee on Foreign Relations before issuance of an export license. By concurrent resolution Congress may, within 30 calendar days of the receipt of such notice, forbid the transfer.

The initial procedure calls for a paper describing the proposed transfer, which is circulated to the Department of Defense, the Department of State, and the Arms Control and Disarmament Agency. If there is disagreement among the groups on the acceptability of the proposed transfer, the final decision is made by the Secretary of State or his representative, unless the matter is of sufficient importance to go before the National Security Council or the President.

B. Inadequacies of the Present Procedure

This procedure is inadequate. Although there are published statements of principles to be applied, most decisions appear to be made *ad hoc,* in response to the pressures of the moment. Admittedly, each program and each country involve particular circumstances, but overall programs like those in recent years for Iran and Saudi Arabia (described below) raise difficult problems if measured against what is desirable in the long run. The State Department arms transfer policy has been unsupported by any coherent, long-term plan. Rather, it stems from pragmatic short-term efforts to maintain a balance of world power.

The Arms Control and Disarmament Agency has played a minor role in spite of new laws giving it the right to participate. In August 1976, ACDA submitted to Congress eleven classified impact statements on major weapons programs, including the cruise miissile, the B-1 bomber, the Trident submarine, and advanced missiles and shells.[11] The eleven statements were largely repetitions of earlier descriptions of technical characteristics of the weapons. Only one statement was more than a page long. Congressman Aspin of Colorado, a Democrat and a member of House Armed Services Committee, described the statements as "totally useless because they are absurdly superficial."[12]

The executive branch must report any major arms transfer program to the Congress, which may ask for additional information. Sometimes there is informal discussion between members of Congress or committee staff and the executive branch, which may result in a modification. Examples of modification occurred as to transfers of Hawk missiles to Jordan (the amount transferred was reduced), the transfer of C-130s to Egypt, and a program of air-to-air and air-to-ground missiles for Saudi Arabia.[13]

V. THE PROS AND CONS OF ARMS TRANSFERS

A. The Proponent's Arguments

Some of the arguments made in favor of arms transfers are listed here.

1. Production in excess of the orders placed for the United States military services is likely to increase corporate profits, provide employment, and produce other advantages resulting from greater volume.

2. Under present legislation, the cost of the items that the United States purchases for itself will be reduced by the share of research and development and production costs included in the purchase price paid by the foreign government.

3. Production beyond the needs of the United States military services may bring lower unit costs and longer maintenance of the production line, providing a greater period during which additional units may be purchased.

4. The foreign government and its military services want an adequate defense capability and more advanced equipment, preferably the most advanced available, for reasons of prestige as well as of utility.

5. An improvement in the American balance of payments will result from cash sales, and there may be more secure access to needed raw materials, particularly petroleum. The oil embargo and subsequent price increases imposed by the Organization of Petroleum Exporting Countries (OPEC) obviously motivated greater American arms sales. Unfortunately, the dependence of the United States and many of its allies (*e.g.,* NATO and Japan) on petroleum as a source of energy has been increasing.

6. In areas of confrontation, such as the Middle East, and the adjacent OPEC countries, United States foreign policy requires the bolstering of the defense capability of certain states. There are foreign policy motivations, including ensuring access to petroleum and containment of Communism, for arms transfers to each Middle Eastern country.

7. A foreign country will tend to be more friendly to the United States if arms, spare parts, training, and, perhaps, maintenance are carried out by American personnel.

In addition to these arguments there is the fear that if the United States does not supply an item, a substitute, even if not of equal quality, will be obtained from another arms exporting country. The Soviet Union, France, Great Britain, and, to a smaller extent, other Communist and Free World countries have become substantial exporters or arms. If the Soviet Union, the People's Republic of China, or another Communist country supplies arms, and perhaps spare parts, maintenance and training, the acquiring country, especially if in the "Third World," may be drawn into the Communist orbit.

B. The Opponent's Arguments

1. Given reasonable notice and advance planning, the companies and the localities involved in defense production can usually convert employees and facilities to production of non-military items; the manufacture of civilian products is fundamentally more useful to society than the production of articles designed to destroy people and goods.

2. If sophisticated equipment is transferred (and sophistication is a relative matter, depending on country and region), there may be an increase in the risk of conflict; and if one develops, it is likely to be more severe.

3. Some purchases may set off a local arms race with neighboring countries.

4. The recipient, particularly if a developing country, may have insufficient resources for the social needs of its people—for example, in the fields of education, health, and welfare; therefore, it should not increase military spending.

5. Arming neighboring countries that are hostile to one another may increase the probability and severity of hostilities, resulting in a greater risk of interruption of petroleum supplies and of Communist intervention.

6. There is an appreciable risk to the United States and its allies in the furnishing of arms to countries that may not remain friendly or abide by restrictions on transfers of weapons to countries not authorized to receive them.[14]

7. The presence of United States personnel, whether civilian or military, brings a risk of their unwanted involvement. For instance, three American civilians, employed by Rockwell International of California, were ambushed and shot to death by Iranian rebels in August 1976.[15]

8. There are risks that some of the countries acquiring American weapons, particularly sophisticated attack weapons, may become involved in a war that could require our military intervention. If Iran were to become embroiled with the Soviet Union, Iraq, or Afghanistan, a serious problem would arise for the United States. Israel faces varying degrees of hostility from Saudi Arabia, Egypt, Syria and Jordan. American weapons are being transferred to some of those Arab countries as well as to Israel.

VI. CONCLUSION

The preceding discussion has given some indication of the great size and breadth of the United States arms transfer program and has presented some arguments for and against such a vast program. Thorough reconsideration of this program has begun, and some moves to alter and perhaps diminish it have been made. There is a new law, but the new executive branch personnel and organization, at least in the Department of State, have not sufficiently been tested. The effect of the congressional "veto power" is not yet clear. President Carter will certainly influence future programs. The energy question, as well as OPEC price changes, could affect the pressure on the United States to offset balance of payments deficits caused by petroleum purchases with sales of arms for cash.

One must hope that we will not continue with mindless arms sales. "The present policy clearly creates unacceptable risks of American military involvement that may, if not quickly checked, be beyond the control of Congress or future Administrations."[16]

It is difficult to form a valid general opinion about arms transfers because applicable considerations differ in particular cases, depending upon, among other things, (a) which country is involved, (b) the situation at the time of the transfer program, (c) the region and neighbors of the country, and (d) the quantity and degree of sophistication of the arms to be transferred.

In any one case, there will be American foreign and defense policy considerations, economic considerations for both the United States and the recipient country, the question of the degree of dependence by the recipient upon the United States as its arms supplier, and the availability and nature of other potential sellers. Different and special factors apply to a NATO ally, to Israel, to suppliers of oil and other critical commodities, to Iran and Saudi Arabia and other countries in that part of the world, which are believed to constitute barriers against Soviet or other Communist expansion in the free or uncommitted world, and to Japan and West Germany, which are subject to treaty limitations on the right to manufacture arms domestically.

The United States generally has been motivated by a strong streak of idealism. It has often supplied large amounts of food and other necessities to less fortunate countries, particularly in times of disaster or crisis. Notable examples are the relief program for Western Europe immediately after World War I, and the Marshall Plan, not long after World War II.[17] Is the sale of large quantities of expensive weaponry consistent with the moral standards of the United States? During the war between India and Pakistan, both sides used weapons made by the United States as well as weapons from other Western countries and from the Soviet Union and its allies. In past hostilities between Israel and nearby countries, we have heavily and generously armed Israel as well as her opponents. The American contribution to the casualties is troubling to many.

It is also repugnant to many Americans to observe the United States supplying arms to governments that are unsavory by our standards. It sometimes seems as if the unsavory becomes savory when it appears to be on our side as against Communism. So far, we have not supplied Communist countries, except unintentionally on occasions like the defeat of Chiang Kai-shek by the Chinese Communists, when the latter captured enormous stocks of American arms that we had supplied to Chiang Kai-shek, or like the defeat of our recent allies in Indochina.

To reduce arms transfers, the following steps must be taken:

1. American consumption of energy in the form of petroleum products must be reduced through conservation and the development of alternative sources of energy, with due regard to problems of pollution and safety. This will eliminate the principal economic pressure for arms transfers.

2. The United States should actively seek an international agreement curtailing arms transfers. The other nations should first include other non-Communist suppliers, such as NATO allies and Israel; and then a proposal should be made to the Soviet Union and its allies and to the People's Republic of China. No encouragement should be given to the development of indigenous arms production in the "Third World" countries.

---

[1]90 Stat. 729 (1976).

[2]22 U.S.C. § 2301 (1970).

[3]U.S. ARMS CONTROL AND DISARMAMENT AGENCY, 93d CONG. 2D SESS., REPORT TO CONGRESS ON THE INTERNATIONAL TRANSFER OF CONVENTIONAL ARMS (Comm. Print 1974).

[4]The Departments of State and Defense assisted in the preparation of this report.

[5]22 U.S.C. § 2571 (Supp. II, 1970).

[6]SENATE COMM. ON FOREIGN RELATIONS, INTERNATIONAL SECURITY ASSISTANCE AND ARMS EXPORT CONTROL ACT OF 1976, S. REP. No. 605, 94th Cong., 2d Sess. (1976).

[7]The Act should be read in conjucntion with the Joint Committee Print entitled "Legislation on Foreign Relations, with Explanatory Notes." HOUSE COMM. ON INTERNATIONAL RELATIONS & SENATE COMM. ON FOREIGN RELATIONS, 94TH CONG., 2D Sess., LEGISLATION ON FOREIGN RELATIONS (Comm. Print 1976).

[8]90 Stat. 729 (1976). In the following discussion all sections analyzed are from the 1976 Arms Export Control Act unless otherwise noted.

[9]Foreign Assistance Act of 1961, 22 U.S.C. § 2301 (1970).

[10]This provision is similar to 89 Stat. 756 (1975), the Foreign Relations Authorization Act, Fiscal Year 1976, effective Nov. 29, 1975, which added to § 414 of the Mutual Security Act of 1954, 22 U.S.C. § 1934 (1970), paragraphs emphasizing "coordination" with the Director of ACDA. It requires decisions whether to issue export licenses to "take into account the Director's opinion as to whether the export of an article will contribute to an arms race, or increase

the possibility of outbreak or escalation of conflict, or prejudice the development of bilateral or multilateral arms control arrangements.''

[11]N.Y. Times, Sept. 12, 1976, § 1, at 30, col. 4.

[12]*Id.* See also SCIENCE, Oct. 1, 1976, at 36; DEFENSE SPACE DAILY, Sept. 27, 1976, at 141.

[13]As to the last-mentioned case, there had been an earlier agreement to transfer for cash to Saudi Arabia 1,000 Maverick TV-guided missiles or bombs. A second installment of 1,500 Mavericks was proposed by the executive branch. Negotiations between the legislative and executive branches, after the notice procedure, obtained a reduction to 650. Subsequently, the Senate Committee on Foreign Relations voted eight to six to block the sale of 650. After intense lobbying by representatives of the executive branch, reported to include Vice-President Rockefeller, and oil andmanufacturing corporations which are doing business with Saudi Arabia, and, of course, the pro-Israel lobbyists on the other side, the Committee vote was reversed, ensuring for all practical purposes that the program for 650 Mavericks would not be stopped. Washington Post, Sept. 28, 1976, at A1, col. 4; Washington Post, Sept. 2, 1976, at A10, col. 1.

[14]There have been examples recently in the Middle East of the use of weapons received from NATO countries, including the United States, by countries engaged in war against our close ally, Isreal. And there have been instances as far back as 1949, in the case of China, when large quantities of arms supplied by the United States have been captured by Communist countries and used against American or friendly forces. This occurred in China before the Korean War and recently in Indo-China.

[15]N.Y. Times, Aug. 30, 1976, at 1, col. 1. As of February 1976, there were reported to be 1,438 United States Department of Defense personnel assigned to Iran, with 1,941 dependents accompanying them. *Id.*

[16]N.Y. Times, Aug. 11, 1976, at 34, col. 1.

[17]The Marshall Plan help was financial and technical and was accompanied by substantial help for the defense of Western European countries, chiefly through NATO.

U.S. Military Exports and the Arms Export Control Act of 1976:

The F-16 Sale to Iran

Henry Billingsley II

There can be no war without weapons. Yet the trend of history strongly suggests that mankind is far from ready to part with either. Since the end of the Second World War, there have been 55 significant armed conflicts throughout the world.[1] Further, the international marketing of increasingly destructive weapons of war has expanded at an unprecedented rate. Total yearly international sales of conventional weapons have grown from $300 million in fiscal year 1952 to an estimated $20 billion in fiscal year 1975.[2] Although the proliferation of nuclear weapons may appear to be a matter of greater urgency, it should be stressed that the astronomical market figures just outlined reflect the trade in conventional, not nuclear weapons. More important, the death and destruction that has attended post-war armed conflict has resulted exclusively from the use of conventional weapons.

The history of efforts to curb the international trade in conventional arms is not a success story.[3] Attempts to limit the arms trade through the League of Nations and the United Nations have been so ineffective that they have served " . . . merely as symbolic gestures of disapproval."[4] There may be many reasons for this lack of success. George Thayer advances an explanation which should be considered:

> Member countries of the U.N. will gladly vote for "disarmament" and nuclear restrictions because it is good public relations, but few would be affected by the decisions. They may vote for an arms embargo against

"U.S. Military Exports and the Arms Export Control Act of 1976: The F-16 Sale to Iran," Henry E. Billingsley II, attorney, 9 CASE W. RES. J. INT'L L. 407 (1977). Reprinted with permission of the Case Western Reserve Journal of International Law.

> South Africa, but only because it is a specific reaction against an un-
> popular and vulnerable nation and few will be affected. But any across-the
> board vote to restrict their own lifeblood—arms—would be dismissed as in-
> appropriate.[5]

By default, the responsibility for initiating and executing policies to control the international trade in conventional weapons has fallen on the
producing nations individually.

The United States leads the world in exports of conventional weapons.
United States exports in fiscal year 1975 reached $9.5 billion—up from
$798 million in fiscal year 1968, and increase of 1,200 percent.[6] Further,
in the ten year period from 1965 through 1974, the United States exported $24.5 billion in conventional weapons to underdeveloped nations,
an amount representing 53 percent of the total arms shipments to the
Third World.[7]

It is not just the quantity of exports that has changed. There has also
been a significant change in the quality of the arms exported. Sales of
the most advanced United States conventional arms to foreign buyers, including nations of the Third World, are becoming common.[8] This trend
has been the subject of sharp criticism. Senator Edward Kennedy has
suggested that the trend of international sales of conventional weapons
by the United States indicates an " . . . apparently indiscriminate Administration policy of selling as much military equipment as foreign
countries will pay for."[9] This criticism was firmly restated by Senator
Nelson, with particular emphasis on United States weapons sales to the
Mideast:

> More than half of our foreign military sales in recent years have been
> made to the oil-rich Persian Gulf and Mideast. Such sales have major
> foreign policy implications, but there is little if any evidence that the Ad-
> ministration has given adequate thought to the long-range diplomatic or
> military consequences of such weapons transfers.[10]

This criticism has been met with the assertions that United States sales of
conventional arms are both a useful instrument for conducting foreign
policy and an important economic asset.[11]

What is the policy of the United States regarding the sale of conventional weapons to the Third World? How is the policy being implemented? On June 30, 1976, President Ford signed into law the International Security Assistanced and Arms Export Control Act of 1976.[12] The
International Security Assistance and Arms Export Control Act of 1976
amends two older laws: The Foreign Assistance Act of 1961,[13] and the
Foreign Military Sales Act.[14] Both pieces of legislation deal with the subject of conventional arms sales. Section 503(a) of the Foreign Assistance
Act authorizes the President to make sales of weapons as an option in
establishing a program of military assistance to a friendly nation. The

Foreign Assistance Act seems much more applicable to U.S. participation in foreign military programs than to sales of U.S. arms to foreign nations. The Foreign Military Sales Act, in contrast, is concerned exclusively with the sale of United States conventional weaponry to foreign countries. The Foreign Military Sales Act purports to " . . . consolidate and revise foreign assistance legislation relating to reimbursable military exports."[15] The amendments contained in Title II of the International Security Assistance and Arms Export Control Act of 1976, together with the Foreign Military Sales Act present the most current consolidation and revision of U.S. law governing the sale of conventional weapons to foreign nations. Therefore, the Foreign Military Sales Act, and the amendments in Title II will be the focus of this inquiry. It should be noted that section 201 of Title II provides that the Foreign Military Sales Act is to be renamed the Arms Export Control Act. Because Title II amends the Foreign Military Sales Act, the original Act and the amendments will be treated as one.[16]

This Note will examine the recently approved[17] $3.8 billion sale of 160 F-16 fighter aircraft to Iran[18] as a case study of the operation of the Arms Export Control Act of 1976. The purposes of this examination are to determine: (1) What the United States policy is regarding conventional arms sales to underdeveloped nations; (2) how this policy has been implemented in the current, major sale of a sophisticated warplane to Iran; and (3) what changes might be necessary to bring arms sales into line with the stated purposes and goals of the legislation.

The Arms Export Control Act of 1976, the authority under which the letter of offer for the purchase of the F-16 was approved, makes reference to the goal of achieving a world " . . . free from the scourge of war and the dangers and burdens of armaments. . . . "[19] Reflecting the continuing effort to realize this goal, the Act states an ongoing policy commitment of the United States " . . . to encourage regional arms control and disarmament agreements and to discourage arms races."[20] The Act stresses, however, that the cost and complexity of modern defense equipment may place intolerable burdens on the ability of a foreign country, particularly an underdeveloped nation, to meet " . . . all of its legitimate defense requirements from its own design and production base."[21] Recognizing this inability, the Act provides that the United States will enter into cooperative international relationships with friendly countries for the purpose of satisfying mutual defense requirements. To further facilitate the common defense the Act authorizes the United States Government to make sales of military equipment, subject to enumerated restraints.[22] It seems that two important general policy statements are made in the Arms Export Control Act. First, there is a recognition of the need to restrain the sale of conventional arms, particularly where the sales may provoke a regional arms race, or bring about economic instability within the recipient country. Second, there is emphasis placed upon the desirability of allowing friendly nations to assess their own defense requirements and to assume a larger role in meeting these national defense requirements. To this end, the Act provides for foreign purchases of U.S. conventional arms. It seems clear that there is no notion in the statements of policy that arms shipments are evil *per se,* but that arms sales can only be made under close supervision.

The main thrust of the limitations on the ability of individual foreign nations to purchase arms is contained in section 3, entitled "Eligibility."[23] No sale of any weapon or defense service[24] shall be made unless: (1) The President determines that world peace and United States security will be enhanced by the sale; (2) the recipient country agrees to make no transfer of any defense article sold without express prior consent of the President; and (3) the recipient nation will provide adequate security for all weapons purchased.[25] Having defined the eligibility requirements for nations seeking to buy weapons from the United States, section 4 presents a limitation on the purposes for which the weapons may be used. Providing for internal security and national self-defense, as well as meeting the requirements of collective security arrangements are the only appropriate uses of purchased conventional weapons.

Complementing the restrictions on the eligibility of recipient nations to enter the market for United States arms, and restrictions on the use of purchased weapons are a body of restraints on the United States arms market itself. Section 21(a) authorizes the President to make sales of arms from Department of Defense stocks to any eligible foreign country if payment for the arms is to be made in United States dollars.[26] In the case of defense services sold to a foreign nation, amended section 21(c) prohibits United States personnel from performing duties of a combatant nature. Duties of a combatant nature would include " . . . training, advising, or otherwise providing assistance regarding combat activities. . . . "[27] This provision seems to emphasize that the justification for allowing arms sales is to enable the recipient nation to meet legitimate defense requirements, not to give the recipient nation the ability to wage a war of aggression with the aid of purchased weapons and technical guidance. Like the provisions against resale of weapons by the recipient country contained in section 21(a), section 21(c) is intended to produce effective end-use control.

Section 22, entitled "Procurement for Cash Sales," directly governs the financial details of the sale of the F-16. Section 22 applies particularly to this sale because the F-16 is not an item in Department of Defense stocks, nor does Iran require credit financing for the purchase. Section 22(a) authorizes the President to enter into procurement contracts for the sale of weapons or defense services providing that the recipient country makes a dependable undertaking to meet the obligations of the contract. The requirements of a dependable undertaking are: (1) Protection from any loss of the United States on the contract; and (2) an understanding that the recipient nation will release funds as required to meet contract payments or to compensate for costs resulting from cancellation.

As demonstrated, the Arms Export Control Act of 1976 imposes restrictions on the abilities of prospective recipient nations to buy and on the abilities of the United States Government to sell defense services and weapons. But these provisions would have little efficacy without new sections 21(f), 25 and 36. These three sections are action-forcing provisions in that they require that all sales made pursuant to the Act be disclosed to the public and the Congress. Under section 21(f) the public is to be informed of all arms sales " . . . to the fullest extent possible consistent with the national security of the United States."[28] Sections 25 and 36 impose requirements on the President to inform Congress before the sale of conventional weapons may proceed.

Paragraphs (1), (3), and (4) of section 25(a) require the President to give specific estimates of arms sales expected to occur as a part of his fiscal year proposal for security assistance programs. Paragraph (1) requires the President to report estimates of the amount of sales to be made to each country under sections 21 and 22. The report of estimates must include " . . . a detailed explanation of the foreign policy and United States security considerations involved in expected sales to each country."[29] Under paragraph (3) the President is required to demonstrate how each sale " . . . will strengthen the security of the United States and promote world peace."[30] Finally, paragraph (4) provides that the President must also prepare an arms control impact statement for each purchasing country. This impact statement should include an analysis of the effect of the sale on arms control efforts in the purchasing country and the region in general. Part (b) of paragraph (4) gives authority to the Speaker of the House and to the Chairman of the Senate Foreign Relations Committee to receive additional information from the President within 30 days of their request.

Section 36(a), as amended, requires the President to present a quarterly report to the Speaker of the House and to the Chairman of the Senate Foreign Relations Committee.[31] The report is to be presented within 30 days of the close of each quarter. The quarterly report must set forth, in part: (a) A list of all unaccepted letters of offer to sell defense equipment for any amount exceeding or equal to $1 million; and (2) a listing, by country, of all letters of offer that have been accepted and the total dollar value of the weapons or defense services sold. The advantage of these provisions is that a full record of unaccepted letters of offer as well as of all arms sales is maintained, continuously updated and regularly presented to Congress.

The notice provisions of sections 36(a), 21(f) and 25 are essential elements of the effort to understand and direct the arms selling operations of the United States. But these provisions only call for the transmission of information relating to arms sales. Amended section 36(b)(1) may be the most significant part of the Arms Export Control Act of 1976 because it is designed to give Congress the ultimate authority to stop the issuance of a letter of offer to a purchasing nation. In order to secure an approved letter of offer either for the sale of weapons or defense services valued at $25 million or more, or for the sale of major defense equipment worth $7 million or more, the President must provide a "certification" to the Speaker of the House and to the Chairman of the Senate Foreign Relations Committee.[32] Following delivery of the certification, Congress has 30 calendar days in which to review the certification. If, before the expiration of the 30 calendar day period, Congress adopts a concurrent resolution of objection to the sale the letter of offer for the sale will not be issued. The President may override this resolution only if the certification states that an emergency exists requiring the sale as a means of protecting the security interests of the United States.

It seems essential to recognize that the Arms Export Control Act does not state any specific dollar limitation on *cash* sales of conventional arms to eligible foreign nations.[33] It is also significant that the Act contains no restriction against cash sales of the most advanced conventional weapons.[34] A nation which currently satisfies the eligibility requirements of section 3 and which has sufficient funds to pay cash for weapons may proceed to the limits of those funds. It is the responsibility of Congress, acting on information supplied at the direction of the President, to pass on the wisdom of the sale. Therefore, the extent to which the Arms Export Control Act can succeed in controlling arms sales is a measure of the diligence of the President in ensuring that the full information is given to Congress and of the ability of Congress to evaluate that information.

The sale of the F-16 to Iran is a major sale, but not the first. Statistics indicate that Iran is the best customer for United States arms in the Mideast. U.S. sales of weapons to Iran have expanded from $113 million in 1970 to a high of more than $3.9 billion in 1974.[35] The Shah of Iran makes the final decisions on all arms purchases.[36] The Shah is a pilot himself, and seems to take a particular interest in military jet aircraft.[37] However, United States sales of conventional weapons to Iran run the gamut of available types of conventional weaponry, including missiles, tanks, artillery, fixed wing aircraft, helicopters, and warships.[38]

The F-16 is billed as the "swing force fighter of the 80's."[39] Technically designated as an air combat fighter, the F-16 is a product of the Air Force lightweight fighter program.[40] The F-16 has been judged an outstanding performer, combining high speed and superior maneuverability, advanced avionics and ordnance delivery systems, and, surprisingly, a low cost.[41] Projected figures indicate a unit price in the area of $6 million compared to a cost of $15 million each for the McDonnell Douglas F-15, another air combat fighter.[42]

The proposal to issue a letter of offer for the sale fo the F-16 to Iran was but one item in a massive certification reported to Congress on September 1, 1976.[43] The September 1 report contained 37 individual letters of offer for the sale of $6.024 billion in conventional weapons to 11 foreign nations.[44] The proposed letters of offer were received with alarm by some members of the Congress, owing to the size of the reported proposals and the timing of their delivery. Senator Bumpers commented:

> Waiting until so late in the legislative session—to deluge the Congress with this gargantuan commitment—tells us one of two things— Either arms sales are indeed out of control as most critics believe, or the administration is utilizing the tactic of swamping the Congress with proposed sales all at one time in hopes that we will find the task of careful examination within the required thirty days impossible.[45]

It should also be noted that the Labor Day recess and weekends, during which there were no sessions, resulted in even fewer days available for consideration of the proposals. Assuming Congress could devote every available day exclusively to consideration of the proposals, which it could not, the available time seems insufficient. It is unlikely that there was enough time to allow for the kind of effective review of arms sales that is required by the Arms Export Control Act. The facts relating to the timing of the notification of Congress support the conclusion that the sale of the F-16 to Iran may have been approved with little more than a rubber stamp.

There is also evidence suggesting that Congress would not have had enough information to fully review the F-16 sale even if there had been sufficient time. The first hearing on the proposed sale of the F-16 to Iran took place before the Subcommittee on Foreign Assistance of the Senate Foreign Relations Committee on September 16, 1976. In his opening statement, Senator Humphrey sharply criticized the Executive Branch for its failure to provide information to the Committee.[46] Senator Humphrey went on to charge that much of the information that had been received was so superficial that it could " . . . not be regarded as a serious response to the Committee's inquiries."[47] Senator Humphrey concluded that this absence of cooperation indicated " . . . an almost total lack of respect on the part of the Executive Branch for the Committee's role in considering arms sales matters."[48]

Senator Humphrey's statements are not the only indication that the Executive Branch may not have met the obligation imposed by the Arms

Export Control Act of 1976. Senator Nelson stated that the justifications for the letters of offer in the September 1 report were "flimsy" and " . . . totally inappropriate to the magnitude of the impact these sales would have on U.S. security and peace in the world."[49] The Senator emphasized that the paucity of information delivered seemed particularly unacceptable given the resources at the command of the President:

> [T]he [E]xecutive [B]ranch is well supplied with manpower in the arms sale field who are working in various offices, bureaus, and divisions of the different services of the Pentagon and in the State Department, National Security Council, Office of Management and Budget, and Arms Control and Disarmament Agency.[50]

The Senator also made reference to two unfinished reports: The National Security Staff Memorandum on arms sales and a comprehensive study on the Persian Gulf region, neither of which had been completed at the time the F-16 sale was considered. Calling attention to the 1975 restriction on arms sales to Israel pending a program reassessment, Senator Nelson expressed concern that despite the lack of any comprehensive analysis demonstrated by the Executive Branch, massive sales to the Persian Gulf were still being proposed.[51]

The disquietude in the Senate Foreign Relations Committee as expressed by the statements of Senator Humphrey reflects a concern that, regardless of the Arms Export Control Act, sales of conventional weaponry to foreign nations are not being fully examined and justified. The concern that the law is not producing its intended results seems more pressing in view of the U.S. sales of conventional weapons to Iran. The most complete examination of the history of United States arms sales to Iran is the Staff Report to the Subcommittee on Foreign Assistance.[52] The report examines the evolution of present arms sales and indicates a major turning point was reached in May of 1972. At that time, President Nixon assured the Shah of Iran virtual *carte blanche* to purchase weapons from the United States.

> The President informed the Shah (1) that the U.S. would sell Iran the F-14 or F-15 aircraft; and (2) that in the future, the U.S. would, in general, sell Iran *any conventional weapons system that it wanted.* The decisions were confirmed in instructions to the bureaucracy.[53] (emphasis added)

The decision to allow the Shah of Iran a free hand to purchase weapons from the United States was made to further President Nixon's "twin pillar" policy of assuring a stable Mideast through United States defense sales and cooperation with Iran and Saudi Arabia. The Nixon Administration decided to rely on local powers in the Mideast rather than an increased U.S. military presence to fill the security gap opened by the exit of the British in 1968.[54] The 1972 decision of President Nixon to remove restrictions on conventional arms sales to Iran has brought about a tremendous increase in arms sales to Iran.

> Although these decisions are consistent with the "twin pillar" policy, they marked the beginning of an arms sale boom to Iran. The bureaucracy ceased its careful scrutiny of requests by Iran except for the most sophisticated systems involving release of state-of-the-art and highly classified technology. The dramatic increase in oil prices in 1973 provided Iran with the means to buy what it wanted.[55]

Further, the original decision to exclude arms sales to Iran from normal scrutiny has never been reconsidered in light of the oil price increase.[56] The Foreign Assistance Subcommittee Staff Report concludes that arms sales to Iran were "poorly managed" and "out of control" for at least 3 years.[57] There seems to be nothing in the facts relating to the approval of the F-16 sale to Iran which suggests that there has been any change, regardless of the Arms Export Control Act of 1976. Congress did not pass a concurrent resolution objecting to the sale within 30 calendar days. The letter of offer for the $3.8 billion sale was approved *automatically*.

The facts surrounding the F-16 sale are irreconcilable with the previously discussed policy statements of the Arms Export Control Act. The Act requires that arms sales be approved only after thoughtful, informed decision-making. In the approval of the sale of the F-16, the decision-making was rushed and based on inadequate information. Therefore, Congress could not provide the overview that the Act is designed to ensure. The F-16 approval so directly contradicts the policies expressed in the Arms Export Control Act that one might well ask if the avowed commitment of the United States to the control of conventional arms sales is more than a facade. If the United States is committed to the stated policies of the Arms Export Control Act, these policy goals might be achieved more effectively by changing the law.

The Arms Export Control Act requires the Executive Branch to inform Congress regarding conventional arms sales. Congress is responsible for reviewing the information. As discussed previously, the success of the Act must be measured by the completeness of the information received by Congress and by the ability of Congress to evaluate the information fully within 30 calendar days. If Congress is pressed for time, it is possible that incomplete or unverified information will go unchallenged in the haste. Three changes in the Arms Export Control Act might alleviate this problem. The first change would be to extend the time limit for consideration of the letters of offer from 30 calendar days to 30 *session* days. This would eliminate the problems arising from a certification being delivered immediately before a recess. Regardless of the timing of delivery, arms sales would receive 30 full days of review.

A second means of ensuring full review would be to limit the number of letters of offer that could be reported at one time. As indicated the September 1, 1976, report to Congress contained proposals for the sale of 37 weapons to 11 foreign nations, for a total of $6.024 billion. A provision limiting the size of the report by number of weapons to be sold, number of individual nations intending to purchase, or dollar amount would protect the Congress from becoming swamped in arms sale proposals.

The third change would be the most significant. Presently the burden rests on Congress to raise objections to a letter of offer or to request additional information from the Executive Branch. In the absence of a request for additional information, or a concurrent resolution of objection, the letter of offer passes without challenge. The proposed change would involve shifting this burden directly to the Executive Branch, providing that all letters of offer subject to amended section 36(b) will be presumed *disapproved* until justified. Under the proposed change the Executive Branch would be required to obtain a concurrent resolution of approval from Congress in order to proceed with the sale. If this change were made, the Executive Branch would more likely be held to its obligation under the Act to provide adequate information to Congress. Any incentive to hinder a full review of a letter of offer would be eliminated by this shifting of the burden.

Arguments can be made against the adoption of any of these three proposals for change. The first of these arguments might be that the change would sacrifice the flexibility presently existing in the field of arms sales, making these sales a less useful instrument of foreign policy. Further, increasing the time and effort required to process a letter of offer might hinder the conduct of foreign policy by casting doubt on the reliability of the United States as a supplier of conventional weapons.

It should be noted that the specific requirements relating to the substance and quality of certifications and reports would not be altered by any of the proposals for change. The only change would be the extent to which the Executive Branch would be encouraged to diligently meet existing requirements. Appropriation requests for the United States defense budget carry no presumption of approval. There seems to be little justification for giving foreign sales of conventional arms a higher priority. Further, Senator Humphrey has pointed out that the automatic reporting requirements written into the Act had been kept to a minimum to allow the President greater flexibility, but that the lack of cooperation of the Executive Branch had hindered the review process rather than helped it.[58] The assertion that the proposals for change would reflect negatively on the reliability of the United States as a supplier raises two considerations. First, it seems doubtful that reliability, by itself, is a virtue. Reliability is desirable only if it follows a careful, informed decision to sell conventional weapons to the particular country in question. The reliable, uncontrolled delivery of weapons to a foreign nation lends no credibility to an assertion by the United States that it is committed to a policy of arms export control. Second, it is suggested that reliability may not be as important as candor in dealing with prospective purchasing nations. Thus, informing the Shah of Iran of inherent economic and technical problems that might militate against the purchase of a highly sophisticated weapon might enhance a friendly relationship.[59]

The loss of the economic advantages for U.S. balance of payments might be advanced as a reason for rejecting proposals for more control over conventional arms sales. As a corollary to the first assertion, one might point to the advantage of reduced weapons procurement costs for the United States as a result of longer production runs due to foreign sales. This argument assumes an ordering of United States policy priorities that is incorrect. There is no indication in the policy statements of the Arms Export Control Act that a favorable balance of payments or a decreased procurement cost is to be offered as a justification for United States arms sales. Sales are authorized to enable recipient nations to meet legitimate defense needs, without placing a burden on their national economies.[60] It is true that adoption of the proposals for change might lessen the economic advantages of arms sales. But U.S. economic advantage is made subordinate to the goal of bringing about control of the sale of conventional weapons, as expressed in the Arms Export Control Act.

The facts of the sale of the F-16 indicate that, despite the Arms Export Control Act of 1976, the United States is not yet prepared to assume its promised role as leader in the campaign to put an end to the massive, indiscriminate trade in conventional implements of war.

---

[1]G. THAYER, THE WAR BUSINESS 2 (1969).

[2]Mayer, Norman, Scott, *Anatomy of the Arms Trade,* NEWSWEEK, Sept. 6, 1976, at 39.

[3]STOCKHOLM INTERNATIONAL PEACE RESEARCH INSTITUTE, THE ARMS TRADE WITH THE THIRD WORLD 86-131 (1971). Chapter 2 traces the history of international efforts to control the trade of arms.

[4]R. HARKAVY, THE ARMS TRADE AND INTERNATIONAL SYSTEMS 221 (1975).

[5]G. THAYER, *supra* note 1, at 375. In a television interview conducted on Jan. 3, 1964, U.S. Secretary of State Dean Rusk stated substantially the same point:

> I recall that at the United Nations General Assembly, at a time when all the members were voting unanimously for disarmament, 70 members were at that moment asking us for military assistance.

[6]U.S. DEP'T OF DEF., FOREIGN MILITARY SALES AND MILITARY

ASSISTANCE FACTS 14-15 (1975).

[7]U.S. ARMS CONTROL AND DISARMAMENT AGENCY, WORLD MILITARY EXPENDITURES AND ARMS TRANSFERS 73 (1976).

[8]Klare, *The Political Economy of Arms Sales,* BULLETIN OF THE ATOMIC SCIENTISTS, Nov., 1976, at 12.

[9]121 CONG. REC. S2409 (daily ed. Feb. 22, 1975) (remarks of Sen. Kennedy). See also Kennedy, *The Persian Gulf: Arms Race or Arms Control,* 54 FOR. AFF. 14 (1975).

[10]122 CONG. REC. S15526 (daily ed. Sept. 10, 1976) (remarks of Sen. Nelson).

[11]Loosbrock, *Keeping Foreign Military Sales in Perspective,* AIR FORCE, Feb., 1976, at 4-5. See also Gray, *Traffic Control for the Arms Trade,* 6 FOR. POL'Y 153 (1972).

[12]International Security Assistance and Arms Export Control Act of 1976, Pub. L. No. 94-329, 90 Stat. 729 (1976) [hereinafter cited as International Security Assistance and Arms Export Control Act of 1976].

[13]Foreign Assistance Act of 1961, Pub. L. No. 87-195, 75 Stat. 424 (1961).

[14]Foreign Military Sales Act, Pub. L. No. 90-629, 82 Stat. 1320 (1968) [hereinafter cited as Foreign Military Sales Act].

[15]*Id.*

[16]In the interest of clarity a textual reference to the Arms Export Control Act of 1976, the Arms Export Control Act or, simply, the Act will include both the Foreign Military Sales Act and the amendments presented in Title II. If a specific provision of the older law or an amendment under Title II is quoted, it will be cited as such.

[17]The notification of the letter for the sale to the Government of Iran was made by the President to the Speaker of the House and to the Chairman of the Senate Foreign Relations Committee on Sept. 1, 1976. Under amended section 36(b)(1) of the Arms Export Control Act of 1976 the letter was automatically approved in the absence of a concurrent resolution of Congress objecting to the sale.

[18]*Supra* note 10.

[19]Foreign Military Sales Act § 1.

[20]*Id.*

[21]*Id.*

[22]*Id.*

[23]*Id.* § 3.

[24]International Security Assistance and Arms Export Control Act of 1976 215(4). A defense service includes any " . . . service, test, inspection, repair, training, publication, technical or other assistance . . . "

[25]Foreign Military Sales Act § 3(a)(1), (2), (3).

[26]International Security Assistance and Arms Export Control Act of 1976 § 205.

[27]*Id.*

[28]*Id.*

[29]*Id.* § 209(a). See Appendix A.

[30]*Id.*

[31] *Id.* § 211(a).

[32] *Id.* See Appendix B.

[33] International Security Assistance and Arms Export Control Act of 1976 § 202(a)(1). This section provides that sales of arms and defense services are not to "exceed current levels" in any fiscal year. However, if one considers the size of the sales now being approved a restriction to current levels seems like no restriction at all. The provision adds nothing to the ability of the law to control the makings of arms sale decisions. Further, the provision states a sense of Congress. As such the limitation does not carry the force of law.

[34] Foreign Military Sales Act § 4. There are limitations on credit sales of sophisticated weaons.

[35] Center for Defense Information, *U.S. arms to the Persian Gulf: $10 Billion Since 1974,* THE DEFENSE MONITOR, May, 1975, at 2.

[36] From a statement of the Shah, as reported in 122 CONG. REC. S15526 (daily ed. Sept. 10, 1976).

[37] Military jets, particularly fighters and fighter bombers, represented the largest portions of Iran's military purchases: $2.71 billion from 1970 to 1974. Center for Defense Information, *supra* note 35, at 5.

[38] *Id.* Iran has also been given permission to purchase the newest DD 993 modified *Spruance Class* destroyer.

[39] Carroll, *F-16: The Swing Force Fighter of the 80's,* AIR FORCE, Oct., 1976, at 33.

[40] *Id.* See also Rider, *Y-F-16 Pilot Report,* AIR FORCE, Oct., 1976, at 33.

[41] Carroll, *supra* note 34, at 31.

[42] *Id.*

[43] *Supra* note 10.

[44] *Id.*

[45] 122 CONG. REC. S15543 (daily ed. Sept. 10, 1976) (remarks of Sen. Bumpers).

[46] *Hearings on the Proposed Sale of 160 F-16 Aircraft to the Government of Iran Before the Subcommittee on Foreign Assistance of the Senate Foreign Relations Committee,* 94th Cong., 2d Sess. (Sept. 16, 1976) (Statement of Sen. Humphrey) [hereinafter cited as the *Humphrey Statement*].

[47] *Id.* at 3.

[48] *Id.*

[49] *Supra* note 10.

[50] *Id.*

[51] *Id.*

[52] REPORT ON U.S. MILITARY SALES TO IRAN BY THE STAFF OF SUBCOMM. ON FOREIGN ASSISTANCE OF SENATE COMM. ON FOREIGN RELATIONS, 94th Cong., 2d Sess. (Comm. Print 1976) [hereinafter cited as SUBOMM. REP.].

[53] *Id.* at 5. Italics mine.

[54] *Id.*

[55] *Id.* at 6.

[56] *Id.*

[57] *Id.* at XII.

[58]The *Humphrey Statement, supra* note 46, at 2.
[59]SUBCOMM. REP., *supra* note 52, at 50.
[60]FOREIGN MILITARY SALES ACT § 1.

The Transfer of Arms to Third World Countries and Their Internal Uses

Asbjórn Eide

INTRODUCTION: THE END OF THE MONOPOLY STAGE OF VIOLENCE

This article should start with an apology. One of Africa's most outstanding political scientists once observed, paraphrasing a famous dictum by Lenin, that imperialism was the monopoly stage of violence.[1] During the period in which Europe and North America underwent a technological revolution which also brought about tremendous changes in armament technology, most of what is now called the Third World was brought under colonial control and prevented from obtaining its own armaments. Not many decades ago, it was still prevailing opinion in the industrialized countries that the rest of the world should be kept disarmed. Surprisingly, the notion seems to have been widespread that the white race was more responsible and more able to control its weaponry than the peoples of Africa and Asia. Already before the outbreak of the Second World War, Kenyatta had the following remark to make about this notion:[2]

> The European prides himself on having done a great service to the Africans by stopping the 'tribal warfares, and says that the Africans ought to thank the strong power that has liberated them from their 'constant fear' of being attacked by the neighboring war-like tribes. But consider the difference between the method and motive employed in the so-called savage tribal warfares and those employed in the modern warfare waged by the 'civilized' tribes of Europe and in which the Africans who have no part in their quarrel are forced to defend so-called democracy.

From *International Social Science Journal*, Vol. XXVIII, No. 2, 1976, pages 245-265. Copyright © 1976 Unesco. Reprinted by permission of Unesco.

The intention of this article is therefore to argue that the Third World is not inherently less capable of controlling their weaponry than the industrialized world, and hence not less entitled to have armed forces. What will be stressed is that there are a number of negative consequences which are and will be experienced by the Third World in seeking to militarize by developing armed forces through the acquistion of 'modern' military technology.

The vast majority of Third World countries would benefit infinitely more by maintaining a relatively modest and technologically simple army while at the same time insisting at international forums on the achievement of comprehensive and general disarmament through which the industrialized States also dismantle the military machineries which they have erected. If such world-wide disarmament is not obtained, there will be no way of halting the militarization of the Third World, whatever negative consequences one may be able to point to in advance.

The effort to maintain a monopoly of violence by the European powers found expression several times during the nineteenth century, in which efforts were made to prohibit transfers of arms to Africa and parts of Asia. The declared intention was to prevent what were called 'tribal wars,' but the effect was that the Third World peoples were unable to resist colonial occupation. Of particular interest is the Brussels Act adopted by an international conference in 1890, regulating the export of arms to Africa. The prohibitions are found in Article VIII of the Act, which it is illuminating to quote *verbatim:*[3]

> The experience of all nations that have intercourse with Africa having shown the pernicious and preponderating part played by firearms in operations connected with the slave tràde as well as internal wars between the native tribes: and this same experience having clearly proved that the preservation of the African population whose existence it is the express wish of the powers to protect, is a radical impossibility, if measures restricting the trade in firearms and ammunition are not adopted, the powers decide, so far as the present state of their frontiers permit, that the importation of firearms, and especially of rifles and improved weapons, as well as of powder, ball and cartridges, is, except in the cases and under the conditions provided for in the following Article, prohibited in the territories comprised between the 20th parallel of North latitude and the 22nd parallel of South latitude, and extending westward to the Atlantic Ocean and eastward to the Indian Ocean and its dependencies, including the islands adjacent to the coast within 100 nautical miles from the shore.

The hypocrisy of this justification is not difficult to detect. The Act was the culmination of regulations applied by individual European governments, to prevent the transfer of arms to the various small African States which over a large part of the nineteenth century maintained independence on the territory which now forms the Union of South Africa.

Since there was no similar prevention of transfer to the white settlers and the colonial army, this policy was a major factor in facilitating racial domination.

Efforts in the same direction were still being made after the First World War, including the Saint Germain Convention of 1920, which prohibited the transfer weapons to the whole of Africa except Algeria—then under French occupation—Libya, and the Union of South Africa.[4]

It should be noted that these efforts were made during a period which coincided with severe and brutal colonial warfare in several parts of Africa and Asia. Mention could be made of the German war of extermination in South West Africa at the beginning of this century, or Portuguese warfare in Angola which lasted at least until 1919 before full colonial control was established.

It was the Second World War which gave the first major impetus to militarization of the Third World. As reflected in the statement by Kenyatta quoted above, the driving force was the interest of industrialized countries to utilize manpower from the Third World in the massively violent confrontation between the industrialized powers which took place from 1939 to 1945.[5] Such efforts were made in different parts of the world. After its occupation of Dutch East India, Japan armed Indonesian nationalists. In the Indian subcontinent, armament was carried out by the United Kingdom, and the French and British set up armed forces in several parts of Africa. This process was intensified after the Second World War, and initially very much related to the cold war confrontation. The West sought to build a collective security system consisting of a chain of military alliances bordering the Soviet Union and China. The countries bordering the two major socialist countries were designated as 'forward defence areas' and received three-quarters of major weapon exports by the United States to Third World countries. This heavy militarization culminated in the formation of SEATO and the Baghdad Pact, later to become CENTO, in 1955. Bilateral mutual defence treaties were established with other countries in the area. Similarly, in the Middle East, military assistance was provided partly in order to persuade countries to join the Western collective security arrangement.[6]

During this early period, practically no transfers took place from the Soviet Union except to China, the Democratic People's Republic of Korea and later to the Democratic Republic of Viet-Nam.

The weapons transferred by the United States to the forward defence area were intended for military confrontation with the socialist countries. Several of the recipient governments, however, joined into these collective security arrangements mainly in order to develop their capacity for fighting local international conflicts and for purposes of internal control.[7]

Armament transfers from the Soviet Union experienced their first major increase from 1955. The first area to be supplied was the Middle East, where the objective mainly was to resist the efforts of the West to organize an anti-Soviet military alliance. Later on, the transfers by the Soviet Union became increasingly related to the conflict between Israel and the Arab countries, in which the Soviet Union catered for the weapon demands of several Arab countries.

Thus, the militarization of certain Third World countries during the Second World War and up to 1960 was mainly caused by major industrialized countries for their own strategic interests. The consequences of this militarization for the recipient countries was hardly given much attention.

A part of the fading monopoly of violence was the system of military bases. The origin of this system can be found in the formation of colonial empires. Trading posts were established, in turn leading to fortification, and gradually a chain of bases were established by the major colonial powers throughout Africa and Asia and on islands in between. The competition and sometimes violent confrontation between the colonial metropolises (in particular the United Kingdom and France) intensified the need for such bases. Notions of geo-politics formed central parts of the justification of these bases. Inherent in geo-political notions is the assumption that major industrialized countries are entitled, for their own strategic interests, to police overseas. With the advent and growth of air forces, the need for air bases became dominant. During the Second World War, in particular as a consequence of the war between Japan and the United States, a far-flung system of air bases was created and much of it maintained after the end of the war. These bases were planned for two purposes: partly to protect all possible air routes to the United States through the overseas basing of defensive fighters, and for deterrence with bases close enough to all potential enemies so that bombers could reach targets within the strategic heartland of any potential adversary.[8]

Thus, the two decades beginning with the Second World War and ending 1960 were characterized by a proliferation of weapons throughout the Third World, but mainly contained within a system of control by the major industrialized countries, directly (in the form of bases) and indirectly (in the form of collective security arrangements).

By 1960, therefore, the monopoly of violence held by some few industrialized countries was being weakened, while still not seriously challenged.

CURRENT CHANGES

During the past fifteen years, important changes have taken place, among which the following seem to be the most important here.

On one hand, the orientation of military assistance from the West (and in particular the United States) has changed. The focus is no longer on collective defence and the deterrence of external attacks, but has increasingly concentrated on internal control in Third World countries. At the beginning of the 1960s, the assumption was that this had to a large extent to be carried out through direct military intervention. Towards the end of the decade there was a change of emphasis towards strengthening the capacity of the police and the military of the Third World for local control by their own forces, but with equipment and training from outside.

Another change has been a substantially increased military assistance by the Soviet Union to a wider number of states, and also increasing support to liberation movements. This support has gone, in particular, to movements in southern Africa and in Indo-China through the Democratic Republic of Viet-Nam.

The third, and probably most important change has been the increasing assertion of autonomy in the use of the armed forces by the governments of many Third World countries.

The emphasis on internal uses of the armed forces had already been a dominant feature in the colonial wars since 1945. Dutch actions in Indonesia, French wars in Indo-China, and later in Algeria, the British in Malaya, and—much later—Portuguese warfare in its African colonies all had this in common: the use of force was not for the purpose of defence against external attack (which would have been legitimate under the United Nations Charter), but designed tro maintain established control and to resist the struggle for self-determination. At the beginning of the 1960s, the internal use of armed force became a more accepted doctrine under the name of 'counter-insurgency.' It evolved, in particular, as part of the doctrine of flexible response adopted by the United States during the administration of President Kennedy. Part of this strategy was the effort to provide the United States military establishment with a 'rapid reponse' capability allowing for deployment of United States troops on the guerrilla battlefield at the first sign of an insurgent uprising.' Several requirements arose from this: an extended network of military bases, the construction of giant transport aircraft, fast supply ships, and a wide range of other weapon developments.

This doctrine, in its original form, ran its full course in the Indo-China war which saw the widest range of counter-insurgency weapons ever deployed on any battlefield. However, it ended in ultimate disaster. Developments took a different turn in other parts of the world, particularly in Latin America. At an early stage of the counter-insurgency programmes, it was found desirable to equip and train the internal military and police forces rather than to prepare for direct external intervention. Under the Military Assistance Programme (MAP), the forces responsible for maintenance of internal security were to be subsidized. These ideas, initially developed in the early 1960s as a consequence of experiences in Viet-Nam, found their place into the Military Assistance Programme from 1963 onwards. The programme became intensified after the visit of Rockefeller to Latin America, where he encountered considerable turbulence.[10] His evaluation of the unrest was that there was a need for stronger government. He claimed that pluralistic forms of government would often be incapable of maintaining the proper balance between development and stability in nations undergoing the process of modernization. The question, he argued, was less one of democracy or a lack of it, than of an orderly way of doing things. He argued that the United States should learn to live with the military strongmen in Latin America, and to understand that a new type of military man was coming to the fore and becoming a major force for constructive social change in the American republics.[11]

In the counter-insurgency programme which followed, military bases were equipped for the gathering of intelligence and for military training, and comprehensive programmes of counter-insurgency training were also set up in the United States itself. In this process, the legitimacy of military intervention in the political systems of Third World countries was actively propagated. Whatever hesitation might have been felt by officers, as a consequence of their traditional professional ethics, was quickly eroded.

At the same time, another process of legitimation was proceeding in a different forum: the struggle for liberation against colonial and racial regimes, particularly in southern Africa, found increasing support in the United Nations. In a series of increasingly pointed resolutions, the United Nations organizations legitimized support to the armed struggle of the liberation movements. Such support, in the form of weapons, came mainly from the Soviet Union, and to some extent also from China. These were weapons designed for guerrilla forces defending themselves against the counter-insurgency actions of the former Portuguese regime, the illegal Smith regime of Rhodesia, and South Africa. In the same period, transfers to independent countries also accelerated rapidly.

It is important to note, also, that there has been a change in the nature of the transfers. During the early years, much military equipment was provided free of charge. In the past decade, most of it has been provided on a regular trade basis, which means that the weapons (increasingly expensive because of their sophistication) have to be paid for. This has had serious economic consequences. Countries in which large military establishments were created through gifts (particularly in the so-called 'forward defence areas') had to continue to live with these military establishments even when they had to pay for them. Due both to the local arms races between neighbouring States generated by the militarization, and also to the strength of the military in the political systems of certain countries, it was impossible to undo what had been created. Having to pay for all the weapons, these countries experienced severe economic problems which in turn required the accumulation of a surplus by the groups controlling the State. This surplus had to be obtained from somewhere in society, which led to exploitation and unequal development, which in turn caused serious disruptions in several countries.

Some of the major Third World States, and particularly those with some industrial base, have started their own domestic arms production. In some cases, this is simply part of the present international division of labour, where multinational companies involved in arms production carry out some production in Third World countries where the labour is cheaper. In other cases, there is a determined effort by Third World countries to obtain autonomy in armaments from the more industrialized countries of the north. For a number of reasons, this autonomy is almost impossible to obtain: studies carried out so far indicate that technological dependence continues and may even become intensified as a consequence of domestic arms production.[12]

Nevertheless, the total effect of all these changes is that Third World countries have become relatively more autonomous in their uses of the armed forces than was previously the case. The northern monopoly of violence has been broken.

The Third World accounts for close to 10 per cent of world military expenditures, more than $20 billion annually, which is three times the level of official foreign development assistance. The main suppliers are the two superpowers, the United States and the Soviet Union. However, an increasing number of middle powers are entering into this trade. France is taking an increasingly large share of it, and other major suppliers are the United Kingdom and the Federal Republic of Germany. In the decade 1963-73 armed forces in Africa and the Middle East increased by 100 per cent, in East Asia by 50 per cent and in South Asia by 40 per cent.

There remains, however, a very obvious armament hierarchy in the global system. The most sophisticated weapons are controlled by very few States. This applies not only to nuclear armaments technology, but also to a wide range of other major weapons. Practically all such weapons are produced in the industrialized countries. The development of new arms, which require heavy investment and a solid scientific and technological base, takes place almost solely in the United States and the U.S.S.R. World expenditure on military research and development is concentrated to an extreme degree in few countries. As much as 85 per cent of total military research and development funds are spent by the

United States and the U.S.S.R. Four other countries are involved, but to a much smaller degree, in the development of new weapons: United Kingdom, France, Federal Republic of Germany and China. These countries—and in particular the superpowers—will therefore necessarily remain in the lead in the qualitative arms race and provide the main impetus for armament dynamics.

The accelerating import of weapons and domestic producton of armament nevertheless have changed important aspects of the power relations in the world today. Yet, it is more than doubtful that this new-won capacity to pursue violence is to the benefit of the peoples of the Third World countries themselves. This is the question to which we now turn.

COERCION AND SOCIAL DEVELOPMENTS:
THE NEGATIVE CONSEQUENCES

There is only one fully legitimate function of armed forces. This is to defend a country and its people against external aggression. Other functions are either clearly illegal under present-day international law, or of doubtful legitimacy under the emerging international normative order, in which the protection of human rights forms a central component.

Starting with colonial warfare against peoples opposing alien domination, the use of armed force in the Third World has to a very large extent been directed inwards and had the main function of repression. A study carried out by Istvan Kende examining all armed conflicts between 1945 and 1969 showed that practically all of them took place in the Third World, and that the vast majority consisted of anti-regime wars with foreign participation mainly on the side of the regime. These were, in his words, wars of independence or class wars (Kende, 1971).

The colonial heritage had left a legacy in certain parts of the world of the need for 'civilized' forces to protect stability against encroaching 'natives' or 'primitive people.' A number of techniques were developed in this context which have found more comprehensive use in our days. Compulsory civilian resettlement, food control, aerial control, were all elements of this colonial legacy. In particular, the control of civilians has always formed a major part of colonial warfare. In the context of resistance against colonial occupation, there was no clear distinction between civilians and those who joined the armed liberation struggle. Control of civilians by the colonial power aimed at the isolation of those joining the liberation struggle, and for this purpose the whole population of the colonial territory was subjected to emergency regulations. Techniques included compulsory transfer of the civilian population into camps or villages which could most easily be described as concentration camps, terrorizing those who did not accept this transfer, food control programmes aimed at preventing the forces of the liberation movements from eating, and having the effect in many cases of subjecting large parts of the civilian population to famine conditions. The introduction of aircraft to back up such policies put greater emphasis on the technological aspects of counter-insurgency warfare: terror attacks against recalcitrant populations became possible over a vast territory even for a power which had safe control only over some central bases in the colonial territory. Most recently, the repressive nature of counter-insurgency warfare in a colonial context was displayed by the former Portuguese regime in its African colonies. The creation of *aldiamentos,* villages that were under continuous surveillance, together with bomb attacks and massacres by heliported troops (Wiriyami)[13] are present-day manifestations of a strategy which has deep roots in the colonial tradition.

Similar strategies are utilized by racial regimes. The consequences of militarization is particularly obnoxious in countries with racial suppression, of which South Africa and Rhodesia today are the main examples. In Rhodesia, as well as in Namibia, traditional counter-insurgency strategies are pursued. Internal repression in Rhodesia centres around the use of helicopters, the great asset of any counter-insurgency force. The helicopters utilized in Rhodesia, most of them on loan from South Africa, provide the racial minority with a vastly superior mobility to that of the liberation forces, and also facilitate the much greater fire-power of the incumbent (but illegal) regime.

There is one peculiar aspect of the counter-insurgency activities of minority racial regimes, as demonstrated particularly by South Africa: the exceptional visibility of the parties to the conflict. Since the Government of South Africa, entirely based on the white population, pursues a policy of complete racial segregation, this means that all non-whites are actual or potential enemies of the regime. This facilitates surveillance and control by the whites which has also been utilized fully by the South African Government, through a comprehensive system of repressive legislation. It includes the passport laws, narrowly circumscribed freedom of movement for non-whites, the assignment of most of the non-white population to Bantustans, and the physical segregation of the non-white labour force in the white areas into special quarters or districts. These measures have made it possible, so far, to maintain control largely by the use of para-military police. The large and almost completely white armed forces of South Africa, equipped with highly modern weapons, serve mainly as a second-line threat— if resistance to continued racial subjugation should reach proportions which the police is unable to control, the armed forces will be brought into action. If they are however, they will have a simple task: the densely populated and segregated areas of the non-white population, separated from the areas inhabited by the whites, are very easy targets for aircraft and the gunners of the armoured cars.

The South African organization of society can, from one perspective, be considered as a long, careful preparation for counter-insurgency warfare.[14]

South Africa, however, is not only preparing for counter-insurgency action within its own territory. Beyond supporting the regime in Rhodesia, and carrying on traditional colonial warfare in the illegally occupied territory of Namibia, South Africa is also posing a threat to its neighbouring countries, the main purpose of which is to deter them from supporting liberation movements. At the time of writing, South Africa has even openly and directly intervened with substantial military forces in the internal conflicts in Angola. One of its purposes is to eliminate the bases of the Namibian liberation movements in southern Angola.

The militarization of South Africa, which started during the period of British colonial administration and developed further as part of the joint imperial defence of which Britain was the centre, has accelerated since 1960 due to the need for internal repression, but has at present reached proportions which has made South Africa into what is sometimes called a 'sub-imperial' power.[15] This term refers to major and heavily armed States in the Third World which are able to develop a local hegemony directed against their neighbours. South Africa is not the only sub-imperial power in the Third World; there are others which are even more heavily armed and may in the future pose even more serious threats to surrounding States, but South Africa is the most visible due to its racial policies. For the large majority of Third World States, it is urgent to resist, through international action, the development of sub-imperial powers, otherwise the security of the smaller powers will be increasingly threatened and may force them to undergo a process of militarization, however wasteful and undesirable this may be.

Counter-insurgency operations can sometimes be extremely capital-intensive, which is possible only when major industrialized States are directly involved. The most dramatic proportions were reached during the Indochinese warfare. There are various calculations about the cost of that war, including a *per capita* expenditure of $L700$ or, for each of Indo-China's 184 million acres, an expenditure of $L170$. Other calculations show an incredible $L124$ per second for the entire eight-year period, or the equivalent in explosive energy of 570 Hiroshima or Nagasaki bombs . . . one every six days![16]

This is not the place to discuss the various aspects of these actions, including the tremendous ecological disruptions, and the suffering of the civilian population. We shall focus here only on the development, in the context of Indo-China, of the notion of automated battlefield techniqes. These techniques, outlined in a famous speech by General Westmoreland in 1969, conceived of an all-computerized control of vast areas with the capability of unleashing instant and enormously destructive force without human involvement. Such automated battlefield techniques can be used mainly against technologically less sophisticated adversaries. If utilized against technologically advanced countries, tremendous problems in gaining air supremacy and of maintaining, without interruption, the electronic system of surveillance and communication, will arise.

The automated battlefield techniques, therefore, can allow rich and technologically advanced powers to maintain coercive control over large masses in distant parts of the world even if politically unacceptable. It is probable, however, that such control is only temporarily possible, due to the strong counter-forces which are generated by the very nature of such warfare. Countervailing forces develop even within the industrialized countries as a result of the indiscriminate and brutal nature of warfare.

Frequently, there exists a vicious circle of militarization and dependence on coercion rather than democratic participation. This applies, first, to civilian regimes maintained by military forces. Reference can here be made to racial minority regimes, where the armed forces do not try to take over political power because it is unnecessary. In these cases, there is a clear congruence of interest between the armed forces and the civilian government in maintaining control over the majority of the population through coercion. The reliance on coercion, however, seemingly eliminates the need to make political concessions and to involve the majority in democratic processes. Since the necessary concessions, required by the development of society, are not made, social tensions increase and the need for coercion becomes more acute. This stimulates terrorism, torture, informers, secrecy, and continuously increasing exclusion from participation in decisions. Increasing opposition on grounds of conscience develop even within the racial minority, with increasing dissatisfaction and thereby also further strangulation of democratic participation even among this privileged minority. Consequently, there will be police actions against dissidents within the minority, increased secrecy, censorship, and the other elements familiar to conflict escalations. Reliance on coercion therefore has its own built-in limitations, and leads to severe perversion of the political system.

Much the same is the case in countries where the military takes over power from civilian regimes. This happens as a consequence of many different causes. On a general level, factors like economic problems, corruption, political schism and general disillusionment have combined to create the climate in which coups can successfully take place.[17] It may generally be said that military takeovers are manifestations of urban discontent, but they also reflect certain characteristics of the military communities in the countries concerned. These characteristics differ vastly, and further generalizations are dangerous. We could nevertheless distinguish between two kinds of military takeovers. Some are more or less pre-planned, within a general logic of counter-insurgency. International training for counter-insurgency has increased the legitimacy of military intervention in domestic political affairs. The emphasis on 'stability' and 'orderly development' rather than on democracy in such training create a distaste among officers for the difficult and time-consuming civilian political processes. Much counter-insurgency training may in fact be seen as coming very close to preparations for military takeovers.

In other cases—particularly in Africa—military coups have not sprung so clearly out of internationally planned counter-insurgency, but have taken place due to more particular local factors. Officers sometimes develop a distaste for civilian politicians. They overemphasize signs of corruption, profiteering, and fractionism which certainly does occur in Third World politics—as well as in the industrialized world. Anti-democratic notions of 'strong government,' of which Europe has also had its rich share in the past, easily come to the surface when it is actively legitimated in the international community. At the early stages of military intervention, the officers may sometimes see themselves as the only uncontaminated force in the State, possessing virtues superior to those of the civilians. In many cases, their identification with the former colonial metropolis creates difficulties when the civilian government pursues a policy of confrontation. The statement made by Colonel Afrifa of Ghana,[18] who was involved in overthrowing Nkrumah is revealing: he reacted to the policies pursued by Nkrumah with regard to Britain's non-action in Rhodesia:

> I knew personally that Her Majesty's Government of the United Kingdom was quite capable of dealing with the Rhodesia situation. I' felt that Nkrumah was making too much noise about the whole issue.

Later, he said:

> I have been trained in the United Kingdom as a soldier, and I am prepared to fight alongside my friends in the United Kingdom in the same way as Canadians and Australians will do.

Another point to be stressed in this regard is probably even more important: with technological developments in armaments, the armed forces of the Third World are the institutions which, more closely than any other, become replicas of the industrial world. Centralization, technological modernization, hierarchical organization which intensifies social stratification, are all important aspects of the social processes which follow upon militarization. If surrounding society develops in ways different from that of the military organization, this becomes a threat to the military, and thereby an additional cause of intervention to change directions. Also, when civilian authorities seek to limit military budgets in favour of other necessary charges, this can be seen as a direct threat to the military, and an additional factor for the intervening of military power.[19]

Whatever the initial cause of military intervention in civilian politics, the long-range effect invariably tends to be extremely unfortunate. In some cases, it is that the officer group itself takes over not only political power but also control over much of the economy by appropriating, at a personal level, the ownership or control of production.[20] In this way, parts of the officer groups become a social class in themselves, with vested interests, which they seek to protect through the use of armed coercion in the face of opposition. Corruption is definitely not something to which officers are lastingly immune.

Even when officers avoid such pitfalls and maintain their purity and austerity at the economic level, their continued rule nevertheless creates serious problems. Over a short period, authoritarian rule without democratic processes may on the surface seem useful and provide stability to facilitate economic growth. In the long run, however, it will be discovered that 'national economic problems do not consist of clear-cut choices between obvious alternatives.'[21]

A society undergoing rapid change necessarily experiences substantial conflicts of interest, which cannot be solved by 'strong' governments, but only through consultation with and participation by all segments. Failure to do so necessarily leads over time to the perversion of political power, with spiralling repression, political imprisonment, secrecy, and the consequent lack of creative participation which is necessary if a society is to remain a living and coherent organism. Whatever the initial good intentions of the military which intervenes in civilian politics, the long-range effect tends to be a reliance on coercion as a substitute for creative change.

There can hardly be any doubt that militarization is directly and indirectly wasteful. It is directly wasteful when weapons are used for maintaining control in the fact of large-scale opposition. The devastating ecological and social effects of capital-intensive counter-insurgency has been demonstrated, above all, in the case of Indo-China, but similar effects are experienced to a lesser extent in many other cases of armed repression. Militarization, however, is also indirectly wasteful due to the misuse of resources. Most weapons have to be imported, and for that purpose products have to be exported which could otherwise have been utilized for local consumption. Military developments in the Third World are significantly more negative than in the industrialized countries, with regard to manpower. The armed forces absorb a substantial part of the skilled manpower, which is one of the most serious bottlenecks for the acceleration of social and economic developments. It has been estimated that the amount invested in transportation, subsistence and training of one solider would suffice to provide general education and industrial training for a civilian.[23]

> Weapons or weapons instruction is not consumed by the workers (in the periphery) and can never be. It can never enter the productive process in those countries, however indirectly. It is utterly sterile. What the exchange has done is to shift potentially productive surplus from India to Russia, or from Brazil to the United States, or the Middle East to Britain and waste in the opposite direction. From the point of view of the capitals involved, it is a one-way transfer of investable surplus which takes place even on the assumption of equal exchange.

Even if the weapons are partly produced in Third World countries themselves, there is a wasteful diversion of productive processes. Armament production is never production to cover basic needs. For the major industrialized States, armament production is a tool for the maintenance of political control and the unequal division of labour. For some few of the major Third World States, domestic arms production may become a tool for exerting local hegemony with some degree of autonomy from the superpowers. Even so, these arms-producing Third World countries will remain technologically dependent on the major industrialized countries, due to the tremendous difference in the capacity for research and development.[23]

Efforts have been made to examine whether militarization represents a burden on the economic development of a country.[24] Unfortunately, they have so far not posed the questions in a meaningful way, which is why we do not have a satisfactory answer. One approach has been to examine the growth rates of the gross domestic product (GDP) of individual countries, as compared to their military expenditures. This approach, however, for easily understandable reasons has yielded any interesting elements, which can be explained by taking the following propositions into account.

Militarization is most advanced where social tension is greatest; and a major cause of social tension is inherent in labour-repressive systems. These frequently maintain a small but privileged working class, and a large and exploited one. In such societies there may be considerable economic growth, but at the expense of most of the population. There may even be considerable welfare-spending on the privileged groups, while the underprivileged may be increasingly exploited or marginalized. South Africa may serve as an extreme but nevertheless highly revealing case. The relation between military expenditure and gross domestic product would here provide a very superficial analysis. It is evident that, in South African society, military expenditure is doubly detrimental to the non-white majority. First, it is an instrument to prevent change towards democratic participation and equality: it serves to maintain an extreme case of labour repression. Secondly, military expenditure represents waste of a significant part of the surplus obtained through the labour of the majority. This surplus could have been turned into badly needed welfare and education. To argue, therefore, that high military expenditure may be consonant with economic growth, is to add insult to injury. While South Africa is extreme, it is not difficult to find similar characteristics in a number of other countries.

ARE THERE POSITIVE ASPECTS OF ARMAMENTS?

So far, we have examined some of the negative consequences of militarization. Nevertheless, under the present world military structure, we must accept that some amount of armaments will be required for highly legitimate purposes in many Third World countries. First, the elimination of colonialism would in many countries not have been successful without partial resort to an armed liberation struggle. In the process of political and social mobilization, the liberation movements of the former Portuguese colonies had to defend themselves against the military forces of the Portuguese. Without the arms which brought down some of the Portuguese aircraft and hampered the movement of the colonial forces, efforts to create liberated zones would have been extremely difficult. Similarly, it will be difficult to bring to an end the illegal occupation by South Africa of Namibia, unless the liberation movements obtain some equipment to stop the repressive operations of South African armed forces. Beyond this, there is a legitimate need for defence against expansionist sub-imperial powers.

There are some, however, who go further and claim that the development of armed forces has positive consequences for society. This is a relatively new notion, which coincided with the development of the strategy of flexible response, including the preparation for counter-insurgency.[25] In the early 1960s, Western sociology and political science was dominated by theories of structural functionalism. The theory of development and underdevelopment, at that time rather naive as compared to present theories, was understood as the degree of deviation from the most advanced industrialized countries. According to this notion the greater the difference as compared to the leading countries, the greater the degree of underdevelopment. It followed that there were stages of growth or development, and that there existed bottlenecks which had to be resolved in order to modernize. 'Development' was equated with 'modernization,' and one important art of 'modernization' was 'nation-building.' As part of this theory, it was claimed that the armed forces could play an important role in modernization, and hence—by definition—for development. This is not surprising, since it is uncontested that armed forces represent the institution within Third

World countries which is most similar to comparable industrial institutions. Most Third World armies have been patterned on the industrial model, which is not only a product of cultural imperialism, but also a consequence of the weapon technology chosen. This technology has been developed in the industrialized countries, primarily for the purposes of the industrialized armies, and when transferred to the Third World requires institutions similar to those of the originators. The theory of modernization through the armed forces contains the following elements.

Military organization is the most suitable tool to alter traditional society and promote social change, because of its hierarchical structure, its emphasis on discipline and the unity of command, and because of its control over the coercive instruments. Further, knowledge and the skills in technology and administration makes the armed forces into a more advanced institution than the rest of society. Since the officers were largely recruited from the middle classes, and given a solid professional training, the military has more internal cohesion than other groups in the society.

With hindsight, these theories proved to be untenable. First, the theory of development on which they were based crumbled when analysed by scholars from the Third World. Authors like Samir Amin (1971), Andre Gunder Frank :1971), Gustavo Lagos (1963) and Osvaldo Sunkel (1972) developed the theory of dominance and dependence[26] which claims that the penetration of Western-based capitalism of Third World countries had led to an international division of labour, where control rests with the major industrial States. Such control is made possible by subordination to this division of labour, and is upheld by existing bridgeheads in the Third World countries, elites whose interests are served by continuation of subordination. Hence, efforts to break out of the system of dominance and unequal division of labour mainly occur as domestic conflicts between peripheral and elite groupings inside Third World countries. The metropolises come to the assistance of their bridgeheads, the power elites in the Third World countries, through direct military intervention, arms delivery, provision of counter-insurgency expertise, and economic aid.

Subsequent developments have shown that this is also too simplistic a theory, particularly since governments of many Third World countries are increasingly autonomous in regard to the 'metropolises' of the north. The lasting value of the theory of dominance and dependence, however, is probably its underlining of the continuously unequal division of labour which results from submissive technological situations. Even when Third World governments pursue policies of nationalization, extending State ownership to the means of production, this does not change the division of labour as long as the economy remains structurally dependent on the world market. So long as the armed forces of the Third World seek to become   replicas of the armies of the industrialized world, they will always lag behind and be the main instrument for preserving structural dependence.

Let us briefly reflect on the notion of nation-building, which has also figured prominently in discussions on the role of the armed forces. 'Nation-building' has much too frequently been ascribed a positive value, without examining its possible contents. There are two fundamentally different versions of nation-building. On one hand, there is the centralized building of the nation where the elite seeks to mobilize the periphery for policies defined by the centre in a directive way. Such a pattern easily degenerates into a system by which the centre exploits the periphery for its own benefit, creating increasing inequalities in the process. The other version of nation-building is generated from the periphery, in a decentralized way, and gradually mobilizes increasingly wider segments of the population in a co-ordinated effort to improve the social, political and economic conditions under which they live. Nation-building of this kind occurred in connexion with some of the liberation struggles against colonialism in parts of the Third World, but not always: some liberation movements were purely military organizattions, not capable of mobilizing the population for social and economic change. Others were only incidentally involved in armed struggle, primarily carrying out social transformation. In so far as they succeeded in mobilizing wide sections of the population for creative participation in development—in political, social, and economic terms—these countries may, after independence, become alternative models for development in the Third World.[27]

Returning to the question of the role of the armed forces, it is important to understand the relationship between the form of force and social formations.[28] In the advanced industrialized countries, the form of force is characterized by a permanent arms race, possessing two features of particular importance. One is that the armed forces are organized around the weapon system: the technology of weapons is the most important factor, and the soldier is of secondary importance, serving technology. In the arms race, there is also a built-in tendency towards expansion. As pointed out by Barnaby in the present issue, arms dynamics today are characterized by a qualitative race. The continuous development of new weapons, which makes other weapons more or less obsolete, require continuous replacement. To the extent that Third World armies adopt these forms, they become permanently dependent on technological developments in the industrialized countries. As previously pointed out, this will apply even if they try to develop some domestic arms production.

The liberation struggle, particularly in the former Portuguese colonies, indicated that there are opportunities for a different military technology. Against the relatively advanced weapon technology of the Portuguese forces, the liberation movements utilized smaller weapons which by necessity had to be carried manually. Much of this weaponry, and particularly the surface-to-air missiles, nevertheless proved to be increasingly effective as a defence against the Portuguese forces. It was possible, throughout the struggle, to maintain an egalitarian, non-hierarchical liberation force with a technology more congruent with the conditions of the country. It is possible that this can provide a lesson for a different kind of military organization, compatible with social equality and balanced development.

CONCLUSIONS

In this article, I have not sought to challenge the obvious, legitimate right of Third World countries to defend themselves against external aggression in consonance with the United Nations Charter. The main argument has been that the militarization which many of these countries are at present undergoing has a number of negative consequences. One of them is that the armaments are mainly used for internal and frequently repressive purposes. Another, and interlinked, observation is that militarization is likely to increase the structural dependence of Third World countries on the industrialized north. The 'modernizing' function of Third World armed forces then becomes a euphemism for the intensification of dependence.

In the quest for genuine self-determination, Third World countries are therefore probably best advised to pursue the two following roads.

On one hand, to opt for a different kind of armed force than that of the industrialized countries, less capital-intensive and with a less complex technology. It would have to make the human being (the individual soldier) into the master and the weapon into the servant of armed action. It should also be harnessed solely to serve actual needs of defence, and not made into a military establishment with its own dynamics and interests. The other task which it would be highly desirable for the Third World governments to undertake, is to push much more strongly than in the past for disarmament on a global level. The tremendous technological superiority of the industrialized States and some sub-imperial powers in the Third World, must be eliminated. Since this cannot possibly be carried out by a process in which the Third World countries seek to match the present armaments of the north, it has to be achieved through far-reaching, general and comprehensive disarmament. As pointed out by Marek Thee in this issue, proposals have already been tabled by the United States and the Soviet Union. For the majority of Third World States the task ahead must be to push, with all their vigour, the United Nations to convene a world conference on disarmament and from there onwards lead the pressure on negotiations until present military establishment have been substantially reduced and equalized. They will find many supporters in the north, though not always in government circles.

---

[1]Ali A. Maxrui, quoted in Gingyera-Pinycwa and Mazrui (1974), p.129.

[2]In *Facing Mount Kenya,* as quoted in Gingyere-Pinycwa and Mazrui (1974), p.129.

[3]Texts of the Brussel Act, the Saint Germain Convention and other documents from the same period can be found in Chamberlain (1929).

[4]Text in Chamberlain (1929).

[5]Another cause of military growth and arms transfer was the repressive function of the colonial army—increasing with growing resistance from the colonial population. In many places, the colonial army incorporated soldiers and non-commissioned officers—sometimes also officers—recruited from among the local population. These persons were socialized into identifying with the colonial army in repressive action against their own people. Where decolonization came about without armed liberation, it was this local component of the colonial army which became the nucleus of the new army of the independent country. Sometimes this army continued to serve the same external interests, mainly economical, and to identify with the former metropolis. Revealing is the formulation used by Colonel Afrifa of Ghana, quoted in the text on page 317.

[6]SIPRI, Arms Trade (1971).

[7]Some States decined to join the Western-led collective security system, but nevertheless carried out a substantial armament programme in order to face the real or imagined threat from neighbouring countries, which were bering militarized through Western inducement. This happened, for example, with India: that country started its long road towards heavy militarization partly as a consequence of the strong arming of Pakistan by the United States. A study of India's militarization can be found in Wulff (1974).

[8]A survey of the causes and functions of military bases is forthcoming in Milton Leitenberg's contribution to *IPRA Study 1976.*

[9]An examination of this doctrine can be found in Mike Klare (1972).

[10]This eventful visit took place in 1969.

[11]The arguments are reviewed in Klare (1972), p.271-3.

[12]An analysis of the growth, causes and consequences can be found in the study by Albrecht, Ernst, Lock and Wulff (1976) (forthcoming).

[13]An investigation of some of these practices can be found in United Nations Inquiry (1974).

[14]Further details on counter-insurgency in southern Africa will be forthcoming in Eide (1976). A comprehensive study of militarization and conflict dynamics in southern Africa is found in Backstrom-Landgren (1976).

[15]On the notion of 'sub-imperialist powers' and the role they are likely to play inthe future international system, see Vayrynen (1975) and, with particular reference to armaments, Oberg (1975). Among sub-imperial powers are normally included—in addition to South Africa—Brazil, India and Iran.

[16]There exist many studies on the nature, scope and consequences of counter-insurgency warfare in Indo-China. Condensed information will be found in the contribution by Marr to the *IPRA Study 1976,* from which the above figures are taken.

[17]A recent study of these causes can be found in Gutteridge (1975).

[18]Afrifa (1966), p.104 and 112.

[19]Interesting initial results corroborating such a thesis, based on material from several African States, have been presented by Jan Jørgensen in a project outline entitled *Government Expenditures on Peace and Violence in Six African States, 1915-1973.* Available from the International Peace Research Institute, Oslo.

[20]Documentation with regard to Indonesia is found in Creyghton (1976) and with regard to Uganda, Jørgensen (1974).

[21]Gutteridge (1975), p.11.

[22]Kidron (1974), p.108.

[23]For a fuller discussion, see the study by Albrecht, Ernst, Lock and Wulff (1976).

[24]A survey of such efforts can be found in Kennedy (1975), Chapter 10.

[25]Most wellknown for his espousal of the positive functions of militarization, including increasing technologization of the army, is Lucian Pye (1962). A compilation of arguments on this direction can be found in Kennedy (1975).

[26]A survey of the works demonstrating the relationship between dominance and dependence can be found, for exmaple, in Eide (1974).

[27]I have in mind, in particular, the PAIGC of Guinea Bissau and FRELIMO of Mozambique.

[28]This point will be further elaborated in the introduction to *IPRA Study 1976,* based on (unpublished) works by Mary Kaldor.

REFERENCES

AFRIFA, A. A. 1966. *The Ghana Coup, February 24th 1966.* London.

ALBRECHT; ERNST; LOCK; WULFF. 1976. Arms Production in the Periphery. In: *IPRA Study 1976* (forthcoming).

CHAMBERLAIN, J. P. 1929. The Embargo Resolutions and Neutrality. *International Conciliation,* No. 25, June 1929.

CREYGHTON, I. 1976. Army and Economy in Indonesia. In: *IPRA Study 1976* (forthcoming).

EIDE, A. 1974. International Law, Dominance, and the Use of Force. *Journal of Peace Research,* Vol. XI.

_____. 1976. Southern Africa: Repression and Transfer of Arms and Arms Technology. In: *IPRA Study 1976* (forthcoming).

EL-AYOUTY, Y. 1974. Legitimation of National Liberation: The United Nations and Southern Africa. In: Yassin El-Ayouty and H. C. Brooks: *Africa and International Organization,* The Hague, M. Nijhoff.

GINGYERE-PINYCWA and MAZRUI. 1974. Regional Development and Regional Disarmament: Some African Perspectives. In: Tandon and Chandarana (eds.): *Horizons of African Diplomacy.* Nairobi/Dar-es-Salaam/Kampala.

GUTTERIDGE, W. F. 1975. *Studies in African History—11. Military Regimes in Africa.* London.

IPRA Study 1976: Transfers of Arms and Arms Technology to Third World Countries (forthcoming). Contributions include papers referred to in this list by Albrect *et al.,* Creyghton, Eide, Kaldor, Leitenberg. (Oslo.)

JØRGENSEN, J. 1975. The Political Economy of the Economic War: The Amin Regime 1971-74. *Structural Dependence and Economic Nationalism in Uganda 1890-1974,* Chapter 7,. Oslo. (PRIO Publication No. 26-23.)

KALDOR, Mary. 1976. Introductin to *IPRA Study 1976,* by Albrecht *et al.*

KENNEDY, G. 1974. *The Military in the Third World.* London.

KIDRON. 1974. *Capitalism and Theory.* London.

KLARE, M. T. 1972. *War without End.* New York, American Planning for the Next Vietnams.

LANDGREN-BACKSTROM, Signe. 1976. *Southern Africa. The Escalation of a Conflict. A Politico-Military Survey.* Stockholm.

LEITENBERG, Milton. 1976. Overseas Military Bases. In: *IPRA Study 1976* (forthcoming).

ØBERG, J. 1975. *Third World Armament. Domestic Arms Production in Israel, South Africa, Brazil, Argentina and India from 1950-75.* Lund University, Department of Peace and Conflict Research.

PYE, L. W. 1962. Armies in the Process of Political Modernization. In: J. J. Johnson (ed.), *The Role of the Military in Underdeveloped Countries,* Princeton.

SIPRI. Arms Trade 1971. *The Arms Trade with the Third World.* Stockholm.

SIPRI Yearboks. *World Armaments and Disarmament.* 1968/69, 1969/70, 1971, 1972, 1973, 1974, 1975. Stockholm.

United Nations Inquiry. 1974. *Reports of the Commission of Inquiry on the Reported Massacres in Mozambique. General Assembly. Official Records. Twenty-ninth session.* Supplement No. 21 (A/9621). New York.

VAYRYNEN, R. 1975. Subimperialism from Dependence to Suborganization. Paper presented to the Sixth General Conference of the International Peace Research Association, 15-18 August 1975, in Turku (Finland). Tampere Peace Research Institute.

WULFF, H. 1975. Indien: Militarisierung und der Aufbau einer autonomen Rustungsproduktion. *Internationales Asienforum,* Vol. 6, No. 3, p.272-301.

III
U.S. Aid and
Human Rights:
Do We Really Mean It?

Human Rights and U.S. Policy Issue

Vita Bite

ISSUE DEFINITION

The basic issue is whether another government's treatment of its own people should be an important factor in U.S. foreign policy formulation and practice. There is wide disagreement between those who feel that the U.S. government should define the human rights conditions of individuals in foreign countries as being within the internal affairs of that country and therefore outside the appropriate consideration of U.S. foreign policy, and those who favor strict sanctions against governments that violate the basic human rights of their citizens.

BACKGROUND AND POLICY ANALYSIS

During the past few years the topic of human rights has become a very conspicuous and controversial issue in the U.S. Government. Congress has, through hearings, drawn attention to the violation of human rights in other countries and has instituted legislative mechanisms aimed at assuring that U.S. foreign policy actions include consideration of the status of human rights in other countries. Over strong objections by the Ford Administration, Congress wrote human rights provisions into foreign military and economic assistance legislation. It cut off military aid to Chile and Uruguay. It established within the Department of State

---

From Hearing before the Subcommittee on International Organizations of the Committee on International Relations, House of Representatives, October 25, 1977, No. IB77056, U.S. Government Printing Office.

a position of Coordinator for Human Rights and Humanitarian Affairs to be appointed with the advice and consent of the Senate. During the 94th Congress, hearings were held on the status of human rights in some eighteen countries.

In his inaugural address President Carter gave significant attention to the importance of a U.S. commitment to and respect for human rights. The outspoken quality of the President and his Administration in subsequent statements on the status of human rights in certain countries has stirred further controversy as to the role that the human rights of foreign citizens should play in U.S. foreign policy. Official U.S. expressions of concern about violations of human rights in particular countries have been viewed by some as threatening U.S. national security, economic, political or other interests. While the promotion of human rights is accepted as a serious social concern, there is considerable disagreement as to whether it is realistically feasible to give substantial weight to human rights concerns in a U.S. foreign policy which deals with sovereign nations and whose purpose is to safeguard the power and international position of the United States.

One of the most difficult problems involved in the issue of international human rights is that of human rights standards. Societies differ substantially in their consensus understandings of basic rights to be accorded all persons. Should the United States apply a single human rights standard to all nations—primitive and advanced, big and small, friend or foe, neutral or vital national security partner? Some argue that it is neither practical nor appropriate for the United States to be the moral judge for a world in which U.S. and Western concepts of human rights differ markedly from the human rights priorities of other nations and cultures. Others claim that violations in some countries are on such a wide scale and threaten such basic human needs that they transcend cultural and political differences among nations.

Some critics have voiced the opinion that without establishing the notion of minimum substantive rights for every citizen of the globe (a minimum calory intake to sustain life and health, minimum shelter, minimum employment possibilities, etc.) the procedural rights that Americans cherish, and which are widely violated around the world—freedom of speech, assembly, press, religion, and thought—will remain irrelevant for a majority of mankind and probably unattainable as well. Others suggest that maintenance of a basic level of human rights is not inconsistent with the requirements of economic development, even in the most needy nations.

Once a decision is made to take some form of action on a human rights issue, the question arises of how to go about doing so. It is in the area of productive approach that efforts to maintain a single standard, if there can be or should be such, are most sorely tested. Different countries, different cultures, different priorities, and different U.S. interests, may require different U.S. responses. Another problem related to the question of approaches is whether any action by the United States does, in fact, result in a positive change in the human rights practices of another country.

Traditional options exercised in the past have included "quiet diplomacy," public statements or denunciations in international forums, and requests that an international organization take action. Quiet diplomacy was the favored approach of previous Administrations, but was criticized by many as ineffective unless it were made clear that other approaches would be used if quiet diplomacy failed. Moreover, since such actions were taken in private by diplomats who were interested in maintaining working relationships with their counterparts from an "offending nation," "quiet diplomacy" has often generated skepticism as to whether U.S. objections to human rights violations were forcefully conveyed. The case for "quiet diplomacy" is that no government is likely to accept meddling in its internal affairs but may bargain and consider internal changes that it visibly initiates.

Another approach is that of multilateral or unilateral economic sanctions. Rhodesia, the only country against which the United Nations currently imposes economic sanctions, is considered by many to be guilty of violating human rights by its opposition to self-determination for its black majority population. The United States modified its adherence to the Security Council sanctions by permitting the importation of Rhodesian chrome under section 513 of the Military Procurement Act of 1972. After repeated efforts to repeal the amendment, the 95th Congress enacted legislation to halt U.S. importation of Rhodesian chrome (P.L. 95-12, see Archived Issue Brief 74031, Rhodesia: U.S. Imports of Chrome Ore, for further information).

An approach which has been used recently by both Congress and the Carter Administration has been to limit or cut off provision of economic and/or military assistance to certain countries deemed in gross violation of certain human rights. Another approach which the United States may take to express its displeasure with the human rights situation in a given country is to sever or limit U.S. diplomatic representation.

Two aspects of U.S. policy on human rights have caused particular controversy in recent years. One was silence on repression of dissent in Communist countries, especially the Soviet Union. The second source of controversy was U.S. economic and military assistance to several regimes that had been widely accused of grossly violating the human rights of their citizens. The Ford Administration acted on the premise that U.S. silence on human rights in Communist countries was linked to good relations with the Soviet Union and to progress in world peace and arms limitation agreements (for more information see issue brief 77031 Human

Rights in Soviet-American Relations). The Ford Administration also took the position that any cut in aid made on the ground of human rights would be counterproductive, and that aid programs allowed the United States to maintain continued influence in those countries.

The Carter Administration rejected the linkage of human rights and detente by vociferously speaking out against human rights violations in the Soviet Union and Eastern Europe. The Carter Administration has stressed that it is trying to be evenhanded in its public comments on human rights in all countries. However, repeated Administration criticism of human rights violations in the Soviet Union has brought the charge that the Soviet Union is receiving a disproportionate amount of such criticism, while other countries that are friends or allies of the United States are not being chastised.

There is a problem of consistency in U.S. words and actions compounded by Secretary Vance's announcement on Feb. 24, 1977, that military aid to Argentina, Ethiopia and Uruguay is to be reduced because of human rights violations, while assistance to the Republic of Korea is to be maintained because of U.S. national security interests. No mention has been made of human rights in countries such as Iran and the Philippines, other examples of countries where U.S. interests and concern for human rights arguably conflict.

EARLIER INVOLVEMENT

Recent Executive action on human rights issues has been preceded by a very considerable record of congressional involvement through both legislative and investigative functions in issues of international human rights as a factor in U.S. foreign policy. While Congress has not come forward with a specific definition of human rights, it has provided a framework for consideration of human rights issues. Thus the International Development and Food Assistance Act of 1975 (P.L. 94-161) relies on language that is frequently used in United Nations resolutions:

> Consistent pattern of gross violations of internationally recognized human rights, including torture or cruel, inhuman, or degrading treatment or punishment, prolonged detention without charges, or other flagrant denial of the right to life, liberty, and the security of person . . .

The International Security Assistance and Arms Exportation Control Act of 1976 (P.L. 94-3291) also relies on standards and criteria that have been established by the international community. Furthermore, this Act declares that it "is the policy of the United States . . . to promote and encourage increased respect for human rights and fundamental freedoms for all . . . To this end, a principal goal of the foreign policy of the

United States is to promote the increased observance of internationally recognized human rights by all countries."

The Charter of the United Nations and the U.N. Universal Declaration of Human Rights are referred to in legislation. The U.N. Charter established fundamental obligations of the United Nations and its member States to protect human rights. The Charter also set forth in article 2(7) the principle of nonintervention by the United Nations in matters within the domestic jurisdiction of any State. This important article has frequently been cited as conflicting with the implementation of the human rights provisions of the Charter.

The Universal Declaration of Human Rights is one of the most widely accepted statements identifying basic human rights. It does not place binding obligations on states since it is not a treaty or international agreement, but rather it declares a common standard of achievement for all people. The Declaration was adopted on Dec. 10, 1948, by a resolution of the U.N. General Assembly and was conceived as the initial part of an international bill of rights in which the human rights covenants or treaties would form the binding portion. Two covenants—one on civil and political rights and the other on economic, social, and cultural rights—were adopted in 1966 and came into force in 1976. The United States, however, is not a party to either one of these major human rights treaties.

Even before 1945, many American officials and non-governmental organizations stressed the relevance of human rights to international peace and to other common international purposes and insisted that international law and institutions protect such rights; these efforts secured a place for human rights in the U.N. Charter and led to the establishment of the U.N. Human Rights Commission. Eleanor Roosevelt led U.S. efforts in the creation of the basic document on human rights, the Universal Declaration of Human Rights, and in the late 1940's the U.S. was among the most active proponents of U.N. human rights activities.

Thus, while the United States deserves much of the credit for bringing about the inclusion of human rights provisions in the U.N. Charter and adoption of the Universal Declaration of Human Rights, and while there may not be many nations whose domestic systems for the protection of human rights are as well developed as are those of the United States, nevertheless, the United States has ratified only a small number of the international human rights instruments: five U.N. human rights treaties and five OAS treaties. There are at least 30 human rights treaties the United States has not ratified. Moreover, none of those which the United States has ratified is considered among the major international human rights instruments. The following chart lists international human rights conventions and U.S. action of their ratification:

Convention	U.S. Action
United Nations Conventions:	
International Covenant on Economic, Social and Cultural Rights	Signed, but not submitted to Senate
International Covenant on Civil and Political Rights	Signed, but not submitted to Senate
Optional Protocol to the International Covenant on Civil and Political Rights	None
International Convention on the Elimination of All Forms of Racial Discrimination	Signed, but not submitted to Senate
International Convention on Suppression and Punishment of the Crime of Apartheid	None
Convention on the Prevention and Punishment of Genocide	Signed, pending before the Senate
Convention on the Non-applicability of Statutory Limitations to War Crimes and Crimes Against Humanity	None
Slavery Convention (League of Nations)	Acceded
Protocol Amending the Slavery Convention Signed at Geneva on 25 Sept. 1926	Ratified
Supplementary Conventary Convention on the Abolition of Slavery, the Slave Trade, and Institutions and Practices Similar to Slavery	Acceded
Convention for the Suppression of the Traffic in Persons and of the Exploitation of the Prostitution of Others	None
Convention on the Nationality of Married Women	None
Convention on the Reduction of Statelessness	None
Convention Relating to the Status of Stateless Persons	None
Convention Relating to the Status of Refugees	Acceded
Convention on Consent to Marriage, Minimum Age for Marriage and Registration of Marriages	Signed, but not submitted to Senate
Convention on the International Right of Correction	None

Convention	U.S. Action
Convention on the Political Rights of Women	Acceded

International Labor Organization Conventions:

Convention	U.S. Action
Freedom of Association and Protection of the Right to Organize Convention	Pending in U.S. Senate
Abolition of Forced Labor Convention	Pending in U.S. Senate
Employment Policy Convention	Pending in U.S. Senate
Right to Organize and Collective Bargaining Convention	None
Equal Remuneration Convention	None
Discrimination (Employment and Occupation) Convention	None

United Nations Educational, Scientific and Cultural Organization (UNESCO) Conventions:

Convention	U.S. Action
Convention against Discrimination in Education	None
Protocol Instituting a Conciliation and Good Offices Commission to be reponsible for seeking a Settlement of any Dispute which may arise between States Parties to the Convention against Discrimination in Education	None

Inter-American Conventions:

Convention	U.S. Action
Convention Establishing the Status of Naturalized Citizens Who Again Take up their Residence in the Country of their Origin	Ratified
Convention between the American Republics Regarding the Status of Aliens in their Respective Territories	Ratified, with the exception of articles 3 and 4
Convention on the Nationality of Women	Ratified
Convention on Extradition	Ratified, subject to reservations
Inter-American Convention on the Granting of Political Rights to Women	Ratified
Convention on Asylum	None
Convention Relative to the Rights of Aliens	None

Convention	U.S. Action
Convention on Nationality	None
Convention on Political Asylum	None
Inter-American Convention on the Granting of Civil Rights to Women	None
Convention on Diplomatic Asylum	None
Convention on Territorial Asylum	None
American Convention on Human Rights	Signed, but not submitted to Senate

Many critics say that the United States has over the years completely lost its leadership in shaping international human rights programs and policies. While some parts of the U.S. Government and many citizens saw and acted on the need for improvement in human rights in the United States, neither the U.S. Government, nor most citizens, thought U.S. human rights problems would benefit from international standards or international interventions. The domestic civil rights movement and U.S. foreign policy on human rights remained largely discreet and unrelated. Even those considering themselves victims of human rights violations in the United States sought international protection, not urged U.S. participation in international programs out of sympathy with victims elsewhere.

In the late 1940s and 1950s a strong constituional opposition developed in the U.S. Congress to human rights treaties or similar international law obligations for the United States. In 1953 Secretary of State Dulles gave assurances to Congress and publicly notified the United Nations that the United States did not intend to become a party to the proposed U.N. Covenants on human rights or other international human rights instruments.

President Kennedy and subsequent presidents reversed this policy and urged U.S. adherence to international human rights conventions. In practice, however, little changed. Few treaties have been ratified in the last 17 years. Constituional objections continue to be raised against these treaties by opponents who argue that the treaty power may be used only to regulate matters of international concern and that human rights are not properly matters of international concern. It is interesting to note, in this connection, that the American Bar Association, which had since 1949 officially opposed U.S. ratification of the U.N. Genocide Convention (for further information see Issue Brief 74129, Genocide Convention), reversed itself in February 1976 and now supports U.S. ratification.

CONGRESSIONAL RESPONSES TO HUMAN RIGHTS VIOLATIONS, 1973-76

Congressional interest in human rights conditions in other countries has increased substantially over the past four years. This interest has been exhibited in different ways and has gone beyond hearings examining human rights conditions in various countries and U.S. executive branch actions in response to blatant and systematic foreign denials of human rights. During recent years the congressional response to human rights violations in other countries has been to assure greater attention to these violations and to the role of human rights in U.S. foreign policy considerations. Congress has passed legislation to limit the provision of assistance to countries in particular circumstances. The Foreign Assistance Acts of 1973 and 1974 both included sections linking the recipt of foreign assistance to the protection of human rights. Sec. 32 of the Foreign Assistance Act of 1973 (P.L. 93-189) provided:

> It is the sense of Congress that the President should deny any economic or military assistance to the government of any foreign country which practices the internment or imprisonment of that country's citizens for political purpose.

Sec. 46 of the Foreign Assistance Act of 1974 (P.L. 93-559) added Sec. 502B urging the President to reduce or terminate security assistance to any government which consistently violates internationally recognized human rights. Violations of human rights were defined as:

> . . . including torture or cruel, inhuman or degrading treatment or punishment; prolonged detention without charges; or other flagrant denials of the right to life, liberty, and the security of the person.

Congress also requested that the President advise it of the circumstances making it necessary to provide security assistance to such governments.

Section 310 of the International Development and Food Assistance Act of 1975 (P.L. 94-161) amended section 116 of the Foreign Assistance Act to: (a) provide that economic assistance may not be given to any country which consistently violates internationally recognized human rights, (b) require the President to submit to Congress a written report explaining how assistance would directly benefit the people of such a country, and (c) stipulate that if either house of Congress disagrees with the President's justification it may take action to terminate economic assistance to that country by a concurrent resolution. In compliance with the provision indicated in item (b) above, the Agency for International Development (AID) on March 5, 1976, submitted a report which said, "While in future years, we will conduct a more comprehensive review, we are satisfied tht development assistance programs as now proposed for FY77 comply, in good faith, with the requirements of section 116.''

Sec. 301 of the International Security Assistance and Arms Export Control Act (P.L. 94-329) (1) established within the State Department a Coordinator for Human Rights and Humanitarian Affairs to be appointed by the President with the advice and consent of the Senate; (2) required the Secretary of State to submit reports each fiscal year on human rights practices in each country proposed as a recipient of security assistance; (3) required upon request of either the House or Senate or of either foreign relations committee that the Secretary of State prepare with the assistance of the Coordinator a statement on a designated country's human rights practices; (4) established that if such a statement on a designated country is not transmitted within 30 days, security assistance to that country will cease until the statement is transmitted; and (5) provided that after the requested statement is transmitted Congress may reduce or end security assistance to the designated country by adoption of a joint resolution.

Congress also enacted legislation directed at problems in specific countries. For example, in 1974 Congress limited military assistance to Korea for FY75 "until the President submits a report to the Congress . . . stating that the government of South Korea is making substantial progress in the observance of internationally recognized standards of human rights" (sec. 26, Foreign Assistance Act of 1974, P.L. 93-559). The International Security Assistance and Arms Export Control Act of 1976 expressed the concern of Congress for the erosion of civil liberties in South Korea and requested the President to communicate this concern in forceful terms to the South Korean Government (section 412, P.L. 94-329). This concern was conveyed to the Korean ambassador in Washington on August 30, 1976.

Appropriations for U.S. assistance to Chile on several occasions prohibited or limited by Congress to express its concern over human rights in Chile. In 1973 Congress included in the Foreign Assistance Act of 1973, section 35, which provided that the President (1) request Chile to protect human rights, (2) support United Nations and Red Cross activities to aid political refugees and investigate detention facilities, (3) support and aid voluntary agencies in emergency relief needs, and (4) request the Inter-American Commission on Human Rights to investigate "recent events in Chile" (P.L. 93-189). In December 1974, Congress passed the Foreign Assistance Act of 1974 (P.L. 93-559): section 25 prohibited all military assistance to Chile and limited assistance to $25 million during fiscal year 1975. In 1975 Congress limited economic assistance to Chile in fiscal year 1976 to $90 million (P.L. 94-161). Section 406 of the International Security Assistance and Arms Export Control Act of 1976 (P.L. 94-329) terminated military assistance to Chile, including a prohibition of military education and training, placed a ceiling on economic assistance of $27.5 million during the transition quarter and fiscal year 1977, and specified conditions relating to human rights under which economic assistance might be increased by an additional $27.5 milion.

Congress also enacted legislation aimed at addressing human rights problems in the Soviet Union and Eastern Europe. Section 402 of the Trade Act of 1974 (P.L. 93-618: approved January 3, 1975) tied MFN (most-favored-nation) treatment to trade in products from nonmarket economy countries to the maintenance of freedom of emigration from these countries. In addition, Congress created a Commission on Security and Cooperation in Europe (P.L. 94-304: approved June 3, 1976) to monitor actions of signatory nations to the Final Act of the Conference on Security and Cooperation in Europe (the Helsinki accords) and especially the provisions relating to cooperation in humanitarian fields (see IB76068, Helsinki Final Act, for more information on the Helsinki agreement).

The Congress stipulated in section 505 of the Foreign Assistance and Related Programs Appropriations Act, 1977 (P.L. 94-441, October 1, 1976) that no funds were to be used to provide military assistance, international military education and training, or foreign military credit sales to the Government of Uruguay. This prohibition was provoked by congressional concerns for the status of human rights in Uruguay.

During 1976 Congress also enacted legislation authorizing and directing the U.S. executive directors of the Inter-American Development bank and the African Development Fund "to vote against any loan, any extension of financial assistance, or any technical assistance to any country which engages in a consistent pattern of gross violations of internationally recognized human rights, including torture or cruel, inhumane, or degrading treatment ór punishment, prolonged detention without charges, or other flagrant denials of the right to life, liberty, and the security of person, unless such assistance will directly benefit the needy people in such country."

Congress has also sought by holding hearings to identify and bring to public attention the extent of human rights violations in specific countries and to clarify and focus executive branch efforts and policies on these problems. Among the most active groups has been the Subcommittee on International Organizations of the House Committee on International Relations which started its hearings in 1973 and issued a report on human rights and U.S. foreign policy in 1974. During the 94th Congress this subcommittee conducted a total of 40 hearings relating to human rights problems in 18 different countries.

EXECUTIVE BRANCH HUMAN RIGHTS ACTIVITY, 1973-76

In the face of congressional action, Administration policies on international human rights underwent significant changes in the 1973-76 period. The 1973 human rights hearings of the Subcommittee on the International Organizations and Movements of the House Foreign Affairs Committee marked the first time in the decade that Congress directed serious consideration to current developments in the international human rights field. They examined proposals designed to strengthen the role of the United Nations in protecting human rights, and to explore the advisability of giving human rights a higher priority in the hierarchy of U.S. foreign policy objectives. In the spring of 1974 from those hearings emerged a report, entitled, "Human Rights in the World Community: A Call for U.S. Leadership," giving 29 recommendations addressing the human rights issues of the day.

Later that year, Congressman Fraser, Chairman of the International Organization Subcommittee, reported that many of the organizational changes recommended in the report had been adopted by the Department of State. Among such recommendations was the designation of human rights officers in all State Department geographic bureaus. A further recommendation for creation of positionof special assistant on human rights in the Deputy Secretary's Office, to insure the consideration of human rights factors at the policy making level, was implemented in mid-1975 by creation of an Office of Humanitarian Affairs. A new position of Assistant Legal Adviser for Humanitarian Rights responsible for legal matters affecting human rights was also created.

Another arena where official U.S. policy appeared to follow the recommendations of the International Organization Subcommittee was in voicing a stronger concern for human rights violations in such international organizations as the United Nations. In March 1975, U.S. Representative to the United Nations, Ambassador John Scali, in a speech which deplored the lack of progress in human rights made by the United Nations in over 30 years, announced that the United States would take a new approach to human rights at the United Nations. He explained that on Feb. 6, 1975, Secretary Kissinger had instructed the U.S. Delegation to the Human Rights Commission in Geneva to support the Commission's conduct of thorough studies on alleged human rights violations anywhere in the world in response to complaints to the Commission that indicated a consistent pattern of gross and reliably attested to violations. The new policy would mean that the United States would support international inquiries into alleged human rights violations in nations regarded as friends as well as adversaries. In following this new policy the United States announced support for the U.N. Human Rights Commission's study of the situation in Chile.

Subsequent U.S. statements in various international forums also called for strengthened international programs and machinery for the promotion and protection of human rights. Thus on November 24, 1976, U.S. Representative to the United Nations, Ambassador William Scranton, charged that needed action on human rights violations by the U.N. Human Rights Commission had died amid procedural difficulties and suggested tha the Third Committee establish effective mechanisms that could initiate control on a particular abuse of human rights before it becomes a global issue. Similarly on June 8, 1976 Secretary of State Kissinger in an address before the General Assembly of the Organization of American States (OAS) meeting in Santiago, Chile condemned Chile's violations of "elemental international standards of human rights," warning that U.S. relations with Chile would be impaired until changes were made. He also called on the OAS to broaden the powers of its Human Rights Commission.

Yet, in an October 20, 1976 speech Secretary Kissinger said that the United States must recognize its limitations in dealing with the issue of human rights violations in other countries. He stated that "quiet diplomacy" often is more effective than a "public crusade." Caution was also reflected in State Department responses to congressional initiatives in the human rights area. Thus in response to section 502B of the Foreign Assistance Act of 1974 by which the President was to advise the Congress of extraordinary circumstances necessitating security assistance to any government engaging in gross human rights violations, an unsigned, summary report, entitled, "Report to the Congress on the Human Rights Situation in Countries Receiving U.S. Security Assistance," was transmitted on Nov. 14, 1975 to Congress. The report concluded that human rights violations were common events throughout the world occurring both in countries receiving U.S. assistance and in those which did not:

> In view of the widespread nature of human rights violations in the world, we have found no adequately objective way to make distinctions of degree between nations. This fact leads us, therefore, to the conclusion that neither the U.S. security interest nor the human rights cause would be properly served by the public obloquy and impaired relations with security assistance recipient countries that would follow the making of inherently subjective U.S. Government determinations that "gross" violations do or do not exist or that a "consistent" pattern of such violations does or does not exist in such countries.

The report concluded tha "quiet but forceful diplomacy" continued to be the best way to improve human rights matters.

HUMAN RIGHTS ACTIVITY DURING THE CARTER ADMINISTRATION

President Carter began his term with a clear commitment to human rights both at home and abroad. In his first few months in office he spoke out about human rights abuses in the Soviet Union and Czechoslovakia, wrote a letter to Soviet dissident, Andrei Sakharov and received the exiled Vladimir Bukovsky at the White House. Moreover, aid reductions to Ethiopia, Argentina, and Uruguay were announced because of their human rights policies.

President Carter in his Mar. 17, 1977 speech at the United Nations called for strengthening of the U.N. Human Rights Commission and for the implementation of a 12-year-old proposal for the establishment of an independent U.N. Commissioner for Human Rights. He also pledged his intention to seek approval for U.S. ratification of some of the U.N. human rights instruments—namely, the Covenant on Economic, Social and Cultural Rights, and the Covenant on Civil and Political Rights as well as the U.N. Genocide Convention and the Convention on the Elimination of All Forms of Racial Discrimination.

President Carter also unequivocally stated the position that the U.S. Government considers human rights to be a matter of international concern:

> All signatories of the U.N. Charter have pledged themselves to observe and respect basic human rights. Thus no member of the United Nations can claim that mistreatment of its citizens is solely its own business. Equally, no member can avoid its responsibilities to review and to speak when torture or unwarranted deprivatgion of freedom occurs in any part of the world.

Less than a month later the President, in a Pan American Day speech on April 14, pledged increased support for the Inter-American Commission on Human Rights, his intention to sign the American Convention on Human Rights, and support for broadened programs for aiding political refugees. In addition, human rights reports on 82 countries were submitted to Congress in March 1977 by the Department of State in compliance with the requirement in section 502B of the Foreign Assistance Act of 1961 as amended, that such a report be transmitted annually as part of the presentation materials for security assistance programs. In protest to this State Department report on their human rights practices and the earlier U.S. announcement of aid reductions to three countries because of their human rights activities, five Latin American countries, El Salvador, Argentina, Brazil, Guatemala, and Uruguay renounced U.S. military aid.

At the end of 1976 Congress had also required, under section 502B (c) of the Foreign Assistance Act of 1961 as amended, that the Department of State submit reports on human rights and U.S. policy in six countries—Argentina, Haiti, Indonesia, Iran, Peru, and the Philippines. These were submitted to Congress as required in December 1976. As outlined in the law, Congress may now decide to adopt a joint resolution terminating, restricting or continuing security assistance to any of the six countries listed. The joint resolution procedure would require the approval of the President or the override vote of Congress in case of a Presidential veto.

During the spring of 1977 Administration statements on human rights emphasized realism and limits on U.S. action in this area. In a speech on April 30, 1977 Secretary of State Vance, while emphasizing the U.S. commitment to human rights, explained that the promotion of human rights must be realistic, avoiding rigidity and an attempt to impose American values on others. He noted that there are constraints on U.S. policy in this area and that U.S. policy should be determined flexibly on a country by country basis. Secretary Vance also defined human rights as consisting of three parts—integrity of the individual, fulfillment of basic human needs, and civil and political liberties. He listed questions which the United States might ask in deciding its human rights policy toward each individual country. Attempts are being made within the State Department to elaborate on the principles outlined in this speech. Until such elaboration is completed, the speech forms the basic guideline for State Department activity in the human rights area.

Recent Administration actions and statements on human rights seem to reflect a more cautious position. Public statements criticizing human rights conditions in other countries have not been issued. The quiet diplomatic approach in advocating improvements in human rights situations in other countries appears to be the recent Administration course. U.S. officials in various contacts with foreign counterparts (for example, Secretary of State Vance during his November 1977 trip to Brazil, Argentina, and Venezuela) are reportedly discussing human rights in private, but little is said publicly. In contrast to his March 1977 speech, President Carter's October 4, 1977, speech at the United Nations did not mention the topic of human rights at all.

President Carter did sign (as he pledged in his spring of 1977 speeches) the American Convention on Human Rights on June 1, 1977, and the U.N. International Covenants on Economic, Social, and Cultural Rights and on Civil and Political Rights on October 5, 1977. None of these international human rights treaties have, however, yet been submitted to the Senate for approval.

The Carter Administration has differed with the Congress and the two Houses of Congress have differed with each other on some human rights legislation enacted during the 95th Congress. On April 6, 1977, the

House by voice vote agreed to human rights amendments to H.R. 5262, authorizing U.S. contributions to international financial institutions. One of these amendments required U.S. officials of all international lending institutions to vote against extending financial assistance to any country found to have a consistent pattern of gross violations of human rights. This amendment was agreed to despite the opposition of President Carter who described such an approach to human rights "at once too lenient and too rigid." The President had favored an amendment which encouraged (but did not require) American representatives to international lending organizations to seek to channel loans to countries other than those engaging in a consistent pattern of gross violations of internationally recognized human rights. The Senate on June 14, 1977, agreed with the President's position not requiring automatic rejection of aid to nations found violating human rights, and so the Senate version of H.R. 5262 contained no section comparable to the above-cited human rights provision in the House bill. The committee of conference retained the House version of the measure except for the mandatory "no" vote. The bill as finally enacted (P.L. 95-118) required U.S. representatives to these institutions to "oppose" all assistance to countries engaging in a consistent pattern of gross violations of human rights unless such assistance directly serves the human needs of the citizens of such country.

A similar divergence in congressional and executive views arose over provisions in the Foreign Assistance and Related Programs Appropriations Act, 1978 (P.L. 95-148). As finally worked out after intercession by President Carter, the measure prohibited direct U.S. aid for Uganda, Vietnam, Cambodia, Laos, Angola, Mozambique, and Cuba. The House had voted in June to prohibit international financial institutions from using U.S. funds for assisting the above listed countries, because of their poor human rights records.

In August, after World Bank President Robert McNamara warned that that institution would not accept U.S. funds under the restrictions specified by the House-passed measure, the Senate deleted such a provision from the bill. After a House-Senate conference was unable to resolve the issue, President Carter (opposed to the House version) met with congressional leaders on September 30, 1977, to work out a compromise, On October 6th the President wrote a letter to Clarence Long, Chairman of the Foreign Operations Subcommittee of the House Appropriations Committee, in which Carter promised to instruct the U.S. representatives to international lending institutions to oppose and vote against any loans to the seven named countries during FY78. The legislation as finally enacted into law prohibited *direct* U.S. aid to the seven countries.

Legislation

P.L. 95-88 (H.R. 6714)
International Development and Food Assistance Act of 1977.
Section 111 of the International Development and Food Assistance Act of 1977 revised section 116 of the Foreign Assistance Act to require the Administrator of AID in consultation with the Coordinator for Human Rights and Humanitarian Affairs to consider specific actions which have been taken by the President or Congress relating to multilateral assistance or security assistance because of human rights practices or policies. It also revised the existing reporting requirement mandating that the Secretary of State transmit to Congress by January 31 of each year a full report on the status of internationally recognized human rights in the countries receiving development assistance.

Section 203 of this legislation added a new section 112 to P.L. 480, title I programs which prohibited entry into any agreement under that title to finance the sale of agricultural commodities to the government of any country which engages in a consistent pattern of human rights violations, unless such agreement would benefit the needy people in such country.

P.L. 95-92 (H.R. 6884)
International Security Assistance Act of 1977.
Section 8(d) of this legislation expressed the sense of the Congress that the United States supports "an internationally recognized constitutional settlement of the Rhodesian conflict leading promptly to majority rule based upon democratic principles and upholding basic human rights." Section 11 prohibited assistance, credits or sales to Argentina. (The House bill had amended section 502 of the Foreign Assistance Act to prohibit military assistance and sales which would aid the efforts of foreign governments to repress the legitimate rights of their citizens contrary to the Universal Declaration of Human Rights. This provision was deleted by the Congress Committee.)

P.L. 95-105 (H.R. 6689)
Foreign Relations Authorization Act, FY78.
Section 109(a) of this legislation elevated the Coordinator for Human Rights and Humanitarian Affairs to an Assistant Secretary of State for Human Rights and Humanitarian Affairs. It also required the Secretary of State by January 31, 1978 to transmit to Congress a comprehensive report on the Office of the Assistant Secretary "including its current mandate and operations, the mandate and operations of its predecessor offices, and proposals for the reorganizations of the Department of State that would strengthen human rights and humanitarian considerations in

the conduct of United States foreign policy." Section 503(a)(4) called on the United States to consider proposals for reforming and restructuring the U.N. system which would improve coordination of and expand U.N. activities on behalf of human rights.

Section 511(b) expressed the sense of the Congress that Cuba's disrespect for the human rights of individuals must be taken into account in any negotiations toward normalization of relations with that country.

P.L. 118 (H.R. 5262)
Authorization for International Financial Institutions

Section 701 provided that the U.S. government shall advance the cause of human rights through those organizations by seeking to channel assistance to countries other than those which show a consistent pattern of gross violations of human rights. The United States is to seek to channel assistance to projects which address the basic human needs of the people of the recipient country. The Secretaries of States and Treasury are to submit an annual report to Congress on programs in achieving the human rights goals in this section. The U.S. Executive Directors of the international financial institutions are to oppose any loan, any extension of financial assistance or any technical assistance to countries engaging in a consistent pattern of gross violations of internationally recognized human rights or providing refuge to individuals committing acts of international terrorism by hijacking aircraft, unless such programs serve basic human needs. Section 703 required the U.S. Government to initiate consultations with other nations to develop a standard for meeting basic human needs and protecting human rights and a mechanism to insure that the rewards of international economic cooperation are especially available to those subscribing to such standards.

P.L. 95-143 (H.R. 6415)
Export-Import Bank Act of 1945 Amendments.

Section 2 amended section 2(b)(1)(B) of the Export-Import Bank Act of 1945 relating to the policy of the United States on loans by requiring the Board of Directors to "take into account, in consultation with the Secretary of State, the observance of and respect for human rights in the country to receive the exports supported by a loan or financial guarantee and the effect such exports may have on human rights in such country."

P.L. 95-148 (H.R. 7797)
Foreign Assistance and Related Programs Appropriations Act, 1978.

Title I barred military education and training funds for Argentina.

Section 107 prohibited direct U.S. aid to Uganda, Vietnam, Cambodia and Laos; section 114 prohibited such aid to Angola and Mozambique; and section 506 prohibited assistance to Cuba.

Section 503A prohibited military assistance, international military education and training, or foreign military credit sales to Ethiopia and Uruguay. Section 503B prohibited foreign military credit sales to Argentina, Brazil, El Salvador and Guatemala. Section 503C limited appropriations for the Philippines to $18,000,000 for military aid, $1,850,000 for military credit sales, and $700,000 for training.

Section 113 prohibited security assistance to any country for aiding directly the efforts of the government of such country to repress the legitimate rights of the population of such country contrary to the Universal Declaration of Human Rights.

Section 507 expressed the sense of Congress that U.S. representatives to international financial institutions oppose loans and other aid to nations systematically violating human rights, except when the President determined that rights would be better served by not voting against such assistance or when the aid was intended to go directly to the impoverished majority of the country.

Operations and Mandate of the Bureau of Human Rights and Humanitarian Affairs

BILATERAL RELATIONS

The Bureau has helped communicate our human rights policy to foreign governments and representatives by supporting and complementing the role of our Embassies abroad and the regional bureaus in Washington.

The Assistant Secretary has visited Argentina, El Salvador, Bolivia, Brazil, Uruguay, Indonesia, Singapore, the Philippines, Thailand, and Yugoslavia, and has held discussions with the highest government officials in those countries. She has also met with local groups and organizations familiar with human rights conditions in these and other countries. She attended the Belgrade CSCE meeting and has had intensive discussions with NATO representatives on human rights issues. The Deputy Assistant Secretary for Human Rights, and other human rights officers, also have met with high officials of other governments to communicate our specific concerns on the human rights situation in their countries, and to seek where possible to work with them on efforts to enhance the respect for human rights.

Consultations are expanding with other governments on ways to increase international cooperation and concern for human rights around the world. These discussions include consultations on human rights con-

Excerpt from *Report of the Secretary of State to the Congress of the United States (January 31, 1978) Regarding the Operations and Mandate of the Bureau of Human Rights and Humanitarian Affairs (as Required Under Section 109 of Public Law 92-105);* Hearings before the Subcommittee on International Organizations of the Committee on International Relations, February 15, 16, 28; March 7 and 8, 1978. Printed for the use of the Committee on International Relations.

ditions in individual countries and specific human rights initiatives in international organizations and in the international financial institutions.

These actions by the Bureau and its officers have complemented representatives and communications by our Embassies overseas and the Department in Washington. There is a continuing exchange between the Bureau and other regional and functional bureaus in the Department on both immediate operational questions and long range strategies to achieve our policy objectives.

BILATERAL ECONOMIC ASSISTANCE

The Bureau of Human Rights and Humanitarian Affairs plays a continuing role in advising AID on human rights conditions in particular countries.

It also has worked closely with AID in the Inter-agency Committee on Human Rights and Foreign Assistance. In addition to working with AID to respond more fully to development needs in countries with positive human rights records, we have collaborated with AID in devising new ways to support non-government groups and individuals concerned with the international human rights movement. In the past, AID has provided varying forms of assistance to legal aid and legal assistance programs in developing countries. These efforts are now being expanded and special attention paid to women's rights. Finally, the Bureau is discussing with AID ways to identify and support programs and activities which will encourage or promote increased adherence to civil and political rights in the spirit of Section 116 of the Foreign Assistance Act.

The Administrator of AID, and the Department as a whole, have considered the human rights record of potential recipient countries an important factor in determining the funding level of bilateral development assistance programs, including PL-480.

We intend to pursue our human rights policy objectives even more systematically in future years, giving particular attention to using our development assistance as a positive incentive to governments which are seriously attempting to improve their human rights situation.

Where countries engage in practices which seriously violate the human rights of their citizens, the Bureau has worked with AID to bring about a reduction or halt in our aid programs, except in cases where those programs directly benefit needy people. In such cases we have worked with AID to insure that help for the needy is the primary purpose of the project and that the needy will be the principal beneficiaries of a program. During the course of the year, the Bureau has helped develop guidelines to assist overseas posts in determining whether bilateral projects benefit the needy. The definitions of "needy people" continue to be those established in AID's 1975 report to the House of Representatives on implementing New Directions.

In 1977 AID projects were delayed or halted in some countries, and the bilateral economic assistance program was linked to expressions of our concern over human rights conditions in other countries.

Provisions were also adopted in PL 95-88 to require consideration of human rights conditions in extending PL-480 Title I assistance. In furtherance on this policy the Bureau advises AID and the Department of Agriculture on human rights conditions in the relevant countries. The Inter-Agency Committee also reviews PL-480 allocations. Thus far in FY 1978, we have instructed our missions in some recipient countries to negotiate an additional provision to our PL-480 agreements to insure that the food or the proceeds of the program will go directly to the needy. In two countries adjustments were made in the allocation level to proposed PL-480 recipients.

SECURITY ASSISTANCE

The Bureau advised the Arms Export Control Board, the Under Secretary for Security Assistance and the Secretary of State concerning human rights conditions in countries for which security assistance was proposed. Human rights factors were also considered, under section 502B, in the preparations for the submissionof the FY 1979 budget, and in the allocation levels for the security assistance program.

In administering the security assistance program approved by the Congress for FY 1978, we plan to consider current human rights conditions prior to the actual implementation of particular country agreements. The Bureau also will examine the recipient agency within each country and the character of the equipment or arms involved in transfers in order to reduce or eliminate the identification of the United States with human rights violations.

INTERNATIONAL FINANCIAL INSTITUTIONS

Under Section 701 of PL 95-118, the Executive Branch is charged with using its voice and vote in the IFIs " . . . to channel assistance toward countries other than those whose governments engage in a consistent pattern of gross violations of internationally recognized human rights." The Bureau advises the Treasury Department, through the Inter-Agency Committee, on human rights conditions in countries before the U.S. position on particular loans is decided and, in conjunction with other appropriate Bureaus within the Department of State and the Department of the

Treasury, has participated in a series of consultations with other nations to discuss the role of human rights in the IFIs.

During the past year, the United States opposed loans to several countries because of the human rights situation in those countries. In other instances, after advising the country that the United States would oppose loan applications if they were presented to the governing boards of international financial institutions, the countries chose to withdraw their applications.

IV
Select Bibliography

Select Bibliography

BOOKS

Amstutz, Mark. *Economics and Foreign Policy: A Guide to Information Sources*. Gale, 1977.

Bauer, Robert A., ed. *The Interaction of Economics and Foreign Policy*. University of Virginia Press.

Behrman, Jere R. *Development, the International Economic Order, and Commodity Agreements*. Reading, MA: Addison-Wesley Publishing Company, 1978.

Bergsten, C. Fred and Thomas Horst. *American Multinationals and American Interests*. Brookings, 1978.

Cahn, Anne et al. *Controlling Future Arms Trade*. N.Y.: McGraw, 1977.

Chachiliades, Miltiades. *International Trade: Theory and Policy*, 2nd ed. N.Y.: McGraw, 1978.

Charles River Associates. *International Cartels: Policy Implications for the U.S.* Praeger, 1979.

Cohen, Stephen. *The Making of U.S. International Economic Policy: Principles, Problems, and Proposals for Reform*. Praeger, 1977.

Conover, Helen. *A Guide to Bibliographic Tools for Research in Foreign Affairs*, 2 vols. Gordon Press.

Coppock, Joseph. *International Trade Instability*. Lexington Books, 1977.

Council on International Economic Policy. *Special Report: Critical Imported Materials*. Washington, D.C.: U.S. Superintendent of Documents, 1974.

Deville, Lawrence. *American Foreign Policy and American Business*, 2 vols. Feb., 1979.

Drucker, Peter. *Age of Discontinuity*. Harper-Row, 1978.

Eckes, Alfred. *The U.S. and the Global Struggle for Minerals*. Austin, TX: University of Texas Press.

Friesen, Connie. *The Political Economy of East-West Trade*. Praeger, 1976.

Frank, Charles and Stephanie Levinson. *Foreign Trade and Domestic Aid*. Brookings, 1977.

Goldberg, Ray. *International Agribusiness Coorindation.* Ballinger.

Gray, Peter. *International Trade, Investment and Payments.* Houghton Mifflin, 1979.

Green, Robert T. and James Lutz. *The U.S. and World Trade: Changing Patterns and Dimensions.* Praeger, 1979.

Harkavy, Robert. *The Arms Trade and International Systems.* Ballinger, 1975.

Hawkins, Robert G., ed. *The Economic Effects of Multinational Corporations,* Vol. 1. Jai Press, 1979.

Hudson, Michael. *Global Fracture: The New International Economic Order.* Harper Row, 1977.

Lortie, Pierre. *Economic Integration and the Law of GATT.* Praeger, 1975.

Marer, Paul, ed. *U.S. Financing of East-West Trade: The Political Economy of Government Credits and the National Interest.* Indiana University Press, 1976.

Melman, Seymour. *The Permanent War Economy.* S&S, 1974.

Miles, Marc. *Devaluation, the Trade Balance, and the Balance of Payments.* Dekker, 1978.

Monroe, Wilbur. *The New Internationalism: Strategy and Initiatives for U.S. Foreign Economic Policy.* Lexington Books, 1976.

Osborne, Harrison. *Foreign Economic Invasion of the U.S. and the Drastically Changed Character of the International Economic Structure.* Institute Economic Policy, 1978.

Putnam, Blueford and D. Sykes Wilford, eds. *The Monetary Approach to International Adjustment.*

Rangarajan, L. N. Commodity Conflict: The Political Economy of International Commodity Negotiations. Cornell University Press, 1978.

Richardson, Neil R. *Foreign Policy and Economic Dependence.* University of Texas Press, 1978.

Rom, Michael. *The Role of Tariff Quotas in Commercial Policy.* Holmes and Meier, 1978.

Sampson, Anthony. *The Arms Bazaar: From Lebanon to Lockheed.* N.Y.: The Viking Press, 1977.

Stern, Paula. *Water's Edge: Domestic Politics and the Making of American Foreign Policy.* Greenwood, 1979.

Tyler, William. *Issues and Prospects for New International Economic Order.* Lexington Books, 1977.

United Nations. *Disarmament Yearbook 1976; Disarmament Yearbook 1977; Disarmament Yearbook 1978.* U.N.: appropriate years.

Yeager, Leland and David G. Tuerck. *Foreign Trade and U.S. Policy: The Case for Free International Trade.* Praeger, 1976.

ARTICLES

Abegglen, James C. and Thomas M. Hout. "Facing Up to the Trade Gap with Japan." *Foreign Affairs* (Fall, 1978) 146-68.

Alexander, Archibald. "Arms Transfers by the United States: Merchant of Death or Arsenal of Democracy." *Vanderbilt Journal of Transnational Law* (Spring, 1977) 249-67.

Avery, Wiliam P. "Domestic Influence on Latin American Importation of U.S. Armaments." *International Studies Quarterly* (March, 1978) 121-39.

Baranson, Jack. "Technology Exports Can Hurt US." *Foreign Policy* (Winter 1976-77) 180-94.

Barnaby, Frank. "The Dynamics of World Armaments: An Overview." *International Social Science Journal* (1976) 245-65.

Bart, Richard D. "Developments in Arms Transfers: Implications for Supplier Control and Recipient Autonomy." Rand Corp. (Sept., 1977).

Bauser, Michael. "United States Nuclear Export Policy: Developing the Peaceful Atom as a Commodity in International Trade." *Harvard International Law Journal* (Spring, 1977) 227-72.

Benson, Lucy Wilson. "Controlling Arms Transfers: An Instrument of U.S. Foreign Policy." *Dept. of State Bulletin* (August 1, 1977) 155-59.

Billingsley, Henry. "U.S. Military Exports and the Arms Export Control Act of 1976: The F-16 Sale to Iran." *Case Western Reserve Journal of International Law* (Spring, 1977) 407-24.

Bowers, Edwin W. "Antitrust Rules Bog U.S. as World Trader." *Iron Age* (August 28, 1978) 53-55.

_____. "U.S. Trade Ailments Infect the Economy." *Iron Age* (August 14, 1978) 30-32.

Brusca, Robert. "U.S. Export Performance." *Federal Reserve Bank of New York Quarterly Review* (Winter, 1978-79) 49-56.

Busniak, Jan. "Reconstruction of the System of International Economic Relations." *International Relations* (1977) 36-53.

Campbell, Robert M. "The Foreign Trade Aspects of the Trade Act of 1974." Parts I and II. *Washington and Lee Law Review* (Spring and Summer, 1976) 325-92 & 639-99.

Coccari, Ronald. "Alternative Models for Forecasting U.S. Exports." *Journal of International Business Studies* (Spring/Summer, 1978) 73-84.

Cohen, Stephen D. "The Causes and Consequences of the U.S. Trade Deficit in 1978." *Business Economics* (May, 1978) 52-56.

Cooper, Richard. "A New International Economic Order for Mutual Gain." *Foreign Policy* (Spring, 1977) 66-120.

"Come to the Aid of Foreign Aid." *Economist* (June 24, 1978) 25-26.

Commerce America. Biweekly publication U.S. Dept. of Commerce.

Direction of Trade. Excellent trade statistics.

"Economics of Special Interest Politics: The Case of the Tariff." *American Economic Review* (May, 1978) 261-63.

Eide, Asbjørn. "Arms Transfer and Third World Militarization." *Bulletin of Peace Proposals* (1977) 99-102.

_____. "The Transfer of Arms to Third World Countries and Their Internal Uses." *International Social Science Journal* (1976) 307-25.

"First Half Deficit Larger Despite Faster Export Rise, Oil Import Drop." *Commerce America* (August 14, 1978) 7-9.

Foreign Agricultural Trade of the U.S. U.S. Dept. of Agriculture.

Gelb, Lesli, H. "Arms Sales." *Foreign Policy* (Winter, 1976-77) 3-23.

Graham, Thomas R. "The U.S. Generalized System of Preferences for Developing Countries: International Innovation and the Art of the Possible." *The American Journal of International Law* (July, 1978).

American Journal of International Law (July, 1978).

Grzybowski, Kazimierz et al. "Towards Integrated Management of International Trade—The U.S. Trade Act of 1974." *International and Comparative Law Quarterly* (April, 1977) 283-323.

Helscher, David. "Public Law 480, American Agriculture and World Food Demand." *Case Western Reserve Journal of International Law* (Summer, 1978) 739-60.

Hillman, J.S. "Nontariff Barriers: Major Problem in Agricultural Trade." *American Journal Agricultural Economics* (August, 1978) 491-501.

Hoyt, Ronald E. "East-West Trade Growth Potential for the 1980s." *The Columbia Journal of World Business.* (Spring, 1978) 59-70.

International Commerce.

International Economic Indicators. U.S. Dept. of Commerce monthly stats international trade.

International Economic Review.

"International Mineral Trade" whole issue *Journal International Law and Economics* (August, 1978).

Johnson, K. "Arms Exports Increase 60% in Decade." *Aviation Weekly* (July 31, 1978).

_____. "Congress to Expand Arms Sales Monitoring." *Aviation Weekly* (August 14, 1978) 14-15.

Journal of International Economics.

Katz, Julius. "International Mineral Trade: U.S. Commodity Policy." *The Journal of International Law and Economics* (1978) 243-46.

Kim, Cae-one. "Transformation of the International Economic Order Seen Through the Natural Resource Crisis." *Korean Journal of International Studies* (Summer, 1977) 35-46.

Kyrolainer, Hannu. "An Analysis of New Trends in the U.S. Military Training and Technical Assistance in the Third World." *Instant Research on Peace and Violence* (1977) 167-83.

Lange, Irene and James Elliott. "U.S. Role in East-West Trade: An Appraisal." *Journal of International Business Studies* (Fall/Winter, 1977) 5-16.

Luttrell, Clifton. "Imports and Jobs—The Observed and the Unobserved." *Federal Reserve of St. Louis* :June, 1978) 2-10.

McKinlay, R.D. and R. Little. "A Foreign Policy Model of U.S. Bilateral Aid Allocation." *World Politics* (Oct. 1977) 58-86.

Metzger, Stanley D. "Cartels, Combines, Commodity Agreements and International Law." *Texas International Law Journal* (Summer, 1976) 527-39.

Meyer, Herbert L. "Those Worrisome Technology Exports." *Fortune* (May 22, 1978) 106-109.

Morisse, Kathryn. "Recent Developments in U.S. International Transactions." *Federal Reserve Bulletin* (April, 1978) 255-64.

Oswald, Rudy. "Trade: The New Realities." *American Federationist* (July, 1978) 12-14.

Passman, Cristy. "The International Security Assistance and Arms Export Control Act of 1976." *The International Trade Law Journal* (Summer, 1977) 169-77.

"The Politics of Protection." *The Economist* (June 24, 1978) 85-86.

Roschke, Thomas. "The GATT: Problems and Prospects." *Journal of International Law and Economics* (1977) 85-103.

Runge, Carlisle Ford. "American Agricultural Assistance and the New International Economic Order." *World Development* (August, 1977) 725-46.

Scholl, R.B. "International Investments Position of the U.S.: Developments in 1977." *Survey Current Business* (August, 1978) 53-59.

Smith, G.W. and G.R. Schink. "International Tin Agreement: A Reassessment." *Economics Journal* (Dec., 1976) 715-28.

Sneath, William. "The U.S. and International Trade—A Realistic Look at the Future." *National Journal* (April 29, 1978) 693-99.

Streng, William P. "Government Supported Export Credit: U.S. Competitiveness." *The International Lawyer* (1976) 401-24.

Stepanek, Jiri. "Economic Cooperation Between Socialist and Capitalist Countries." *International Relations* (Prague) (1976) 43-60.

Todd, Shelly. "Trade Between Developed and Less Developed Countries: North-South Trade." *The International Trade Law Journal* (Summer, 1977) 255-61.

Warnecke, Steven. "The U.S. and the European Community: The Changing Political and Economic Context of Trade Relations." *Journal of International Affairs* (Spring/Summer, 1976) 21-36.

Volcker, Paul. "The Challenges of International Economic Policy." *Federal Reserve Board of NY Quarterly Review* (Winter, 1977-78) 1-6.

Weissbrodt, David. "Human Rights Legislation and U.S. Foreign Policy." *Georgia Journal of International and Comparative Law* (1977) 231-287.

Westerfeld, Janice. "Commodity Agreements: The Haves vs. the Have Nots?" *Federal Reserve Bank of Philadelphia Review* (Nov. Dec., 1977) 11-18.

Wolpin, Miles. "Military Dependency vs. Development of the Third World." *Bulletin of Peace Proposals* (1977) 137-41.

World Trade Annual.

Wood, Geoffrey E. and Douglas Mudd. "The Recent U.S. trade Deficit—No Cause for Panic." *Federal Reserve of St. Louis* (April, 1978) 2-7.

Yergin, Daniel. "Politics and Soviet-American Trade: The Three Questions." *Foreign Affairs* (April, 1977) 517-538.

GOVERNMENT DOCUMENTS

CBO. *U.S. Balance of International Payments and the U.S. Economy.* Washington, D.C.: U.S. Government Printing Office, Feb., 1978. Y10.9:In8.

U.S. Congress. House Agriculture Committee. *Export of U.S. Agricultural Commodities,* Oct. 12, 1977.Washington, D.C.: U.S. Government Printing Office. Y4.Ag8/1:Ex7/8.

U.S. Congress. House Appropriations Committee. *Foreign Assistance and Related Agencies Appropriations for 1978,* Washington, D.C.: U.S. Government Printing Office. Y4.Ap6/1:F76/3/978.

U.S. Congress. House Appropriations Committee. *Foreign Assistance and Related Agencies Appropriations for 1979.* Washington, D.C.: U.S. Government Printing Office. Y4.Ap6/1:F76/3/979.

U.S. Congress. House Appropriations Committee. *Foreign Assistance and*

Related Programs Appropriations Bill, 1979. House Report 95-1250. Washington, D.C.: U.S. Government Printing Office.

U.S. Congress. House Appropriations Committee. *Making Appropriations: Foreign Assistance FY 1979.* Oct. 10, 1978. House Report 95-1754. Washington, D.C.: U.S. Government Printing Office.

U.S. Congress. House Banking, Finance, and Urban Affairs Committee. *Implications of Our International Trade Policy for American Business and Consumers.* Oct. 8, 1977. Washington, D.C.: U.S. Government Printing Office. Y4.B22/1:In8/39.

U.S. Congress. House Banking, Finance, and Urban Affairs Committee. *Trade Policy and Protectionism.* July-August, 1978. Washington, D.C.: U.S. Government Printing Office. Y4.B22/1:T67/2.

U.S. Congress. House Committee on International Relations. *Rethinking U.S. Foreign Policy Toward the Developing World.* Aug.-Nov., 1977. Washington, D.C.: U.S. Government Printing Office.

_____. *Review of the President's Conventional Arms Transfer Policy.* Feb., 1978. Washington, D.C.: U.S. Government Printing Office. Y4.In8/16/C76/3.

_____. *Report on Human Rights Practices in Countries Receiving U.S. Aid.* Feb. 8, 1979. Washington, D.C.: U.S. Government Printing Office. Y4.F76/2H88/9.

_____. *Export Licensing.* June, 1978. Washington, D.C.: U.S. Government Printing Office. Y4.In8/16:Ex/7/7.

_____. *Agricultural Exports and U.S. Foreign Economic Policy.* April June, 1978. Washington, D.C.: U.S. Government Printing Office. Y4.In8/16:Ag8.

_____. *International Transfer of Technology.* Dec., 1978. Washington, D.C.: U.S. Government Printing Office. Y.4.In8/16:T22/5.

_____. *Evaluation of FY 1979 Arms Control Impact Statements: Toward More Informed Congressional Participation in National Security Policymaking.* Jan. 3, 1979. Washington, D.C.: U.S. Government Printing Office.

_____. *International Security Assistance Act of 1978.* Sept. 7, 1978. Washington, D.C.: U.S. Government Printing Office. House Report 95-1546.

_____. *Agricultural Trade Act of 1978.* Sept. 14, 1978. Washington, D.C.: U.S. Government Printing Office. House Report 95-1338.

_____. *Foreign Assistance Legislation for FY 1979.* Washington, D.C.: U.S. Government Printing Office. Y4.In8/16:F76/8/979.

_____. *International Security Assistance Act of 1978.* May 12, 1978. Washington, D.C.: U.S. Government Printing Office. House Report 95-1141.

_____. *Dept. of Defense Policy Statement on Export Control of U.S. Technology.* Oct. 27, 1977. Washington, D.C.: U.S. Government Printing Office. Y4.In8/16:Ex7/5.

_____. *U.S. Arms Transfer and Security Assistance Programs.* March 21, 1978. Washington, D.C.: U.S. Government Printing Office. Y4.In8/16:Un35/16.

_____. *Export Stimulation Programs in Major Industrial Countries.* Oct. 6, 1978. Washington, D.C.: CRS print.

U.S. Congress. House Committee on Ways and Means. *Causes and Consequences of U.S. Trade Deficit and Developing Problems in U.S. Exports.* Nov. 3, 1977. Washington, D.C.: U.S. Government Printing Office. Y4.W36;95-44.

———. *Multilateral Trade Negotiations.* July 18, 1978. Washington, D.C.: U.S. Government Printing Office. Y4.W36:95-90.

———. *Oversight of the Antidumping Act of 1921.* Nov. 8, 1977. Washington, D.C.: U.S. Government Printing Office. Y4.W36; 95-46.

———. *Task Force Report on U.S.-Japan Trade.* Jan. 2, 1979. Washington, D.C.: U.S. Government Printing Office. Y4.W36:WM CP-95-110.

———. *Trade Agreements Reached in the Tokyo Round of Multilateral Trade Negotiations.* Jan. 15, 1979. Washington, D.C.: U.S. Government Printing Office. House Document 96-33.

———. *Unfair Trade Practices.* Sept. 5, 1978. Washington, D.C.: U.S. Government Printing Office. Y4.W36:WMPC 95-99.

———. *U.S. International Trade Commission Authorization for FY 1979.* Feb. 21, 1978. Washington, D.C.: U.S. Government Printing Office. Y4.W36:95-62.

———. 15th, 16th, 17th et al. *Qtrly Reports to the Congress and East-West Foreign Trade Board.* Washington, D.C.: U.S. Government Printing Office. Y4.W36:2/15-17 et al.

U.S. Congress. House Interstate and Foreign Commerce Committee. *Report on the Activity of the Committee on Interstate and Foreign Commerce 95th Congress.* Jan. 2, 1979. Washington, D.C.: U.S. Government Printing Office. House Report 95-1831.

U.S. Congress. Joint Economic Committee. *Anticipating Disruptive Imports.* Sept. 14, 1978. Washington, D.C.: U.S. Government Printing Office. Y4.Ec7:Im7.

———. *Issues in North-South Dialogue.* June 21, 1977. Washington, D.C.: U.S. Government Printing Office. Y4.Ec7:D54.

———. *Trade Deficit: How Much of a Problem? What Remedy?* Oct., 1977. Washington, D.C.: U.S. Government Printing Office. Y4.Ec7:T67/6.

———. *1978-1979 Economic Report of the President.* (See sections foreign trade, balance of payments, etc.) Washington, D.C.: U.S. Government Printing Office. Y4.Ec7:Ec7/2/978 and 979.

U.S. Congress. Senate Appropriations Committee. *Foreign Assistance and Related Program Appropriations FY 79.* Washington, D.C.: U.S. Government. Printing Office. Y4.Ap6/2:F76/7/979.

———. *Foreign Assistance and Related Programs Appropriations.* Sept. 15, 1978. Washington, D.C.: U.S. Government Printing Office. Senate Report 95-1194.

U.S. Congress. Senate Armed Services Committee. *Consideration of Stockpile Legislation.* March, 1978. Washington, D.C.: U.S. Government Printing Office. Y4.Ar5/3:St6/8.

———. *General Stockpile Policy.* Sept. 9, 1977. Washington, D.C.: U.S. Government Printing Office. Y4.Ar5/3:St6/7.

U.S. Congress. Senate Banking, Housing, and Urban Affairs Committee. *Export Policy.* Washington, D.C.: U.S. Government Printing Office. Y4.B22/3:Ex7/25.

———. *Financing of Foreign Military Sales.* Jan. 30, 1978. Washington, D.C.: U.S. Government Printing Office. Y4.B22/3:M59.

U.S. Congress. Senate Commerce, Science & Transportation Committee. *Na-

tional Export Program. Sept. 28, 1978. Washington, D.C.: U.S. Government Printing Office. Y4.C73/7:95-113.

U.S. Congress. Senate Foreign Relations Committee. *American Foreign Economic Policy: An Overview.* March-April, 1977. Washington, D.C.: U.S. Government Printing Office. Y4.F76/2:Ec7/6.

_____. *International Security Assistance Program.* Washington, D.C.: U.S. Government Printing Office. Y4.F76/2:Se2/11.

_____. *International Security Assistance Act of 1978.* Washington, D.C.: U.S. Government Printing Office. Senate Report 95-841.

NTC Contemporary Issues Series

 NTC *NATIONAL TEXTBOOK COMPANY • Skokie, IL 60077 U.S.A.*